MW01069682

MUSSOLINI'S WAR

Fascist Italy's Military Struggles from Africa and Western Europe to the Mediterranean and Soviet Union 1935–45

Frank Joseph

Map of Italy

MUSSOLINI'S WAR

Fascist Italy's Military Struggles from Africa and Western Europe to the Mediterranean and Soviet Union 1935–45

Frank Joseph

Helion & Company Ltd

Helion & Company Limited
26 Willow Road
Solihull
West Midlands
B91 1UE
England
Tel. 0121 705 3393
Fax 0121 711 4075
Email: info@helion.co.uk
Website: www.helion.co.uk

Published by Helion & Company 2010

Designed and typeset by Farr out Publications, Wokingham, Berkshire
Cover designed by Farr out Publications, Wokingham, Berkshire
Printed by The Cromwell Press Group, Trowbridge, Wiltshire

© Frank Joseph 2009
All photographs from the author's collection except for photograph of Mussolini on rear
cover © Bundesarchiv (101I-316-1181-11). Maps retrieved from public access sources and
amended by Farr out Publications.

ISBN 978 1 906033 56 9

British Library Cataloguing-in-Publication Data.
A catalogue record for this book is available from the British Library.

All rights reserved. No part of this publication may be reproduced, stored in a
retrieval system,or transmitted, in any form, or by any means, electronic, mechanical,
photocopying, recording or otherwise, without the express written consent of Helion &
Company Limited.

For details of other military history titles published by Helion & Company Limited
contact the above address, or visit our website: http://www.helion.co.uk.

We always welcome receiving book proposals from prospective authors.

Contents

Foreword

Frank Joseph has asked me to write a forward for his new book, *Mussolini's War*. I am certainly most happy to do so. Although I am not an academic or military historian, as a former U.S. Marine who enlisted in 1964 and retired in 1992, I certainly have an interest all things military. And this book is right up my alley. It is packed with military minutia, but written in such a way that it reads like an action novel. The author's extraordinary gift for original research and the ability to weave detailed accounts into readable works is exceptional.

He is a gifted researcher, and pulls most of his information from source documents. By doing so, those who think they know World War Two history will be pleasantly surprised to learn an incredible array of new details about the entire scope of that conflict, and not just as it related to Italy. And I guarantee that it will completely change general, preconceived notions of the Second World War. It certainly changed mine. A great read!

Forrest P. Patton
Lieutenant Colonel, United States Marine Corps Reserve (Ret.)

Introduction

The First Casualty of War

Words are indeed splendid things. But rifles, machine-guns, ships,
airplanes and cannons are even more splendid. Right remains an empty
word, if it is not backed by power, and your great countryman, Niccolo
Machiavelli, has predicted that unarmed prophets will perish.

Benito Mussolini, Florence, May 1935[1]

According to Ernle Bradford in his *Siege: Malta, 1940-1943*, "The stories of (Italian) cowardice carried in the British press, like all things else in wartime, were designed for home consumption by civilians." [2] Writing of the Italian pilots who flew against Britain in 1940, aviation historian, Peter Haining, concluded that "many of them fought with skill and bravery against daunting odds." Haining recounts that an RAF commander, angry and embarrassed by newspaper distortions of his unit history, said "there was no truth in the claims of the press that the Italians had run away at the first sight of a *Hurricane*." His men, he added, "admired the Italians for their bravery and courage in inferior aircraft."[4]

Mussolini's War belongs to these multiplying reassessments, but differs from them in that it does not focus on a single campaign or theater, but for the first time attempts to encompass the entire conflict from the perspective of Italy's true role in the fighting. In so doing, its fresh examination of the Italian military in North Africa, on the Eastern Front, in the air and at sea, reveals a story radically at odds from standard assumptions about the *Duce* and his men, unknown to most readers, particularly outside Italy. Forgotten, too, are Italian achievements in aircraft production, such as her *Veltro*, or 'Greyhound', equal to the best Allied fighters, and so admired by Luftwaffe top brass they equipped an entire *Gruppe* with the swift airplane.

However, *Mussolini's War* does not attempt to sanitize the memory of a man capable of waging modern warfare on pre-literate East Africans. Since 1945, countless published biographies and film documentaries have enumerated this and many other morally reprehensible acts associated with 20th Century's Italy's most infamous son. The present investigation will not re-hash his all-too-familiar reputation as a murderous bully, but endeavor to separate it from his abilities as a *dux bellorum,* or Roman war chief, which gave birth to his popular title, *Il Duce.* In so doing, the real performance of his troops stands forth.

Unfortunately, their remarkable military record is still obscured by historical exaggeration. Even dispassionate researchers interested only in the truth continue to view Italy's role during World War Two through the distorted lens of Mussolini's despised ideology. Instead, this history strives to illuminate him, not from a 21st Century perspective, but within the context of the crucial times he lived in and impacted. Today is not yesterday. A world died in 1945, followed by a new epoch, ours, with which it had little morally in common. The wholesale gassing of African tribesmen by European imperialists, now an

Adolf Hitler and Benito Mussolini appear together at the
balcony of the Palazzio Venezia in May 1938.

unthinkable atrocity, was hypocritically criticized at the time as a kind of embarrassment
to the League of Nations, whose own member-nations had gassed many more thousands
of British, French and Germans on the Western Front, just seventeen years earlier. There
are two sides to every story, even Mussolini's story.

His perceived political or moral failings are the kind of issues largely left to other
investigators by this examination in its determination to discover the real nature of
Italy's participation in the Second World War. Even students already familiar with
that monumental conflict will be surprised to learn how the British Royal Navy was
defeated and driven from the Central Mediterranean; or how, on 7 June 1942, infantry
of the Italian X Corps saved Rommel's 15th Brigade near Gazala, in North Africa, from
otherwise certain annihilation.

No less remarkable was history's last, victorious cavalry charge undertaken by Italian
horse-soldiers on the Eastern Front, or Mussolini's incredibly successful offensive against
the Americans before the final curtain of the Italian theater in World War Two. Far more
unfamiliar were Italian plans to attack New York City, Winston's Churchill's secret,
wartime correspondence with the *Duce*, and Italy's own atomic bomb project.

Mussolini's War describes what actually happened from the blazing tank battles of
North Africa and the desperate fight for control of the Mediterranean Sea, to the blood-
stained snows of the Eastern Front. Here, too, is the real account of Mussolini's death, and

how an Italian submarine scored the concluding Axis victory of the Second World War. Most startling of all is how remarkably close he came to overcoming the Allies. During several pivotal crises, his forces were within a hair's breadth of winning the war. In these fleeting moments of truth, he held the key to final victory. How he lost it is the question posed by this investigation.

Mussolini's War is a blow-by-blow recreation of the Second World War from the Italian perspective divested of its dated propaganda trappings, resulting in an unsuspected revision of our understanding of the *Duce's* armed forces, their performance in North Africa, the Mediterranean, France, Britain and Russia, together with his own leadership abilities. The picture that emerges differs from mid-20th Century caricatures repeated by conventional historians of a malevolent clown strutting in the role of an *ersatz* Caesar, a brutish coward trampling the existence of defenseless little peoples, like Ethiopians or Albanians, but easily beaten in a fair fight. The real-life image was far more complex – of a Faustian figure as much molded by the force of events, before and during his own lifetime, as he willfully shaped them himself.

When he visited Germany in 1937, while his troops and airmen were fighting and dying in faraway Spain, he signed a Berlin guestbook with the words, "History makes men." Below, on the same page, Adolf Hitler wrote, "Men make history."[4] This mirror concept reflected the Italian *dux bellorum's* fundamental dichotomy, the well-spring of his behavior. It recurs throughout this examination of his alchemical attempt to transmute the base matter of defeat into shining victory through armed struggle – Mussolini's war.

1

Crossing a 20th Century Rubicon

Blood alone moves the wheels of history.
Benito Mussolini[1]

The roots of Mussolini's War go back fourteen years before he was born at 2:00 in the afternoon, 29 July 1883, in the Varano dei Costa, a farmhouse at Dovia di Predappio of central Italy's Forli province. While other European powers were carving up most of the 'Dark Continent' into colonial empires of their own, a private Italian trading company purchased Assab, a relatively insignificant East African territory in Eritrea, from its native chief. The venture was a modest success, attracting some settlers and merchants from Italy, until their numbers eventually grew into a small community. Perennial banditry and inter-tribal quarrels endemic to the this part of the world made life on the frontier somewhat hazardous, so it was sold to the Italian government, which dispatched a pair of military expeditions to Massawa.

From its Eritrean port they marched inland, pacifying the region by way of a few minor clashes that ended in 1889 with the Treaty of Ucciali. This was an agreement with local native governors establishing their autonomy and making Ethiopia – or Abyssinia as it was – also an Italian 'protectorate', but in name only. Italian forces were confined to Assab and a few outposts on the Indian Ocean coast, but allowed to range throughout the country in pursuit of troublemakers. The Italian garrisons had been established four years earlier with permission granted by the Sultan of Hobyo, who became a staunch ally of the Italians.

In sharp contrast to the colonial ambitions of her fellow European states, Italy had expressed only modest imperialist interest in Africa, fairly purchasing the little she controlled there. Her relatively low profile in Eritrea was not enough to keep her out of trouble, however. Among the Ethiopian 'governors' who signed the Treaty of Ucciali was Sahle Mariam, who granted the Italians mineral rights to his country's rich deposits of tungsten, platinum and gold if they would support his bid for power. He eventually owed his crown to them, and knew it would be lost without their continued military presence. 'Menelik II', as Sahle Mariam now styled himself, soon developed into a cruel despot with outlandish dreams of his own African empire. As king, he was the wealthiest slave-owner in East Africa, where involuntary servitude was to endure well into the next century. But to realize his own imperialist dreams, the Italians, who so recently helped him to the throne, must go.

Menelik inflated the size of his motley military forces, mostly through public examples of torture and mass-murder. In February 1896, these unruly, dangerous mobs of armed men began amassing near the north central town of Adowa. On the 7th, their movements were reported by Italian scouts to General Oreste Baratieri, the governor of Eritrea, on the north coast. He felt intimidated by the great number of gathering, angry Ethiopians, and planned to evacuate all soldiers and civilians alike from East Africa. However, orders to the contrary from Premier Francesco Crispi, in Rome, demanded he put down the uprising at once.

The General obediently marched his 20,000 ill-equipped, poorly organized troops to Adowa, where more than four times as many tribal warriors awaited them. On 1 March, the Italians were decimated in a savage melee that lasted most of the day. They avoided total massacre only by fighting their way from the battlefield over the bodies of thousands of dead Ethiopians. Showing that incredible resilience their 20th Century descendants were to later demonstrate in Africa and other theaters of war, the Italians regrouped to pulverize the victory-intoxicated hordes of Menelik in battles of near-annihilation at Monte Mocram, Tucruf, Gina Guna, Bacharit and Cherseber. The success of each engagement brought Baratieri's survivors to the Red Sea coast at Eritrea, where they were evacuated by the *Regia Marina*, the Italian Royal Navy. But Menelik was victorious, and for the first time in history, a European colonial power had been forcibly expelled from foreign lands by their native people.

The debacle at Adowa festered in Italian national consciousness for decades thereafter, and was hardly helped by defeats in the Alps at the hands of outnumbered Austrian forces during World War One. As before, the undoubted personal courage of Italian soldiers had been squandered by poor leadership and worse organization. Their commanding officers belonged to Italy's ruling elite in the House of Savoy, a collection of moth-eaten aristocrats more interested in operatic uniforms and military pomp than proper training and modern equipment. Raised by his father as a socialist, who named him after the Mexican radical, Benito Juarez, Mussolini despised these obsolete monarchs, together with their wealthy friends who gave fashionable lip service to liberal causes, and opposed his county's involvement in the First World War. To him, it seemed nothing more than a military extension of capitalist competition, not worth a single drop of Italian blood. But as the conflict progressed, he decided that even this war offered revolutionary possibilities for social change, turned his back on Marxism, and joined an elite corps of sharpshooters, the *Bersaglieri*. Badly wounded when a mortar exploded in his face, the painful operation to save his life was conducted without anesthetic.

During recuperation, he systematized his ideas and experiences into an alternative to Capitalist exploitation and Communist disorder known as Fascism. Its name derived from the Roman *fasces*, a bundle of rods bound together around an axe as the ancient symbol of unity and state authority. Personifying the militant spirit of Mussolini's new ideology were cadres of his followers known as 'Blackshirts'. They made political hay from chaotic social conditions in the wake of the 1918 victory that excluded Italians. For, having switched sides when the Allies were desperately in need of any help they could get, Italy was given short shrift by the French and British framers of the Versailles Treaty. They ignored her claims to new territories needed to offset a postwar national debt of depression-level severity.

Inspired by U.S. President Woodrow Wilson's call for 'world democracy', Italy's postwar politicians set up a government that unraveled in a series of liberal regimes, as impotent as they were numerous. During 1920 alone, the nation was afflicted by 1,880 strikes that paralyzed economic life.[2] From the Soviet Union, Lenin dispatched cadres of agent provocateurs to cull revolution from discontent in cities like Milan and Turin, where unemployed mobs took over factories, sacked banks, and trashed all manner of public buildings, from libraries to post offices.[3] Army units mutinied, while violence spread to towns and villages where local governments were forcibly displaced by Marxist thugs. National dissolution was accompanied by a 'Roaring Twenties' immorality of prostitution, cultural psychoses, and crime – organized or freelance – that characterized the larger cities. War veterans were publicly despised, and Italy's outstanding historical figures held up to ridicule.

Mussolini opposed the politically and culturally chaotic trend of the times with ideological violence and revolutionary rhetoric. In 1921, he commanded nearly a third of a million members in his Fascist Party backed up by 20,000 *Squadristi,* precursors of Adolf Hitler's Stormtroops, commonly armed with cudgels. The following year, when a Communist strike ground public transportation to a standstill, *Squadristi* took over and ran the trolley cars themselves, providing free rides for everyone, thereby winning widespread popular favor. By then, Mussolini was generally regarded as the only personality strong enough to save the country from imminent demise. This recognition, combined with universal disdain for the liberal-democratic government, swept the Fascists into power on 29 October 1922.

At thirty-nine years of age, Benito Mussolini was the youngest, most radical Premiere in Italian history. He did not, however, abolish Parliament with its royal hangers-on, as expected. Of his fourteen-member cabinet, just four were Fascists. "I could have transformed this grey hall into an armed camp of Blackshirts, a bivouac for corpses," he declared menacingly with his first speech before the Chamber of Deputies. "I could have nailed up the doors of Parliament."[4] Instead, he sought to legitimize his reign by maintaining at least the outward forms of the old system. He refrained, too, from dismantling the archaic, fundamentally anti-Fascist House of Savoy, because of its traditional symbolic value for Italians.

But Mussolini's preservation of the crowned aristocracy, however politically attenuated, was a decision he would come to deeply regret toward the end of his life. He wrote near the close of World War Two, "Fascism – generous and romantic as it was in October 1922 – has footed the bill for its mistake in not having been totalitarian tight up to the apex of the pyramid, and for having believed that it was solving the problem of a system which, in its historical applications both recent and remote, has shown itself a difficult and short-lived compromise. The Fascist revolution halted before the throne."[5]

Even his detractors, like U.S. historian, Robert Elston, admitted that "Italy at first responded almost magically to Mussolini's leadership. The strikers went back to work, and the students to their books."[6] Two years after assuming power, the Fascists polled sixty-five per cent of the votes cast in their first national election, the greatest plurality since 1871, when modern Italy was formed. Regarding the results as a mandate, Mussolini abolished the liberal-democratic system altogether as part of his intention to utterly transform Italian society, economy and culture.

His move had also been prompted by press agitation that very nearly toppled the Fascist regime, when the murder of a wealthy Socialist, Giacomo Matteotti, was dilated into a *cause celebre.* "I have tried for more than two years to share power with my opponents, who do nothing but prate about democracy, while digging in their heels against any form of progress that threatens their profits", Mussolini declared on 3 January 1925. "Italy wants peace and quiet, work and calm. I will give these things with love if possible, with force if necessary." Thus was born the modern totalitarian state, in which all life was conditioned and permeated by a definite ideological style and world-outlook. As German Major Walter

Troege was to tell the First European Student and Front Fighter Meeting in Dresden on 17 April 1942, "Mussolini transformed Italy from a museum into a state."[7]

But the national transformation he undertook did not initially extend to Italy's armed forces. Although hailed as *Il Duce*, a modern *dux bellorum*, Mussolini was little interested in military affairs for the first few years of his premiership. After World War One, the Italian Army represented hardly more than a curious collection of First War War equipment and worn-out surplus discarded by the Allies. That conflict had bankrupted the postwar government, which could not even provide basic domestic services, let alone an armed forces. In what he described as "the 6th Year of the Fascist Era", however, the national economy had recovered sufficiently to undertake at least their partial modernization, although there was still not much funding to go around.

An enthusiastic, experienced aviator, with an eventual total of 17,000 flying hours to his credit, Mussolini had given his country its first, independent air force, the *Regia Aeronautica*, on 24 January 1923. Until then, Italian military aviation, which had achieved some brilliant successes during the First World War with its nimble Ansaldo pursuit-planes and gigantic Caprini bombers, had been entirely subservient to the Royal Army. Now the *Duce* waxed grandiloquent at the very thought of an unprecedented air armada: "A flash of green, white and red Italian light will stay in the skies signalling to the Infinite what Italy stands for. Flight constitutes the greatest poem of modern times."[8]

Two years later, he set up an air ministry, demanding from its mostly Fascist commanders progressive and imaginative technical advances. They obediently "produced a force held in high regard," according to a historian of the *Regia Aeronautica* in the Battle of Britain, Peter Haining.[9] Mussolini used his control over tight government expenditures to politicize the army, or *Esercito*, doling out much-needed manufacturing or raw materials to compel the replacement of hostile or indifferent Savoia aristocrats with more ideologically reliable commanders.

But less than twenty years later, poised on the brink of a world war, too many command positions in the Italian armed forces would still be occupied by royalists completely ignorant of modern combat operations and more enamored of their British crown cousins than of Mussolini's plebian rabble. "There is no doubt that the Army Staff was pre-eminently royalist," he declared. "It formed a sort of highly circumscribed if not exclusive caste, on which the Royal House relied absolutely ... The Army was considered as the domain of the Royal House. Its task was chiefly to defend existing institutions, and, also, to make war, in which case the majority of officers considered it not as the long-desired and crowning glory of a mission, but as a regrettable nuisance which everyone wished to avoid ... At the grand military review in the Via dei Trifoni, the *Führer's* suite observed that, while the Queen and her ladies-in-waiting bowed deeply as the Army banners passed, they pretended not to notice the pennants of the Fascist militia."[10]

When Adolf Hitler became German Chancellor on 30 January 1933, the international political climate changed abruptly, forcing Mussolini to take more interest in military affairs. As rearmament and talk of war accelerated throughout the tension-wracked decade, the *Duce* began to exert more of his personal influence on the armed forces, demanding they measure up to modern standards and introduce more 'spirited Fascists' into command positions. Although resisted by the entrenched aristocrats, he was able to make some headway against their conservative policies, particularly among strategists of the *Supermarina*, the naval high command. In the midst of up-grading the Italian military, however, its first challenge arose unexpectedly overseas.

Certainly, there had always been calls to "avenge the dead of Adowa" long before the *Duce*'s rise to power. Resultant nationalism ignited by his Fascist movement only intensified this popular sentiment. But in the years since Adowa, various Eritrean tribal leaders, fearful of Ethiopian raiding parties, welcomed the return of an Italian settlement with its protective garrisons and harbors that allowed the importation of European goods. Local leaders like the Sultan of Hobyo became staunch allies of the Italians. More conscious of the country's commercial potential than avenging 19th Century misdeeds, Mussolini wanted trade with Abyssinia. As early as 1923, he championed that country's admission to the League of Nations, which he still respected. But his attitude would be changed by an ambitious young man's rise to power in East Africa.

Although the 36-year-old Haile Selassie was only one of the Ethiopian Emperor's numerous grandnephews, he had schemed his way to the throne by deposing the rightful heir and marrying the late Menelik II's daughter, Zauditu, who 'appointed' him regent. Within two years, she died under mysterious circumstances, and Selassie, claiming to be a direct descendant of Israel's King Solomon and the Queen of Sheba, had himself crowned Emperor. In honor of his coronation and to maintain amicable commercial relations, the Italian government established Ethiopia's right to procure arms for national defense and internal order. But unbeknownst to Mussolini, the new 'King of Kings' harbored strong anti-Italian feelings. Even the limited presence of Europeans in East Africa was unwelcome, Selassie felt, because they might side with any one of the numerous tribal chiefs who wanted to revenge themselves on this 'Elect of God' for past massacres.

Like his fellow countrymen, he wanted to exterminate the Azebu Galla, natives of Eritrea, who sought refuge from Ethiopian genocide under Italian protection. With fantasies of a Greater East African Empire dancing in his head, he was ambitious to annex Eritrea for liquidation of the despised Azebu Galla and seizure of their valuable port facilities. The Emperor's objective was to literally absorb Eritrea through the sheer force of human numbers, steadily marginalizing the Italians out of East Africa. As early as the First World War, he had planned to stage a 20th Century version of the Battle of Adowa that would expel the Italians once and for all, and win Abyssinia's rightful place in the sun as a military power capable of humiliating a European power.

The *Duce* finally awoke to Selassie's real sentiments in 1928. The two had just concluded a new friendship treaty that allowed Ethiopia favored-nation trade status. But instead of going to Italy for the modernization of his military, as expected, Selassie snubbed Mussolini, making all his arms purchases from French, Belgian, Swedish, Czech and Swiss suppliers. By the early 1930s, they had gone far in out-fitting his half-a-million warriors with weapons that gave the Emperor a huge advantage over his tribal adversaries and seriously threatened Italian holdings in Eritrea and Somalia, where the local sultan was loyal to Mussolini.

Tensions, exacerbated through a number of incidents along the Eritrean frontier, increased throughout 1934. They climaxed on 3 November, when a vital water source, Welwel, used by desert nomads on both sides of the border, was seized by Haile Selassie's troops. An Italian unit dispatched to the scene promptly drove off the Ethiopians two months later after an exchange of gun-fire that left 150 men dead on both sides. Haile Selassie insisted that Welwel was off-limits to all outsiders, but the Eritreans and Italians wanted to make its waters available to everyone. The matter was deferred to the League of Nations, where Italy was also a member, but the deputies continually postponed their verdict. Meanwhile, similar confrontations along the Eritrean border were flashpoints throughout most of 1935.

The League finally reached a decision nearly a year after the early November dispute, exonerating both parties, but failed to address the status of Welwel, the cause of concern. Ironically, Ethiopia had been excluded from the League of Nations after World War One by British liberals on the grounds that slavery was still practiced there. They were eventually forced to admit Abyssinia after a newspaper report revealed that their minister in Addis Ababa refused to discharge his butler, who was also among East Africa's largest slave-holders, because firing him would deprive the Ethiopian of 'his life's savings', i.e., his slaves.

Thoroughly disgusted by "that gavel shop of privileged hypocrites", Mussolini was determined to act, ignoring the League.[11] Border disputes were becoming more frequent and violent, as Italians in East Africa feared a repeat of Adowa was in the making. Ethiopia's re-conquest, "an act of historical justice" long dreamt by revengeful nationalists, could galvanize the whole Italian people behind the Fascist regime, while providing the *Duce* with some of the raw materials, particularly native tungsten, he needed to complete the

Stylized statue of Benito Mussolini cradling the symbol of his
Movement – the Roman *fasces* – as it still appears today on 1930's Columbus
Memorial, just outside downtown Chicago, Illinois, in the U.S.

upgrading of his armed forces. There would, however, be a serious trade-off. Until now, Mussolini was the most popular statesman on Earth. A Gallop Poll of Americans in 1930 showed that they considered him the most brilliant and desirable statesman of the decade.[12]

In the words of the *Encyclopedia Britannica*, "Mussolini remained a hero to his own people and was profoundly respected around the world. He was hailed as a genius and a superman by public figures all over Europe and in the United States, compared to Caesar, to Napoleon and to Cromwell. The American Cardinal O'Connell of Boston said that Mussolini was a genius given to Italy by God. Winston Churchill declared that he himself would have donned the Fascist black shirt, had he been an Italian."[13] In 1934, Mussolini had even stood alone against German attempts to take over Austria. Hitler backtracked when Italian troops were rushed to the frontier. While the Western Allies enthusiastically applauded the *Duce*'s action, he noted bitterly that they left him to confront the Third Reich alone.

Their long honeymoon with the Fascist leader ended quite suddenly when he threatened to invade Abyssinia. Britain's Foreign Secretary, Sir Samuel Hoare, banged the League of Nations' podium, declaring that his country stood "for steady and collective resistance to all acts of unprovoked aggression," referring to Italy. "*Steady and collective resistance to all acts of unprovoked aggression!*", he emphatically repeated to a standing ovation of all members, save Baron Pompeo Aloisi, the Italian representative. In a statement generally understood to threaten war against Italy, Hoare declared, "If risks for peace are to be run, they must be run by all. The security of the many cannot be ensured solely by the efforts of the few, however powerful they may be."[14]

Belgium's representative, Paul Hymans, concluded, "The British have decided to stop Mussolini, even if that means using force."[15]

Mussolini responded, not with words, but by mounting a public display of his armed forces on 18 May 1935. An immense public audience cheered wildly when a large formation of bombers roared over the mock-up of an enemy factory, which exploded into thousands

Regia Aeronautica bombers demonstrate their destructive
power during 1935's display of Italian armed might.

of fragments. Massed corps of flamethrowers spewed great swaths of fire across the staged battlefield. Dozens of the army's largest artillery pieces thundered, while machine-guns rattled at imaginary targets, and whole battalions of infantry were put through their paces.

A *New York Times* reporter covering the military spectacle wrote, "*Signor* Mussolini himself took a hand, and displayed considerable skill in thowing hand-grenades, showing he had not forgotten the lessons he learned in war."[16]

But Sir Hoare was not impressed. To back up his words the day after he uttered them, the Royal Navy sailed 100 warships led by H.M.S. *Hood*, the largest battleship afloat, through the Straits of Gibraltar, into the Mediterranean Sea. The *Duce* did not feel himself intimidated, however, and asserted that Britain was only interested in siding with Abyssinia to preserve the *status quo* of her own colonial holdings around the world. Hoare publicly bristled, "If these suspicions are still in anyone's mind, let him once and for all dispel them. No selfish or imperialist motives enter into our minds at all."[17]

Few, even in the League of Nations, believed him. Indeed, behind the scenes he tried to cut a deal with Baron Aloisi, in which Abyssinia would be carved up between Britain, France and Italy, with Mussolini getting the largest serving, if only he refrained from military aggression. The secret plan had at least the tacit approval of Prime Minister Stanley Baldwin, who may, in fact, have concocted it.[18] "These politicians are truly despicable," the *Duce* told Aloisi. "I don't know how you can keep clean in their presence. I'd need a bath after every meeting with them."[19]

His answer to Hoare's suggestion was delivered from the Fascist Party's Rome headquarters to an immense, expectant crowd gathered beneath its balcony. "Not only is an army marching," he exclaimed on 2 October 1935, as the invasion got under way, "but forty million Italians are marching in unison with this army, because an attempt is being made to commit against them the blackest of all injustices. And it is against our people to whom humanity is indebted for the majority of its accomplishments, and it is against our people – saints, poets, artists, navigators, colonizers and settlers – that they have spoken of sanctions. To sanctions of an economic nature, we will reply with discipline, with sobriety, and a spirit of sacrifice. To sanctions of a military nature, we will reply with war!"[20]

The economic measures he anticipated were soon forthcoming. After almost unanimously condemning him as an aggressor, arms exports to Italy were stopped, trade was cut off, and all financial dealings suspended. Italy manufactured enough aluminum to sell overseas, but other materials vital for military production, such as nickel, tin and rubber, were available only through imports, now canceled. The United States embargoed arms shipments to either combatant, although Italy obtained petroleum from American oil companies whose directors had no misgivings about conducting business with an official 'aggressor nation'. With his rich gold mines and playing on his certified victim status, Haile Selassie could make large credit purchases of materiel, particularly munitions, from the same League states that condemned a less minerally well-endowed Italy.

In defiance of the outside world, more than half-a-million Italian married people donated wedding rings to their country's war effort, a sacrifice compensated by the Fascist government with bands of steel. "This colorless ring is far more precious to me than anything else on Earth," exclaimed the wife of a serviceman on his way to the fighting in Ethiopia, "because it binds us together more closely than the most precious gold."[21]

"I thank Almighty God for permitting me to see these days of epic grandeur," stated the Bishop of Civita Castellana in a public speech, then removed his gold pastoral chain, handed it to Mussolini, and gave him the Fascist salute to the cheers of 12,000 on-lookers.[22]

Italians from many foreign lands, including the New York Metropolitan Opera star, Ezio Pinza, flooded Rome with donations. But other New Yorkers reacted differently.[23] Following a boxing match, in which Primo Carnera, the world's former heavy-weight champion, was knocked out by Joe Lewis, his fellow blacks went on a rampage, looting Italian-owned shops and restaurants in Harlem.[24] Others opposed to Ethiopian slave practices did not join in the rioting. America's celebrated East St. Louis-born entertainer, Josephine Baker, appealed for "a negro army" to help Mussolini "liberate" East Africa.[25]

Some League delegates demanded that the Suez Canal be closed to prevent Italian forces from reaching East Africa. But such a move would have violated world trade agreements allowing free access to all nations, save in the event of military operations against Britain. Short of a declaration of war, which neither the British Prime Minister nor the Fascist *Duce* was willing to make, Mussolini's invasion fleet could pass through the Canal without interference.

Most of Africa had been long before divvied up by the imperial powers, but now Italy, poor in natural resources, was being denied her relatively small portion, just as happened after World War One. The same British and French imperialists who boasted of colonizing foreign peoples, growing rich in the process, Mussolini argued, now had the unmitigated gall to castigate him as an aggressor for following their example.[26] Justified as he felt in these comparisons, henceforward he would find himself increasingly isolated in his relationship with the West. Germany alone of the great powers commended his decision to occupy Abyssinia, the first move in a fateful friendship that bound Hitler and Mussolini together in a shared destiny.

The Italo-Ethiopian War that ensued has since been condemned as the cowardly subjugation of innocent, defenseless primitives by a modern, industrialized dictatorship greedy for their land. Others regarded it as the first step in Axis ambitions to conquer the world, and the worst example of militant racism. Images of a barefoot, indigenous people pathetically striving to ward off Italian tanks with wooden spears are still presented in popular documentaries of the period. But Haile Selassie forbade most of his troops from wearing footgear of any kind in the belief that boots made crossing rough ground more difficult. Only elite members of his Imperial Guard, the *Kebur Zabagna*, were allowed to dress entirely in uniforms, including boots.[27]

A closer look at the conflict reveals it was not the racial confrontation generally imagined. Tens of thousands of tribal peoples from East Africa volunteered to fight for the Italians. Foremost among these were the *Penne di Falco*, or native Askari 'Hawk Feathers', renowned for more than the tall tarbush fez, with its single, long plume. Valued by Italian commanders for their elan, the *Penne di Falco* were effective cavalry, playing an important role in the capture of Dese, Haile Selassie's military headquarters, where they presented arms to the commander of the Eritrean colonial division commander, General Pirzio-Biroli. The *Regio Corpo di Truppe Coloniali* also featured a 'Libyan Brigade' of volunteers from Yemen, and Somali *dubats* ('turbans'), Muslim soldiers led by the Sultan of Olol Dinle, who would capture the city of Geladi for Italy early in the campaign.

Outside participation on the Emperor's side was more pronounced. As David Nicolle, an historian of the Italo-Abyssinian War, remarked, "The role of foreign advisors and mercenaries in the modernization of Ethiopian arms was crucial".[28] Junior officers of the *Kebur Zabagna* were sent to Europe for military education until a cadet school was opened in Haile Selassie's summer residence at Oletta, near Addis Ababa, the capital. The school had been established by a Captain in the Swedish Royal Life Guards, Viking Thamm.

A larger military mission from Sweden was led by General Virgin, who taught the Emperor's warriors about modern deployment, while vastly improving their communications and fortifications on the northern front. In place of the Ethiopian Army's backward medical services, which relied primarily on ritual magic, the Swedes dispatched Red Cross ambulances fully outfitted with doctors, volunteer staff and the latest supplies. These were matched by British, Dutch and Finnish Red Cross units, including assistance from Egypt's Red Crescent.

In 1934, with war on the horizon, the government in Belgium sent military advisors to establish a training centre at Harar for the creation of two modern infantry battalions, plus squadrons of horse-soldiers, camel-mounted infantry, and armored cars. Next year, Colonel Reul led an 'Unofficial Belgian Mission' of professional soldiers to Haile Selassie's Dese headquarters. Experienced veterans from the Belgian Congo, they transformed the Emperor's rag-tag forces into modern armies, often personally leading them into battle, like Captain Cambier, who was killed in one of the first engagements of the conflict.

Swiss advisors turned the Kebur Zabanga into an up-to-date gendarmerie armed with modern Mannlicher rifles purchased from Czechoslovakia. Other firearms came from France, like the Lebel *Fusil Modèle* 1886 M93 bolt-action rifles, which fired soft-nosed 8mm rounds the Italians mistook for banned 'dumdums', because they caused similarly awful wounds. A German arms dealer managed to sell twelve state-of-the-art Pak 35/36 anti-tank guns to Haile Selassie before Hitler learned of the transaction and put a stop to all further sales. By then, the Ethiopian Army possessed 234 pieces of artillery, each one provided with at least 400 shells, plus over 1,000 Colt and Browning machine-guns from America and Britain, respectively. There were substantially more examples of Stokes mortars, used by Imperial Guardsmen with particular skill late in the campaign. Among the most effective weapons operated by the Ethiopians were Oerlikon light anti-aircraft guns, which not only accounted for enemy planes shot down, but were used with telling effect against ground targets. Major Wittlin, from Switzerland, commanded an Oerlikon battery in defense of the strategic Awash River bridge. Over it passed the Addis Ababa-Djibouti railway line, which carried weapons and munitions from French Somaliland.

The Ethiopian Air Force was certainly the least valuable component in Haile Selassie's armed forces, but it did see action. Based at Akaki, its crews operated a relatively new German Junkers Ju.52 trimotor that could fly double duty as a transport or bomber, although only about a hundred 10-kg bombs were available. Four French, unarmed Potez-25 observation planes flew numerous and invaluable reconnaissance throughout the war, while a single Farman monoplane was pressed into service as a message-carrier, together with an Italian Breda sportsplane. For protection, these defenseless aircraft had to rely on just two Dutch Fokker fighters, which, despite their sturdy condition, could not provide escort for every one of its charges at all times.

None of them were at much initial risk, however, because aerial confrontations were rendered infrequent by the vast air spaces in which pilots on both sides were compelled to operate. Only in the final phase of the war were all but two specimens of this bizarre collection destroyed – a single Potez that had been nicknamed 'Bird of the Prince', captured with only minor damage at its Akaki airfield, and the *Ethiopia I*, a radically modified British De Havilland Moth, Haile Selassie's private plane. It is still on display at the Italian Air Force Museum, in Vigna di Valle.

The Emperor's hybrid Air Force attracted equally motley crews. Only the Potez reconnaissance planes were actually flown by Ethiopians. The rest and most ground personnel were foreigners – politically indifferent mercenaries, muddled idealists, or thrill-seeking adventurers from elsewhere, like Lieutenant Micha Babitcheff, the crazy Russian director of the Ethiopian Air Force, and his fellow countryman, Theodore Konovaloff, an electrical engineer. 'Flight Captain' Allesandro del Valle came from Cuba, and Ludwig Weber was a foreign volunteer responsible for transforming the old De Havilland Moth into *Ethiopia I*. A former member of the K.P.D., Germany's Communist Party, he fled Europe in early 1933 just as Adolf Hitler was sworn in as Chancellor. The Emperor's personal pilot before and during the campaign, Weber would be killed during the capture of Addis Ababa.

Another fascist-hater from Germany was a stunt pilot who arrived in a 12-seat, twin-engined American Beechcraft just ahead of the Italian invasion. Previously, Count Carl von Rosen had been disinherited by his family for personal behavior which might only be described as anti-social and irrational *in extemis*. Throughout the campaign, he continued to fly medical supplies to the front and wounded men back to the rear. During one such mission, a low-level strafing run by *Regia Aeronautica* fighters shot up and destroyed von Rosen's doughty Beechcraft on the ground. He escaped unharmed.

Another Count, a French one, was less fortunate. Hilaire du Berrier traveled throughout Europe trying to recruit volunteers like himself for the Emperor's Air Force with less material than moral support. Returning to Abyssinia, he arrived just as the capital was about to fall, and fled for his life, but was captured by the Italians about fifty-five kilometers away. Ordered by Paris to leave East Africa before the war started, some Frenchmen deliberately stayed behind. Lieutenant Pierre Corriger shared Ludwig Weber's duties as Haile Selassie's personal pilot by flying the Emperor around on inspection tours of the most important military bases. Demeaux, Corriger's mechanic, left only after Addis Ababa was taken by the enemy.

Afro-Americans Hubert Fauntleroy Julian and Johannes Robinson spent every dime they owned for travel expenses from New York and Chicago, respectively, arriving at the Akaki airfield months later, flat broke, but full of 'racial solidarity' for their Ethiopian kinsmen. After announcing himself as 'The Black Eagle of Harlem', 'Colonel' Julian rendered himself *persona non grata* to his hosts by cracking up one of their few, serviceable aircraft on an attempted demonstration flight.

More seriously, General Mehmet Wehib Pasha headed a mission from Ankara, and was without doubt the best military mind in Abyssinia. His experience as commander of the Turkish 2nd Army at Gallipoli, where Australian troops were pinned down and massacred in 1915, had been preceded four years by action in Libya against the Italians. Now, in front of Harar, he was fighting them by constructing modern fortifications deemed 'impregnable' at the time, and referred to in the Western press as comprising East Africa's 'Hindenburg Line'.

General Pasha's impact on Haile Selassie's armed forces was to carry forward their modernization at all levels, and delay the invaders long enough for them to be swamped by wave upon wave of the Emperor's feudal levies. With substantial foreign assistance in weapons, munitions, supplies, advisors, and volunteers, the powers at his command were not limited to the primitive tribal warriors wielding spears portrayed in popular histories. Instead, the Abyssinian armed forces comprised a military elite of European leaders commanding ground forces of mostly native peoples outfitted with relatively modern weapons and supplies.

Like their opponents, the Italians did receive some assistance from overseas, although not at all as much as the Ethiopians collected. The Italians purchased 100 Caterpillar tractor vehicles and 450 Ford trucks from the United States. But the technical superiority of their arms, organization and support had to compensate for the distinct numerical advantage possessed by an enemy operating artillery and armored cars. Moreover, some of the Italians' equipment proved either unsatisfactory or disappointing in combat conditions. Breda machine-guns were often clogged by sand sticking to their oil-lubricated cartridges, while rate of fire for the cumbersome, complicated Fiat-Revelli machine-gun was low, a horrible disadvantage when confronted by masses of charging warriors.

Recruited from Italy's mountainous regions, the elite *Alpini* were among the world's finest light artillery troops, but they were handicapped by an otherwise excellent 45mm Mortar Model 35, which shot an inadequately powerful round. Italian artillery, too, was less than ideal. The range of the 65/17 infantry support field gun was poor. The Italian Army's first tank regiment had been established on Mussolini's orders eight years before the East African Campaign, although too many of its units operated the Carro CV 33, nicknamed 'the Italian Oven' by Ethiopian warriors, who commonly jammed its puny treads with tree limbs, setting them on fire after stalling the worthless 'tankette', and cooking its crew trapped inside. How many Italian tankers were the guests of honor at such cannibal feasts during the conflict is unknown.

Despite these significant deficiencies, the invasion foreshadowed things to come in World War Two. Close cooperation between ground forces and *Regia Aeronautica* warplanes was copied by German Wehrmacht tacticians for their attack on Poland, four years later. Also prefiguring Axis tactics under Field Marshal Erwin Rommel in the Libyan Desert, the Italians advanced across Ethiopia in columns, with their aircraft playing a major role in the outcome of the East African campaign, particularly during low-level strafing runs on enemy troop concentrations. Large numbers of Abyssinian infantry were decimated and the morale of survivors unused to the terror of attacks from the sky was badly shaken. Particularly innovative were *Regia Aeronautica* mass drops of parachute-flares to illuminate night-time battlefields. The deployment of motor vehicles in large numbers, most notably armored cars, was used for the first time by the Italian Army.

Important as developing military technology undoubtedly may have been, the Campaign was characterized by a great deal of vicious, hand-to-hand combat and fighting at very close quarters. In these awful confrontations, the courage and will-power of ground troops determined the final outcome. Outsiders observed that "the courage of Ethiopian warriors was found in a crowd, rather than as individuals," according to Nicolle. "They were virtually unstoppable in a massed charge, but were also prone to panic."[29] Haile Selassie's enlisted men nonetheless embodied an enthusiastic offensive spirit, and demonstrated their bravery throughout the war. For their part, they came to regard Mussolini's Italians as better soldiers than their grandfathers, who had been defeated at Adowa.

3 October dawned with Italian forces moving in a coordinated pincer movement against Abyssinia southward out of Eritrea and northward from Somaliland. Despite

their technological advantage in aircraft and armor, the *Duce*'s 300,000 troops were outnumbered by three-to-one odds. Military experts in the West concluded he needed more than a year of hard fighting to subdue Haile Selassie's tribal armies, which would cost him a projected 20,000 casualties.

These estimates heartened League delegates certain their sanctions should grind the Italian economy to a halt by spring 1936, and were confident Mussolini's 'Ethiopian adventure' would provoke his downfall. Indeed, some overseas' observers better acquainted with the heavy European military aid Ethiopia had been receiving during the previous ten years speculated that he might even lose the war or suffer a domestic political crisis, as a consequence.

The *Duce* was himself no less conscious of economic and political deadlines. Over the loud objections of aristocrat careerists in the royal armed forces, he installed younger, more politically reliable officers, instructing them in no uncertain terms to wind up operations before summer: "This is Fascist Italy's first real appearance on the world stage as a military power. We must not disappoint our international audience! Far more than the subjugation of East Africa is at stake."[30]

At the start of the Campaign, these instructions appeared to be fulfilled, as his forces poured across pontoon bridges spanning the Mareb River at the Eritrean border. A 20th Century Rubicon had been crossed. They were heartily welcomed by Azebu Galla tribesmen,

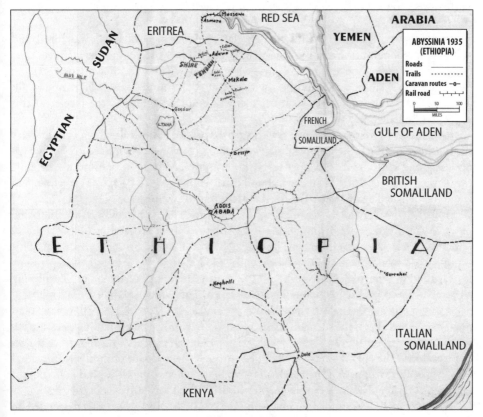

Ethiopia 1936.

who looked upon the Italians as liberators from Haile Selassie's tyranny, and joined them against the genocidal Ethiopians. Abyssinia's counter-invasion strategy depended on large forces poised to overwhelm the Italians at Ogaden, but these were cut off before they could move by a swift advance undertaken by the *Aosta* Lancers, elite units operating in conjunction with regular Army forces. They were led by General Rudolfo Graziani, who would go on to become Italy's most important commander in World War Two. During 1935's first week of October, his pre-emptive strike along the Ogaden front propped open Ethiopia's front door for the main body of the invasion.

Just three days into the Campaign, the 'shame of Adowa' was wiped out when *Regia Aeronautica* warplanes bombed the town into submission. "A new cycle has begun for our country," one volunteer wrote his father back in Italy. "The Roman legionaries are once more on the march."[31] Almost immediately thereafter, however, their 20th Century descendants began to bog down in the country's rough terrain, where its few roads were hardly more than footpaths.

The confusion of desert sinks alternating with steep-sided plateaus and deep gorges was challenging for any modern army, but familiar to the defending natives, who successfully ambushed the invaders on numerous occasions. In a particularly extraordinary encounter, an entire unit of tankettes trying to negotiate a mountain pass was over-run by waves of Ethiopians who tore off the drive-chains with their bare hands. Engagements such as these encouraged Haile Selassie, who still believed he could swamp the Italians with concentrated masses of warriors.

In his first general order of the war, he declared, "Everyone will now be mobilized, and all boys old enough to carry a spear will be sent to Addis Ababa. Married men will take their wives to carry food and cook. Those without wives will take any woman without a husband." He exempted only mothers with infants, "the blind, those who cannot walk, or for any reason cannot carry a spear. Anyone found at home after the receipt of this order will be hanged."[32]

Selassie was sure that time was on his side. Hence, the longer his armies could delay the Italians, the greater their supply problems owing to League of Nations' sanctions, which needed about half-a-year to take effect. Morale continued to be very high in Abyssinia throughout the war. The Italians, it was universally believed, had been beaten before, and would be defeated again, regardless of their temporary advances.

But the 'Lion of Judah' was having internal problems of his own. With spreading news of the invasion, long-smoldering inter-tribal rivalries erupted in bloodshed and plundering across his heterogeneous Empire, while thousands of subjects resentful of his brutality fled to aid the foreigners. Meanwhile, the Italian juggernaut rolled irrepressibly forward, taking the ancient Abyssinian capital of Axum on 15 October, and destroying a powerful motorized Ethiopian relief column near Hamaniei less than a month later.

Caught off balance since the day the Italians crossed the Mareb River, Ethiopian forces finally collected themselves for an offensive on 15 December. Their tactics were simple: To throw the largest horde of men possible at a single target again and again, regardless of losses, until the enemy was overwhelmed through sheer weight of numbers. Six years later, Mussolini's troops and their Axis allies would experience the same kind of battlefield encounters on the Eastern Front, when confronting tidal waves of Soviet soldiers.

On the same day Axum fell, immense hordes of Haile Selassie's warriors descended on the Dembeguina Pass. Traveling only by night, they had arrived at their assault positions unobserved by *Regia Aeronautica* observer aircraft. With the first morning light, they attacked *en masse*. "There seemed to be more of the enemy than we had bullets," recalled one Italian veteran, as the entire Gran Sasso Division was pushed out of Dembeguina with heavy losses.[33] Ethiopian forces continued to advance for another week, retaking the Scire area. When news of their success reached the Emperor, he was beside himself with joy, vowing a repetition of his predecessors' victory at Adowa. "This time," he promised a press conference of foreign journalists, "we will not expel the Italians, but exterminate them."[34]

Mussolini had the same in mind for the Ethiopians. To break their onslaught at Dembeguina, he ordered the first mustard gas attack since World War One on 22 December. He was also determined to set an example of ruthlessness as a guarantee against future perceptions of Italian weakness. The tribal warriors died like masses of gnats killed by insecticide.

In less than three months since the Campaign began, the Italians were brought to a standstill after a conquest of just 130 kilometers. They had been stopped by virtually impassable terrain far better known to its native defenders, who took their toll on the occupiers with sniping and hit-and-run raids. Addis Ababa still lay some 600 kilometres away.

Advised of the situation, Mussolini granted a leave of absence to his Secretary of the National Fascist Party, dispatching him to Asmara, in Eritrea. Achille Starace was given command of a mixed group of Blackshirts and *Bersaglieri*, which he formed into a mechanized column of truck transports aimed at clearing the way to Gondar, the capital of Begemder Province.

Living up to his reputation as 'the Panther Man', he told his men before setting out, "This is the most risky, most difficult, and most important venture of the Campaign. Don't waste a shot! We are carrying all the ammunition we are going to have on this expedition. Our column must be like an electric live wire. Death to the touch! Truck drivers must learn to keep to the right of the road under pain of severe penalties!"[35]

His *Wikipedia* entry admits, "The road building skills of Starace's men turned out to be of almost equal importance to their military skills. But, on the morning of 1 April, the trucks of his East African Fast Column (*Colonna Celere de Africa Orientale*) entered Gondar in triumph. They had covered approximately seventy-five miles in three days."[36]

Gratified by the Panther Man's achievement, Mussolini ordered his forces to dig in, as Italian engineers built the country's first modern roads. When completed, they could bring up heavy artillery, 150 tanks, and 400 warplanes.

Meanwhile, skirmishes raged around the defensive perimeter, where masses of attacking tribal warriors were mowed down by machine-gun and rifle-fire. Undisciplined as they were, the Ethiopians were effective in close-quarter fighting, particularly members of the Emperor's elite Imperial Guard, singled out by Marshal Pietro Badoglio for their "remarkable degree of training combined with a superb contempt for danger."[37] Italians unfortunate enough to be taken dead or alive by the Ethiopians, however, were routinely decapitated or mutilated, just as their Emperor promised.

Through the testimony of a prisoner-of-war, the Italians learned that contraband was being smuggled into Ethiopia disguised as 'humanitarian aid' by Christian evangelicals from Scandinavia. When crates with false bottoms for concealing pistols and ammunition were found covered by stacks of Christian bibles, Mussolini angrily ordered his commanders, "I authorize you to drive away the Swedish missionaries!"[38] His native allies were not above irregularities of their own, however, as the castrated genitals of enemy warriors figured prominently in the dowry of Azebu Galla brides.

Shortly after New Year's Day 1936, the roads were ready for renewed conquest. A four-day battle beginning 12 January climaxed at Genale Wenz with destruction of the Abyssinians' southernmost army. Inexplicably, the Italian victory prompted many thousands of Christian Askaris in Somalia to desert from the Royal Colonial Troop Corps and join up with the freshly defeated Ethiopians. Haile Selassie embraced their desertion as a sure sign of ultimate triumph. Victory seemed confirmed a few days later, when his forces surrounded the Italians at the Warieu Pass with what appeared to be the entire male population of East Africa. Elsewhere, a column of the invaders was trapped in the Ende Pass by Ethiopian ingenuity, when some concealed Amharan tribesmen sowed confusion and chaos among the invaders by skillfully mimicking Italian bugle calls!

Mussolini's legionaries were not slow to collect themselves, however. Hordes of rifle-wielding Ethiopians were cut to ribbons by mortar grenades and fragmentation bombs falling from diving Fiat warplanes. A major contributor to the slaughter was squadrons of Lancia armored cars. Their twin-barreled turrets spewed out heavy machine-gun fire concentrated enough to often break a massed charge of foot soldiers. By 24 January, the only barrier forbidding the Italians from resuming their advance had been formed by enormous mounds of enemy dead.

The Ethiopians' last major counter-offensive was the turning-point of the war, when an immense army led by Haile Selassie's own Imperial Guard fell on the enemy at Maych'ew on March 31st. By then, Italian snipers knew that if they could bring down a tribal leader, even in the midst of apparent success, his followers lost all heart for continuing the fight. As one headman after another fell to Fascist sharp-shooters, Ethiopian resistance began to melt away in sections.

The process was accelerated by relentless machine-gun fire on the ground and from the air, until the shattered remnants of the *Kebur Zabagna*, together with the rest of the army, abandoned Abyssinia's final offensive. They held their positions against renewed Italian assaults on 2 April, eventually breaking and running after forty-eight hours of relentless shelling. Surviving *Kebur Zabagna* officers stopped the route with spear-points and bullets long enough to collect their panicked forces for another effort. Their desperate counter-attacks beginning on 24 April put off Italian attempts to seize Degeh Bur, but, less than a week later, the city fell, and, with it, all Ethiopian resistance in the south.

On 9 May, Marshal Badoglio, who had assumed overall command from General Emilio De Bono the previous November, paraded through Addis Ababa surrounded by tanks and armored cars, with squadrons of warplanes flying in formation overhead. Meanwhile, Haile Selassie entrained with his entourage of wives and retinue of slaves for French Somaliland, where the British had a warship waiting at the port of Djibouti to complete his rescue.

The following night, on the other side of the world, an expectant crowd of nearly half-a-million people was jammed shoulder to shoulder in the capacious Piazza Venezia, overflowing into the streets beyond. Twenty centuries earlier, this date had been celebrated as the Roman *Lemuria*, when the spirits of the dead returned annually to the world of the living for propitiation. Tonight, several powerful air-raid spotlights focused on the high, deserted balcony hung with scarlet Medieval tapestries. Suddenly, a tremendous shout went up from the anxious multitude, as the *Duce's* familiar, stocky figure appeared on the brightly illuminated balcony.

One of his British admirers was a woman radio announcer, who described the scene for B.B.C. listeners, her enthusiastic voice dramatically competing with the 'live' sounds of an immense, hysterically jubulent crowd intermixed with the strains of martial music: "The *Duce* has told them them that the war is over. And now they will go back to their homes, and they will realize that in seven months, Italy has acccomplished one of the greatest military feats known in history. You will hear now that the band in the square playing, and the people are still calling him, and the balcony is still lighted. And he will appear again. Yes, he has just appeared at this moment, standing on the balcony, this lonely figure of a man, who has led thirty-four millions to this colossal victory in spite of sanctions, in spite of the hostility of the world."[39]

Mussolini waved the agitated masses into silence, then declared, "Blackshirts of the Revolution! Italians in the Fatherland and the world – Listen! With the decision you will learn of in a few moments – a decision approved by the Fascist Grand Council – a great deed has been accomplished. The destiny of Ethiopia has been sealed on this day, the 9th of May, in the fourteenth year of the Fascist Era. All knots have been cut by our shining sword. The African victory stands in the history of our Fatherland as whole and pure as the fallen Legionaries and their survivors who had dreamt and wanted it. Italy finally has her empire!"[40]

His success came sooner than military experts in Europe and America had expected, and much to the chagrin of League of Nation members, who counted on a long war to bring down the Fascist regime. The twenty-seven-week campaign had cost the Italians only 1,500 dead. The Ethiopians suffered ten times as many fatalities. Toward the climax of the fighting, the *Regia Aeronautica* operated 386 warplanes of all types, 72 of which were lost to accidents and enemy ground-fire, including 122 aircrew casualties. No less valuable than the mineral riches won in the Ethiopian conquest was Italy's revived military reputation. For the first time since World War One, Italy was taken seriously as a world power, able to victoriously assert her will, even in the face of world opposition. The *Duce's* prestige, if not his popularity, soared abroad. At home, he was hailed as a 20th Century Caesar.

A few days after peace was declared, Mussolini engaged in an acrimonious interview with an outspokenly anti-Fascist woman reporter from Britain's famous newspaper, *The Daily Mirror.* "While other, enlightened nations are no longer expanding colonial holdings and, in fact, many of their own citizens and leaders urge an end to imperialism altogether as inhumane," she scolded him, "your government barges ahead with its obsolete notions of empire-building. Why is Italy so behind the times?"

In a measured tone that ill-concealed his impatience, the *Duce* lectured her, "Fascism sees in the imperialistic spirit – especially in the tendency of nations to expand – a manifestation of their vitality. In the opposite tendency, which would limit their interests to the home country, it sees a symptom of decadence. Peoples who arise or re-arise are imperialistic." In a pointed reference to the reporter, he said, "Renunciation is characteristic of dying peoples."[41]

During early June, Haile Selassie appeared in Geneva, Switzerland at the League of Nations, which had been convened in special session at his request. As he began to tell of Abyssinia's plight, some Italian journalists present set up a ruckus by jeering and whistling at him. Their antics were featured around the world in newsreels contrasting the dethroned

Emperor as a quietly dignified statesman with the apish behavior of Fascist bullies. These enduring images of the pre-World War Two era were in the minds of European and American leaders who lavished foreign aid on Ethiopia for the next thirty years.

Little of their assistance, however, ever reached the masses of East Africans enduring the worst effects of famine and squalor. While they were crushed under decades of unrelieved misery, the Emperor outfitted floating palaces for himself, and ruthlessly put down a revolt by young intellectuals and army officers demanding an end to oppression in 1960. Fourteen years later, they finally succeeded in deposing the despised 'King of Kings' and killed him. Far many more Ethiopians – upwards of nearly two million – had died under his despotism than the 15,000 who fell in the mid-1930s' conquest of their country. Today, the name of Haile Selassie is far more hated in Ethiopia than memories of Benito Mussolini. Indeed, while the assassinated 'Elect of God' is almost universally condemned throughout East Africa, at least some descendants of tribal warriors, like the Somalis, Askari, and Eritreans who fought against the Emperor, still recall the *Duce* with nostalgia, if not reverence.

Italian rule lasted until Haile Selassie was set back on the throne by British forces in 1941. But during Fascism's brief administration, hospitals and schools had been built, general hygiene institutionalized, modern agriculture introduced, inter-tribal warfare ceased, and many adult males found employment in a new, immense colonial army. Less than a year after the fall of Addis Ababa, the Italian military presence in Abyssinia was drastically reduced, as the former enemy state settled down to become an imperial holding. The first campaign of Mussolini's War was the success he envisioned, but it set him on a course to far greater trials than he could imagine.

2

Flying Rats

Struggle is the origin of all things, for life is filled with opposites: love and hate, white and black, day and night, good and evil. And as long as these opposites do not maintain a balance, struggle will determine human nature as the final power of fate.

Mussolini[1]

With victory over Abyssinia, Italy erupted in jubilation. Adowa had been avenged. The Italian tricolor waving over Addis Ababa was a glorious sight to the *Duce's* fellow countrymen. But henceforward, with only two brief intervals, they would be at war for the next nine years.

The smoke of battle had hardly cleared over East Africa when Mussolini received an urgent appeal for help from Francisco Franco, leader of the Nationalist cause in Spain. In February 1936, a liberal-leftist coalition calling itself a 'Popular Front' won the country's national elections by a slim margin. Immediately thereafter, radical socialists in the coalition pushed loudly for revolution. All political organizations and newspapers outside the far Left were criminalized, churches vandalized, nuns raped and priests beaten to death by incensed mobs raging through the streets of Madrid and Barcelona. Strikes spread everywhere, as military uprisings reduced the country to anarchy. On 26 July, the watchful Soviet leader, Josef Stalin, took advantage of Spanish internal distress, which he saw as an opportunity for establishing his long-dreamt-of foothold in Western Europe.

He dispatched more than 2,000 'military advisors' to the new government leaders, who liquidated their liberal predecessors in the best Stalinist tradition, then set up an openly Marxist regime in Madrid, calling themselves, 'Republicans'. Soon, 240 warplanes, 1,200 artillery pieces, and 700 tanks poured into Spain from the USSR. Soviet aid did not come cheap though, and Stalin had no qualms about bilking fellow Communists for more than $315 million, which represented Madrid's entire gold reserve.

To counter the influx of men and arms from Russia, the Nationalists needed to transfer their army, stranded by these chaotic events in Morocco, to Iberian battlefields at once. But they lacked the means to do so. "Could we Fascists leave without answer that cry," the *Duce* asked, "and remain indifferent in the face of the perpetuation of such bloody crimes committed by the so-called 'Popular Fronts'? No. Thus our first squadron of warplanes left on 27 July 1936, and that same day we had our first dead."[2]

For his part, Hitler ordered an air fleet of transport planes to North Africa, from which they ferried the Nationalist army to Spain. He thus envisioned and enacted the first military airlift in history. As the *Führer* remarked later, "Franco ought to build a monument to the Ju-52".[3] The Junkers Ju-52, affectionately known as *Tante Ju*, or 'Aunty Ju', by its crews, was the aircraft that flew in Nationalist troops from North Africa. In fact, aviation was to play a more pivotal role in the Spanish Civil War than any previous conflict, and proved to be its decisive factor.

Most mainstream historians, discounting another influential component – ideological rivalry – have long insisted that Hitler, Mussolini and Stalin were only interested in the conflict as an opportunity to test their weapons for a future, more serious confrontation. But larger considerations were actually at stake. Hitler eventually regretted his aid to the Nationalists, because Franco later declined to reciprocate when Germany wanted Andalusian bases for the capture of Gibraltar. Mussolini was genuinely alarmed at the prospect of a Red presence in the Mediterranean, however. The venerable Continent seemed about to be surrounded, especially in view of Stalin's oft-repeated promise to transform the world into "a dictatorship of the proletariat" (i.e., the Soviet state) during his lifetime.

Franco's appeal for help coincided with important, not unrelated events inside Italy itself. Beginning three years earlier, Mussolini had been faced with the most serious challenge to his power since he became Prime Minister. *Giustiziae e Liberta* was a well-financed, competently led underground of dedicated anti-Fascists formed in Turin. Although propaganda activities took place mostly in the city's working class districts, specifically targeting the important Fiat manufacturing plant there, its leadership was made up mostly of upper middle class intellectuals, many of them with influential university positions.

They did not confine themselves to surreptitiously distributing handbills critical of the regime, but sought recruitment for its violent overthrow. Assassination of Fascist leaders, not excepting the *Duce* himself, was advocated and planned, and activists were busy infiltrating several important institutions, especially newspapers and schools. Although *Giustiziae e Liberta* organizers seemed to steer an indefinite political middle-road, the movement's Marxist sympathies were not easily disguised, and their appeal to former leftists was beginning to attract followers among academics at some major northern universities.

Giustiziae e Liberta was a child of its time. With Adolf Hitler's rise to power in January 1933, Stalin was concerned that Fascism, no longer confined to Italy, was spreading, and needed to be stopped. Similar movements during the 1930s were active in virtually every European country, where supporters, like those of Britain's Sir Oswald Moseley or Holland's Anton Mussert, ran, collectively, into the hundreds of thousands. Soviet operatives were watched with growing concern by agents of OVRA, the *Organizazione Vigilanza Repressione Antifascismo*, or Fascist secret police. When moderate Fascists expressed misgivings about the implications of such a clandestine arm of government, Mussolini reminded them that even the benevolent Emperor Hadrian found need for a similar organization, the *frumentarii*. "Whenever respect for the State declines," he said, "and the disintegrating and centrifugal tendencies of individuals and groups prevail, nations are headed for decay."[4]

After three months of investigation, the authorities were alarmed to discover that *Giustiziae e Liberta* was a hybrid underground of native Italian Communists and professionally-trained propagandists (some of them expert saboteurs) who had covertly entered the country from the Soviet Union. And the anti-Fascist underground found particularly fertile ground among the country's numerically insignificant Jewish communities, mostly in Turin. One of its members later immigrated to England, where Massimo Coen's *Parla Londra!* ('London Calling!') was a series of radio broadcasts blasting Mussolini in the Italian language and which were heard around the world. In fact, the founder of *Giustiziae e Liberta*, Tancredi Duccio Galimberti, was himself a Jew.

From its inception, however, Fascism was not inherently anti-Semitic, with minimal Jewish participation in its revolution, although some Jews held key positions in government, like the Grand Rabbi of Rome, who was likewise the capital's political leader. During an interview in 1932 with the famous German-Jewish author and journalist, Emil Ludwig (patronym Cohn), Mussolini condemned anti-Semitism as divisive and "not part of the new Italy. Race: it is a feeling, not a reality. Ninety-five per cent a feeling". Yet, he spoke out against the Jews in no uncertain terms for the first time just a year later, in August, when he felt his regime was seriously jeopardized by *Giustiziae e Liberta*. The following month, as some indication of his change of sentiment, he sent a personal delegation to the Nazis' national congress in Nuremberg. It was headed by Professor Arturo Marpicati, Vice Secretary of the Fascist Party, who was allowed to address the delegates in Italian, and, for the first time, publicly broached the subject of cooperation between the two ideologically kindred movements.

In standard biographies of Mussolini he is portrayed as initially indifferent to the Jews, and only assumed the guise of anti-Semite in 1938 to curry Hitler's favor. Actually, it was his fear of *Giustiziae e Liberta* with its Communist activists that elicited his first hostile statements about the 'Jewish Question' in 1933. The Race Law he passed five years later was exceptionally mild in comparison with Germany's Nuremberg Laws, and did little more than forbid marriages between Italians and Jews.

The armed forces, police and all Fascist organizations were henceforward closed to Jews, but the royal House of Savoy, which effectively controlled the Army and Navy, prevented all Jews already enlisted from being removed. Even in the Fascist Party and government, their few Jewish members mostly continued to serve unmolested. During the war, Adolf Eichmann complained to his SS superiors that the French, Yugoslav and Greek zones occupied by Italians had become 'Jewish refuges'. Italy's Race Law mostly impacted Italian education, where schools of every level were required to teach students about 'Jewish perfidy'.

Years before the passage of this anti-Semitic legislation, Mussolini was an ardent Zionist, going so far as to initiate important contacts with leading figures in the movement, including Bernard Baruch. The *Duce* heartily agreed that the only solution to the 'Jewish Question' was the creation of a Jewish state, where the world's Jews could be resettled. At one time, he even proposed setting aside territory in conquered Abyssinia as ideally suited for the creation of a 20th Century Israel, if only because large numbers of Falasha Ethiopians already regarded themselves as Jewish. Baruch declined the offer on the grounds that urbanized Jews in the United States or Europe would never consent to living in East Africa. The *Duce* was somewhat put off by his rejection.

"If Ethiopia is good enough for my Italians," he sniffed, "why isn't it good enough for your Jews? You tell me they have been horribly persecuted in many parts of the world. If so, I imagine they would be happy to find refuge anywhere they can live in peace. Well, no one can say I didn't try. It will take a more adept statesman than myself to solve this age-old problem to everyone's satisfaction."[5]

Henceforward, Mussolini's ardor for Zionist solutions noticeably cooled.

For nearly three years, an intense, underground war was waged between determined OVRA operatives and elusive *Giustiziae e Liberta* subversives. whose influence in northern Italy appears to have peaked by mid-1935. War in Ethiopia that year generated a national wave of patriotic fervor that mostly extinguished anti-Fascist activism, succeeding where

OVRA's counter-subversive measures failed. Even Vittorio Emanuelle Orlando, the prominent and outspokenly anti-Fascist liberal politician ousted from office by Mussolini after the March on Rome, arose from the obscurity of his legal practice to loudly praise the Ethiopian Campaign.[6] Thanks to majority public support for the invasion, the fires of resistance were effectively dampened, although they were not entirely extinguished, and smoldered unseen until, eight years later, the changing winds of Mussolini's fortune fanned them to life once again.

As some measure of *Giustiziae e Liberta*'s impact on the regime, of the 4,000 persons in Italy arrested for anti-government activities between 1927 and 1940, more than half took place from 1933 to 1936, the underground movement's brief years of florescence. So too, eight of the ten men and women executed by the Fascists in that same thirteen-year period belonged to *Giustiziae e Liberta*.

Despite accusations of political oppression, Mussolini showed an early clemency toward his opponents he later came to regret. His most public enemy prior to achieving power in 1922 was Palmiro Togliatti, founder of the Italian Communist Party. After the March on Rome, Togliatti was unmolested until 1926, when, frustrated by Fascism's spreading popularity, he began working underground for a Socialist revival. When that also failed, he fled to Moscow, but, courtesy of the Anglo-American invasion of Italy, returned during March 1944 to reestablish the Communist movement there.

Many government officials particularly criticized Mussolini for his mild treatment of Amedeo Adriano Bordiga. It was deemed too extreme even for his fellow Marxists, who expelled Bordiga from the Italian Communst Party; he was briefly interned in 1925, later freed under police surveillance.

The last arrests of *Giustiziae e Liberta* adherents had just been made when Mussolini received Franco's request for help to defend his country from the same internal forces that bedeviled Italy. The *Duce* was hardly alone in his concern for events in Spain. They deeply touched most Italians, who regarded the Spaniards as not only fellow Latins, but Catholics suffering a wave of church desecrations and bloody atrocities at the hands of a militantly atheist government. People worried that the Russian calamity of 1917 was about to repeat itself, and this time not that far away. They clamored for a modern crusade to extirpate the Communist infidel from Western European soil.

But Italy's military had been worn out by the Abyssinian experience. The Army and Air Force were in need of refitting. Mussolini was at first able to spare Franco only nineteen warplanes, which would be up against far more enemy aircraft. These included sixty French Breguet XIX reconnaissance bombers, forty Nieuport-Delage Ni.52 fighters, fourteen Dewoitine D. 371 and ten D.373 pursuit planes, plus 65 Potez Po.540 medium bombers, together with twenty British Vickers Wildebeest torpedo-bombers. Aiding the Italians were nine, wheezing biplane fighters which comprised the entire Nationalist Air Force, and ten German tri-motor transports.

On 29 July, the *Morandi* sailed from La Spezia for Melilla, a port in Spanish Morocco. The large freighter carried abundant supplies of ammunition, bombs, aviation fuel and aircraft for Franco's forces. The next day, a flight of nine Savoia-Marchetti SM.81 bombers landed at Nador outside Melilla, the first of some 720 aircraft and 6,000 aircrews Mussolini dispatched to the Nationalist cause. They were intended to support the more than 70,000 Italian soldiers that would eventually serve in Spain.

Throughout most of the Spanish Civil War, the Republicans continued to enjoy a numerical edge over their opponents, thanks to help from Russia and covert armaments smuggled across the Pyrenees by a sympathetic French Premiere, Leon Blum. At the behest of the League of Nations, along with most other world leaders, he had signed a non-intervention agreement that excluded outside involvement in the Civil War for the expressed purpose of containing hostilities in Iberia, thereby preventing them from widening into a general conflict. Although publicly avowing non-participation in the sharply drawn ideological struggle, Blum covertly slipped French arms and supplies to the Republicans, and allowed his border patrols to look the other way when leftist volunteers wanted to cross the mountains into Spain.

But other heads of foreign governments likewise paid little more than lip-service to official non-participation. U.S. President, Franklin Roosevelt, who vigorously condemned the Nationalists, did not prevent thousands of Americans from joining something called the 'Abraham Lincoln Brigade'. This was an armed assortment of socialist intellectuals, fire-breathing Communists, bored dilettantes, desperately unemployed men, one-world idealists, and Jews alarmed at the rise of European anti-Semitism who fought on the Republican side.

With its Wagnerian name, Operation *Feuerzauber* ('Magic Fire') was supposed to have been nothing more than a training exercise provided to Franco's mechanics by a handful of German aeronautical 'advisors' at the Tablada airfield, near Seville. From these humble, thinly disguised beginnings, however, a *Kondor Legion* of Messerschmitt fighters and Stuka dive-bombers swiftly evolved. League of Nations deputies entrusted with international enforcement of the non-intervention agreement had no control over Mussolini after he stomped out of their Geneva headquarters over the Ethiopian affair, and the Soviet Union was not a member, never having been asked to join, so neither Italy nor Russia were constrained from sending men and equipment to Spanish battlefields and airfields.

Republican warplanes unquestionably dominated the skies from the beginning of the conflict. But they were challenged during August by the arrival in Seville of Savoia Marchetti and Caproni Ca.135 aircraft in two bomber squadrons. Together with the original dozen Fiat fighters dispatched by Mussolini, they comprised an early nucleus for the Italians' *Aviazione Legonaria*, which eventually fielded 250 aircraft of various types. And their pilots would achieve distinction as the world's best during the mid-1930s.

Some, like Maresciallo Baschirotto, became aces, shooting down at least five enemy a piece. His experience in Spain prepared him for duty in World War Two, when he destroyed six more Curtiss P-40s, Beaufighters, and Hawker Hurricanes during the North African Campaign. Baschirotto's last victory was over a Spitfire near the island-fortress of Pantelleria, on 20 April 1942. "It was a happy birthday present to the German *Führer*," he told a reporter for one of Italy's oldest, most widely read newspaper, the *Corriere della Sera*.[7] Hitler had on that day celebrated his 53rd birthday.

His comrade in Spain was Group Commander Ernesto Botto, who received the Gold Medal for downing four Republican aircraft. Although he lost a leg during their destruction, he volunteered for frontline flying two years later, when Italy went to war against Britain. Botto went on to claim another three 'kills' in the skies over the Libyan Desert, earning him the nickname, *Gamba di Ferro*, or 'Iron Leg'.

The aircraft men like Maresciallo Baschirotto and Ernesto Botto were supposed to fly for Franco were not always as physically fit as themselves. The SM.81, for example, had already seen service during the Abyssinian Campaign in transport and reconnaissance duties. Its three 700-hp Piaggio P.X RC.35 nine-cylinder radial engines gave the *Pipistrello*, or 'Bat', as the rugged aircraft was affectionately known by its crews, 340 km/hr at 9,800 meters, with a range of 2,000 kilometers carrying a bomb payload of 1,000 kilograms – not bad for 1936. The Caproni was a more modern, twin-engine medium-bomber with a sleek fuselage and twin-boom tail. Faster by 60 km/hr than the *Pipistrello*, and able to deliver an additional 1,000 kilos of bombs, its three 12.7mm machine-guns in nose, dorsal and ventral turrets foreshadowed future developments.

For escort, the bombers were protected by the Fiat CR.32, generally considered the best pursuit model at the beginning of the war, "soon gaining a reputation as one of the outstanding fighter biplanes of all time," according to British aviation historian, David Mondey.[8] Agile, quick and tough, the Fiat's extraordinary aerobatic characteristics and top speed of 375 km/hr at 3,000 meters enabled its pilots to take on maneuverable 'double-deckers' like itself, such as the Soviets' *Super Chata*, or more modern monoplanes, including the formidable *Mosca*. Eventually, 380 CR.32s participated in the Spanish Civil War. But during the conflict's first months, just a handful of Italian bombers and fighters were General Franco's first and, for some time, only support aircraft. Terribly outnumbered as they were in 1936, their technological superiority over the Republicans' French and British machines, together with the Ethiopian experience of their aggressive crews, made the *Aviazione Legonaria* a force to be reckoned with from the start.

During late August 1936, the Italian airmen launched their first sorties against enemy strongholds in the north, where the Fiats swatted Nieuports and Dewoitines, while the *Pipistrellos* and Capronis were dead-on target with their destructive payloads. To combat these intruders, a famous French Communist author, Alfred Malraux, helped raise twelve million francs for the purchase of new warplanes as needed additions to his *Escuadrilla España*. Based in occupied Madrid, his fiery oratory attracted foreign volunteer pilots from France, Britain and Czechoslovakia. Not to be outdone, Mussolini rushed additional squadrons of CR.32s to Seville.

They arrived just in time to confront a major enemy offensive during September, and contributed decisively to the battle. Malraux's elite squadron was badly mauled, as the Popular Front offensive folded under the bombs of SM.81s and CA.135s. By December, with half its aircraft destroyed, the *Escuadrilla España* disbanded; survivors melted into the regular Republican Air Force. Replacements came in the form of fifty Russian SB-2 *Katuska* bombers and I-15 *Chata* fighters. Later, after the New Year, Leon Blum quietly slipped another twenty state-of-the-art Loire 46 pursuit planes across the Pyrenees. More troublesome for the Italians was the appearance of a remarkably advanced Soviet bomber, the Tupelev SB-2, over Cordoba. It was faster than the quick Fiats, and could even out-climb them after dropping its bombs.

For weeks, the unassailable Tupelevs ranged over Nationalist territory, wrecking havoc on troop concentrations and supply depots. All attempts to intercept them met with failure. In January 1937, a Spanish pilot, Garcia Morato, noticed that the bombers were in Cordoba skies every morning at precisely the same time and altitude. Jumping into his CR.32 before they arrived, he climbed to 5,030 meters, well above the lower-flying enemy. They appeared like clock-work, and Morato pounced on them, his 7.7mm Breda machine-guns blazing. Two of the swift Russian aircraft fell flaming to earth, and the rest frantically jettisoned their payloads to beat a hasty retreat. Nationalist fighter pilots learned from his experience. If they were given sufficient advance warning, their Fiat fighter-planes, with remarkable service ceilings of nearly 8,840 meters and a swift rate of climb, could dive on the redoubtable Tupelevs from above.

But the speedy bombers were not the only quality aircraft sent from the USSR. Squadrons of nimble biplane fighters, the Polikarpov I-15, arrived in Madrid, together with numbers of an altogether different design, the I-16. The stubby monoplane more physically resembled a trophy-racer of the era than a military machine. It was the product of a prison experience endured by Dmitri Gregorovich and Nikolai Nikolayevich Polikarpov.

By late 1932, their new I-15 was despised by Red Air Force test-pilots unhappy with its instability at high speeds, and its gull-wings which prevented the airmen from seeing the horizon while in flight and obscuring the ground on approach, making landings hazardous. Enraged by the negative reports of his test-pilots, Stalin threw Russia's leading aeronautical inventors into prison, together with every member of their design teams, until they came up with a fighter for the Soviet Union at least as good as contemporary examples from other nations. With their freedom and, ultimately, their lives at stake, the hapless engineers, still behind bars, put their heads together for the creation of an aircraft ahead of its time.

The I-16's successful debut on New Year's Eve 1933 coincided with the designers' release from behind bars. An innovative, retractable landing-gear made it the first monoplane of its kind to enter service. The cantilever, or internally braced, low metal wing, plus all-wood monocoupe fuselage, resulted in a solid form easy to maintain in frontline conditions, able to take terrific punishment, and strong enough to survive the high-speed maneuvers that broke apart lesser aircraft. As one commentator observed, "its rolls and loops could be quite startling." Powered by a 1,000-hp M-62 radial engine, Polikarpov's best effort

A Soviet Polikarpov I-16.

flew higher by 670 meters and faster by 115 km/hr than Italy's finest fighter, and totally outclassed the Heinkel 51, Germany's early rival for Spanish skies.

Yet, the wonder plane had serious flaws. It was said to have killed more of its own airmen than the enemy, an exaggeration spawned by the aircraft's chronic instability under all three axes. Requiring constant attention while in flight, it suffered from a fatal tendency to stall out in a glide or during approach, requiring the hard work of skilled operators. In tight combat maneuvers, the I-16 was known to unexpectedly spin out of control on occasion. Russian pilots gave it the tongue-in-cheek name of *Ishak*, 'Little Donkey', for its unpredictability and sometimes rough ride. Republicans in Spain during the Civil War dubbed it the *Mosca*, or 'Little Fly'. To their Nationalist opponents, it was simply *Rata*, the 'Rat'.

Until enough *Ishaks* left production to make a difference in the fighting, Stalin unloaded a whole squadron of the earlier I-15, the plane that landed Polikarpov in jail, on desperate if grateful Popular Front pilots. For all the gull-wing's blind spots and high-speed instability, the inexperienced Republican flyers found the *Chata* better than the older French Nieuports or Dewoitines, easier to fly and more forgiving on rough landings at the improvised airfields they were forced to use.

Soviet advisors sent to Spain watched the *Chatas* in action, then sent their reports back to Polikarpov, who made numerous changes to his original design. The result was a vastly improved version, the I-15bis, or 'second variant', minus the earlier model's defects, including the obscuring gull-shape. Hundreds more of the up-graded I-15bis, the *Super Chata*, were manufactured and dispatched to the Republicans. They made good use of these and other supplies received from the USSR in February 1937, just in time to oppose a large-scale Nationalist operation against Madrid.

On the 13th, the new Soviet aircraft were given their baptism of fire in Iberian skies. No less than forty *Chatas* bounced sixteen Nationalist planes of the *Aviacion del Tercio* returning from a mission to their base at Tablada. The Italians suddenly found themselves not only terribly outnumbered, but confronted by an opponent 100 km/hr faster than their own mounts. Deprived of defense, Giuseppe Ruzzin tried to save himself by putting his sturdy biplane through a dazzling aerobatic display that lost his pursuers and somehow freed up his previously jammed twin 7.7mm Breda-SAFAT machine-guns.

He was convinced his Fiat CR-32 was "the best fighter in the world, easy to fly and very maneuverable," so he returned to the fray, engaging in the fight of his life to shoot down a *Rata*, before making an emergency landing at Getafe. Climbing out of his open-air cockpit, Ruzzin counted some 150 bullet holes in the aircraft's fuselage alone. But he was elated to learn that his squadron had accounted for a total of nine kills that day, with no losses to themselves. Besting an enemy decidedly advantaged in both numbers and performance demonstrated that the *Legonaria*'s superior flying skills could cancel out any numerical or technological deficiencies.

During March, however, its pilots were unable to save Italian forces from being decimated at Guadalajara by relentless swarms of Communist *Chatas*. The troops had been caught in the open on barren terrain that provided no cover from aerial assault. Beyond the reach of Nationalist fighters, the defenseless columns were strafed and bombed for days. The carnage was terrible, and losses were so high Franco had to call off his offensive. The hour Mussolini learned of the disaster, he dispatched additional squadrons of Meridonali aircraft to his airmen stationed at Majorca. Decidedly inferior in every way to the newer

A CANT 'Heron'.

Soviet Polikarpovs, the rugged biplanes were fitted with undercarriage racks for 180 kg of bombs, and relegated to the ground-attack role, in which, however, they excelled beyond all expectations.

The Meridonali were accompanied by two outstanding seaplanes. The Z.501 manufactured by CANT (*Cantieri Riuniti dell'Adriatico*) twice won the distance record for aircraft of its type, first in October 1934, when the company's chief, Mario Stoppani, flew from his base at Monfalcone, in Trieste, to Massawa, Eritrea, a distance of 4,120 kilometers. His record was marginally surpassed by French aviators soon after, but he regained it during July the following year in the same aircraft by flying 5,000 kilometers to Berbera, in British Somaliland. When a squadron was assigned to the 2nd *Escuadrilla*, *Gruppo* 62 of the *Agrupacion Espanola* – the Nationalist Air Force – the type was known as the *Gabbiano*, or 'Seagull', and became famous for the anomalous turret with 7.7mm machine-gun stationed incongruously atop the center of its parasol wing.

Joining the *Gabbiano* was another CANT record-holder, the Z.506. After achieving a load-to-height precedent of 10,155 meters carrying a 1,000-kg. payload, the *Airone*, or 'Heron', covered 7,022 kilometers non-stop from Cadiz to Carevalas, in November 1937. A variant, the Z.508, went on to break a number of speed records. The technical advantages of these outstanding aircraft were constantly needed to off-set the numerical superiority possessed by the Republicans until the last year of the war.

Although the slaughter of Italian troops at Guadalajara had forestalled the conquest of Madrid, Franco still had something of a stranglehold on the capital. Accordingly, a major effort to relieve this pressure by attacking the Nationalists in overwhelming numbers near the town of Brunette was undertaken in July. Squadrons of aircraft and pilots from Germany, Italy, Poland, Russia, France, Britain, Ireland, America, Portugal, Holland and Mexico participated in the largest air battle of the Spanish Civil War. The Republicans threw in 150 bombers and fighters. All but 50 were destroyed between the Italian *Aviazione Legionaria* and German *Kondor Legion*. Nationalist losses totaled just twenty-three aircraft. Despite this crushing defeat, the Republicans still outnumbered their opponents by 122 warplanes.

Following up on his success at Brunette, Franco captured the strategic city of Bilboa in June, when Italian units redeemed the defeat at Guadalajara through their contribution to this important victory. They were aided by the arrival of the first Fiat BR.20, a fast medium-bomber with an extraordinary range of 3,000 kilometers. Graceful handling characteristics earned it the nickname *Cicogna*, and the 'Stork' became a common sight in the skies over the Teruel front, where they frequently attacked enemy concentrations of troops and vehicles with bomb-loads of up to 1,600 kg. At 430 km/hr, it could out-run all Republican interceptors, save the over-powered *Rata*.

Assigned to escort the *Cicognas* was the new Breda Ba.65, an *aeroplano di combattimento*, intended to perform multi-purpose roles as interceptor, light-bomber, reconnaissance and attack aircraft. In reality, it could fulfill none of these requirements, and eighteen specimens equipping the 65th *Squadriglia* were used only to go after lightly defended ground targets at Santander. As many *Super Chatas* and *Ratas* in defense of the city exacted a fearful toll on the slower Ba.65s. It was here, however, that the Italians achieved the decisive victory of the Spanish Cili War.

Republican strength was most importantly concentrated in the Army of the North, with heavily-fortified Bilbao and Santander as military and political lynchpins. The Reds continuously reinforced defences here to not only render them impregnable, but to make the north a staging region for a major offensive aimed at overwhelming Iberia in a single operation, as soon as enough materiel had been received from the Soviet Union.

Italy's Ettore Bastico was placed in charge of dealing with this threat. During early spring 1937, he began husbanding troops and supplies for an offensive of his own. Its objective was not the conquest and consolidation of territory, but defeat and annihilation of enemy forces, even though they would outnumber his by at least two-to-one odds. A dozen Basque brigades were bolstered by another twelve of the Republican Army and twenty-seven Asturian brigades. These were covered by more Republican aircraft than operated over any other front, and munitions piling up for the intended Red offensive provided more than adequate defence.

Undeterred by these challenges, General Bastico subjected his men to a period of intense preparations and instruction, emphasizing tight interdependence between Spanish and Italian troops, together with close coordination of arillery and air power. Everything

A Fiat 'Stork'.

was to be swept forward in an irrepressible movement. "There are to be no hold-ups," he admonished his commanders. "We die or advance, but stop for nothing but victory."[9]

Months of hard training and the arrival of new warplanes plus field artillery instilled high morale throughout the Nationalist troops. When they attacked the front between Valdecebollas and Cuesta Labra on the morning of 14 August 1937, their assult was so ferocious it unnerved the defenders. The Republicans regrouped and fought back furiously the following day, but were beaten within twenty-four hours. Italians took the strategic El Scudo Pass on the 17th, enabling Republican Army battalions to be surrounded a few days later at Campo. One town after another fell in rapid succesion until the 24th, when Basque forces surrendered to the Italians. Two days later, the Nationalists entered Santander, but resistance continued until 1 September, when 17,000 Republicans were taken prisoner in the city. Many of them were executed almost immediately. Of the Reds' original fifty-one brigades, twenty-three had been obliterated, amounting to the loss of 60,000 troops. National losses were high, but not correspondingly so, and less than anticipated.

With Bilbao's capture during the same operation, the Army of the North virtually ceased to exist, crippling the Republican cause. The neat precision and rapid advance of the Nationalist attack had stunned the defenders, never giving them an opportunity to catch their breath. In little more than two weeks, they had been overrun by aggressive troops, concentrated artillery and air power closely coordinated to achieve common objectives in as little time as possible. General Bastico had not only carried out the first *Blitzkrieg*, but irreversibly turned the tide of the Spanish Civil War in the Nationalists' favor.

Unfortunately for him – and for Italian fortunes in the next war – his triumph engendered envy among Italian General Staff officers, who shunted him into the background as the Governor of Libya. After their humiliation in his province at the hands of outnumbered British forces, Mussolini prevailed in having him replace an inept Italo Gariboldi as Commander-in-Chief of Italian Forces for North Africa in July 1941. Rommel admired Bastico more than any other Italian officer, and the two desert foxes would combine their expertise to win many victories throughout the Desert Campaign.

The few Breda warplanes that survived the fighting at Santander nevertheless went on to play important roles by striking railway and road junctions in the course of strafing artillery batteries and troop concentrations. In July 1938, after structural improvements made by mechanics in the field, the Ba.65s performed for the first time as dive-bombers, knocking out pontoon-bridges thrown across the Ebro River by Republican forces, and helped to decisively turn the tide against them seven months later in the Catalonia offensive. By the time the Bredas' last missions in the Spanish Civil War were flown on 24 March, twelve of the original twenty-three examples sent to fight with the 65th Squadron had been lost in the process of carrying out 368 ground-strafing attacks and fifty-nine dive-bombing missions. These last Ba.65s were donated to the *Agrupacion Española*.

They did not participate in military aviation's first round-the-clock bombing, when Caproni and Savoia-Marchetti tri-motors operating from airfields on Majorca attacked Barcelona from 16 through 18 March 1937. Despite widespread destruction and panic, the defenders refused to capitulate, and held out until Italian forces, supported by Navarrese and Moroccan troops, finally took the city on 26 January the following year.

By early 1939, the Reds were down to less than 100 aircraft against 600 flying for the Nationalists. Madrid finally fell in March, and the Spanish Civil War ended with a Republican surrender at month's end. The *Duce* declared that Western Civilization had been saved from Soviet imperialism by the combined efforts and sacrifices of continental Fascists and pro-Fascists.

To be sure, Stalin would have had his desired foothold in Spain, save for intervention by the German *Kondor Legion*, together with the 37,000 Italian troops, plus 750 pilots and ground personnel in the *Aviazione Legonaria*. During nearly three years of fighting, its crews carried out one of history's most successful aerial campaigns, racking up 1,921 sorties, including 59 bombing runs and 368 strafing attacks. The Legionnaires suffered 196 fatalities and 86 aircraft lost to enemy fire, but destroyed 903 enemy planes on the ground and in the air. Losses in Republican air personnel exceeded 2,000 dead. Italian military prestige at home and abroad soared.

Such a decisive victory seemed to confirm Mussolini's capable leadership and the superiority of his armed forces. Neither he nor Hitler had allowed themselves to be outflanked by Stalin at the western extremes of Europe. As Colonel McCormack observed in his *Chicago Tribune* editorial for 2 April 1939, "like it or not, Germany and Italy have prevented the Old World from going Communist. How America might have fared against a colossus that must have otherwise stretched from Vladivostok to Madrid is hardly open to question."[10]

Privately, however, Mussolini expressed concern that the Spanish Civil War had actually been the first skirmish in a future, much larger confrontation between Europe and the Soviet Union. And he wondered how his military, wearied by two consecutive campaigns, would perform if confronted by the largest military power on Earth.

3

A Modern Gallic War

Sometimes history grabs one by the throat and forces a decision.
Mussolini[1]

A lone, Italy would be unable to oppose the unloosed hordes of the Soviet Union, a fear that drove Benito Mussolini into a military alliance with Hitler's Germany. The 'Axis' they created was supposed to be the center-post of opposition to the USSR around which other nations were invited to combine their armed forces in the event of war with Stalin. Such a confrontation seemed unavoidable, given recent events in Spain. Important allies like the Japanese, oil-rich Rumanians and tough Finns eventually became Axis partners, but Mussolini doubted anything could really stop the Red Army after it completed modernization, anticipated for sometime in the early 1940s.

It was his concern over this growing colossus in the east that made him strenuously oppose another European war. Relatively small, localized conflicts, such as the one he fought in Spain, or campaigns far removed from the continent, like his conquest of Ethiopia, offered little danger of sparking a general conflagration. But it seemed obvious to him that another serious confrontation between the European states would be just what Stalin was waiting and preparing for off-stage. In truth, the moustachioed Marshal had publicly predicted the inevitability of just such a golden opportunity on several occasions.

According to the *Encyclopedia Britannica*, "Mussolini understood that peace was essential to Italy's well-being, that a long war might prove disastrous."[2] As he himself explained, "In one of the many articles which I published at that time (during the mid-1920s) in the American Universal Service press, and devoted to the study of the various aspects of the European situation, I pointed out the dilemma: either a minimum of European solidarity, or else war, with the consequent crumbling of the common values of civilization."[3]

He always had a soft spot for the Americans, who he looked to as the only potential mediators in Europe's endless squabbles. Shortly after the East African Campaign's conclusion, he told audiences in the U.S. via a Fox Movie-tone newsreel in clear English, "I will speak to you in a few, brief words of a serious problem which interests the whole of mankind; namely, peace or war. I know what war means. The terrible personal sacrifices of an entire generation of young people have not vanished from my memory. I have not forgotten, nor will I permit myself to forget it. I was myself severely wounded. Then and now, as man and Prime Minister, I have before my eyes an awful panorama of the political, economic, moral and the spiritual consequences of war. Italy will never make any policy in supporting war. On the contrary, we heartily welcome the prospect of our own disarmament in mutual accord with all others, as an international goal. Italy needs peace – a long, secure era of peace to be able to exploit and consolidate the concrete results of our Fascist government. Fascism wants to assure the cooperation of the Italian nation with all other peoples for a future of prosperity and peace."[4]

On 27 August 1928, Mussolini enthusiastically endorsed the Kellogg Pact, the first article of which condemned "recourse to war for the solution of international controversies, and renounce it as an instrument of national policy in their relations with one another."[5] At the time, he was no doubt sincere in his desire to avoid another military confrontation, if only because the Italian armed forces were clearly unready for war against another European power, much less a combination of such powers. Mussolini's often-stated position made him the matrix in summit talks over 1938's Czech Crisis.

Of the four heads of state meeting at Munich, he only was conversant in every language spoken at the conferences, a fluency he skillfully employed to defuse an international situation that would have otherwise resulted in war. As he recalled six years later, "the question of the Sudeten peoples, that is, of the Germans incorporated into Czechoslovakia, seemed at one point as if it must prove the famous spark which fired the powder. To prevent an explosion, the Big Four met, for the first and last time in Munich. Italy's action was recognized as of prime importance in the peaceful solution of the problem. When it was known that an agreement had been reached, the nations breathed again."

"On leaving the room, a French journalist accosted me, and said, 'You have given an oxygen tank to a sick man.' I replied, 'It is the normal practice in serious cases.'

"Daladier, the President of the Council, who had been accorded friendly, popular demonstrations in Munich, was received in Paris by an enormous crowd and carried in triumph. The same happened to Chamberlain in London. Returning to Rome, I was received with perhaps the greatest popular demonstration in the whole twenty years of Fascism. The *Via Nazionale* was overflowing with crowds, hung with flags and strewn with laurels."[6]

But Mussolini had not been impressed by the British statesmen he met at Munich. "These are the tired sons of a long line of rich men," he confided to his son-in-law, Galeazzo Ciano, "and they will lose their Empire."[7] Nor was he disillusioned by their real motives: "In reality, France and England wished simply to gain time. During 1938, the atmosphere was already extraordinarily lowering."[8]

Indeed, both Western Allies needed the grace period conveniently extended by 'appeasement', as the newspapers called it, to complete their own rearmament programs, which would not be finalized for another two or three years. Had Hitler, in fact, gone to war over the Czech Crisis, as he wanted, he would have been better prepared than his opponents on the battlefield. Although long after excoriated for his 'peace in our time' agreement with the Nazis and Fascists, post-war reassessment of Neville Chamberlain's 'umbrella diplomacy' at Munich reveals his negotiations were primarily aimed at delaying any military showdown – even by sacrificing the Czechs – to provide time for upgrading Britain's armed forces.

Mussolini was not allowed a moment to relax. The same month in which the Spanish Civil War ended, he was informed that the Albanian parliament had voted a moratorium on its debt payments to Italy. The news could not have come at a worse time. The Italian economy had been stretched to the limit by two recent wars, and depended on the repayment of loans extended to King Zog. He was notified in March 1939 that payments would have to continue, according to agreements signed by the monarch himself fourteen years earlier. Relations had been traditionally good between the two nations, with a treaty of friendship and twenty-year defensive military alliance offered by Italy. Such protection was deeply appreciated by the Albanians, who would have been victimized by their neighbors in the same kind of the kind of 'ethnic cleansing' for which Yugoslavia is ill-famed.

Mussolini's investment in the otherwise undeveloped Balkan backwater had been high. "What a prodigious work was achieved during a few years in Albania," he exclaimed, "where the Albanians were given equal rights and the same duties as Italian citizens, in keeping with Roman tradition! Here, one may see the great motorway from Durazzo to Tirana, the new buildings in the capital, the reclamation of the Musachia ... there, the almost completed plan for a main railway from Durazzo to Elbassan which, had it been continued from Lake Ochrida, would have put us into direct communication with Sofia and the Black Sea."[9]

In exchange for fending off Albania's enemies and bringing her into the modern world, he was granted access to "the petroleum wells of Devoli – Italy's only source of this raw material – the iron mines near Elbassa, the bitumen, copper, and chromium mines", all of which made up for Italian lack of these absolutely vital natural resources.[10] Even so, he refrained from undermining the Albanian monarchy and seizing the country outright. Cooperation was cheaper than occupation.

But the man he was forced to deal with had the mentality of a local chieftain, who filtered foreign aid through his family and followers to become fabulously wealthy, while the rest of his country wallowed in traditional squalor. Radio Bari would later refer to the sycophants surrounding King Zog as part of a "court which can only recall the remote days of absolute kings and vampires battening on an unfortunate people."[11] In early 1939, the prefect of Durazzo, Marko Kodeli, spoke out publicly, wondering why nearly twenty years of Italian assistance had not improved the lives of ordinary Albanians. According to the King's biographer, Jason Hunter Tomes, "unable and frankly unwilling to have much faith in any group of his people, Zog strove to keep all classes in unstable equilibrium. Through hours of hideously convoluted talk, he obsessively manipulated his assorted underlings (nearly all older than himself) in an effort to exercise personal control from seclusion."[12]

None of this particularly bothered the *Duce*. But when he learned that Zog was meddling in Balkan affairs, intriguing with Greece to extricate himself from debt, Mussolini acted to prevent instability in that inherently combustible region, especially where Italy's oil and mineral interests were at stake. Critics dismiss his move against Albania as nothing more than an act of international aggression to show Hitler that the Fascists could also gobble up little countries with impunity. But it is clear that Mussolini's abiding concern for the constant importation of Albanian oil and metals, suddenly jeopardized by Zog's tribal megalomania, was his chief motivation.

Accordingly, early Friday morning, 7 April 1939, Albanians living along the sea coast awoke to behold an armada of warships just offshore. The first Italian soldiers to step off in Durazzo were politely stopped by a local policemen, who asked to see the foreigners' passports. "We have none," the soldiers laughed. "We've come to occupy your country."[13] As more and more troops disembarked from their transports, the frantic gendarmes suddenly opened fire on them with a pair of machine-guns. The police were soon after joined by some 300 Albanian soldiers, who scattered after a brief, booming bombardment fired by the Italian battleships. Thereafter, General Guzzoni, in charge of operations, leisurely put ashore two divisions of four Bersaglieri regiments, backed up by a tank battalion.

Zog made impassioned appeals by radio for a patriotic uprising against the invaders, his former benefactors of almost two decades. His dramatic words were heard by more

Americans than his own people, however, because few Albanians owned receivers. Instead, the plight of the besieged King was broadcast across the U.S. as a pitiful example of yet another, innocent, little nation swallowed by Fascist rapacity. In reality, "too many Tirana intellectuals spent Easter weekend not fighting for their country, but debating whether Zog was worth having," Tomes writes. "Very few Albanians showed any willingness to fight for him. The majority apparently accepted the Italian occupation in a spirit of resignation which verged on indifference."[14]

While Americans were still glued to their radio sets, listening to Zog's defiant, if pre-recorded speeches, the King had already fled with his wife and son across the Greek border in a long caravan of limousines over-loaded with gold bars, furniture, crates of cigarettes, evening gowns, and assorted luxury items. Sporadic fighting lingered on for a few days, killing five Italians and three times as many defenders, until Albania was incorporated into the Italian Empire on 16 April.

Although mainstream historians continue to deprecate Mussolini's seizure of that country as the victimization of yet another helpless people, events there had been very closely followed by British intelligence agents, who concluded that Italy's timely, rapid conquest scotched an imminently explosive situation with consequences not unlike those that ignited World War One in the same region. As soon as Albania was pacified, Mussolini received a personal telegram from the British foreign secretary, Sir Anthony Eden, thanking him for his correct action and affirming Great Britain's support in the matter.[15]

The *Duce* received no such telegrams from the French, whose relations with Italy had been in decline throughout the 1930s. They regarded the Albanian crisis with alarm, a move whereby the *Regia Marina*, the Italian Navy, had secured its rear in the east to threaten them in the west. By the end of the decade, Paris was more likely to make war on Mussolini than against Hitler. During the Spanish Civil War, Italians fighting too close to the Pyrenees had made the French nervous. They were jittery, too, about Italian military installations on the Libyan coast, where the French fleet was widely believed to be suddenly compromised. There was little Mussolini could say to assuage these objections.

"What do they want of me?" he asked an American reporter interviewing him for the *Chicago Tribune*, "Pack up our ships and get out of North Africa just to accommodate their navy? We would be happy to oblige them, if only they agreed to do the same. Disarmament, like universal peace, is a wonderful idea, but it must be mutual to work. I have been saying for years I will be happy to take the first step in that direction, but I can't go it alone. In the meantime, the Mediterranean is a large body of water, big enough for several fleets. We are not challenging the French or anybody. We operate a fleet for the same reason as they; namely, to protect overseas' colonies. We want nothing from the French, but to be left alone." And, repeating an old theme, "They have their empire, which they think a glorious thing, but they object to Italy having one, and a very much smaller version, I might add, than theirs!"[16]

Recriminations such as these did not exactly soothe international feelings. On 22 May 1939 Germany and Italy cemented their alliance in the Pact of Steel, solidifying their alliance, although it did nothing to improve suspicions of military ambition nurtured by the Western Allies. The similar ideological forces driving both nations combined with either's growing isolation from most of the outside world, resulting in closer ties. But throughout that long, hot summer, Italy's relations with France continued to simmer, threatening to boil over.

"The Fascist loves his neighbor," Mussolini told the world, "but the word 'neighbor' does not stand for some vague, amorphous conception. Love of one's neighbor does not exclude necessary educational severity. Fascism will have nothing to do with groundless, universal embraces (an ill-concealed jibe at the still-despised League of Nations). As a member of the community of nations, it looks other peoples straight in the eye. It is vigilant, and on its guard. It follows the behavior of others in all their manifestations, and notes any changes in their interests. And it does not allow itself to be deceived by mutable or fallacious appearances."[17]

The guarded, defensive tone of such language reflected the growing mutual mistrust of the times. But attention shifted suddenly from the Mediterranean to Eastern Europe on 1 September, when Hitler's Wehrmacht stormed through Poland. To Mussolini, the invasion seemed like another localized conflict, but with potential for a broader conflagration, in view of the assurances that had been given the Poles by Britain and France. He immediately contacted diplomatic representatives in London and Paris, asking for a suspension of any war declarations until "the root causes as found in the Treaty of Versailles" had been re-examined.[18] A four-power conference, such as the one that settled the Czech Crisis, should be convened at once. While opposed to a replay of Munich-1938, Hitler offered to withdraw his forces, save for the city of Danzig, which had been severed from Germany twenty-one years before by the victors at Versailles.

But the Western Allies would have none of it this time. Mussolini pointed out to them the futility of their position. No one could save Poland now. And according to their own sworn pledge, Britain and France were compelled to fight "any nation (without publicly specifying Germany) that violated Polish sovereignty". Yet, they were obliged under the same agreement to declare war on Russia which occupied eastern Poland two weeks after the German invasion began. The *Duce* called for a moratorium on the fighting, "before the situation becomes yet more dangerous. During the last ten days of August," he recalled five years later, "Italy made what might be called a desperate effort to try and avert the catastrophe. This was acknowledged by all parties in books and speeches, even by our present enemies."[19]

By 10 September, Ciano had already made several attempts at intermediating peace, assuring the British ambassador, Percy Loraine, that Mussolini could persuade Hitler to suspend operations in Poland for the sake of negotiations regarding Danzig, over which the war had begun. "It seems ludicruous, macabre that an entire world must incinerate itself because of one, small, remote city," the Count almost laughed.[20] Loraine contacted Lord Halifax, who discussed the Italian offer at a war-cabinet meeting, where Winston Churchill, a new cabinet member, scotched all further diplomatic feelers: "If Ciano realises our inflexible purpose, he will be less likely to toy with the idea of an Italian mediation."[21]

Mussolini was less inflexible. "I did not want war," he stated. "I saw it approaching with the deepest anguish. I felt that it was a question-mark hovering over the whole future of the nation. Three military undertakings had ended successfully: the Abyssinian War, the Spanish Civil War, and the union of Albania with Italy. I thought that a pause was now necessary in order to develop and perfect the work. From the point of view of human loss, the figures were modest, but the financial and administrative strain had been enormous. Nor must one forget the nervous strain of a people which, save for short intervals, had been at war since 1911! It was therefore high time to give people's nerves a rest; it was high time to apply the nation's energy to works of peace."[22]

The French deigned not to respond to Mussolini's proposals for a ceasefire, while British diplomats maintained cordial, if cagey relations with Italy. As Germany's uncommitted ally, Mussolini felt he was in the best position to broker an end to the fighting during the so-called 'Sitzkrieg' of inactivity that lasted from Poland's defeat until the onset of the Western Campaign, the following spring. At first, Hitler gave the nod to Mussolini's behind-the-scenes peace efforts, which fell on deaf French ears. The British were at least willing to listen, but the upshot of their diplomatic conversations was always the same. They invited Mussolini to change sides, promising him the Tyrol (long a contentious issue between Italy and Germany), Austria in its entirety, and portions of Bavaria, together with all previously neglected demands, after the Third Reich was destroyed.

"The Italy of 1940 is not the Italy of 1914," he told them. "We've heard that story before, much to our regret. Why should we believe you now? Besides, these territories are not yours to give away. In any case, I doubt their inhabitants have been consulted about the matter, anymore than you asked the natives of India or Africa for permission to colonize them, for their own good, I am sure!"[23]

In March, he met with Hitler, symbolically enough, at the Italian frontier near the Brenner Pass, where the *Führer* urged him to join him against the Western Allies. But Mussolini was reluctant to fight an Anglo-French coalition. He confessed that his armed forces, still recuperating from military campaigns in East Africa, Spain and Albania, would not be ready for at least another two or three years. Meanwhile, he would continue diplomatic efforts to stop the war. Hitler respected his decision, and got on with his plans for an April offensive in the West. Before it exploded with the ferocity of a sudden spring storm, British attempts to sway Mussolini to their side with tempting morsels of Tyrolean, Austrian and Bavarian real estate had obviously failed. Alarmed at his meeting with Hitler, "Paris and London announced their intention of seizing all shipments of German coal intended for use in Italian industries in mid-Channel".[24] The news came as a shock to the Italians, who had managed to stay out of the fighting while preserving relations with both sides.

Threatening sanctions again was a provocation that particularly riled Mussolini. "Italy is a neutral nation," he bristled, "and, as such, may trade with whomever she chooses. Seizing our goods on the high seas violates the very premise of international law. There is a word for such action. It is called 'piracy'. As our own recent history shows, economic sanctions invariably constitute a prelude to war. From today on, the world recognizes the identity of the real aggressors." He lamented the solemn pledge made just eleven years before by forty-five nations – including Italy, Germany, Britain and France – to abandon war as a means of settling international disputes. The Kellogg Pact had "found its way to the graveyard of sensible initiatives which have failed."[25]

From the Allies' point of view, immediate war with Italy was desirable before she had time to up-grade her armaments, now that British diplomats were convinced they could not tempt Mussolini with promised German territories. While strategists in both London and Paris correctly assessed the Italian Armed Forces' condition of unreadiness, they wrongfully equated it with the Wehrmacht. They dismissed the Third Reich's apparent strength as so much propaganda that would be swiftly debunked on the first day of battle. Since the early 1930s, Allied rearmament continued to outpace military production in 'the totalitarian states'.

During 1939, the year the war began, the French government outspent Germany on armaments, while its large air force was more heavily funded than Hermann Goering's Luftwaffe. Beginning in February 1934, according to U.S. journalist, Doug Brinkley, Paris was spending a billion francs annually for its air force alone.[26] Five years later, it fielded more than 3,000 aircraft, somewhat less than the Luftwaffe, but combined with the sizeable and modernized Polish, Dutch and British air forces, the Germans would be outnumbered in the air. Altogether, army reserves in Poland, the Netherlands, France and Britain totalled some ten million men, outnumbering German reserves by five to one.

At sea, the Allies had twenty times the warships possessed by the German Navy, the Kriegsmarine. But a resurgent Italy combined with German technological advances might constitute a serious challenge in the next decade. The French Army and British Navy were the mightiest organizations of their kind on Earth. Better to use them now, while their ascendency was still unquestioned.

The *Duce* hurriedly convened his military chiefs of staff for an assessment of Italy's ability to wage a prolonged war against the British and French Empires. On paper, Italian prospects looked good. 1,630,000 men served in seventy-three Army divisions comprising 166 infantry regiments, a dozen *Bersaglieri*, or light infantry regiments, another dozen cavalry, ten *Alpini* mountain regiments, nineteen of engineers, thirty-two artillery and five tank. Mussolini was not told, however, that just twenty divisions – less than a third – were fully equipped and manned. Generals in the *Commando Supremo*, the Italian High Command, assured him that upgrading of the armed forces was far ahead of schedule. The *Esercito*, *Regia Marina* and *Regia Aeronautica* were quite capable or undertaking anything asked of them, they stated confidently. Their splendid performance during the recently concluded Spanish Civil War was held up as proof of their efficacy.

This rosy portrayal was mostly a deception, however. Only the navy, with five new or modernized battleships protected by numerous cruisers, and 122 destroyers was in a relatively satisfactory state of preparedness, although these vessels would be badly outnumbered by the combined fleets of Britain and France.

Elements of the Regia Marina during pre-war maneuvers off Naples,
as seen from the bridge of the heavy cruiser Trento.

True, the *Esercito* possessed almost 8,000 pieces of artillery, but Mussolini was not informed that only 246 of them had been manufactured after 1930. Most were not even made in Italy, but First World War field-guns received from the defunct Austro-Hungarian Army as part of reparations provided by the Treaty of Versailles in 1919! To cover their antiquity, Army brass secretly ordered the original wooden spokes of the carriage wheels replaced with shiny steel, a deliberate fabrication that deceived Mussolini and the outside world.

Francesco Pricolo, the Major General of Aviation, boasted he had 3,296 warplanes at his disposal. But this impressive figure was misleading. In fact, Italy operated only 166 modern fighters, Fiat G.50s and Macchi-200s, and both types were inferior to French and British frontline interceptors. The *Regia Aeronautica's* remaining 1,334 aircraft were outnumbered and mostly out-matched by the Allies.

Ciano suspected that division strength had been multiplied beyond actual availability, just as the number of men serving in the infantry was grossly exaggerated to cover the failure of army brass. "Fantasies are being woven around the Air Force," he wrote in his diaries. "I have advised an investigation by the Prefects. They are to count the aircraft in the hangars, and get at an accurate figure, which should not be an impossible undertaking. Up to today, we have not succeeded in getting at the truth."[27]

Sixty years later, Romano, Mussolini's son, remembered that "the reports Il *Duce* received talked about 'flawless aeronautical equipment fully prepared to meet future challenges.' In reality, the Spanish exploits had drained Italy's arsenal, which had been greatly reduced during the Ethiopian War."[28] It was the success of these two campaigns after all, that engendered over-confidence in man like Pricolo, who were additionally anxious to camouflage their failings and neglect with bloated statistics.

Had Mussolini known his commanding generals were lying to him about Italy's lack of military preparedness, he would have doubtless refrained from entering the fray when he did. As he later regretted, "I took the airmen's word for it, who, after all, were the experts who ought to have known more than I did. For that matter, Marshal Badoglio, who was Chief of General Staff for seventeen years, never pointed out these mistakes or that situation to me."[29]

Most Italian equipment was worn out, steeped in obsolescence, or sub-standard. By the end of World War Two, most Italian artillery still dated to the First World War or earlier. There were some state-of-the-art field-pieces in the *Esercito*, such as the *Cannone* 18 Models 35 and 37, firing 75mm shells with efficiency equal to German assault guns. But their numbers were never sufficient enough to replace the old artillery. The vast majority of Italian artillery shells were badly understrength. The Carcano *Modello* 91, the Italian soldier's standard bolt-action rifle, dated back to 1891, before the Battle of Adowa! Its small, 6.5mm caliber made it altogether inferior to the English Lee Enfield or French *Lebel*. Even after the 91/38 version firing a 7.35mm round was introduced, Germany's old-standard 8mm Mauser still out-classed it.

Italy's worst deficiency by far was her inadequate armor. Again, things seemed good on paper. Her 700 tanks were numerically comparable to most other major powers in 1940. But she began World War Two with no heavy or medium tanks. Crews of the L.6 were poorly protected, while its short-barreled 37mm gun lacked punch. Worse yet, the Italian Army still relied on its *Carro* CV 33, which had performed so poorly on Abyssinian and Spanish battlefields. Some 2,000 of these 'tankettes' and their similarly worthless

CV 35 variants were manufactured to be slaughtered with impunity by the British in the Libyan Desert.

In at least one military vehicle, however, the Italians excelled: the Camonietta 42 or *Sahariana*. Bristling with 20mm Soluthurn and 47/32 anti-tank guns, plus 13.2mm heavy machine-guns, the armored car was far ahead of its time, comparable to early 21st Century 'Humvee' all-terrain patrol cars. Strong, fast and reliable, it operated within an incredible range of 970 kilometers. Also excellent was the 81/14 Model 35. Able to throw a heavy bomb at 1,500 meters or a light one at 4,052 meters with pinpoint accuracy, the 81 mm mortar was the finest in the Second World War. Captured specimens were highly prized spoils of war by British soldiers, who knew to their misfortune that the Model 35 seriously outclassed their own versions. Throughout the war, in every campaign the Italians fought, their mortar teams were invariably the best, and often redeemed otherwise disastrous confrontations with the enemy.

One more bright spot in Italy's mostly bleak military condition was the 'Voluntary Militia for National Security' (MVSN), the Fascist Party's military arm, composed of ideological fanatics as young as 17 years old or into their 50s. Regarded as a fourth armed service, it escaped the corruption and incompetence of House of Savoy dynasts in charge of the Army, Navy and, to a lesser extent, Air Force. As such, MVSN personnel coalesced into a kernel of military renovation after the royal failures of 1940. As some indication of the popularity of Mussolini's war in Ethiopia, enough men volunteered to flesh out seven MVSN divisions. Another four campaigned in North Africa, where they were virtually annihilated in the first months of combat, attesting to their fearlessness. Battle-hardened survivors and new recruits formed the 'M Battalions', known for their ruthless hunting down of partisans in Yugoslavia and victory-or-death attitude on the Eastern Front. Meanwhile, MVSN volunteers contributed to the sorely needed reorganization of the Italian military, beginning in 1941. Worse even than its materiel deficiencies, the Italian army chain of command was badly organized, and *Regia Aeronautica* cooperation with the navy was virtually non-existent, leaving the *Supermarina* almost blind at sea.

Mussolini's foreign enemies were well aware of these deficiencies. According to historian Alexander Gibson, closing the English Channel to his trade with the Third Reich was a deliberate provocation by the Allies to force the *Duce* into the war while he was still unprepared.[30] French and British politicians were convinced Italy would link up with Hitler as soon as she was ready; hence, their determination to bring Mussolini into the fighting when he was still militarily disadvantaged.

While the outside world believed Fascism wanted to conquer the Earth, Mussolini knew that entering into hostilities with the 'plutocratic West' would be no ordinary war. It was a contest not over trade or territory, but between diametrically opposed ideologies for global domination, a life-or-death struggle between fundamentally different worldviews and those who believed in them. With his declaration of war against France and Britain on 10 June, Mussolini described the coming struggle as "the logical development of our Revolution. We have actually been at war since 1922 – that is, from the day when we lifted the flag of our Revolution, which was then defended by a handful of men against the Masonic, democratic, capitalist world."[31]

Allied success, he explained, would mean Italy's re-enslavement by international capitalists and the debasement or even outright obliteration of European culture under the spell of gross materialism. War with France and England was perceived as a fight for existence against international financial oligarchs. "This conflict must not be allowed to cancel out all our achievements of the past eighteen years," he declared, "nor, more importantly, extinguish the hope of a Third Alternative held out by Fascism to mankind fettered between the pillar of capitalist slavery and the post of Marxist chaos. The proponents of these obsolete doctrines must understand that the Fascist sword has been unsheathed twice before, in Ethiopia and Spain, with known results."[32]

Despite his confident rhetoric, Mussolini knew from the beginning that something was wrong. Mobilization proceeded with maddening slowness. Hitler's triumphant campaign in Scandinavia came and went, but still the *Esercito* was far from ready. In May, the German Panzer armies flashed through France, scoring one victory after another, as officers of the Italian General Staff still struggled to line up their forces. Cowed by Mussolini's enraged impatience, they lied again, assuring him that everything was at last in readiness. Once more misled, he immediately declared war on the Western powers.

From a propaganda perspective, the timing was awful. The French Campaign was winding down, with just two weeks of fighting left. Allied newspapers announced that Mussolini, sure of a cheap and easy victory, joined the invasion only after France was already on her knees. It certainly did look that way. But even after his general staff officers told him the army could move out at his command, General Badoglio confessed that the army needed at least another twenty five days to mount any kind of offensive. In a towering rage, the *Duce* demanded that an invasion commence at once through the Alps, ready or not. Meanwhile, he was ridiculed throughout the West as a cowardly bully riding on Hitler's coat-tails, attacking the French when they were already vanquished. President Roosevelt, referring to Mussolini, told Americans in a radio broadcast, "the hand that held the dagger has struck it into the back of its neighbor."[33]

If the Italians were still mired in organizational chaos, their new enemies were not slow to act. As early as 31 May, Churchill had discussed the Allied response if Italy entered the war. "I proposed that we should strike by air-bombing at the northwestern industrial triangle enclosed by the three cities of Milan, Turin and Genoa," he later recalled his discussion with French generals in Paris. "Many Italians were opposed to war, and all should be made to realise its severity."[34]

Twelve days later, Wellington medium-bombers took off from airfields in France. Meeting no resistance as they crossed into northern Italy, they tried to knock out Fiat's corporate headquarters and home manufacturing plant in Turin. The bombs went wide of their targets, exploding near the city center, killing fourteen non-combatant men and women, and badly injuring another thirty, including children. No air raid alarms sounded, and not a shot had been fired at the enemy aircraft, which returned to France without encountering a single interceptor.

The American historical writer, Nicholson Baker, tells how "the Italians took some foreign correspondents on a bus tour of the bomb damage in Turin and Milan. Four British bombs had fallen in a square in a poor section of Turin, near an oil tank," where ten civilians died. In Milan, reporters saw the Breda airplane factory, the Pirelli tire factory and a steel mill. All were undamaged. Five bombs had, however, hit a building at a Catholic children's home."[35]

From the Italian perspective, the raid was a deliberate act of terrorism aimed at innocent civilians, and national hatred for the British erupted. Until then, most Italians were not entirely sure why their country found itself at war with the West. They had been virtually unanimous in their support of military operations in Ethiopia, Spain and Albania, where the issues seemed unambiguous. Hostilities with Britain and France appeared far less clear until the Wellingtons' air raid.

With the 'terror attack' on non-combatant men and women, however, Mussolini got the popular support he needed from his fellow countrymen. They cried out for retaliation, and pilots of the *Regia Aeronautica* were glad to oblige. Less than twenty-four hours after the Turin 'massacre', Fiat *Cicognas* struck at Toulon, Hyeres, Saint-Raphael, Calvi, Bastia, and Bizerta. Their bombing accuracy was spoiled, however, by intense anti-aircraft fire, which broke up their formations. Little damage was incurred by the Allies in these attacks.

Units of Fiat fighters were hurriedly posted near Turin to intercept future enemy sorties, but, lacking night-interdiction capabilities, the antiquated double-deckers failed to oppose another appearance by the foe, this time by French Potez bombers, which struck the city after dark. *Regia Aeronautica* commanders then hastily improvised a *Sezione Caccia Notturna*, or 'Night Fighter Flight', of just three almost wholly inadequate CR.32s fitted with extended exhaust manifolds to shield tell-tale exhaust flames from the engine. Based at Rome's Ciampino airport, the trio of specialty biplanes did not have long to wait.

On the evening of 13 August, the British returned, but only one of the Fiats was able to make contact with them. It was flown by *Capitano* Giorgio Gaffer, who closed on a twin-motor Whitley. At the critical moment, his guns jammed, so he rammed the enemy airplane, then bailed out. The British pilot struggled to keep his critically damaged bomber airborne, but, gradually disintegrating during the return flight, it crashed into the English Channel. For his dramatic interception, Gaffer received the Bronze Medal. He went on to become an ace with another four victories during the Greek Campaign, where he was killed in a dogfight with Gloster Gladiators over Delvinakion three months after deliberately colliding with the Whitley bomber. Mussolini posthumously awarded him Italy's highest citation, the Gold Medal for Military Valor.

On dawn of the day after *Capitano* Gaffer's debut with the *Sezione Caccia Notturna*, heavy cruisers of the French Navy's 3rd Squadron, escorted by a flotilla of light cruisers, opened fire on the port of Genoa. Potez ground-attack aircraft joined in the attack, bombing the industrial areas of the ancient city defended only by several, slow-firing coastal batteries. One of these lobbed a 152mm shell at the French destroyer, *Albatros*, which then disengaged from the action after this near miss. Her companion vessels – the *Foch, Algerie, Dupleix* and *Colbert* – proceeded unscathed, leaving Genoa under a pall of smoke.

"Where is the *Regia Marina*?!" people demanded. Only the *Calatafimi*, a mere destroyer-escort, plus some motor torpedo boats from the 13th *MAS Squadrilla*, tardily approached the enemy cruisers, which ignored them, and turned away to renew their mission by blasting the helpless ports of Savona and Vado with impunity. Down to their reserve shells, the 3rd Squadron warships returned to Toulon minus any serious interdiction from either sea or sky.

A worse blunder was committed by the *Regia Marina* even before the first shots had been fired by the French fleet. *Supermarina* commanders had failed to alert Italian captains overseas before Mussolini's declaration of war, which would have allowed the merchant men time to return to Italy. As a consequence of this unpardonable neglect, the Allies effortlessly seized 212 freighters, tankers and transports of various kinds amounting to 1,236,160 tons the moment hostilities officially began. A quarter of the Italian merchant marine was lost without a fight in one, fell swoop. To prosecute the war, the Italians had been suddenly reduced to 604 serviceable ships totaling 1,984,292 tons.

With French warships' almost leisurely bombarding Italy's west coast, the *Regia Aeronautica's* thorough inability to defend its homeland from attack was now all too apparent. There were not enough warplanes in the entire Italian Air Force to shield half of the country's major cities. Every type of aircraft had been committed to the campaign in the West, leaving the country virtually unprotected. Meanwhile, two more French cruisers, the *Duquesne* and *Tourville*, sortied from their base at Alexandria, Egypt, to shell Italian holdings in the Aegean, again without encountering any opposition. A week later, destroyers sank the first Italian submarine lost in the war, the *Provana*. By then, the French suffered their sole loss in the Mediterranean when one of their own submarines, the *Morse*, struck a mine.

On 16 June, the Breda Aviation Company's much-heralded though over-valued Ba.88, the *Lince*, got its baptism of fire when a dozen of the *aeroplano di combattimento* of the 19th *Gruppo Automono* bombed and strafed airfields at Corsica, losing a trio of the twin-engine planes to French ground-fire. Three days later, the remaining nine Ba.88s descended on Corsica once more. All survived the raid, but inflicted only light damage on the enemy.

So far, the war had been conducted exclusively by warships (predominantly French) and aircraft (mostly British). Even at Mussolini's emphatic insistence, the army could only get a move on for another eleven days after his declaration of war. Marshal Badoglio was right. The *Esercito* was woefully unprepared. It did not even have enough pots and pans with which to feed its troops, let alone equipment sufficient to carry forward a real offensive. In spite of these grave inadequacies, nineteen of the thirty-two divisions massed in the Alps lurched at designated enemy positions after dawn. In overall charge of the invasion was Prince Umberto, heir to the throne – a bad omen for Italian prospects, which would suffer the worst effects of royal duplicity for the next three years.

Naturally, much of southern France's regional defense had been siphoned off long before to fight the Germans, who now threatened the Alpine Army's rear by marching down the Rhone Valley from the northwest. By splitting his forces to fend off the Wehrmacht, General Orly, the French commanding officer, could oppose the Italians in the southeast with only half of his already severely diminished strength. In the brief campaign that followed, soldiers on both sides fought with extraordinary fortitude. While Mussolini's troops sought to compensate material draw-backs with death-defying determination, the French were entrenched and resolute.

The Italian invasion began promptly on 21 June at 0530 hours with a heavy barrage aimed at La Turra. But Italy's World War One-vintage shells bounced off the defiant fort. Italian guns performed no better at Briancon, where French 280mm howitzers silenced Italian fortifications at Chamberton. The *Regia Aeronautica* was called in to break the defenders, but the pin-pointed targets were beyond the accuracy of level-flight-bombers, which passed overhead without effect. Italian aviation needed an efficient dive-bomber, but its sole attempt – the *Lince* – had been a complete failure.

Against the Bourg-Saint-Maurice, Mon, Petit Saint-Bernard and Seigne passes, defended by just four battalions and forty four pieces of artillery, the Italians advanced with a dozen battalions, retracing the route Hannibal took more than two millennia before to invade Italy. Coming to the aid of General Orly's outnumbered men was a freak snow-storm of almost cataclysmic proportions. The invaders' light tanks bogged down, and ordinance froze in place. All aircraft were grounded, and the Italian infantry suffered 2,000 cases of frostbite.

In the midst of extraordinarily inclement conditions, the poorly out-fitted Italians succeeded in surrounding a fortified post near the Petit Saint-Bernard pass, but were unable to take it. They stormed Modane in an effort to breach the passes at Bellecombe, Clapier, Mont-Cenis and Solliers, but were rebuffed. A pair of Italian battalions outflanked French reconnaissance units, which retreated to the La Tuille dam, then Le Planey. But by the end of the first day of fighting, the Italians had been stopped all along the front, save at the Le Queyras headland, where they encircled Abries, a fortified village.

The next day was better for the Italians, but not much. Although they took the eastern approaches of Menton, the rest of their renewed advances were frustrated. The arrival of substantial reinforcements on the 22nd afforded them no headway. By the 24th, they were still unable to move forward when, at 2100-hours, came word of the armistice with Germany.

An hour later, General Orly stated, "Of the thirty two divisions of the Italian army, nineteen were wholly or partly engaged against the outposts, and, in a few cases, the main elements of our six divisions. We were outnumbered seven to one at Tarentaise, four to one in Maurienne, three to one in Brianconnais, twelve to one in Queyras, nine to one in Ubaye, six to one in Tinee, seven to one in L'Aution and Sospel, and four to one in Menton. Our adversary only made contact with or approached our main positions in Tarentaise and near Menton. All our fortified advance posts held out, even when encircled."[36]

Against 40 French soldiers killed, 84 wounded and 150 unaccounted for, the Italians lost 631 dead, 2,361 wounded, and 600 missing. After four days, the invasion had crawled a scant five miles from the French border with Italy before being stopped.

At least, the *Regia Aeronautica* had gone farther. Its airmen flew 1,337 sorties, carrying out 715 raids to drop 276 tons of bombs with precision and effect, representing extraordinarily intense activity compressed into only two weeks. Even so, the Italians' antiquated biplanes were decidedly inferior to Dewoitine, Bloch and Morane-Saulnier interceptors. On 15 June, for example, a dozen *Falcos* of the 23th *Gruppo* were bounced by half as many Dewoitine D.520s of GCIII/6's fifth squadron. Its Vice-Commander, Adjutant Pierre Le Golan, immediately shot down a pair of CR.42s before his flight accidentally strayed into another formation, from which he downed a third Fiat over Hyeres.

Returning to base, he discovered it was under attack by the 75th *Squadriglia*, and promptly destroyed the first enemy plane he could catch in his sights. It belonged to *Capitano* Luigi Filippi, the *Squadriglia's* Commanding Officer. Le Golan's success represented the *Regia Aeronautica's* blackest day of the Campaign, during which its fighter pilots flew 1,770 hours over the front, carried out eleven strafing runs, and were credited with ten 'kills' in aerial combat. Nearly a third were claimed in a single combat, when Giuseppe Ruzzin, the noted Spanish Civil War veteran, shot down a trio of Bloch MB.152 fighters in cooperation with three other Falcons.

Dozens more warplanes of all types belonging to France's *Armee de l'Air* were destroyed on the ground at Provence, together with airfield supplies and facilities, by Savoia-Marchetti and CANT bombers. Their important success was the *Regia Aeronautica's* high-point in an otherwise less than brilliantly executed invasion, and justified Mussolini's faith in tactical bombing. Indeed, his aviators' relative success may have saved their comrades on the ground from something worse than a stalemate. During the brief campaign, the

Regia Aeronautica lost twenty-four airmen killed, but destroyed an additional fifty French aircraft on the ground.

On 30 June, the *Duce* drove to Lanslebourg, in Maurienne, where he frankly congratulated his troops at the Alpine front for their valor in spite of sub-zero conditions, sub-standard equipment and insufficient supply.

"Looking into their fatigued, joyful faces," he admitted to Ciano, "I swore then that I would have a military we could be proud of once more, no matter what the cost in career officers!"[37]

Driving from the Mont-Cenis pass, he was surprised to see the French tricolor still fluttering over a battered installation. An army advisor informed him that this was the same La Turra fort that had successfully resisted bombardment and encirclement from the first hour of the invasion. It continued to be defended by Sub-Lieutenants Prudhon and Chandesris with nine NCOs, plus forty-one *Chasseur* riflemen and gunners. After a moment of poignant silence, the *Duce* ordered the French heroes freed and given special honors of war with his compliments.

He had more trouble with Paris politicians. They refused to recognize his contribution to their defeat, until he threatened to renew aerial attacks against Merton. That brought them back to the negotiation table, but their capitulation offered small compensation for the exceedingly poor performance of his ground forces. The Allied historian, Raymond Klibansky, concluded that Mussolini's "attack on an almost defeated France, far from bringing the Italian Army any laurels, had revealed it parlous state."[38]

4

King Of Beasts By The Tail

War alone keys up all human energies to their maximum tension, and sets
the seal of nobility on those peoples who have the courage to face it.
Mussolini[1]

In September, still itching to hit back at the British for their 'terrorist' raid on Turin, Mussolini dispatched a *Corpo Aereo Italiano* to German-occupied Belgium for operations against targets in southeast England. But revenge was the C.A.I.'s least important motivation. Tactically, its primary mission was to damage harbor facilities at Folkstone, Harwich, Foulness, Ramsgate, Margate, and other port cities, because the war against the British Empire was fundamentally a naval campaign.

More broadly, the Italians' strategic goal was to divert aircraft and personnel of the RAF's already overstretched resources from defending London and other, industrial centers then being heavily attacked by the Luftwaffe. The mere appearance of *Regia Aeronautica* bombers over the south coast of England was sufficient to justify their participation for every Hurricane or Spitfire they could distract from the real Battle of Britain raging in the north. With these objectives, the C.A.I. crews would prove remarkably effective, contrary to Allied propaganda, which had them effortlessly slaughtered minus any successes whatsoever.

Three *Stormi* of eighty-seven fighters, five reconnaissance planes, and seventy-eight bombers originally made up the Italian Air Corps. These forces were later expanded with the addition of another *Squadriglia* that included CANT Z.1007bi long-range reconnaissance tri-motors, several Caproni Ca.164 communications planes, and one Savoia-Marchetti S.M.75 all-purpose transport, bringing the total number to somewhat less than 300 aircraft.

Their 6,600 personnel of all ranks were led by Air Marshal Rino Corso-Fougier. A brilliant officer and skilled pilot, his recent experience during the French Campaign would prove invaluable. Having personally engaged British fighters over southern France, he fully appreciated their superiority over the Fiat biplanes and poky bombers with which he was expected to make a name for himself in British skies.

Thanks to Corso-Fougier's diplomatic sense, relations with Luftwaffe personnel were cordial, even friendly, especially as the Battle of Britain wore on and both Luftwaffe and C.A.I. flyers suffered losses in common. "Nothing can better make the lasting relations between peoples animated by mutual ideals," Mussolini declared at the time, "than bloodshed in the common cause and sacrifices shared."[2]

At first sight, the Germans laughed at their Italian allies' old-fashioned-looking warplanes. But several Luftwaffe pilots invited to test the Fiat *Falco* for themselves were impressed by its 430-kph-speed, much faster than they imagined for any biplane, and admired its robust agility. Ironically, the first victims of World War Two to fall under the CR.42's twin Breda Safat 12.7 mm machine-guns had been German. The few Fiat fighters Belgium's *Aeronautique Militaire* had purchased for its *IIème Group de Chasse* had acquitted themselves well during the Wehrmacht invasion of the Low Countries the previous May, shooting down five Luftwaffe planes for the loss of two 'Falcons'. Their victories against state-of-the-art Messerschmitts should have told the British that the little double-decker was not to be dismissed as a toothless antique.

"Extremely light on the controls," commented Field Marshal Albert Kesselring, in charge of the German aerial offensive, "it is a delight to fly, and will hold its own against the enemy until Italian aviation can come up with a modern replacement. The *Falco* should be as much a surprise to the British as it was to us."[3]

It was indeed. An RAF Intelligence report issued to Prime Minister Winston Churchill and the War Cabinet warned, "The maneuverability of the CR.42s, in particular their capacity to execute an extremely tight half-roll, has caused considerable surprise to other pilots and undoubtedly saved many Italian fighters from destruction."[4] The report was seconded by Captain Eric Brown after putting a captured *Falco* through its paces. The British test pilot found the biplane "remarkably fast" with "a marginal stability which is the mark of a good fighter." He deemed it "brilliantly maneuverable, an aerobatic gem, but under-gunned and very vulnerable to enemy fire."[5]

C.A.I. pilots had similar views of their opponents. According to Flying Officer Giulio Giuntella, "the English .303 bullet was not very effective. Italian aircraft received many hits which did no material damage, and one pilot even found that his parachute pack had stopped a bullet."[6] A man similarly protected was Flight Sergeant Franco Campanile of the 83rd *Squadriglia*, whose pack absorbed several rounds from a Spitfire. As further testimony to the weakness of British machine-gun fire, another 83rd *Squadriglia* veteran took no less than three bullets in the lungs, but still flew his damaged aircraft back across the North Sea to ditch near a Belgian beach. Warrant Officer Felice Sozzi recovered from his ordeal to win the *Medaglia d'Argento al Valore* and resume his flying career.

Weak enemy firepower and the *Falco's* superior maneuverability combined with Italian skill and courage was all Corso-Fougier could hope for against an otherwise superior enemy. The Supermarine Spitfire was arguably the finest interceptor of its time, outclassing anything comparable in the *Regia Aeronautica*, but the Hawker Hurricane actually destroyed more Axis aircraft. Faster than the *Falco* by 102 kilometers per hour, and armed with eight Browning machine guns, its high rate of climb made it a particularly lethal opponent in the hands of skilled pilots.

And there were many in the 46th Squadron that tangled with the C.A.I. on 11 November, when forty 'Falcons' escorting ten *Storks* of the 43rd *Stormo* attacked Harwich during daylight. Three CR.42s and as many Breda bombers were shot down with no RAF casualties. The British pilots who fought this action were combat-experienced, bloodied veterans of encounters with the Luftwaffe during the previous September, when they scored nineteen 'kills', but lost twenty of their own.

The Italians were additionally disadvantaged by the short-range capabilities of their own aircraft, which allowed them little more than ten minutes flying time over southern England. This restrictive window-of-opportunity contributed significantly to the low number of aerial victories won by C.A.I. pilots, who were often forced to break off an engagement for lack of fuel. The low-wing G.50 was a more modern fighter than the biplane *Falco,* but its radius of action was just 445 kilometers, even without armor protection for the pilot or armored fuel tanks. Round-trip operations from bases in Belgium to targets in southern England took 275 kilometers, cutting the Italians' combat time short.

But the most important factor working against them was the British interception of Axis radio traffic that provided ample warning of an impending raid, so much so, the approaching Italians often found the RAF already waiting for them before they neared their targets. Aileen Clayton belonged to a group of Wireless Units listening in on enemy transmissions, and recalled how their "conscientious monitoring would be largely responsible for British fighters being so well placed they were able to effect a crushing defeat on the first Italian sortie of note on 11 November."[7] Flight Sergeant Luigi Gorrini remembered how this system of radio location "enabled them to find our forces before we reached the English coast and attack us from directions we least expected."[8]

The truly daunting odds faced by the men of the *Corpo Aereo Italiano* put their struggle over the English Channel into proper perspective. As historian Peter Haining concluded, "Out of almost a thousand missions of all types flown from the Belgian bases, this figure does credit to the skill of the C.A.I pilots, no matter what their achievements may have amounted to."[9]

After Kesselring presented Corso-Fougier with a Fieseler *Storch* command plane for his personal use, both men agreed that *Luftflotte* 2 would control the target sectors allotted to the Italians and facilitate inter-service communication, an important feature, because only three C.A.I. planes were equipped with radio; the rest lacked instrumental navigation of any kind. The 13th *Stormo* B.T., together with the 172nd Reconnaissance Squadron, flew out of the Melsbroek airfield, while Ursel was home to the 43rd *Stormo* B.T. The 22nd *Gruppo* C.T.'s fifty 'Falcons' operated from Maldeghem.

On 22 October, Corso-Fougier reported his *Stormi* were ready for action, and, three days later, eighteen *Cicogna* bombers took off to raid Felixtowe and Harwich after nightfall, returning to their Belgian airstrip without suffering any losses. Back home, Italy's major daily newspaper, Il *Gionale D'Italia*, featured a front page article about the C.A.I.'s first raid headlined, "British Aggression Answered by Italian Might". The story read, "By boldly executing attacks with well-aimed bombs, Italian aircraft have obtained great success against harbor works in the east of England. This marks the beginning of action against the metropolitan territories of Great Britain as a reprisal and severe warning against aggression of the RAF over the territories of northern Italy."[10]

To celebrate the eighteenth anniversary of Mussolini's 'March on Rome', a stronger effort was made on 29 October against Ramsgate Harbor in a somewhat bizarre daylight raid. Fifteen *Cicognas* escorted by thirty-four Fiat G.50s and thirty-nine *Falcos* approached in a low-level pass virtually wing-tip to wing-tip, as though performing in an air show. This theatrical effect was augmented by the warplanes' own gaily painted camouflage in pale green and bright blue colors, which were doubtless appropriate for a Mediterranean setting, but made the C.A.I. warplanes resemble a flying circus in the somber skies of autumnal England. British anti-aircraft personnel were so awestruck by the approaching formation they needed several minutes to recover from their surprise before opening fire. When they saw the *Cicognas* and *Falcos* escorted by a group of more seriously camouflaged German Messerschmitt Me 109 fighters, some gunners thought the Italian planes "stood out like peacocks among eagles".[11]

On the afternoon of 8 November, twenty-two G.50s flying an offensive patrol between Dungeness, Folkstone, Canterbury and Margate held their own against RAF fighters, although no claims were made by either side. That same day, radar detected *Cicognas* approaching the English coast, and Hawker Hurricanes from the 17th and 257th Squadrons were scrambled to join up with other fighters of the 46th Squadron already airborne and patrolling near Foulness. British interceptors converged on the approaching bombers, mauling them badly.

The following day, RAF Bomber Command, in response to the Italians' presence over the Channel, dispatched a flight of Wellingtons in a return raid on Turin, the same city where the retalitory air strikes had begun the previous June. Only two hospitals – one military, the other maternity – had been bombed, including a sanitorium. When C.A.I. crews leaned of the attack, they presumed it had been carried out to draw them away from Belgium, back to the defence of their homeland. If their supposition was correct, they must be more effective than they knew.

Trusting in a diversionary tactic, Corso-Fougier ordered the daring, daylight operation for the next day. While unescorted *Alcione* bombers without escort struck Great Yarmouth on 11 November, ten *Cicognas* and as many German *Stuka* dive-bombers protected by forty 'Falcons' struck Harwich. The decoy tri-motors fulfilled their mission without interference, save for ineffectual anti-aircraft fire, while the main body of attacking Axis warplanes was intercepted by Hawker Hurricanes. In the resulting melee, three Italian bombers and as many fighters were shot down, the Germans and British suffering no losses, but the objective was bombed. Returning with severe battle damage, another trio of BR.20s was forced to crash-land outside the base at Ursel.

Subsequent raids usually involved eighty Fiat *Cicognas* of the 13th and 43th *Stormi* escorted by fifty *Falco* fighters from the 18th *Gruppo*, together with fewer numbers of Fiat G.50s. Their purpose was to get the bombers through to the target, not challenge the RAF. But the nimble 'Falcons' showed what they could do in a tight situation. Spitfire pilots found their prey dangerously elusive.

"As I fired," Lieutenant Edward Preston Wells recalled, "he half-rolled very tightly, and I was completely unable to hold him, so rapid were his maneuvers. He immediately disappeared into the cloud sill, and was not seen again. I attacked two or three more, and fired short bursts, in each case the enemy aircraft half-rolled very tightly and easily, and completely out-turned me. In two cases, as they came out of their rolls, they were able to turn in almost on my tail, and opened fire on me ... they seemed to be able to pull their noses up very high to enable them to get in a short burst, without stalling, at a Spitfire climbing at maximum range."[12]

Experience taught that the Italian pilots could still prevail over their opponents. "I realized that in a maneuvered flight the CR.32 could win or survive against Hurricanes and Spitfires," concluded Flying Officer Giuntella, "though we had to be careful of a sweep from behind."[13]

In one of the Second World War's most macabre episodes, a CR.42 returning to Belgium over-shot its home runway and settled to a rough landing not far beyond the base in a farmer's field. When C.A.I. personnel sprinted to the stranded aircraft, they were horrified to find the pilot's headless body slumped over the controls. Only after the close of hostilities, five years later, did they learn that their comrade had been decapitated during close combat with a Hurricane. When he ran out of ammunition, the frustrated Canadian Flight Commander Peter 'Cowboy' Blatchford had rammed the *Falco* with his propeller. He needed all his piloting skills to control the shuddering Hurricane, which was vibrating itself to pieces after the collision. He did manage to effect a safe landing, but his ground mechanic pointed out that six inches were missing from one propeller blade, and nine inches from another. As incredible testimony to the damaged CR.32's inherent stability, it continued eastward by itself on a straight course like a free-flight model airplane, carrying its dead pilot back to Belgium.

Notwithstanding the Canadian 'Cowboy's' decapitation of an enemy combatant, relations between British and Italian pilots were generally gallant, a relationship that was to deteriorate in the years to come. When, for example, Pietro Salvadori, a sergeant in the 95th *Squadriglia* flying out of Ursel, was forced to make an emergency landing on the beach at Orfordness after the engine of his CR.32 over-heated and quit, he waved at a low-flying Hurricane pilot, who waggled his wings in greeting.

Corso-Fougier ordered another audacious daylight operation on 23 November, when a flight of twenty-nine 'Falcons' swept over the Channel coast between Ramsgate and Folkstone, looking for trouble. They found it, as twenty British fighters rose to meet the challenge. The old-fashioned Italian biplanes shot down two Hurricanes for a pair of their own lost.

Six days later, ten Fiat BR.20s of the 13th *Stormo* lifted off Melsbroech airfield at 17.45 in an audacious night-raid against two important seaports. Without fighter escort, and carrying a combined payload of 16,000 kilograms of high explosives, the twin-engine *Cicognas* could reach a respectable maximum speed of 430 km/hr, but their single 12.7mm machine-gun in the nose and 7.7mm machine-guns mounted one each in a dorsal turret and ventral position provided inadequate protection. They eluded enemy detection, and crossed the Channel without interception.

The heavily-laden *Storks* split up just before reaching the coast. Against blinding searchlights and anti-aircraft fire as accurate as it was intense, half of the flight attacked Lowestoft between 5,000 and 6,000 meters to drop their bombs on the Richards Shipyard. Great Yarmouth no less vigorously defended itself against the other five *Cicognas*, which inflicted damage on the city's harbor works. Three bombers were hit by ground-fire, but altogether the formation scored a combined total of sixty-one hits on both facilities. As the BR.20s banked into the east beyond the reach of the searchlights, they were pursued by, though successfully fought off a tardy interception of RAF night-fighters, returning to Belgium without loss.

Throughout December, British resistance in the air seemed to be on the wane, as the Italian bombers returned to pound Harwich several times with impunity, at least where the RAF was concerned, although the Channel ports' ground defenses remained strong. In fact, attrition had so reduced the number of Spitfires and Hurricanes by the end of 1940, they were thinly spread along the eastern approaches to London, leaving other cities sorely underdefended and, in most instances, completely unprotected. Both C.A.I. and Luftwaffe personnel were confident that the steady erosion of Britain's airpower must culminate in the island's surrender not long after the New Year, obviating the need for invasion.

As some indication of the RAF's dwindling capabilities, all it could muster on 19 December was a single light bomber to attack Ursel airfield. One of the 107th Squadron's remaining, serviceable machines based at Wattisham, in Suffolk, a lone Bristol Blenheim flew across the Channel at just after sunset to drop a quartet of 115-kg. bombs on several hangers and a line of parked enemy aircraft. The twin-engine Blenheim escaped with impunity into the gathering darkness, leaving behind a few damaged *Cicognas* and holed hangers, but no casualties. Its sortie revealed that the British were indeed beginning to feel pressure enough to risk one of their last operational warplanes in a desperate attempt at blunting the C.A.I.'s strike capabilities, contrary to lingering propaganda tales of light-hearted British indifference to the Italians.

Either unable or unwilling to risk any more aircraft from its depleted arsenal, the RAF ventured no further attacks against Corso-Fougier's forces. Instead, he launched a quartet of Fiat *Cicognas* from the 13th *Stormo*, which left Melsbroech airfield in a night mission against Harwich on 2 January 1941. Over the Channel, they ran into heavy snow flurries, a serious situation, because the Fiat BR.20 was not fitted with de-icing equipment. A pair of *Stork*s had to turn back when their wings began to ice up, but the other two pressed on, taking the enemy defenders by complete surprise to accurately drop ten 100-kg. incendiaries on the port, "causing considerable damage in the harbor area," according to Haining.[14] The bombers returned to Belgium without further incident, but their raid climaxed the history of the *Corpo Aereo Italiano*.

Just eight days later, its flight crews began leaving Belgium to conclude their country's participation in the West. Pilots and planes were needed to defend Italian positions in North Africa from a major British offensive rolling across Cyrenaica. Even so, two squadrons of the 20th *Gruppo* stayed on at the Channel front until April 1941. Altogether, the doughty *Cicognas* had unloosed 54 tons of ordinance over southern England, Mussolini's revenge for RAF bombs dropped on Turin the previous June.

More than three months of mostly night-time raids damaged 22% of the C.A.I.'s aircraft, not a particularly high rate, considering the 883 missions flown by fighters alone. Enemy fire from the ground accounted for just two Italian bombers. Only ten *Falcos* had fallen in combat, a testimony to the flying skills of 18th *Gruppo* pilots. They gave as good as they got, losing fifteen fighters and bombers of all types for as many Spitfires and Hurricanes accounted for. In somewhat more than 1,800 flying hours, the Italians carried out 1,076 operations against Britain for the loss of twenty-one airmen.

Contrary to Allied portrayals of Italian participation in the Battle of Britain as a ludicrous failure, the *Corpo Aereo Italiano* achieved all the objectives initially assigned to it at a relatively low cost in human life and lost aircraft. The last of its pilots missed joining in the biggest raid against England by just one month, when Herrmann Goering's Luftwaffe marshalled more than 500 bombers in May to divert the attention of the world from Hitler's mobilization for invading the Soviet Union. Until then, Mussolini's men would have to attend to more pressing business far removed from both Britain and Russia.

5

Snatching Defeat from
the Jaws of Victory

The road to failure is the road to fame.
B.H. Liddell Hart, in *Greater Than Napoleon: Scipio Africanus*[1]

The British were not slow to act after Italy's declaration of war on 10 June. The next day, their armored cars raced across the Egyptian frontier into Libya, ambushing and destroying unarmed Italian trucks near Fort Capuzzo. After three days of fierce fighting, Capuzzo and another Italian fort (Maddalena) were captured. While units of the British Army and the RAF launched a series of relentless raids throughout the Italian-held territories, British engineers excavated a powerful defensive line at Mersa Matruh, 483 kilometers west of the Suez Canal. The conquest of North and East Africa was under way.

Responding to these incursions, Mussolini and his General Staff devised a strategy calling for a massed offensive of infantry, accompanied by anti-tank guns and field artillery screened by advancing units of tanks, and covered by fighters and bombers of the *Regia Aeronautica*. They had high hopes for the campaign, so long as the initiative was maintained. A prolonged struggle would only work to the advantage of the British, who were richer in war materials. Unlike the undersupplied divisions hastily thrown together for the invasion of France, Italian forces in Africa had had four years to organize and equip themselves since the capture of Ethiopia. They comprised fourteen divisions divided between the 10th Army in the east and the 5th Army in the west.

The *Armata Azzurra*, as the Italian Air Force was known in North Africa, was not, however, very substantial. Just 88 fighters – all of them Fiat CR.32 and CR.42 biplanes – accompanied 125 bombers. Britain's Western Desert Air Force was only slightly larger and no less antiquated, with heavy reliance of its own biplane, the Gloster Gladiator. Combined British forces totaled 86,000 infantry against Italy's 280,000 troops. Equipment disparity was yet more uneven. Against 1,500 Italian guns, the British had 150 of field artillery, and their 45 tanks faced 300 operated by the Italians.

Mussolini's forces seemed overwhelmingly strong. But appearances were misleading. With few exceptions, like their *Sahariana* armored cars, virtually all their weapons were obsolete, poorly manufactured, and unreliable. Their machine-gun, the 'knuckle-busting' 8mm M1935 Fiat *Revelli*, was an updated version of an early World War One-vintage original, given to unexpectedly 'cook off' rounds chambered during lulls in operation. Italian armor was sub-standard. The M13 was supposed to be a medium tank, but was small enough to pass for a featherweight in most other armies.

British equipment was not much better, however. The Matilda, a strong, powerful tank, was nevertheless a ponderous, easy target, unable to keep up with the faster Cruiser Mk 6, itself dogged by mechanical breakdowns which often left it vulnerable. Worse for the Italians, 70% of their armies in Africa were made up of native troops. While known to generally fight well in close combat, they could be counted upon to panic under an artillery barrage or aerial assault. Moreover, they could hardly have been expected to serve with much enthusiasm or loyalty for their European conquerors. The British operated far fewer colonials in their ground forces, and possessed a decided technological advantage, at least in the air. Their Supermarine Spitfires outclassed anything flown by the *Regia Aeronautica*. Aware of these dire difficiencies, Mussolini dispatched an extra squadron of improved M-11 medium tanks to Marshal Rodolfo Graziani, commanding his armies in Libya.

Graziani began the invasion of Egypt on 13 September, intending to squeeze the enemy between both offensives. His five divisions with 200 tanks stormed across the border, taking Sollum, while the British Western Desert Force, consisting of the 7th Armored and 4th Indian Divisions, fell back. Just two days later, the Italians had penetrated sixty miles, overrunning Sidi Barrani. After four days on the march, Graziani halted the 10th Army eighty miles west of British defenses dug in at Mersa Matruh. He complained of the heat and anti-tank guns that awaited his armor, suggesting the offensive be renewed in October when his equipment replacements would be completed.

"That might be too late!" the *Duce* railed at him. He agreed that the struggle was difficult, and losses would probably be high. But the Italians must not lose their momentum now. "He who advances to the attack with decisiveness has victory already in his grasp!" The Italian 10th Army, seven divisions strong, must push on another 480 kilometers to capture the port of Alexandria, still under defended. With its seizure, the Campaign would be as good as won. 1940 was its best and perhaps only chance to succeed. "Time is working against us," Mussolini urged Marshal Graziani. "The loss of Egypt will be the *coup de grâce* for Great Britain."[2] Still, Graziani hesitated, while Mussolini fumed helplessly and sent him more supplies.

The *Duce*'s impatience was not without cause. During late August, in the very midst of the Battle of Britain, when her every resource was pressed to the limit, Britain dispatched a large convoy carrying abundant munitions, artillery, aircraft, and 150 tanks to their beleaguered forces in North Africa. Since the Italian Navy still dominated the Mediterranean Sea, British freighters had to be routed the long, time-consuming way around the Cape of Good Hope. Mussolini knew that a fat convoy was on its way that would tip the scales against him. The moment to resume the attack was now or never.

Finally re-equipped with additional armor and Fiat CR-42 fighters, Marshal Graziani relit the offensive with initially good success, only to halt again after a few days, this time to build a series of fortified camps, allowing General Wavell, commanding British forces, opportunity to organize his own counter-attack. The *Duce* was furious, and demanded the advance be resumed at once. Incredibly, Graziani refused. Time, as Mussolini argued, was running out for the Italians in North Africa. On 24 September, more than a month after it set out, the heavy-laden convoy reached the British Western Desert Force. Wavell now had 31,000 troops, 120 guns, sixty armored cars, 150 aircraft, and 275 tanks, including fifty new Matildas and 100 Cruisers. Meanwhile, Graziani, still reluctant to resume the attack, worked at strengthening and expanding his fortified camps around Sidi Barrani.

Faced with an insubordinate commander and a re-supplied enemy, Mussolini was desperate to do something that would re-tilt the balance of the desert struggle in his favor. A lone alternative seemed to be a bold operation that must irk the only other major European power on Italy's side, while risking yet another military humiliation. Yet, if it

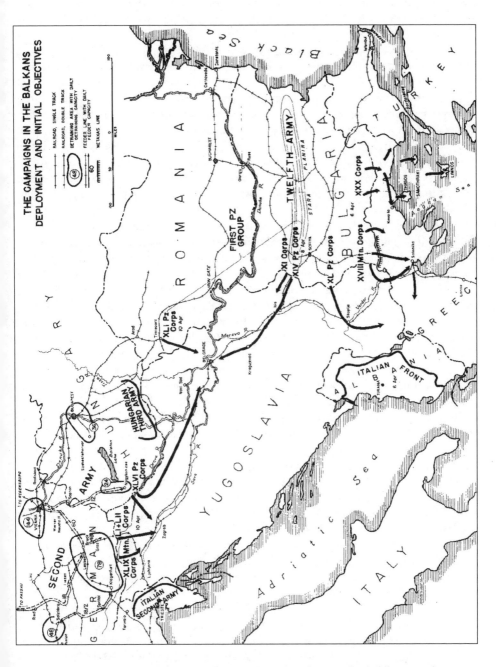

The campaigns in the Balkans, showing the Italian fronts in both Albania and
Dalmatia, and their interrelations with Hitler's strategy against Russia.

succeeded in its ulterior purpose, the effort would justify all sacrifices. Accordingly, he decided to invade Greece as a major diversionary strategy, hoping the British would draw away enough of their forces to make a critical difference in Africa. Italian reversals in Greece would even work on behalf of the diversion, making it yet more alluring to Prime Minister Winston Churchill, himself short of victories these days.

As Rex Trye, a historical investigator of 'Mussolini's Afrika Korps' observed, "The Greek campaign was to siphon off vital men and equipment needed in North Africa."[3]

There were other important considerations that urged invasion. King George II and his parliamentarians were outspoken Anglophiles busily transforming Greece into a headquarters for anti-Fascist spies and saboteurs from various parts of the world. For more than two years, OVRA directors had warned Mussolini about Greek-based espionage in Italy, and even urged at least some punitive military action against King George before the outbreak of World War Two. "From maps discovered by the German General Staff in France," Mussolini added, "it has been established that as early as May, Greece had offered to the British and French all her naval and air bases. It was imperative to put an end to this situation."[4]

The country's real leader was General Ioannis Metaxas, an ultra-royalist responsible for modernization of the Greek army. Since the Italian take-over of Albania the previous year, Metaxas had substantially enlarged and strengthened his ground forces in preparation for an inevitable clash at the border. Greece was a definite liability at Italy's unguarded eastern door. An unexpected thrust through it, with Italian attention fixed on overseas' events, could have awful consequences for the homeland. Marshal Badoglio told Mussolini he would need twenty divisions to overcome the 150,000 Greek troops, who enjoyed a superiority in the number of machine-guns. But all the *Duce* could spare were nine divisions which at least possessed more mortars, very useful in Alpine combat.

For operations against Greece, the *Regia Aeronautica* fielded nine squadrons of forty Fiat G.50s, forty-six *Falcos* and fourteen CR.32s. While not executing ground attacks, they were expected to escort twenty-four SM.81 and thirty-five SM.79 bombers. Additional air support could be flown in from Brindisi, where 119 assorted bombers, twenty German Junkers Ju.87 Stuka dive-bombers built under license in Italy, and fifty-four fighters were stationed. The Italians would appear to have badly outnumbered and outclassed the Greeks' biplane defenders – six Czech Avia B.534s and two British Gloster Gladiators – nine, less antiquated French Bloch MB151 fighters, and thirty-six PZLP.24 open-cockpit, high-wing monoplanes from defeated Poland. Three squadrons were equipped with twenty-five Bristol Blenheim IV, Fairey Battle Is, and French Potez 633 light bombers, together with six Hawker Horsley torpedo-bombers.

Known as 'Contingency C', the original Italian plan aimed at limited territorial gains into the Epirus region intended to provoke a British reaction. Only if the invasion moved quickly to cover more ground could subjugation of the entire country be considered, a secondary objective. Mussolini knew that "the rugged mountains of Epirus and its muddy valleys do not lend themselves to a lightning war, as the incorrigible experts of a comfortable armchair strategy would suggest."[5] Had he been properly informed about the level of Greek preparedness, however, he would have searched for an alternative diversion to distract Churchill. Three weeks before 'Contingency C' was launched, Italian agents at the Greek frontier alerted Rome that Metaxas had more than a quarter of a million men under arms, most of them laying in wait along the Albanian border.

Days later, Colonel Mondini, the Italian Military Attaché, reported that the Greeks had already mobilized a full sixteen divisions. This vital information was withheld from Mussolini by the privately anti-Fascist General Visconti Prasca, who repeatedly assured him that Greece was defended by no more than 30,000 troops, an assertion confirmed by the Chief of the General Staff, Pietro Badoglio. "Serving the *Duce* and the Fascist cause as long as success was on their side," writes Klibansky of the Marshal, "he withdrew and turned against them once their fortune declined."[6] Mussolini was to recall, "He drew away from the regime and began to premeditate his revenge after the start of the Greek campaign, when he was relieved of his appointment as Chief of General Staff."[7]

Just as the generals had grossly inflated the actual number of Italian warplanes available, now they deflated the real size of enemy troop strength. It was based on their statements that Mussolini had implemented his strategic actions. Promised a quantitative advantage over the Greeks, his men would find themselves badly outnumbered. "All the Army Staff, Badoglio included," he bitterly remembered four years later, "were convinced that the campaign would be a success. Visconti Prasca was positively lyrical. The information they gave me about the enemy armed forces was such that victory seemed assured in a few days, if not a few hours."[8]

In October 1941, the *Duce*'s chief concern was relieving British pressure on his beleaguered forces in North Africa by provoking their attention elsewhere. But more than Churchill would be provoked. Hitler did not want anyone to disturb the Balkans, where he was forging alliances with Bulgaria and Yugoslavia for Operation *Barbarossa*, his up-coming invasion of the Soviet Union. He thought highly of the Greeks, and had no intention of making an enemy of General Metaxas, whom he personally admired. More critically, nothing must upset his friends in nearby Rumania, Germany's most important source for oil. It was with some horror then, that Hitler received Mussolini's greeting, "*Führer*, we are on the march!"[9] Il *Duce* rightly anticipated the German leader's strenuous objections to the invasion by not informing him of it in advance.

On 23 October, the Italian 9th and 11th Armies' seven divisions advanced in four lines from occupied Albania into Greece through a driving rain. Mussolini wasted not a moment in telegraphing Marshal Graziani still digging fortifications in the Libyan Desert. "Renew the offensive against Alexandria at once!" he commanded. "With the world's attention focused on events in Greece, you have been offered a golden opportunity to move forward with new prospects of success."[10]

An impatient Mussolini told his Chiefs of Staff, "I should be in favor of advancing Graziani's attack by a few days. Then the conquest of Mersa Matruh would make the possibility of such help still more remote, especially in view of the fact that we shall not stop there. Once the cornerstone of Egypt has been lost, the British Empire will fall to pieces, even if London can still hold out. India is in a state of unrest, and the British would no longer get help from South Africa or by the Red Sea lifeline. There is the consideration of morale to be added, to the effect that a success in Africa would give a fillip to our men in Albania."[11]

Meanwhile, 'Contingency C's' *raison d'être* quickly materialized with the arrival of the first RAF forces in Greece. Just days after the Italian attack began, Nos. 30, 70, 80, 84, and 211 RAF Squadrons arrived with some 400 Wellington medium bombers and Hurricane fighters desperately needed in North Africa. Over the strenuous objections of General Wavell, Anthony Eden and virtually all his military advisors, Churchill committed

British assistance to opposing the Italian invasion, dispatching men and materiel from the fighting in the Libyan Desert. Churchill's committment in Greece would eventually deprive Wavell of more than 50,000 troops. But Graziani was still not certain if he should wait for more supplies, or follow Mussolini's demand to attack. The reluctant Marshal had been gifted with an historic opportunity. Instead, he frittered away his last chance by continuing to indecisively wait for the British behind his fortified camps.

At last, on 9 December, warships of the Royal Navy pounded Maktila. The early morning bombardment coordinated with an offensive comprising the 7th Armoured Division, 4th Indian Division, and 7th Royal Tank Regiment. They were led by General Richard O'Connor, assessed by many historians as among the British Army's ablest, and certainly most aggressive field commanders of World War Two. At 0735 hours, his forces attacked the garrison at Nibeiwa, where they surprised and swiftly annihilated a large number of M11s whose crews had just begun warming up their engines. Although taken entirely unawares and suddenly deprived of all their tanks, the Italians fought back with intense ferocity, refusing to leave their guns, even as they were being overrun. They were, Trye wrote, "horrified by the lack of effect their weapons had on the enemy armour," but nonetheless fought to the death.[12]

According to 16th Battery Sergeant Major Robert Donovan 2/2 Australian Field Regiment, Royal Australian Artillery, 6th Australian Division, "The Italian artillery was definitely good at their trade ... We were saved from serious casualties because of the amazingly poor quality of the projectiles, many failed to burst, and those that did were ineffective. The gunners fought their guns to the last, many were found dead in their gun emplacements. The Italian dead were everywhere. The guns were piled around with empty cases where men had fired to the very last. The Italians fought like hell at Nebeiwa."[13] The same fate befell the Tummar garrisons, weakly defended as they were by puny L3 tankettes.

Only the Italian 37mm and 47/32mm guns, always in short supply, were capable of effectively piercing the new enemy armor. On the first day of the fighting, the British lost fourteen Cruisers to Tummar's defenders, and warriors of the Maletti Group, whose tanks had been slaughtered in the opening minutes of the attack, knocked out thity-five of the fifty-seven attacking Matildas. All the rest were destroyed in battles for the vital ports of Bardia and Tobruk. The Italians put up a determined defense at Bardia, beginning on 21 December. Outnumbered, outgunned and down to their last supplies, they fought off the tough Australians for more than two weeks.

At Sidi Barrani, where the Italians were so taken by surprise, General Pietro Maletti, still dressed in his pajamas, was killed while shooting his machine-gun at waves of oncoming British troops. Their offensive rolled irrepressibly into 1941. "The defenders of Derna put up dogged resistance against the attacking Australian infantry," Trye writes, "making them pay for every centimeter of earth in a series of savage rearguard actions. It was the most fierce resistance yet encountered by the Allied troops."[14] The 7th Armored Division cut off Sofafi and Rabia, from which, however, the Italians staged a successful breakout.

On 7 January 1941, the British XIII Corps captured Tobruk within twenty-four hours. By then, the Italian 10th Army had more than 100,000 men taken prisoner. The Italians put up stiff resistance at various strongpoints, but the tide had turned against them. Efforts to block the enemy advance toward Tripolitania at El Aghelia were cut-off by the 7th Armored Division, which reached the coast seventy miles south of Benghazi.

Refusal to obey Mussolini's orders by maintaining the momentum of the offensive had cost Graziani dear. His entire North African Campaign was on the verge of complete collapse with the loss of 320 kilometers of conquered territory.

By mid-February, more than 115,000 of the *Duce*'s men had been captured, along with 845 pieces of artillery, added to the destruction of 380 tanks and 200 of their 564 aircraft. Another 50,000 troops evacuated Gallaba to take up better defended positions on more rugged ground in Agordat and Barentu east of Kassala, which they also abandoned. The huge numbers of POWs, sometimes taken by relatively small British units, helped foster Allied propaganda characterizing the Italians as cowards, or, at any rate, unwilling, unenthusiastic participants in 'Mussolini's war'. But most who surrendered were actually colonial auxiliaries. In its assessment of the fighting across Libya and Egypt, the British VIIIth Army newspaper concluded that "the Black Shirt and *Bersaglieri* Divisions were often comparable in courage and fighting spirit to the best troops in the Campaign."[15]

Just as the Italian armies in the Libyan Desert faced certain annihilation, "the British halted their offensive," writes historian Hans Werner Neulen, "because many of their troops were transferred to Greece."[16]

"This was a major blunder on the Allied side," Trye concluded, "as there were few strong formations left in Tripolitania to oppose them in early 1941. The occupation of Tripoli at that time would have prevented future Axis build-up, and finished the North African Campaign there and then."[17]

Italian holdings in Egypt had been reduced to Sollum, Fort Capuzzi and Sidi Omar, with the loss of hundreds of thousands of troops taken prisoner, their tanks and artillery all but annihilated or captured. Yet, the *Duce*'s men were able to hang on, thanks to the respite afforded them by his successful diversion. Into that breathing-period, Erwin Rommel would arrive with his *Deutsche Afrika Korps*.

Meanwhile, British code-breakers learned of Italian intentions, relaying the information to Metaxas, who knew the day Italy would attack his country. Thus forewarned, the Greek defenders shifted their forces to the Macedonian front, where they would outnumber their opponents. Here, the Italian XXVI Corps, mostly the *Parma* Division, was already undermanned. And British aid soon made itself felt, especially in the air. On 19 November, nine Gloster Gladiators led by Greeks piloting three PZL P.24s jumped a flight of Italian fighters from the 160th and 24th *Gruppi*, respectively.

Three *Falcos* and one G.50 were shot down for the loss of three RAF biplanes. The following month, on the 21st, ten Gladiators of Number 8 Squadron penetrated Italian air-space, where they were intercepted by fifteen CR.42s, both sides each losing two aircraft. While Italian and British airmen traded blow for blow in the skies overhead, the campaign was being decided on the ground by the Greeks themselves.

Metaxas' counter strategy lay along mountain ranges and rivers, using their features as natural defensive positions. Deteriorating weather conditions transfigured roads into muddy paths, slowing vehicular progress, and rising rivers were difficult to cross. Many of the *Centauro* tanks bogged down and had to be abandoned after being stripped of weapons. At every turn the invaders were ambushed or stopped by destroyed bridges. Most of the Italian soldiers were raw recruits, and, when the weather suddenly dropped below freezing, many of them suffered for lack of snow-boots or winter clothing. They nonetheless attacked in a four-pronged advance forty kilometers into Greek territory. The

Tsamouria Corps clawed its way to Kalpaki through the mountains, as the *Littoral* Group advanced along the coast.

To their left, a pair of regimental battle groups, intent on taking the Metsovon pass, marched on either side of Mount Smolikas after splitting away from the *Julia Alpini* Division. In the face of enormous physical difficulties presented everywhere by the terrain and stubborn, persistent resistance from the Greeks, a bridgehead over the Kalamas River was established by the *Littoral* Group and *Aosta* Lancers through sheer force of will. The *Julia* Division was thereby able to thrust a wedge into the enemy line and fended off infiltration attacks mounted by General Papagos in the process of surrounding the Italians. Reinforcements of élite *Bersaglieri* came to the rescue, breaking the Greek attempt at encirclement, but at the cost of many casualties.

In late November, while awaiting re-supply for a planned 5 December offensive, the Italians dug in along the Devoli River and at the base of the Morava massif to safeguard their rear. Here, they were attacked in overwhelming numbers by the 9th, 10th and 15th Divisions of the Greek Army, which forced them out of the mountains and from Koritsa, a vital valley town, on 21 November. Although reinforcements were thrown into improvised counter-attacks, they could not prevent the loss of another key position at Erseke, which exposed the 11th Army's left flank.

Additional Greek divisions struck with an all-out effort, overwhelming the Italians and compelling them to retreat down the coast. Infuriated at being pushed across the border into Albanian territory, they launched a virtually suicidal attack at Monastir, retaking a strategic hill known as Height 731, the hinge-pin of the Metaxas' counter-invasion. As Phillip Jowett observes in his history, *The Italian Army*, "The individual Italian soldier in Greece often fought with heroism, especially in defense."[18] The ebb of Greek forces was stopped and began to flow backward.

10 January 1941 marked the high-water mark of their fortunes, when the important Klisura junction was taken. Filled with self-confidence after having driven some of the Italian invaders from their country, Metaxas refused further aid from Churchill, assuring him the Greeks would soon be marching through the streets of Rome. Just then, however, Italian units, inadvertently assisted by the enemy's over-extended supply lines, frustrated the Greeks on the front south of Vlone, a vital port town. Attempts to capture Vlone achieved initial success, but slowed soon thereafter in the same kind of bad weather that earlier bedeviled the Italians. Now it was the Greeks' turn to cower under the wrath of General Winter, as all air support was grounded. With casualties sky-rocketing and equipment irretrievably lost, King George II was forced to accept Churchill's long-standing offer of more reinforcements on 24 February. The chief aim of Mussolini's Balkan strategy had therefore been achieved, as Britain now poured substantial military aid into the fighting.

But juggling the North African and Greek campaigns had been an oscillating trade-off. Southeastern Italy's important ports on either shore of the Adriatic Sea came well within striking range of the RAF, which, night after night, went after crowds of transports supplying the invasion of Greece. With the *Regia Aeronautica* committed in the Western Desert and on the Balkan front, not a single interceptor was available to shield the Italian ships from streams of Beaufort and Wellington bombers. Protection lay entirely with the *Regia Marina's* anti-aircraft defenses. But the curtain of fire they put up around the harbors was virtually impenetrable. Brindisi was soon known to British flyers as 'the volcano of the lower Adriatic', while they referred to Valona as 'Death's Hole'. In fact, Italian naval batteries saved the entire supply fleet. Not one freighter or tanker was lost to aerial attack, although some received light damage. It was during the Greek Campaign that Italian marksmen established themselves as among the best flak-gunners of World War Two, a reputation subsequently proved again on numerous occasions in other theaters of war. But over-reliance on their admittedly high skills alone would lead to disaster at another harbor later this year: Taranto.

Until then, only two ships were lost to slow-moving Fairey Swordfish torpedo-bombers. These included a destroyer escort, the *Andromeda,* and the *Po*, the first of several Italian hospital ships sunk by British pilots, who sighted-in on the flood-lit, oversized red crosses draping port and starboard flanks to make easy kills. Mussolini's own daughter, Edda, had been serving as a Red Cross nurse aboard the *Po* when it was attacked. He told his wife, Rachele, in a telephone conversation at the time, "Just imagine, she was in the water for five hours, but now she's safe."[19]

RAF attacks against clearly marked non-combatant ships continued into 1941, when five, small sea-rescue vessels used to save pilots downed at sea were deliberately strafed, killing and injuring those aboard, some of them wounded British flyers picked up by the Italians. Several of the defenseless ships were sunk under the bombs and shells of Fairey Fulmars or Sea Furies. They went on to sink the Italian hospital-ships *California* (13,060-ton) in the port of Syracuse on 11 August, and the 8,024-ton *Arno* outside Tobruk less than a month later. These *bona fide* war crimes were never investigated, either during or after hostilities, by legal authorities on either side, since claims for compensation by 'Fascists' against Allied war criminals could hardly have been made with impunity in the postwar climate of the Nuremberg Tribunals.

A single troop ship, the *Sardegna*, was torpedoed on 29 December 1940. All but three of its 200 soldiers successfully abandoned her, as the *Proteus*, a Greek submarine responsible for the attack, was almost immediately thereafter rammed and sunk by a destroyer escort, the *Antares*. But the *Regia Marina's* real success lay in its less dramatic transportation of men and material to Albania for the fighting in Greece. By mid-September, an expeditionary force numbering 40,310 troops, 7,728 horses and mules, 701 vehicles, and 35,531 tons of supplies had been delivered without loss in just ten days' time during one of the most remarkable operations of its kind in the whole war.

Taking advantage of inclement conditions in the Balkans, Mussolini ordered a counter-attack. He threw seven fresh divisions into a 9 March operation between Mount Tommorit and the Vijose River against twice as many enemy divisions holding the Albanian front. The Greeks recoiled, but the counter-offensive suspended ten days later after incurring heavy losses. The Italians now brought up one armored, four Alpine and twenty-three infantry divisions totalling 526,000 men. In April, they coordinated attacks with German forces striking through the Pindus to take Ioannina, forcing the Greek surrender.

Allied propaganda portrayed Mussolini as initially beaten by the Greeks, from who he was saved by Hitler. While the Wehrmacht certainly accelerated events, they were actually brought about, not by the Italo-Greek War, but because sudden replacement of the pro-Axis Yugoslav monarchy with a figurehead sympathetic to Britain precipitated a crisis. As far as Mussolini was concerned, the invasion achieved its purpose when Churchill drained British troop strength into the Balkans, thereby diluting General Wavel's forces in North Africa. Even though Graziani failed to take advantage of this diversion, pressure on Axis armies in the Libyan Desert had been significantly relieved, thereby staving off a general collapse.

The final phase of fighting in the Balkans opened on 6 April 1941, as twenty-eight Italian divisions covered by 320 warplanes advanced in conjunction with the German Wehrmacht toward turncoat Yugoslavia. During the eleven-day Blitzkrieg, *Regia Aeronautica* crews shot down five enemy aircraft, losing as many of their own, but wrecked more than 100 Allied planes on the ground. Earlier, over Greece, the Italians flew over 21,000 hours in 14,000 sorties for sixty-five of their machines shot down, with another fourteen lost through accidents or in enemy raids. 223 airmen were killed or missing, with an additional sixty-five wounded. These sacrifices contrasted with 273 Greek and British bombers and fighters destroyed in aerial combat. Yet again, *Regia Aeronautica* flyers had acquitted themselves with distinction. But their comrades on the ground suffered far greater casualties. They lost almost 14,000 dead, with another 25,000 missing.

After the close of operations in southeastern Europe, Mussolini took over Montenegro, the Dalmatian coast, western Macedonia, Slovenia, and Kosovo. But native armed resistance was so widespread he eventually needed fourteen infantry divisions to occupy the Balkans by July 1943. These were opposed by Josip Broz Tito's Communist partisans and Serbian royalists known as 'Chetniks' led by Dragoljub Mihailovic. The two groups fought each other with greater ferocity than their own enemies, the Axis invaders, so Mussolini took advantage of their mutual hatred by organizing the *Milizia Volontaria Anti-Comunista*. He encouraged nationalist Yugoslavs to join him against the commonly despised Reds, beginning in early 1942. A year later, the MVAC had 30,000 volunteers, and even Colonel Mihailovic eventually went over to the Italians.

In Dalmatia, the *Milizia* comprised eight *bande* made up of 100 men each divided into six Roman Catholic and two Orthodox 'companies'. Dr. Marko Natlacen's *Slovenska Legiya*, or 'Slovene Legion', served under the Italians as auxiliary troops, as did Ernst Peterlin's Slovenian Village Guard and the *Legija smrti*, the 'Legion of Death'. It comprised 1,687 elite, anti-partisan fighters in three battalions – the *Vrnika, Gorjanci* and *Mokronag*, respectively. Organizing of these diverse identities into a common cause against Marxism shifted Yugoslav nationalism away from the Axis occupiers to the Communists, and tended to ameliorate some of the ethnic or religious antagonism endemic to the Balkans.

Remarked one elderly veteran toward the close of the 20th Century, "If the MVAC had prevailed, there would have been no civil war with all its mass-murders at Kosovo and elsewhere, because each group had its own organization within the *Milizia*. Tito's dictatorship only suppressed their divisions for forty years, until they erupted into conflict during the 1990s. If the Allies had not kept him well supplied, we would have won, because he was losing popular support in 1942 and '43."[20] In fact, Anglo-American aid to the Chetniks was terminated after Colonel Mihailovic began collaborating with the Axis.

Mussolini himself contributed to MVAC recruitment with elite Italian veterans who fought under his own initial in the 'M' Battalions. According to Salvatore Vasta writing in *COORTE* magazine, they "proudly wore the red M's and *fascetto* on their black collar-patches as insignia."[21] Their obvious dedication to the cause of pacifying the Balkans with a mixture of force and goodwill renewed the *Duce*'s favorable interest in southeastern Europe:

"I admit I always opposed the very notion of a 'Yugoslavia' as some unnatural coalition of mutually opposed peoples, cultures and faiths indiscriminately cobbled together by the framers of the Versailles Treaty. They manufactured this political abortion out of either evil intentions for future upheaval – to keep our Continent forever in ferment – or from rank stupidity. In place of this monstrosity, I nevertheless propose following the Versailles Treaty at least this one time to the letter of the law by granting the Balkans the 'self-determination' of its peoples. While I regard the very existence of Yugoslavia as a threat, not only to Italy, but to the entire region, and the whole of Europe itself, I enthusiastically welcome a revival of those former states, whose racial, religious, linguistic and cultural identities are individually valuable additions to the Western Civilization we all share in common.

"Croatia and Serbia have already achieved their independence within this New Order of the Balkans. I look forward to the day when the rest of the originally autonomous peoples of that former, synthetic 'Yugoslavia' have regained their liberty and self-consciousness. The present conflict in which we are engaged offers everyone an unprecedented opportunity to achieve that goal, which Italy will forever champion in the name of genuine peace and rational friendship on both sides of the Adriatic."[22]

6

Desert Fox In A Henhouse

*If certain Italian generals could fight as well as they
sing, there would be no need for me to be here.*
General Erwin Rommel in a letter to his wife after arriving in Libya, 19 February 1941[1]

While British forces were being sucked into a vortex of defeat throughout southeastern Europe and the Aegean, the pendulum of war in Libya began to swing back in Mussolini's favor. At the beginning of hostilities, efforts to preserve East Africa and expand its potential for wide-ranging operations seemed good, even though Ethiopia was surrounded by enemy territories and virtually cut off from outside assistance. To off-set their isolated predicament, the Italians struck British Somaliland with a lightning invasion spear-headed by four *squadriglie*. The *Africa Orientale Italiana* faced 370 British and Commonwealth aircraft with 323 of their own, but of these, eighty-one were unserviceable, reducing the odds still further. 19,000 troops in British Somaliland, Kenya and Sudan, covered by perhaps 100 aircraft, faced 200,000 foot-soldiers with an air umbrella of 400 warplanes.

The Italians knew they would have to make up for numerical and technological inferiority with audacity. On 4 July, the offensive began from East Africa when fourteen *Falcos* and thirty two CR.32s staged surprise, low-level raids at Burao, Hergheisa and La Faruk, shooting up Hawker Hurricanes and Bristol Blenheims on the ground before they could get airborne. The doughty Fiats quickly achieved mastery of the skies by destroying the remaining Gloster Gladiators in 'dog fights' reminiscent of First World War encounters between opposing biplanes. Ground forces instantly over-ran the key posts at Kassala and Gallabat on the Sudan borders with Eritrea and Ethiopia, from which the Italians swept into Somaliland.

On 17 August, the British were 'Dunkirked' a second time, when Royal Navy ships evacuated them from the port of Berbera. A few hours later, all of Somaliland fell to the Italians. Their swift and far-ranging advance through the desert allowed them to threaten southern entrances of the Red Sea, seriously jeopardizing Great Britain's oil supplies in the Middle East and her vital lines of communication with India and the Far East through the Suez Canal. From conquered Somaliland, *Regia Aeronautica* bombers ranged out far over the Red Sea, attacking Allied convoys into spring 1941.

By then, the consequences of Graziani's failure meant trouble for Italians throughout East Africa. His reverses in the Libyan Desert encouraged the British to seize Ethiopia on 6 November 1940. Fort Gallabat fell almost at once, "but the *Regia Aeronautica* hit back hard and effectively," according to Neulen.[2] Capture of the Sudanese town was undertaken by Sir William Slim's 7,000 infantrymen with a tank regiment covered by an RAF squadron. While these forces were still on the march, they were spotted by a flight of *Caccia-Bomardiere*, fighter-bombers of *Captano* Antonio Raffi's 412a *Squadriglia*.

He and his fellow pilots promptly downed five Gloster Gladiators without any losses to themselves, then strafed enemy troops, killing forty-two and wounding 125. On 12 December, the same *Squadriglia* destroyed another five aircraft on the ground, while shooting up repair and spare parts facilities in a daring raid on the RAF's Sudan landing field at Gaz Regeb. Italian supremacy over the battlefield was so complete, the British were forced to abandon freshly captured Gallabat. With his tanks shot up and troops under incessant harassment from the air, General Slim called off the offensive and withdrew.

Another attempt was made on 24 January 1941, because General Wavell's imminent capture of Cyrenaica simultaneously allowed the arrival of rich supplies and virtually cut off East Africa from the outside world. Now the British struck from Kenya with far greater supplies and infantry strength, while additional Empire troops attacked Eritrea from Sudan. As before, the Italians were at first successful in blunting the offensive, but attrition took its toll on aircraft which could not be sufficiently replaced. Mussolini ordered the *Servizi Aerei Speciali* to establish an air-bridge for the relief of his forces defending Ethiopia. Formed the previous June, the SAS requisitioned civilian planes for emergency transport duties from Italy's three commercial airlines: *Ala Littoria*, LATI, and *Avio Linee Italiane*. The thirty-one SM.75s, four German Junkers-52s, and single American Douglas DC-2 joined the *Regia Aeronautica's* SM.82 *Marsupiales* in ferrying crated fighters and supplies to Ethiopia and the Sudan, returning to Italy with wounded.

Their pilots demonstrated exceptional courage running the round-trip gauntlet of 12,000 kilometers from Rome to Benghazi, Gondar and Djibouti in unescorted, unarmed transports protected only by Red Cross markings on fuselage and wing surfaces. Unusually lucky was Max Peroli. He completed five of the eighty-two-hour-long relief flights before his SM.82 was caught parked at the Dijbouti landing strip by an attacking South African pilot who shot it into flames. Such efforts, for all their daring, could not keep pace with the far more richly outfitted British, who captured Mogadishu, the capital of Italian Somalia, on 23 February.

Their overwhelming forces breached the southern front at Giuba, then poured over the stronghold of Galla Sidama, the northern front with Sudan, the Italian defensive ring of Kurmuk, Gallabat, and Kassala. The offensive was halted at Cheren, a stronghold from which the Italians resisted from 31 January to 27 March 1941, even though completely cut off and surrounded by enemy infantry and armor. Unable to take Cheren, the British eventually skirted it to threaten the *Regia Marina's* Red Sea naval base at Massaua.

The Italians, meanwhile, had been reduced to defending all of East Africa with a pair of *Sparviero* tri-motors, five *Falcos*, a quartet of aged Caproni Ca.113 bombers, and a single CR.32 biplane. By March, Italian aircraft still flying in Abyssinia dropped to thirteen machines. Defying hopeless odds, their pilots rose to the occasion. But so furious was the opposition put up by the handful of airmen manning their over-stressed fighters that the British offensive dragged on until late the following November! During one and a half years of fighting, seven airmen of the *Africa Orientale Italiana* became 'aces', each one downing at least five aircraft apiece.

The British returned Haile Selassie, seated vindictively in an Italian Alfa Romeo limousine, to Ethiopia. At this low ebb in Italian fortunes, they suddenly and quite unexpectedly reversed themselves when Mussolini realized that the 10th Army suffered for lack of sufficient armor. He moved quickly to organize a *Brigata Corazzato Speciale*, or 'Special Armored Brigade', of M-11, M-13/40 and L.3/35 tanks operating in squads.

They were accompanied by infantry specializing in anti-armor weapons and tactics. This hurriedly improvised force was dispatched to General Valentino Babini just in time to confront the massed assault of 177 *Matilda* tanks and other armored vehicles at Mechili.

During a single engagement, on 24 January, the badly outnumbered soldiers of the Special Armored Brigade quickly knocked out and disabled the first fifteen tanks in as many minutes. The British regrouped, charged again, losing another six tanks almost at once, then fled toward Cairo, the Italians in hot pursuit for another twelve miles before losing contact with the enemy. Soon after, a determined effort was made to wipe out the dangerous BCS with all the armor at Wavell's disposal. When the smoke cleared, twenty of his seventy *Cruiser* heavy tanks, plus twenty-five light tanks, had been reduced to smoldering wrecks, with insignificant damage endured by the *Brigata Corazzato Speciale*. Wavell called a two-week halt in operations, until his losses could be made good.

Based on the example of Mussolini's Special Armored Brigade, his troops no longer wasted tanks in haphazard, individual attacks, but concentrated their armor in motorized groups, acting in unison for the combination and concentration of firepower. As part of these new tactics, improved M.13/40 tanks were backed up by the redoubtable *Sahariana* patrol cars in 'Reconnaissance Units of the Army Mobile Corps', *Reparto Esplorante di Corpo d'Armata di Manovra*, or RECAM. Rethinking and reorganizing was beginning to strengthen the entire Italian command structure, resulting in a gradual improvement of its situation, until it was frittered away under Italy's incompetent Chief of General Staff, Ugo Cavallero.

On New Year's Eve 1941, after three days of continuous fighting, a pair of Indian Divisions and two more Indian Infantry Brigades forced the Italian Army to withdraw from the Keren Plateau. Four days later, 30,000 British troops attacked its 23,000 defenders. First the Indians, then the Scots were beaten back, as the Italians held the line for almost seven weeks. On 27 March, they were forced to evacuate the plateau, leaving behind 3,000 dead. But a general collapse had been staved off, and Graziani's position, however fragile, stabilized. By then, the entire British tank force had been virtually wiped out. Wavell no longer possessed a single medium tank, while most of his heavier Cruisers and light tanks were gutted hulks littering the desert. In fact, his combined motorized forces had been whittled down by 80%. Infantry losses were also high, with one in every twenty five of his soldiers killed in battle and scores wounded.

This was the enemy's condition when General Erwin Rommel arrived in Tripoli with a Panzer and Motorized Infantry Division, initially supported by eighty warplanes of the 10th *Fliegerkorps*. These included the infamous *Stuka* dive-bomber and Messerschmitt ME-109F, then the best fighter in the world. They were eventually joined at Berca by a special model of Messerschmitt's twin-engine ME-110 armed with a MK 101 30mm cannon slung under the fuselage; Focke-Wulf's FW-189 *Uhu*, the 'Owl', for reconnaissance; the versatile Junkers-88 medium bomber; an advanced STOL high-wing command-plane, the Fieseler Fi.156 *Storch*, or 'Stork'; and ground-attacking Henschel 129 bristling with 20mm and 30mm cannons.

The appearance of the well-equipped but very small forces of *Die Deutsche Afrika Korps* set off no alarm bells in London. Army General Perry-Gambia told BBC listeners in mid-February, "The German troops that face us are worth even less than those of 1914-1918. They are by no means what they pronounce themselves to be, a kind of super soldier. They are worth even less, for here they cannot base themselves on any colonial experience or tradition."[3]

At first sight, the newly-arrived German pilots "had a tendency to judge their Italian comrades-in-arms somewhat skeptically," recalled Luftwaffe airmen, W. Girbig and H. Ring. "Later on, the German fighter pilots of I./JG 27 were grateful for every Italian aircraft that helped them to escort the *Stukas*. The Italians were always ready to co-operate in a comradely way with the German fighter pilots."[4] The aircraft they flew almost completely eclipsed anything comparably operated by either the Italians or the British in North Africa, and contributed significantly to a long string of lightning victories achieved by the *Deutsche Afrika Korps* almost immediately after its arrival on 12 February.

Rommel had then at his disposal 111 of the deadly Flak 88 guns, equally effective against ground armor and aircraft; 2,000 assorted vehicles; 130 Panzer tanks; and 9,300 men already aglow with intense *espirit de corps*. Nor were they alone. Landing in Libya at the same time were 6,949 Italian troops, 163 tanks, thirty-six pieces of field artillery, and sixty-one anti-tank guns of the *Ariete* and *Brescia* Infantry Divisions. The new German-Italian units combined with Graziani's resources to give Rommel 100,000 Italian soldiers, 7,000 trucks, 1,000 guns, and 151 aircraft, mostly *Falcos* and *Cigognas*. After his first inspection of the Italians, he confided to his adjutant, "good troops, bad officers. But remember that without them we wouldn't have civilization!"[5]

Less than a week before his DAK set foot in Libya, the British, recovering from defeat at the hands of the *Brigata Corazzato Speciale*, suddenly destroyed eighty Italian tanks and seven generals were taken prisoner at Benghazi. Worse came the next day, when 120 tanks, 200 artillery pieces, and 20,000 troops were captured. Undaunted by these otherwise catastrophic reversals, Rommel went over on the offensive with an imaginative flair rarely encountered in warfare. After little more than two months, he made General Wavell give up all gains won from the Italians. Rommel's unbroken series of victories coincided with an improvement in Italian fortunes.

On 30 April, the same day Greece surrendered to the Axis, paratroopers of the Italian 2nd Battalion jumped from SM.82 transports to seize three strategic Eastern Mediterranean islands. So complete was their surprise attack, they took Cefalonia, Itaca and Zante without firing a shot in what may only be described as a 'textbook operation'. The capture of these Ionian outposts was not only a prerequisite for the coming invasion of Crete, but testified to growing Italian influence in the region and demonstrated that Mussolini had regained the initiative.

But the contest for North Africa was far from decided. To pre-empt a planned Axis attack, the redoubtable O'Connor's Scots Guards killed 592 Italians and 685 Germans on 15 May, but lost seven of ten Matilda tanks. It was the last success, however costly, they would enjoy in 1941. For the rest of spring, throughout summer and into fall, the British Desert Army was kept alive with supplies sent from England and her colonies, while being savaged by the *Afrika Korps* and its Italian ally. Meanwhile, equipment was secretly horded and stockpiled for a major British offensive – *Crusader* – designed to overwhelm Axis forces at Bir El Gobi, beginning in the early hours of 18 November. The RAF assembled 1,311 Hawker Hurricanes and Bristol Beaufighters, plus U.S.-built Curtiss P-40 Warhawks and Douglas Boston light bombers. These first-rate machines were opposed by 200 mostly obsolete Italian aircraft and 120 over-worked German planes.

Neither Germans nor Italians benefited from anything equivalent to the Allies' military intelligence, and were forced to rely on direct observation. For once, it paid off, however, when the crew of an aged Meridionali Ro.37 biplane flying reconnaissance photographed a massive build-up of enemy vehicles and troops fronting the area. Rommel was unsure the images actually portended attack, since the British were supposed to have been too low on supplies for a major operation. He suspected that 'tanks' in the photographs might actually be decoys, and blamed Italian concerns on "excessive Latin nervousness".[6] But the Commander-in-Chief of Italian Forces in North Africa and conqueror of Santander in the Spanish Civil War, General Ettore Bastico, whose advice he respected, convinced Rommel that spreading his armored units around Tobruk at this time would leave them unnecessarily vulnerable. The *Afrika Korps* and Italian *Ariete, Trieste* and *Savona* Divisions were put on alert, and just in time. Next morning, as scheduled, the British attacked Bir El Gobi with a ferocious artillery barrage.

Crusader had not only been well-supplied, but carefully prepared. Teams from the Long Range Desert Group drove some eighty kilometers into Italian-held territory without being detected to destroy parked aircraft. At dawn, they surprised a flight of G.50s sitting at Sidi el Rezeg, the 20th *Gruppo*'s airstrip, capturing sixteen fighters intact. Only three Fiats managed to save themselves by getting airborne in time. Another thirteen monoplanes were blown up on the ground at Ain el Gazala. Undaunted, *Armata Azzurra* pilots of the 9th Group struck back with their new airplane in its debut action, the MC.202 *Folgore*, shooting down seven P-40s without loss to themselves.

In the desert below, the British 22nd Armored Brigade threw 158 Crusader tanks against the *Ariete*'s 137 medium and light counterparts. But the Italians had learned from bitter experience, and their concentrated artillery with improved shells 'brewed up' fifty-five oncoming Crusaders, forcing the survivors to re-group at the Allied rear for the next two weeks. The *Ariete* then went over on its own attack against the fleeing 22nd and 4th Armored Brigades, knocking out 200 enemy tanks and as many vehicles with assistance from the *Trieste* and *Savona* Divisions.

Italians of the *Ariete* Division blast Operation *Crusader's* armour in
this illustration by Kurt Caesar, an eye-witness to the action

Italian *Carabinieri* about to break out of encirlement.
Illustration by DAK *Sonderführer* Kurt Caesar.

Rommel's 21st Panzer joined in the destruction, accounting for another twenty-three Crusaders and Matildas. The onslaught spilled over into the next month, when the British tried a second time to overwhelm Axis forces at Bir El Gobi. Beginning 2 December, an entire army corps struck at the rear of an oblivious *Afrika Korps*. Outnumbered three to one, volunteers in the *Giovanni Fascisti* regiment parried a death-blow blow dealt by the 11th Indian Brigade, foiling General Ritchie's attempt to trap Rommel in Gabr Saleh after assaulting the Germans' southern flank.

The furious desert battles raged for four days, during which the British 4th Armoured Brigade was so severely mauled its tattered remnants retreated twelve kilometres away to recover themselves. The 1st South African Division was similarly knocked out of the fighting. Badly thrashed, the 11th Indian Brigade withdrew minus 100 tanks lost to the 75mm guns of the *Giovanni Fascisti*. Italian covering action undoubtedly saved the *Afrika Korps* at Gabr Saleh. Although the British continued to pour material into the melee, their final attempt at surrounding Italo-German forces was too weak from loss of blood. The *Trieste* and *Ariete* Divisions fought their way through encirclement, destroying another 100 enemy vehicles in the process.

Attrition had depleted both Desert Army troops and RAF pilots, but Churchill ordered another major effort to "catch and destroy Rommel with his Italian lackeys".[7] Operation *Crusader* lumbered forward again on 18 December against the *Ariete*, which was under-supplied after prolonged fighting less than two weeks before. To permit the Division's withdrawal, a *Caribinieri* parachute battalion stopped pursuing British forces at the Elut el Asel fork in the Cerenaic Djebel. The paratroopers allowed themselves to be surrounded, affording the *Ariete* enough time to complete removal to the rear. When it escaped the fighting, the *Caribinieri* shot their way out of encirclement in a bold attack along the Balbia Road, near Lamluda. An entire enemy division and a battalion had slipped through scorched British fingers.

Taking advantage of enemy consternation, the *Afrika Korps* and *Corpo d'Armata di Manovra*, an Italian Mobile Army Corps, combined to inflict serious casualties on the 22nd Armoured Brigade. Of its original 158 tanks, just thirty survived Operation *Crusader*. The *Caribinieri*, who made this Axis victory possible and fought through encirclement against impossible odds, eventually reached Italian lines. They left behind thirty-five dead paratroopers. Another 200 were missing. When word reached Mussolini of their achievement, he ordered the Battalion's flag decorated with the Silver Medal of Military Valor.

Back in London, Churchill blew up in front of his commanders, telling them that the British Army was the laughing stock of the world, and asked bitterly if they did not have just one general who could win battles.[8]

7

Mare Nostro

*It was always a surprise to me how the Italian seamen continued to operate
their ships in the face of the dangers that beset them. They were liable to surface,
submarine and air attacks throughout the whole of their passage from Sicily, and
the fact that they stood up to it should be remembered to their credit.*
Admiral of the Fleet, British Royal Navy, Andrew Browne Cunningham[1]

B y the time their first clash of arms took place in the Libyan Desert, Britain and
Italy had already begun to fight it out on the high seas. On 12 June, two days after
Mussolini's declaration of war, the *Giovanni Berta*, a small gunboat on patrol off
Tobruk, was gunned down by a pair of British cruisers. Within the next twenty-four
hours, a British submarine, the *Odin*, was dispatched by the destroyer *Strale* in the Gulf
of Taranto, followed to the bottom shortly thereafter by her sister-boat, *Oswald*, south of
Calabria under the depth-charges of another destroyer, the *Vivaldi*.

The toll on Royal Navy submarines continued to climb with the destruction of the
Grampus and *Tempest* to depth-charges hurled at them by C-110 and *Circe* torpedo-boats
off Augusta on 24 June; the *Pandora*, blasted by *Regia Aeronautica* bombers at Malta;
and *Phoenix*, which would never rise again after her fatal encounter near Sicily with the
torpedo-boat *Albatross*. Other British submarine losses included the *Triton*, sunk by the
torpedo-boat *Clio* in the Adriatic, together with the *Triumph, Tigris, Triad, Talisman,
Tetrarch, Traveller* and *Trooper*. Eventually, fourteen of the twenty-two boats belonging
to the T-class alone were lost, all but one of them in the Mediterranean.

Italian forces had gone far in extirpating British influence from the Mediterranean Sea,
an achievement made all the more remarkable by the odds stacked against them. When
Italy entered the war, her navy, the *Regia Marina*, was badly outnumbered in its own
home waters by the combined French and British fleets. With the abrupt fall of France,
however, the numerical balance of power shifted suddenly in favor of the *Supermarina*,
the Italian Naval High Command. Despite his late and short-lived invasion of France,
Mussolini's unexpectedly magnanimous behavior, such as his personal tribute paid to
the stubborn French defenders of La Turra, seemed to dissolve previous years of growing
tension between the two nations.

In any case, what he failed to win through force of arms he intended to gain through
diplomacy. The same negotiating skills that won him laurels during the Czech Crisis he
now applied toward France with positive results. A favorable French attitude meant that
Supermarina commanders did not have to worry about a defeated, resentful neighbor
at their back. On the contrary, Vichy France voluntarily assisted the *Regia Marina* in
relaying Royal Navy ship movements and Allied convoy schedules, whenever such priceless
information was made known to them.

But Mussolini had his own convoys to worry about. They comprised the lifeline of
supplies to Italian armies in North Africa, and completed their runs without incident

for weeks after the opening of hostilities. In late June, however, an encounter took place which mystified and alarmed his naval commanders. On the 27th, Captain Baroni was the *squadrilla* commander of three destroyers – the *Espero, Ostro* and *Zefiro* – on a high-speed run out of the *Regia Marina's* chief port at Taranto. Aboard were 120 tons of ammunition, ten anti-tank guns and 162 artillerymen. By the time they reached the open sea, his convoy was complete when the *Pilo* and *Missori*, escort vessels carrying another fifty-two infantry and additional tons of military supplies, joined up. The vessels were shadowed ominously the next day for several hours by a reconnaissance plane which kept its distance, but there was otherwise no sign of the enemy.

As evening descended on the calm sea, a barrage of eight-inch shells flew out of the blinding sunset. An unknown number of warships were attacking from more than twenty kilometers away. Baroni ordered the convoy to make a dash for North Africa, while he covered their escape with his destroyer. Alone, the *Espero* turned to confront the overwhelming firepower of five cruisers closing fast. Through skillful helmsmanship, he distracted the British for nearly two hours of unrelenting maneuvering, so much so they were unable to score a hit on him until their fifteenth salvo. Captain Baroni was last seen saluting his men through the smoke that enveloped his ship, in which he perished with most of her crew. Their self-sacrifice allowed the *Ostra, Zefiro, Pilo* and *Missori* to arrive unscathed in Tobruk with their valuable cargoes.

However, the serious inadequacy – or, in the *Espero's* case, total lack – of Italian aerial reconnaissance had been brought home to *Supermarina*. It began the war with little more than 100 observation planes, deemed a sufficient number on behalf of foreseen fleet operations. But in the reality of war, they were swallowed by the immensity of the Mediterranean Sea. At least three times as many scout-planes were needed. The developing failure of Italian aerial reconnaissance could not be blamed on its crews, whose skill and courage were never called into question. They flew seaplanes by CANT, the single-engine *Gabbiano*, and tri-motor *Airone*, successful veterans of the Spanish Civil War. Rugged construction and respective ranges of 1,000 and 2,750 kilometers made them effective eyes of the fleet, as far as their few numbers allowed. The *Gabbiano* was nearly 65 km/hr faster than its enemy counterparts – the Seagull V or Walrus Mk I and II – and could fly thirty-five kilometers further. It was the tight inter-action between ships and planes, however, that gave a decisive advantage to the British.

Moreover, both the *Gabbiano* and *Airone* were too slow and under-gunned to fight off enemy carrier-based interceptors, like the Fairey Fulmar, with its eight wing-mounted .303mm machine-guns. However, neither Italian aircraft was precisely defenseless, and the extraordinary skills of their crews often made up for technical deficiencies. A case in point was Pietro Bonannini, who served with the 170th *Squadriglia*, 83rd Gruppo, stationed at the Augusta float-plane base on Sicily's east coast. The only non-pilot double-ace in the *Regia Aeronautica*, *Aiutante di Battaglia* Bonannini shot down ten British fighters, warding off an unknown number of others as a gunner aboard *Gabbiano* and *Airone* seaplanes.

Poor inter-service cooperation stemmed in part from the *Regia Aeronautica* attitude that warships had been replaced by aircraft as the decisive factor in the war at sea. To test the hypothesis, a bomber unit specifically trained and equipped for the anti-shipping role began flying out of Libyan coastal bases against enemy vessels in the Mediterranean from late August 1940. Military aviation theorists did not have long to wait for the vindication of their faith in naval warplanes. On 17 September, crews of the *Reparto Sperimentale*

A S.M. 79 'Sparrowhawk' launches its torpedo, as illustrated in 1941 by
Kurt Casear, a *Sonderführer* with the German Africa Corps.

Aerosiluranti disabled a 14,200-ton cruiser, H.M.S. *Kent*, so badly she had to be towed
back to Alexandria. The following month, they crippled another cruiser, the 11,350-ton
Liverpool, with a direct hit on her bow.

These attacks against capital ships were only high-profile success of the 278th
Squadriglia *Autonoma Aerosiluranti*, as the R.S.A. was henceforward known, its torpedo-
bombers accounting for numerous, less glamorous, but more important victims among
the British merchant marine. While the flyers' motto, *Pauci sed semper immites* ('Few, but
always aggressive') accurately characterized the bellicosity of their Squadron, it also pointed
up the lack of sufficient numbers made available for anti-shipping duties. Indeed, Italy's
too few long-range aircraft combined with British radar and the RAF's close protection
of Royal Navy warships to render the *Regia Marina* relatively blind.

Nowhere was this more true than after dark, because the Italians never developed night
air-sea reconnaissance, unlike the British, who excelled in this often decisive technique
from the beginning of the war. Inequalities were compounded further still by the inability
of understrength hydroplane squadrons to achieve comparable cooperation with Italian
warships. Their failure lay primarily in the chain of command itself.

A ship's captain in need of air support appealed to the *Supermarina*, which forwarded
his request to the *Regia Aeronautica*. Officers there convened to appraise the situation
and draw up an appropriate plan. These were then sent on to the appropriate squadron
leaders, who had to formulate their own course of action before actually carrying it out.
By that time, the enemy usually escaped after carrying out his attack. Yet, until 1942,
aerial reconnaissance represented the *Regia Marina's* only early warning system, unlike
the British, who had the benefit of radar from not long after the beginning of hostilities.
Italian commanders operated in a darkness that was no barrier for their enemies.

As Mussolini told his naval chief-of-staff, Admiral Iachini, after the disastrous Battle of Matapan – in which three *Regia Marina* cruisers went down with 2,400 men – "Your ships were like blind invalids being set upon by armed killers."[2] Italy's inability to equip her vessels with radar was among the leading causes for their destruction and even the outcome of the war itself. It seems particularly ironic then, that the inventor of radar was an Italian who proposed such an instrument to American audiences in the same year Mussolini rose to power.

After the Italian air force, the navy was the most Fascist of all services, but conservatives from the House of Savoy still played influential roles in the *Supermarina*. As in the *Regia Aeronautica*, this ideological imbalance manifested itself in stress between traditionalists trusting long-established modes and usually younger officers anxious to incorporate new technologies. These included the application of a device first described in a memorandum presented to members of the American Institute of Electrical Engineers on 20 June 1922 by the renowned inventor of wireless telegraphy.

Guglielmo Marconi believed that radio waves striking any solid object were detected by a receiver in such a way that the target's position could be accurately identified. His proposal was seriously examined by scientists in other parts of the world, especially in Britain, where its transformation into a navigational instrument was the special interest of physicists Richard Appleton and William Barnett just two years later. By 1935, Professor Watson Watt had taken their research so far forward his work won generous funding from the British High Command. The investment paid off after just five years in an early-warning radar network that played its key role during the Battle of Britain.

But Marconi had not been idle. Two years before Dr. Watt won lavish support from Britain's military establishment, Marconi successfully demonstrated history's first operational radar set to high-ranking members of Italy's Commando *Supremo*. His device produced signal fluctuations caused by automobiles passing through a powerful radio transmission on the road between Rome and Castengandolfo. The aristocrat officers were little more than amused, and failed to grasp the instrument's military potential. Only Ugo Tibero, a young sub-lieutenant in the reserves, completing his service at Rome's *Istituto Militare Superiore Trasmissioni*, was excited about what he had seen. Through his encouragement, Marconi continued to develop the new receiver, and it was entirely because of Tibero's influence that the military agreed to another demonstration, this one of an up-graded version referred to as a *radioecometro*.

Its performance was markedly improved over the prototype, but considered too weak to be of any military use in 1935, the same year Professor Watt got the backing of the British High Command. In sad contrast, Marconi's device was consigned to leisurely evaluation tests conducted by an armed forces' commission made up of several different ministries. The commission was badly underfunded, and, by the time Marconi died two years later, his radar invention, referred to unenthusiastically as the 'E.C.', was still granted low priority, and would have certainly died of neglect, had not Professor Tiburo furthered its research and promoted its acceptance. Even so, his only support came in the form of a few technicians and a meager 20,000 lira, about £28,000.

With the success of his 'E.C'. detectors on the eve of World War Two, the *Regia Marina* finally began to take real interest in radar, and an important Milan radio factory was put at Tiburo's disposal. But there were far too few electrical researchers, engineers or technicians available. These rare individuals were already deeply engaged in duties given higher priority. E.C.detectors were still being tested when the disastrous naval battle off Cape Matapan took place. Sure now that the British were using radar aboard their warships, the E.C. prototypes were rushed into service aboard Italian vessels. Emergency accelerated development resulted in improvements known as *Folaga* and *Gufo*; the former was used for coastal surveillance, while the later served aboard ships. Both versions performed with an efficiency that surprised even Professor Tiburo.

Operating at a frequency between 150 and 300 MHz, *Folaga* detected an incoming flight of American bombers in May 1943 during tests at a university campus, and was thereafter ordered into full-scale production. Five months later, Mussolini was deposed. Before that event, the *Regia Marina* received only four *Folagas*, not enough to make a significant difference that late in the war. The delivery of thirteen *Gufos* to the navy was marginally more successful, and plans were actively under way to equip every military vessel, from battleships to torpedo-boats, with radar. Again, such good intentions were too late and overtaken by events that rendered deployment impossible.

The crisis was entirely preventable and should have never arisen, because just four days after Italy joined the Third Reich in fighting the Allies, *Commando Supremo* officers were in Germany being shown the latest technological advances in naval warfare, including the *Freya* radar. After their visit, some of the apparatuses were sent to Italy, where they actually equipped a few warships as early as summer 1940 – long before the *Regia Marina*'s calamitous defeats that could have been avoided by proper use of the devices. Incredibly, the Italians never bothered to develop the *Freya* sets into their own electronic detectors, nor to even operate them with better advantage. Their failure to carry on the lead in this field initiated by Marconi and developed by their generous ally was unquestionably among the most important contributions to ultimate defeat.

Ironically, the Italians led the world in the development of sonar. As early as the Spanish Civil War, the 334-ton submarine chaser, *Albatross*, operated the *petiteo*, an experimental sonar set, under combat conditions. Application of sonar helped the *Regia Marina* score heavily against Allied submarines from the outset of the Mediterranean Campaign, when nine British submarines were lost in as many months during 1940. If the Italians could have developed and perfected sonar, they could have done the same for radar.

But the Mediterranean Theater was the real arena where naval supremacy would be won or lost. At the outbreak of hostilities, Mussolini had at his disposal six battleships against five British counterparts moored at Alexandria, the Royal Navy base. There, Admiral Cunningham operated an additional twenty destroyers, seven cruisers, twelve submarines and one aircraft-carrier, the *Eagle*. But of all the Italian services, only the *Regia Marina* stood at an acceptable level of readiness. Two million tons of fuel oil available could keep its ships in full operation for more than a year before calling upon reserves.

The newly completed *Littorio* and *Vittorio Veneto* were outstanding battleships, the pride of the Italian Navy. Each displaced 45,000 tons and mounted nine fifteen-inch guns in three triple turrets, two fore and one aft. The Italian battleships were superior to their British counterparts not only in firepower, but speed, with a substantial three- to five-knot edge over the *Barham, Malaya, Ramillies, Royal Sovereign* and *Warspite*. The *Conti di Cavour* and *Giulio Cesare* were older, but had been refitted in 1937 with 12-inch guns, and subjected to a thorough modernization process that lasted until called upon to serve three years later. Both could top twenty seven knots, despite an innovative anti-torpedo bulge protruding below the water-line.

The Italian battleships *Littorio, Duilio* and *Vittorio Veneto*.

The twenty-five-year-old *Andrea Doria* and *Caio Duilio* had been similarly rebuilt in 1939, but sailed one knot slower than the Cavour Class battleships. Their main armament was greater, however, and they carried an additional ten 33cm. guns supplemented by fifty-three pieces of naval artillery ranging in fire-power from 13cm. cannons to anti-aircraft guns.

Joining the battleships were six heavy cruisers, including the 13,000-ton *Trento* and *Trieste*. With their high speed of thirty-six knots and 21cm. guns, they gave Admiral Cunningham special cause for concern. Only two knots slower for their additional thousand tons were the equally well-armed *Fiume, Gorizia, Pola* and *Zara*. These impressive capital ships were supported by dozens of destroyer escorts, minelayers, frigates, seaplane tenders, and torpedo-boats. They were supplemented by a particularly large destroyer fleet of 120 ships, greater numbers than either the French or American Navies possessed, and comparable to the British Royal Navy. Mediterranean fleet-carriers were not deemed necessary, since the peninsula, together with numerous Italian islands, supposedly allowed *Regia Aeronautica* warplanes to range across the entire Mediterranean. Italian officers were skilled, crews well-trained, and noted for their high *espirit d'corps*.

The *Regia Marina* was not without problems, however. To achieve their speed advantage, its warships were relatively lightly armored. 14,000 tons of armour protecting the *Littorio* and *Vittorio Veneto* seemed sufficient, but were not impervious to British shells. Italian cruisers and destroyers were narrower at the beam, allowing for faster performance. But there were fundamental trade-offs in stability and proper space for gun platforms, to say nothing of general sea-worthiness. During fleet action on 22 March 1942, a pair of Italian destroyers, the *Lanciere* and *Scirocco*, were lost off Sicily, not to enemy action, but in a gale.

The *Regia Marina's* premiere clash with its British counterparts demonstrated that diligence, skill and élan could sometimes overcome technological deficiency, while at the same time misconceptions regarding the conduct of aerial warfare at sea were debunked. On 6 July 1940, five heavily laden merchant vessels left Naples and Catania for Benghazi under the protection of sixteen torpedo boats, sixteen destroyers, eight light cruisers, and six heavy cruisers, plus the battleships *Giulio Casare* and *Conti di Cavour*. While the primary purpose of this formidable fleet was to ensure safe passage of the freighters to Libya, *Supermarina* commanders were actually spoiling for a decisive confrontation. In fact, a British convoy escorted by fifteen destroyers, the battleships *Malaya, Royal Sovereign*, and *Warspite*, together with the aircraft-carrier *Eagle*, was simultaneously under way from Alexandria to Malta.

Alerted to their position and direction by intercepts of Royal Navy radio messages, Chief of Staff Domenico Cavagnari instructed his forces to veer north toward Calabria in the hope of drawing them within striking distance of *Regia Aeronautica* aircraft. A few hours before his order was received, their squadrons boded well for the immediate future when bombers scored a hit on HMS *Gloucester*, instantly killing eleven ratings and six officers, including two Lieutenant Commanders and the Captain. The bridge was knocked out and damage so extensive that the light cruiser could only be controlled from her aft steering position. Nevertheless, 'the Fighting G', as she had been nicknamed, did not return to Alexandria for repairs, but stayed with the fleet, and participated in the coming battle.

Vice Admiral Inigo Campioni aboard the *Giulio Cesare* signaled Cavagnari for immediate aerial reconnaissance to locate the British ships, plus bombers to interdict them, but none appeared. Meanwhile, Vice Admiral Cunningham and his fleet were closing in south east of Punta Stilo, the so-called 'toe' of the Italian peninsula.

On the morning of 9 July, when the opposing forces were about 140 kilometers from each other, HMS *Eagle* launched flights of Fairey Swordfish against the Italian heavy cruisers, whose maneuvers and defensive fire were so effective, no torpedo-bombers found their mark – luckily for Campioni, whose repeated pleas for fighters still sitting at their bases just 100 kilometers away went unanswered. Lacking spotter planes to provide him with his opponents' location, he had to depend on the naked eye of his look-out, who did indeed find the enemy vessels just in time for the Italian battleships' superior range-finding equipment to direct firing from 21,500 meters, supposedly beyond the ability of Cunnigham's guns, a myth soon to be shattered.

Incoming bombardment came closer with each round, so Vice Admiral John Tovey withdrew his cruisers after *Neptune* received a hit from the *Giuseppe Garibaldi*. Closing the range, *Warspite* fired at the *Alberico da Barbia* and *Alberto di Giussano*. But her rounds fell short, so she divided her main guns between the *Conte di Cavour* and *Giulio Cesare*. A broadside from the latter missed *Warspite*, but straddled a pair of protecting destroyers, *Hereward* and *Decoy*, damaging them both. Immediately after *Warspite* narrowly escaped two near-misses, one of her 381mm shells struck the *Giulio Cesare*'s after deck from a distance of more than 24,000 meters, still a world record for naval gunnery against a moving target.

Aboard the Italian battleship, crews hurriedly evacuated her engine room after it filled with fumes from a fire started by exploding 37mm ammunition. Two seamen had been killed and several others wounded, but with half the boilers shut down, *Giulio Cesare*'s speed fell to eighteen knots. *Conte di Cavour* defended her from *Warspite*, which turned away, while the *Alberico da Barbia* and *Alberto di Giussano* intervened with other destroyers to cloak the stricken *Giulio Cesare* behind a smokescreen.

Cruiser groups of the opposing fleets fired volleys at each other without effect, save for three hits on the *Bolzano* that temporarily locked her rudder and killed two seamen. Equally inconclusive were torpedo attacks engaged in by destroyers on both sides, until both sides turned away from each other. Just then, *Regia Aeronautica* aircraft made their belated appearance, scoring hits on *Eagle*, *Malaya* and *Warspite* without sinking them.

Mutual collateral damage was traded the next day when an Italian destroyer on patrol in the area, *Leone Pancaldo*, was torpedoed by one of *Eagle*'s Fairey Swordfish, and another destroyer – this time, HMS *Escort* – was sunk by the submarine *Marconi*.

The Battle of Punta Stilo (or Battle of Calabria, as it was known to the British) was a draw, because both convoys reached their destinations intact. While it demonstrated that the *Regia Marina* could match the Royal Navy, the *Regia Aeronautica* proved to be a lingering disappointment.

The next month, *Supermarina* commanders were promised air cover for the transfer of the *Bande Nere* and *Colleoni* to the Dodecanese island of Leros, where the Italian base seemed menaced by a build-up of enemy naval forces. Untypically, *Regia Aeronautica* planes were in the sky overhead, reporting clear sailing. At the same moment, a British Walrus Mk I shadowed both vessels. Just off Crete, on the morning of 19 July, they were confronted by a quartet of Royal Navy destroyers, which turned and fled eastward at high speed after Admiral Casardi in command of the light cruisers ordered them to commence firing, but accuracy was hampered by very poor visibility conditions.

Eventually, the pursuit drew parallel with Cape Spada and a thick fog to the north, out of which an unexpected eruption of gunfire straddled the Italian warships. They could only respond by shooting back in the general direction of flashes punctuating the mist. Gradually, an armored cruiser, the *Sydney*, accompanied by HMS *Havock*, a destroyer, emerged from the ghostly curtain, behind which their guns had scored their first hits on the surprised enemy. Suddenly outnumbered by more than two-to-one odds, Admiral Casardi would have been justified in making a break for Leros. Instead, he radioed the island airfield, only a thirty-minute-flight away, for help, and swung around to join battle.

Both sides hammered away at each other for an hour without inflicting any serious damage, until the *Colleoni*'s engine-room exploded, and she came to full-stop. The *Havock* and another destroyer rushed at her, firing torpedoes and 13cm. shells, until the immobile cruiser capsized amid a series of devastating explosions. Alone now, the *Bande Nere* foiled all attacks, finally scoring a direct hit on the *Sydney*, which broke off action in the company of her destroyer escorts. Admiral Casardi made for Bengazi while the going was still good. Only now did Italian warplanes put in their ill-timed appearance by ineffectually bombing the *Havock*, which was busy trying to pick up *Colleoni* survivors. The rescue operation had to be called off, resulting in the abandonment of many Italian sailors at sea.

In sharp contrast, British torpedo-bombers achieved an important success at Tobruk. Unopposed by a single interceptor, they sank the *Zeffiro*, *Ostro* and *Nembo*, then blew off the bow of the *Euro*, which was towed back to Taranto for lengthy repairs. In two separate attacks on 5 and 20 July, the entire Italian destroyer squadron guarding Tobruk had been wiped out. Its annihilation was important to the British, whose coastal flanks had been menaced by the warships.

The Italian destroyers' most valuable contribution came in the form of regular convoys ferrying arms, men and supplies to Axis armies in Libya. When, in late July, Marshal Graziani requested additional materiel to fuel his offensive, the *Regia Marina* responded by launching the first large-scale formation of its kind. Each of its eleven freighters was protected by a cruiser together with twenty-three destroyers and another fourteen escort vessels. The British chose not to interfere with this show of strength, regardless of its importance to the ground fighting, and the convoy arrived intact.

In August, extensive mine-laying operations were methodically undertaken by the *Regia Marina*. It took mine-laying more seriously than any other navy, and with far better results. Immense secret spaces of floating death carpeting vast stretches of the Mediterranean were carefully chartered and used with dramatic effectiveness in connection with surface actions. Only a few weeks after mine-laying began, the fields claimed their first victim on the night of 20 August, when the British destroyer *Hostile* blew up and sank near Cape Bon.

From late July until the end of November, Italian convoys sailed to Libya virtually unhindered. Admiral Cunningham refused to challenge them with his older battleships, and Royal Navy submarines failed to make any impression on the fast enemy freighters. Instead, the *Regia Marina* stepped up its undersea interdiction, sinking the British submarines *Orpheus* and *Rainbow* in quick succession. Attrition among Italian submarines was also high, with thirteen sunk in the Mediterranean, plus four more in the Red Sea. Most were destroyed by enemy aircraft.

Regia Marina commanders learned from these losses, and routed their convoys beyond the range of RAF warplanes. All the Bristol Blenheim medium-bombers could do was to raid Bardia, Tobruk, Derna and Bengazi, where the Italian destroyers *Borea* and *Aquilone* were sunk, and heavy damage was incurred by the destroyer escorts *Cigno* and *Cosenz*, plus a trio of merchant vessels. But these were small prices to pay for the 148,817 tons of supplies and equipment successfully delivered to Marshal Graziani before the end of September.

Early next month, however, a particularly disturbing confrontation took place. During a night patrol north of Malta, the destroyer *Alcione* sighted what appeared to be a large ship and fired a pair of torpedoes from 1,830 meters. Surprisingly, the target easily steered out of harm's way, so the destroyer escort came about for another, closer run, while broadcasting the alarm. She was soon after joined by the *Airone*, which launched her own pair of torpedoes at the elusive enemy, hardly more than a blacker silhouette against the night sky, and missed.

Frustrated, the *Airone* captain fired two more from just 365 meters. When these, too, failed to strike home, he continued to close the range, firing his three 100mm deck-guns. They, at least, landed about seven hits on the mystery vessel, which, except for some fancy maneuvers, refused to defend itself. At just 275 meters, the *Airone* was suddenly blasted by 152mm shells erupting from a fiery broadside that momentarily transformed night into day and stunned the attacking vessel into immobility. Another destroyer escort, the *Ariel*, ran all ahead full at the enemy, simultaneously firing deck-guns and torpedoes, but was almost immediately stopped dead in the water by a direct hit.

A few minutes later, she rolled over and plunged to the bottom of the Mediterranean with most of her crew. By the time *Alcione* had completed her turn for another run, the enigmatic shadow was gone. It had belonged to HMS *Ajax*, a cruiser whose radar-directed guns played havoc with her less electronically endowed attackers. She went on to intercept three more destroyers steaming obliviously at full speed into the battle zone, set the *Artigliere* ablaze, and was in the process of tearing apart the *Aviere*, when, running low on ammunition, the cruiser disengaged from action.

The Italian operation was transformed into a rescue mission of survivors from the *Airone* and *Ariel*. Her devastating fire extinguished, the smoldering, badly wounded *Artigliere* was taken in tow by the *Camicia Nera*. In the early morning, however, they were subjected to a ferocious series of RAF attacks. Emergency calls went out for assistance from the *Regia Aeronautica*, which never responded, as British warplanes came down on the tied up ships, strafing their decks, dropping bombs and torpedoes.

The handicapped destroyers' anti-aircraft was so intense and effective, however, the attackers were driven off without sinking either vessel. Only when the *Camicia Nera* spotted two enemy cruisers approaching with a quartet of destroyers did she cut the doomed *Artigliere* adrift. After evacuating her surviving crew members, she made for home port. When the British force arrived in the area, the helpless destroyer exploded and sank under the pounding of HMS *York*, which used her for target practice. The day would come, however, when the Italians would wreak terrible revenge on this same heavy cruiser.

Until then, the confrontation with *Ajax* was history's first naval action in which radar played a part. Even now, *Supermarina* commanders could not believe the enemy was actually equipping his warships with such a combat-ready instrument, and falsely attributed the loss of their destroyers and destroyer escorts to conventional night-time operational skills acquired by the Royal Navy. Britain's early victories at sea were certainly spectacular and heralded yet greater things to come. But they had little impact on the steady flow of arms, equipment and men streaming to the shores of Libya.

Churchill's patience was at an end, and he shot a rankling telegram at Cunningham, excoriating him for his reluctance to interfere with the busy enemy convoys, which were fueling Graziani's advance toward Egypt. The Prime Minister fumed that his Admiral "had been rather backward in offensive operations against the Italian Fleet", and demanded that he "should do more".[3] Stung by the Prime Minister's insinuations, Cunningham envisioned a bold strike that would radically alter the course of the entire war and go down in history as one of the most influential military operations of all time.

Despite recent set-backs, the *Regia Marina* could still call the Mediterranean *Mare nostrum*, 'our sea'. The mere presence of its capital ships at Taranto, the fleet anchorage, prevented Britain from sufficiently supplying Crete and Malta, the Royal Navy's most crucial bases in this theater. Convoys for British armies fighting in the Libyan Desert had to travel the long way around most of Africa, navigating the Cape of Good Hope, then sailing northward along the entire length of the eastern continent in extended voyages fraught with danger and delay. Cunningham was particularly distressed by the addition of two new vessels to the Italian Fleet. The *Littorio* and *Vittorio Veneto* were among the finest battleships afloat, faster than anything comparable at his disposal. Since 2 August, they rode menacingly at anchor, laying in wait for the next available opportunity to pounce on anything that dared venture forth from either Alexandria or Gibraltar.

Because of Taranto, the life-line of convoys empowering Graziani's offensive could not be interdicted. In a conclusion born of desperation, Cunningham decided that Italy's major naval base would have to be reduced. All too aware of his warships' limitations, he assigned the task to an aircraft its crews referred to with tongue in cheek as the 'String-bag'. The plan was extremely innovative and bold, apparently suicidal. Never before had aircraft unsupported by naval units attempted to knock out an enemy fleet in its own home port.

Already renowned as the war's grand masters of ack-ack, the Italians had fortified Taranto with anti-aircraft defense-in-depth. It comprised twenty-one batteries of 10cm.

guns and eighty-four 20mm and 37mm anti-aircraft cannons, plus 109 heavy calibre machine guns. They were joined by the combined firepower of six battleships, seven cruisers and twenty-eight destroyers in Taranto's inner and outer harbors, numbering more than 600 anti-aircraft weapons. These were directed by twenty two large search-lights designed to illuminate enemy planes and blind their pilots.

Barrage balloons tethered in three rows across the anchorage would be sent aloft at the first sign of a raid. Their draping, almost invisible steel cables, were hung to sheer off the wings of low-flying aircraft. While ninety such balloons were on hand, there was only enough hydrogen available to send a third of them aloft. If in the unlikely event that the enemy attacked with an overwhelming armada of bombers, a heavy blanket of smoke could spread over the facility, obscuring the entire port, which was almost completely ringed by 4,600 meters of heavy steel-mesh anti-torpedo netting. Although Taranto was without radar, it did have highly sensitive sound detection devices able to pick up the noisy flight of slow-moving biplanes long before they arrived, thereby providing sufficient warning.

The entire harbor was a concentric arrangement of truly awesome defenses manned by the best shots in the world. They longed for the chance to show what they could do to an enemy aerial attack. So confident were the anti-aircraft gunners in their weapons and skill, they refused any cover from the *Regia Aeronautica*, arguing that its fighters would probably be mistakenly brought down by friendly fire in the thick curtain of shells sent skyward. Nothing, they were certain, would be able to penetrate their defenses. They were, in any case, deemed necessary only as a last resort, because the Italian fleet was ordered to leave its base the moment any sufficiently powerful enemy force came within 300 kilometers of Taranto.

Aware of the *Supermarina's* contingency plans, thanks to code intercepts, Admiral Cunningham dispatched the aircraft-carrier *Illustrious* in the company of four cruisers and as many destroyers on the afternoon of 10 November, then broke the formation into two directions near the Greek island of Cephalonia. Three additional cruisers simultaneously steamed on a northerly heading to create diversionary maneuvers in the seas between Italy and Albania. There they stumbled upon a World War One vintage destroyer escort, the *Fabrizi*, and an auxiliary cruiser, *Ramb* III, guarding a convoy of four empty freighters returning to Brindisi after having discharged their supplies in Valona. *Ramb* III kept the overwhelming enemy force at bay with nineteen salvos, and made good her escape without damage.

The old *Farbrizi*, however, rushed, guns blazing, at the three cruisers, and was almost immediately disabled by a fusillade of 21cm. shells. In a riddled condition and no longer able to defend herself, she tried to lure the British into a nearby mine-field. But they suspected the ruse, and sank the entire convoy of four ships between themselves. That done, they streamed out of the Adriatic at high speed. *Supermarina* commanders following these maneuvers were duly mystified, and failed to notice that the following day *Illustrious* was 370 kilometers from Taranto. On deck, a flight of Fairey Swordfish were unfolding their fifteen-meter wings.

In service since early 1934, the three-seat open-cockpit biplane was, in late 1940, obsolete by all standards, defended by just two 7.7mm Vickers machine-guns; one fixed forward, the other mounted on a swiveling ring aft in an arrangement out of World War One. For tonight's mission, even this inadequate armament would be reduced by half with removal of the rear gunner's position to allow for the installation of extra fuel tanks. These extended the aircraft's range, but increased its risk of catching fire, while reducing an already unimpressive top speed from 222 km/hr. The long, slow approaches made by Swordfish when on a torpedo run rendered them especially vulnerable to enemy ground-fire, against which their fabric-covered metal frames crumpled and burned like dried parchment.

Despite these formidable drawbacks, it could carry 680 kg of bombs or a single 726-kg torpedo over 1,600 kilometers. Its 750-hp Bristol Pegasus 9-cylinder radial piston engine performed with steadfast reliability under a variety of extreme conditions, from freezing to boiling temperatures, including ice and salt-water spray. The airplane was very stable, forgiving on the controls, and a delight to fly.

"You could pull a Swordfish off the deck and put her in a climbing turn at fifty-five knots," according to veteran pilot, Terrence Horsley. "She would maneuver in a vertical plane as easily as she would straight and level, and even when diving from 3,000 meters, her indicated air-speed never rose much about 200 knots. The controls were not frozen rigid by the force of the slipstream, and it was possible to dive within sixty meters of the water. The approach to the carrier deck could be made at a staggeringly slow speed, yet response to the controls remained firm and insistent. Consider what such qualities meant on a dark night when the carrier deck was pitching the height of a house."[4]

At 2100, *Illustrious* turned into the wind off the northwestern point of Cephalonia, and a dozen airplanes lifted slowly from the deck. Led by Lieutenant Commander K. Williamson, his and five other Swordfish were armed with torpedoes, followed by four more with a mix of flares and bombs. Another two were armed with torpedoes. Over-burdened with these munitions and auxiliary fuel tanks, the first wave launched without incident, but struggled for altitude. Somewhat more than an hour later, the second wave of another nine 'String-bags' rose into the night air. For the first thirty minutes of flight, Williamson's group navigated by instruments alone through thick cloud. Concerned the pilots might lose their bearings, he ordered them to climb above the overcast at 2,200 meters, where they found clear skies illuminated by a crescent moon.

One of the airmen, Lieutenant H. Swayne, had indeed lost contact with the first wave of Swordfish, and found himself heading toward the target alone. The Italians' acoustic early warning system detected his approach, and all available barrage balloons dangling lethal steel cables ascended in the glare of the harbor's combined search-lights. Realizing he was early, Swayne circled just out of ground-fire range until the rest of his comrades appeared. Still far from Taranto, they could see it already spouting fire like a monstrous volcano. Into this inferno, Commander Williamson led the first attack wave.

After the first two Swordfish illuminated the harbor with flares, he dove from the west, then turned southeast over San Pietro Island. His port wing-tip almost brushed against a balloon cable, as he bore down on a battleship, dropping his torpedo a mere ten meters above the water. It raced toward the target, narrowly missing a destroyer, and exploded half-way between the B-turret and bridge of the *Conti di Cavour*. The attacking aircraft banked away, was shredded by machine-gun fire and spun into the sea, but both Williamson and his observer were captured alive.

Two more Swordfish followed the Lieutenant Commander's example, but their torpedoes missed the already sinking *Cavour*, because the pilots had been dazzled by blinding searchlights. They flew through the hellish ground-fire unscathed. But Taranto's defenders also had difficulty seeing their opponents. Burning magnesium parachute-flares dropped by the enemy airplanes created false images and dancing shadows, making target identification extremely difficult. Every gun capable of firing a shot was nonetheless blasting away at the intruders. They could not, however, protect the Italian Fleet's newest battleship. A torpedo strike on the *Littorio* tore a 15- by 10-meter-wide hole in her bow, followed a few minutes later by a hit at the port quarter. Water rushed into its 8- by 2-meter cavity, and the vessel began to go down. At the same time, Lieutenant M. Maund dropped his torpedo toward the *Vittorio Veneto* at 1,300 meters, but a searchlight spoiled his aim, and he missed. The bomb-laden Swordfish unloosed their missiles on several warships. They, too, went wide of their targets, save for a lucky destroyer, which escaped the consequences of a direct hit when a British bomb failed to explode.

Taranto's seaplane base, the eyes of the fleet, was far less fortunate. It was utterly demolished, all its hydroplanes destroyed and invaluable repair shops plus spare parts depot wrecked. As the first wave of attackers turned out to sea, the second one, back on *Illustrious*, got under way with some difficulty. Its last two planes were taxiing to starting positions when they accidentally locked wings, reducing Lieutenant Commander Ginger Hale's flight to just seven aircraft. Undaunted, they took off from the pitching deck to arrive over Taranto for a final, midnight raid.

Numerous targets were brilliantly illuminated by twenty four magnesium flares, and Hale came in at ten meters above the surface of the sea, his torpedo going away at 700 meters toward the already stricken *Littorio*. She shuddered with a direct hit that tore yet another gaping wound in her side. Close behind Hale, Lieutenant G. Bayley dove on the listing battleship to deliver her *coup de grâce*. But before he could release his torpedo, he was caught in the crossfire of perhaps a dozen guns, which literally vaporized his aircraft in mid-air. Lieutenant Bayley's body was never found.

Other *Swordfish* bombed the harbor's precious oil storage facilities, which erupted into a conflagration turning night into day. Clearly illuminated by the ferociously burning depot was another large battleship singled out by Lieutenant Lea. He dove on it, and the *Caio Duilio* lurched with a hit that tore an eleven-by-thirteen-meter hole one meter below her water-line. Lea came in so low his run took him straight over the target's foredeck and between the *Fiume* and *Zara*, two cruisers which, in their eagerness to shoot him down, fired on each other. Lea threaded their cross-fire, then banked for *Illustrious*. He left the *Caio Duilio* in a sinking condition, but she was saved by the frantic efforts of her crew, who ran her aground just in time. Torpedoes dropped by two more Swordfish missed the *Vittorio Veneto*, and an unexploded bomb-hit on the cruiser *Trento* nonetheless ruptured her oil tanks. These last attackers escaped without a scratch.

The Taranto they left behind was a tangle of badly wounded ships illuminated by the glare of burning harbor works. Against the loss of two British planes and four men, forty Italians perished – twenty-three aboard the *Littorio*, sixteen with the *Conti di Cavour* and one on the *Caio Duilio*. Had the defenders operated their smoke-screens, the raid might have been put off. Steel-mesh netting surrounding the ships was sufficient to protect against conventional torpedoes exploding on impact, but at Taranto the British introduced magnetic torpedoes traveling at depths greater than the nets, which only went down to a vessel's maximum draught, to detonate directly beneath a target's keel.

Trying to shoot down even slow-moving aerial targets at night against the shifting glare of drifting magnesium flares spoiled the aim of anti-aircraft gunners. However, they were not entirely to blame for the disaster, because the audacious operation was the first of its kind. Until Taranto, no one would have believed that a handful of 'String-bags' could have single-handedly displaced the balance of power in an entire theater of war. That, in fact, was the result of the attack. Surviving vessels were moved to Naples, too far away from enemy convoys now able to supply Malta and Greece.

Implications were still more far-reaching. For those who understood Taranto as an example of things to come, the era of the battleship had ended. No one learned this lesson better than the Axis leaders. Hitler was so impressed, he wanted to scrap all his capital ships to build more long-range bombers. Mussolini was hardly less disenchanted with the costly, vulnerable battleships, and ordered his naval architects to create a new fleet of more numerous, smaller attack craft, particularly torpedo-boats. To the Japanese, however, Taranto was their inspiration for Pearl Harbor. The success of that raid was possible because the Americans did not learn from the lessons of November 11. They continued to surround the USS *Arizona* and other doomed vessels with the same kind of steel mesh netting used by the Italians with such disastrous effect in 1940.

8

The *Duce's* Dolphins

Going down into the vast sea and to destiny, laughing at Lady Death …
From *Inno del Sommergibili*, 'Hymn of the Submariners'

When Benito Mussolini went to war against the Western Allies, he had at his disposal the world's greatest submarine fleet in terms of tonnage. Only the Soviet Navy possessed a slight numerical edge. He was able to field 172 mostly modern, undersea warships, enough to simultaneously fulfill the numerous duties assigned to them: defending Italian coasts, intercepting enemy shipping, scouting for the surface fleet, transporting essential materials, and laying minefields. Nearly half of them could operate continuously for up to six months, ranging over 20,000 miles, far beyond the capabilities of any other contemporaneous submarines. Their torpedoes were among the best of World War Two; their all-volunteer crews, well-trained, skilled and spirited. If anything could truly make the Mediterranean Sea into Italy's *Mare Nostro*, friend and foe alike believed the *Duce's* submarines would effect the transformation.

Their expectations appeared to be confirmed just two days after his declaration of war, when the *Bagnolini* attacked two enemy light cruisers escorted by a destroyer squadron. A torpedo fired by Lieutenant Commander Franco Tosoni Pittoni struck HMS *Calypso*, sinking her about thirty kilometers southeast of the small island of Gavdo. In September, he escaped detection running submerged through the Straits of Gibraltar and into the North Atlantic. As a testimony to the skill of their operators, none of the Italian submarines that passed out and back into the Mediterranean from 1940 to 1943 were lost in the Straits deemed 'suicidal' by the Germans, who did indeed lose several U-boats around Gibraltar. Tight security in the form of vigilant corvettes and stationary hydrophones made movement through the narrow gauntlet hazardous.

Contributing to these military challenges was a powerful current that carried submerged vessels beyond their depth limits to sometimes collide with the rocky bottom. More than one boat was damaged by this navigational hazard, which was unknown until the first Italian submarine to leave the Mediterranean Sea for operations in the Atlantic Ocean successfully slipped through the Straits of Gibraltar on 13 June. Afterward, the British island-fortress was on high alert to prevent similar escapes. The *Veniero* had deftly infiltrated a formidable barrier of floating minefields and diligent patrols to team up with its U-boat comrades stationed at Bordeaux. British intelligence wrongly assumed she had sailed from Tobruk, where more submarines were supposedly lying in wait. Accordingly, the city was raided repeatedly by RAF Beaufort bombers, until a squadron of Italian destroyers sailed within range of the Egypto-Libyan border to shell British airfields at Salum, cratering the strip, blowing up repair stations, and inflicting irreparable damage on parked warplanes.

While sailing on the surface into the Bay of Biscay, the *Bagnolini* was attacked by a light bomber, but her accurate gunfire drove it away with the Blenheim's starboard engine trailing smoke. On 11 December, Commander Franco Pittoni's vessel joined German U-boats in action against Allied convoys, sinking the British cargo ship, *Amicus*, with a single torpedo. But the Italian submarine wallowed almost uncontrollably in North Atlantic weather, and returned suffering some damage to the Kriegsmarine base at Bordeaux. She sailed from there in early 1944, re-christened UIT-22 (*U-boot-Italien*, reflecting her Italo-German crew) commanded by Oblt.z.S. Friedrich Wunderlich. On 11 March, some 300 kilometers from Cape Town, UIT-22 was on her way to meet with U-178 for refueling, when she was attacked and sunk by pilots of South Africa's 262nd Squadron. Their *Catalina* flying-boats were guided to the rendezvous by German radio messages of the kind British cryptographers had been intercepting the previous two years.

The fate of the former *Bagnolini* in some ways paralleled Italy's entire undersea efforts during World War Two. Like that doomed ship, they got off with a successful start, but were soon hamstrung by a series of failings leading ultimately to disaster. These crucial faults were categorized and analyzed for the first time by Admiral Antonio Legnani, a veteran of the battles at Punta Stilo and Cape Matapan, where he successfully commanded his light cruiser, the *Luigi di Savoia Duca Degli Abruzzi*.

In "A Critical Examination of our Readiness and Results of our Submarine Warfare until early December 1941", he pointed out that Italian boats were too slow: "This deficiency makes the reaching or passing (to then attack) of individual units or a convoy of them impossible." Contributing to an inadequate speed was the drag produced by oversized Italian conning towers, which additionally slowed undersea maneuvers and, while surfaced, became large, visible profiles, unlike much smaller German versions. The U-boats also rode lower in the water, making them more difficult to see than the higher Italian free board. Italian engines were too loud, "with serious consequences in regards to detection by the enemy's hydrophones."[1] Italian submarines were not designed to navigate through high seas, and therefore could not keep up with Kriegsmarine success against Allied convoys.

Germany's Supreme U-Boat Commander, Admiral Karl Dönitz, originally had high hopes for augmenting his operational forces. At one time, "there were actually more Italian submarines than German U-boats operating in the Atlantic," according to naval historian Robert Jackson.[2] But the former handled so poorly in rough seas they achieved little. The final straw came on 25 May 1941, when Captain Giulio Ghiglieri was informed by radio that his submarine was the only Axis warship in the area where the German battleship Bismarck was immobilized and under attack by overwhelming surface forces. He tried to attack a pair of enemy cruisers, but the *Barbarigo* was unable to fire her torpedoes because the seas were too rough for her. Thereafter, Italian submarines were reassigned to the less turbulent Central and Southern Atlantic on solitary patrols.

Admiral Legnani wrote that Italian boats needed two to three minutes to submerge, more than twice as long as German submarines. Their turning radius was 300 meters, "thanks to the installation of a double rudder, where it is about 500 meters on our units."[3] U-boat torpedo-launchers generated no telltale air bubbles; Italian counterparts did. Italian torpedoes ran straight and true, but were sometimes diverted from the target by heavy swells. Worse, they only exploded on contact, when at least half of their blast potential was blown away from the target; German torpedoes were equipped with magnetic detonators that exploded with maximum effectiveness directly beneath an enemy vessel, breaking its keel.

The most distressful defect afflicting Italian submarines came to light at the very beginning of their operations. In early June 1940, serious problems with air-conditioning systems aboard the *Archimede, Macalle* and *Perla* were being attended to by repair personnel. But their efforts were interrupted by Mussolini's declaration of war; a week later, the boats were ordered to the East African naval base at Massaua. During their first day at sea, crewmembers aboard all three vessels began experiencing debilitating nausea apparently caused by the air-conditioning units, which were partially shut down until cases of heat prostration continued to multiply. Conditions aboard *Archimede* were particularly severe, where some of the men, including two officers, suffered heat stroke. With the air-conditioning switched back on, many more exhibited extreme psychological disorders, including deep depression, loss of appetite, euphoria, hallucinations, and maniacal behavior.

On the night of the 23rd, a riot broke out among the crew, four men were killed, and Captain T.V. Signorini aborted his mission after restoring order, landing at the port of Assab. Mechanics rushed in from Massaua determined that methyl chloride – an odorless, colorless but highly toxic gas used as a coolant – had seeped into the ventilation systems and poisoned everyone aboard. It was replaced with relatively harmless freon, but most other Italian submarines continued to use methyl chloride for months thereafter!

A mid-1942 German newsreel documenting life inside the *Barbarigo* shows perspiring officers and crewmembers stripped down to their shorts, because they were reluctant to use the boat's disreputable air-conditioning.

After the *Archimede* was restored to duty, she proceeded through the Red Sea, where she was on station for the next ten months. During that period, the few other Italian boats operating in this theater were virtually on their own, minus significant support from surface warships, with terrible consequences, as exemplified by the *Torricelli*. Enemy forces caught her on the surface outside Massawa during the dangerous daylight hours of 23 June, because malfunctioning ballast-tanks prevented her from diving. A pair of British gunboats and three destroyers converged on the partially disabled submarine, an apparently easy kill.

Hopelessly outnumbered and out-gunned, Lieutenant Commander Pelosi defiantly opened fire at 0530 with the *Torricelli*'s single deck-gun. A direct hit on the *Shoreham*'s deckhouse forced the gun-boat to disengage from the attack and make for urgent repairs at Aden. Taking advantage of the enemy's astonishment, the suicidal *Torricelli* pressed forward at top speed, unloosing a spread of torpedoes at the destroyers. While they turned to avoid being hit, Pelosi directed his furiously firing deck-gun to concentrate its 100mm shells on the *Khartoum*, which erupted into flames.

So successful were the *Torricelli*'s maneuvers that the British were not able to score a hit until 0605, when its steering gear was knocked out and Pelosi wounded. He ordered the boat's troublesome ballast-tanks manually forced opened, and she slipped beneath the surface of the Red Sea with the Italian tricolor still flying from her conning tower. In excess of 700 shells and 500 machine-gun rounds fired at the submarine in little more than half an hour had been unable to destroy her. Standing on the decks of *Kandahar* and *Kingston*, the destroyers that rescued them, survivors of the scuttled *Torricelli* witnessed the still-blazing *Khartoum* explode and sink. So impressed was Captain Robson with the Italians' courage, he received Lieutenant Pelosi aboard the *Kandahar* with military honors.

Meanwhile, pressured between British forces descending from the north in Sudan and coming up from Kenya in the south, East Africa could not be expected to hold out indefinitely. Outside supplies and reinforcements could not reach the Italian defenders. Before the capture of Massaua, the *Archimede* and her fellow submarines made for the

Italo-German base at Bordeaux, France. After passing south through the Gulf of Perim, evading enemy surface units and aircraft, they received enough supplies from a German tanker, the *Northmark*, to complete, in Jackson's words, "an epic journey round the Cape of Good Hope".[4] The four submarines traversed 20,447 kilometers, eluding enemy interdiction and arriving in Bordeaux after sixty-five days at sea, most of them while surfaced, to great popular acclaim.

Their achievement was at least some compensation for the loss of East Africa. During the boat's last cruise, she was under the command of *Tenente di Vacello* Guido Saccardo, prowling the Brazilian coast. On 15 April 1943, a U.S. Navy PBY Catalina piloted by Ensign Thurmond E. Robertson appeared 628 kilometers east-southeast of Natal. Each Italian submarine bristled with a quartet of 13.2mm machine guns, and *Regia Marina* crews often preferred to fight it out on the surface against attacking aircraft, rather than trust to the sluggish dive time of their boats. Saccardo's men were no exception, and they put up such intense, accurate fire, Robertson had to abort a low-level, straight-in bomb-run, thereby affording the *Archimede* an opportunity to crash-dive. But she was too slow.

In desperation, Robertson put his lumbering 'Gooney Bird' into a sixty-degree dive, reaching a speed of 245 knots – far beyond the performance parameters for which the PBY had been designed. At 610 meters, five knots within terminal velocity, he pulled up to release four 160-kg Mk 44 Torpex-filled depth-charges. They exploded on either side of the submarine's hull, smashing all light fixtures, disabling one of the 1,500-hp diesel engines, and blowing two forward hatches off their hinges. Unable to dive, the Italians were no less willing to surrender. For the next hour and twenty minutes, they fought off not only Robertson's Catalina, but four other American flying-boats called to the scene. One of them piloted by Lieutenant Gerard Bradford, Jr. swooped in at a mere sixteen meters above the surface of the sea to drop four depth-charges on the *Archimede*. One tore through her aft hatchway, detonating torpedoes in the stern tubes, and she went down stern-first in a matter of seconds.

A pair of PBYs dropped three life-rafts for the survivors, Commander Saccardo among them. Of his fifty-four crewmembers, twenty-five were still alive, but not for long. Most were so badly wounded, they soon succumbed to their injuries. After twenty-nine days adrift in the company of his dying comrades, Engineer Giuseppe Lococo was washed ashore on Bailque, a small island at the mouth of the Amazon River, where he was found by local fishermen, who nursed him back to health. The twenty-six-year-old Sicilian coxswain was the only survivor.

The outcome of other encounters between attacking Allied aircraft and Italian submarine gunners mostly favored the latter. On 7 March 1941, look-outs aboard the *Argo* traversing the Bay of Biscay observed a Sunderland flying-boat in the distance. While any U-boat commander would have immediately crash-dived his vessel at the first sight of such a lethal threat, the Italians began communicating with the four-engine monster via signal lantern! Once they ascertained its identity, they allowed the Sunderland to approach to within 800 meters before opening fire, spoiling the pilot's bomb run. By the time he resumed his attack, the *Argo* had vanished beneath the waves. A similar incident occurred exactly eight months later, when the *Tricheco*, attempting to make the Sicilian naval base at Augusta, was menaced by a Blenheim that veered away after having been hit by too many 13.2mm rounds. Off the coast of Brazil in early February 1943, gunners aboard the notorious *Barbarigo* caused an American Catalina pilot to prematurely drop his three bombs, which went wide of their target. The previous August 29th, she was attacked in the same waters by several PBYs. One was shot down and the others driven off, but after-gunner Carlo Marcheselli paid with his life for defending the boat.

He was not the only crewman to die in these sub-versus-plane duels, which usually saved the vessel, but not without casualties. Sergeant Michelangelo Canistraro was killed during a machine-gun attack carried out by a Sunderland against his submarine endeavoring to cross the Bay of Biscay on 15 February 1943. The *Cagni* escaped undamaged to complete 136 days at sea, the longest continuous mission undertaken by any Italian vessel during World War Two.

But the *Torelli* experienced the most unique anti-aircraft action of its kind. Among the most successful *Sommergibili Italiani*, she sank seven enemy vessels totaling 43,000 tons, but incurred extensive damage from a British flying-boat on 5 June 1942 in the eastern Atlantic while under way to the Bahamas. Just two days later, while limping back to Bordeaux on the surface, unable to dive, she was attacked again by two more Sunderlands. Their bomb-runs repeatedly spoiled by defensive fire, they strafed the submarine, killing Sergeant Flavio Pallucchini, wounding Captain Antonio de Giacomo and another officer. During a low pass, one of the aircraft was hit, and both turned away.

The following 16 March, the *Torelli* was hunting along the Brazilian coast, when three Catalinas caught her on the surface. Failure of her main shut-off valve on the engine intake prevented the boat from submerging, so she was forced to engage in a ferocious gun battle with the American torpedo-bombers. One was destroyed and the other two driven off, but the deck was badly shot up, and there were casualties. The radio-man had been killed; wounded included the chief engineer, an engineer, and, once more, the captain, this time badly injured, who transferred control to his second-in-command.

Thereafter, the *Torelli* was made over into a long-distance transport. Stripped of all offensive weapons, save her four 13.2mm anti-aircraft guns, her torpedo tubes were used as extra fuel tanks to extend her range and interior extensively renovated. On 14 June 1943, she departed Bordeaux with 150 tons of mercury, steel, and munitions, including 20mm cannons and a 500-kg. bomb. Also on board was Colonel Kinze Sateke, a Japanese officer specializing in telecommunications, who had just finished advanced training in Germany. He was accompanied by a German engineer, plus two civilian mechanics. All of these personnel were to assist in technologically up-grading Japan's war effort. Although Allied intercepts learned of the secret voyage before it got underway, alerted Sunderland and Catalina flying-boats patrolling from Gibraltar to Freetown failed to locate their prey.

The *Torelli* arrived in Singapore without incident on 31st August. Just nine days later, word came of the Badoglio armistice, and she was seized by German authorities, her officers and men interned in POW camps. But when Mussolini established his Social Republic three months later, most of them elected to fight for him again aboard their old submarine, re-named UIT-25 for her Italo-German crew. Assigned to the 12th and later the 33rd U-boat flotilla, she served in the western Pacific until the surrender of the Third Reich was learned on 10 May 1945.

But the vessel's life was not yet finished. She received yet a third designation when drafted into the Imperial Japanese Navy as I-504. Some die-hard European officers and men stayed on board, and for the rest of World War Two, I-504 was manned by a mixed German-Italian-Japanese crew. A few days before the close of hostilities, their boat was approached by a Mitchell B-25 medium bomber. Forty-one years later, when Raffaele Sanzio was 66 years old, he recalled that attack as an engineer aboard the former *Torelli*:

"For the record, I can confirm that it was the 13.2mm Breda machine guns of my submarine that, on August 22nd 1945, shot down the last American twin engine bomber. It happened in Kobe, and it was us Italians who shot it down."[5] Theirs was the last Axis victory of the Second World War.

Although Italian submariners avoided surface combat with warships whenever possible, they did engage enemy submarines, not always by choice. The first such encounter took place on the night of 15 October 1940, when the *Enrico Toti* went full ahead on the surface to investigate a suspicious craft some sixty kilometers off Cape Colonne, Calabria. At about 5,000 meters, the enemy identified himself by opening fire and maneuvering for a torpedo run. A shell struck the base of the Italian boat's conning tower, followed by one torpedo racing just passed the stern. The *Toti*'s four machine-guns replied by raking the stranger's deck with 13.2mm rounds. The target turned, the *Toti* in pursuit, firing both of her 100mm guns at the slightly faster prey over the next thirty minutes. At 0140 hours, the 1,475-ton British submarine, *Rainbow*, went down with all hands.

The *Toti* was something of a sub-killer. The same month she sank the *Rainbow*, her torpedoes found the *Perseus*, near Zante.

The *Sommergibili* often gave Italian morale a boost when most needed. Just three days after 1941's unfortunate Battle of Cape Matapan, the *Ambra* torpedoed HMS *Bonaventure*. A veteran of the raid on Taranto five months before, the battleship keeled over near Crete. That night, two freighters in a convoy bound for Greece were sunk by another Italian submarine, the *Dagabur*, with one, well-aimed torpedo apiece. These successes were broadly publicized to restore general confidence in Italy's war at sea.

Italian submarines carried out less well-recognized but equally important missions. With Axis supply convoys being savaged by Allied interdiction, the *Delfino* transported more than 200 tons of ammunition and fuel to Italo-German troops in Libya from 13 November 1942 to 6 January 1943, shooting down a Sunderland in the process. Joining her was the *Micca*, formerly the flagship of the Italian submarine fleet. As such, she led a famous naval parade in honor of Adolf Hitler's visit to Naples on 5 May 1938. When war came, the *Micca* was assigned to the 16th Squadron of the 1st *Sommergibili* Group, serving as a successful mine-layer off the Egyptian coast. In one such mission alone, on 12 June 1940, she daringly laid forty mines before the approaches to the Royal Navy's Mediterranean Fleet headquarters at Alexandria. As a transport, the *Micca* delivered 2,163 tons of materials to Rommel's Afrika Korps.

While Italian submarines took a beating in North Atlantic gales, their hull integrity was robust, perhaps even more so than their German betters. Crash-diving to escape the destroyer escort of a British convoy the *Argo* was just about to attack on 5 December 1940, she was battered by twenty-four well-placed depth-charges for more than four hours. A storm, not any damages incurred during the previous day's underwater attack, practically swamped the boat and shorted out most of her electrical system, forcing Captain Crepas to make for Bordeaux. Three days earlier, the *Tarantini* endured 176 depth-charges hurled at her for twenty-four hours to emerge scarred but seaworthy. But the *Smeraldo* held the record for survival after escaping another round-the-clock barrage, this time in the Mediterranean, of more than 200 depth-charges between the 7th and 8th of July 1940, returning for minor repairs at the *Regia Marina* base in Tobruk. More impressive, the redoubtable *Torelli* survived an attack that would have broken the back of most other submarines, when two bombs launched at her from a Sunderland exploded under the vessel's keel. Although badly damaged, on fire, with all her navigational aids knocked out, Commander Migliori brought her safely to the Spanish port of Aviles, where the *Torelli* was repaired and went on to fulfill her interesting destiny in the Pacific. Ironically, the *Schnorchel*, an extendable tube that allowed diesel-powered submarines to recharge their batteries without exposing themselves while surfaced, had been invented by an Italian major, Pericle Ferretti, as early as 1922. Like radar, another Italian invention, no one bothered to develop his *Schnorchel*.

These two neglected devices could have altered the course of military history in the *Regia Marina*'s favor. Mussolini's envisioned navy had always included submarines, which received preferential considerations in fuel and production. Even so, Italy lacked the industrial capacity to keep up with attrition. German shipyards mass-produced more than 1,000 U-boats, while just forty new submarines were built by the Italians.

Far more decisive, however, was the unseen battle of military intelligence. An early gift to Allied cryptographers was a copy of the *Sommergibili Italiani* SM 19/S code book retrieved from the *Uebi Scebeli*. Described by Jackson as "among the best Italian submarines to be used during the war, giving good service in a variety of roles ... strong and very maneuverable", she was scuttled by her crew after having been depth-charged to the surface and subjected to the concentrated fire of five enemy destroyers on 28 June 1940.[6] Over the next two weeks, eight more vessels of Italy's sub-surface fleet were sunk in equally quick succession, until *Regia Marina* commanders realized the missing manual was being used to intercept their submarines, and revised all naval codes. Henceforward, Italian undersea successes resumed when a destroyer, HMS *Escort*, failed to survive her encounter with the *Marconi* off Gibraltar on 11 July.

But the power of code-breaking to sway the fortunes of war would return two years later, when the last impediment to the ULTRA secret and its capacity to render all Axis' secrets transparent was removed with the assassination of Reinhard Heydrich, chief of security in the Third Reich. ULTRA code-breaking was in large measure responsible for most of the Italians' eighty-two submarines lost during World War Two. That they were able to sink 724,656 tons of enemy shipping in just three years is a remarkable testimony to their courage and skill, operating as they did at distinct disadvantages not confronted by Allied submarines. The enemy read orders issued by *Commando Supremo* at the same moment they were received by *Regia Marina* captains. As such, virtually every Italian vessel – not only most submarines – was ambushed before it could locate an opponent. Whereas the Italian Navy depended on a few, slow reconnaissance planes of limited range to search the vast Mediterranean Sea for targets, cryptographers sitting in London knew in advance almost every move Axis commanders made.

The *Sommergibili* were additionally confronted by formidable anti-submarine measures, the like of which no Anglo-American boats need ever have feared. The fifty-two U.S. submarines lost in the Second World War escaped the almost invariably innocuous attacks by enemy destroyers to be far more often bombed while surfaced by Japanese aircraft. Britain's Royal Navy Submarine Service lost seventy-five submarines, but sank 1,500,000 tons of merchant shipping, plus 169 warships in all theatres, although during a longer period of time (three more years). Moreover, the vast majority of these successes were made against virtually defenseless Japanese convoys in the South and Central Pacific.

During the first half of World War Two, British submarines operated primarily out of Malta, protecting that besieged, strategically valuable island, and raiding Axis convoys to North Africa. In the course of fulfilling these duties, they were eminently successful, but had they been forced to operate in the North Atlantic, as the Italian submarines did, they would have suffered no less grievously. Hitler's U-boats were true, ocean-going vessels, more advanced than any contemporaries, and Admiral Legnano perhaps mistakenly compared them to his own country's submarines, which had been designed for the less navigationally-challenging Mediterranean Theater.

Had he juxtaposed his *Sommergibili* with American versions, he would have had cause for optimism, because the U.S. Navy's 'Silent Service' was far inferior to Italy's undersea fleet. Beginning after the attack at Pearl Harbor, throughout all of 1942 and most of 1943, American submarines ran up a virtually unrelieved record of failure. Its boats were plagued with stability and buoyancy problems. Their torpedoes ran too deeply and exploded harmlessly, if at all, against an enemy hull in the rare instance they could be made to hit a target. Of the first four torpedoes fired by the submarine *Tinosa* on 24 July 1943 at a Japanese whaling factory ship, two struck the 19,000-ton vessel, which suffered no damage. U.S. Commander Daspit launched two more torpedoes, both of which hit the *Tonan Maru 111* and stopped but could not sink her. At close range, and at right angles to his stationary target, he loosed off nine additional torpedoes. All hit; none exploded.

Solutions were needlessly prolonged by Bureau of Ordinance bureaucrats, who steadfastly stood by the sacred design superiority of 'American torpedoes,' and blamed all failures on human error. An authoritative website additionally points out that "many U.S. submarine captains did not stand up to the rigors of war time command that was demanded of them; in 1942, 30% were removed for lack of fitness or lack of results, and 14% for the same reason both in 1943, and 1944. All were career officers, generally older and thus much more conservative and cautious in combat. Consequently, most of the early offensive maneuvers were made from the safety of deep water by sonar, with predictably dismal results."[7]

Another web site reveals that "the lack of a unified submarine command (in the U.S. Navy) compounded the challenges. Infighting between the Pacific Fleet based in Pearl and the Asiatic Fleet in Manila for manpower and materials accounted for a schism in command that lasted throughout virtually the entire war. But even with the 'heads up' intelligence information being provided (by ULTRA code-breakers), tactical positioning errors by top leadership continued to haunt the submarine fleet. Boats were continually given orders of deployment to stalk the entrances of harbors and ports, ignoring the fact that the bulk of the Japanese shipping was concentrated along established, high seas trade routes. "[8]

Immediately after the war, commanders of the 'Silent Service' announced they sank ten million tons of Japanese shipping, amounting to 4,000 enemy vessels. Subsequent U.S. Navy investigation of the record showed that the total destroyed tonnage was actually half as great, while the number of ships sunk was a third of the original claim. Investigators also learned that of America's 16,000 submariners, 375 officers and 3,331 enlisted men perished at sea – a 22% casualty rate, the highest percentage in all U.S. armed forces.

Properly functioning torpedoes were not introduced until the close of 1943, long after the war had already turned decisively in the Allies' favor. For the remaining twenty months of that conflict, Americans sank the most ships of any submarine service of the war, possibly because they were fighting an enemy whose ability to defend himself was severely hampered.

The Soviet Navy's undersea fleet would have likewise encouraged Admiral Legnano. After having primarily distinguished themselves for most of the war by being sunk by German *Stuka* dive-bombers, the few Russian submarines that survived attacked unarmed passenger liners overcrowded with refugees during the waning days of hostilities. On 30 January 1945, Commander Alexander Marinesko sank the *Wilhelm Gustloff* with the loss of 9,343 wounded soldiers, medical personnel, Baltic families and other civilians – the highest loss of life at sea in recorded history. A similar Soviet 'triumph' was submarine L-3's destruction of the *Goya*, carrying 7,000 Eastern Europeans the following 16 April. Only 183 survived.

The Italian submarine service made up for its deficiencies with some of the most outstanding commanders of the war. Among them was Gianfranco Gazzana Priaroggia. Kriegsmarine admirals were so impressed by him, they awarded *Ursus atlanticus*, as his crew members affectionately referred to their Captain, the distinguished *Ritterkreuz*, or 'Knight's Cross', an honor infrequently bestowed on their own commanders, let alone foreigners. Among his many, perilous exploits, he eluded destroyers dispatched to intercept him, while sinking six Allied vessels, including the *Empress of Canada*, a large British troopship. Before he was killed in action on 23 May 1943, he sank 90,601 tons of Allied shipping, making his *Leonardo Da Vinci* the most successful Italian submarine, with 120,243 tons sunk. Fifty years later, the Italian Navy's new S525 was christened the *Gianfranco Gazzana Priaroggia*.

The last hurrah of the *Sommergibili Italiani* was their desperate defense of Sicily against an overwhelming Allied onslaught. A few managed to get in some significant hits before most of them went down fighting, such as the *Dandolo*, when her torpedoes so badly wrecked HMS *Cleopatra* on 16 July 1943 the anti-aircraft cruiser would never see combat again. Thereafter, aside from a handful of Italian submarines that happened to be operating outside the Mediterranean on 8 September, those in harbor were immediately seized by the Badoglio authorities. All the rest still at sea were ordered, under protocols laid down by the Anglo-Americans, to strictly observe a cease-fire and proceed at once on the surface under a black flag to various assigned ports. A few submarines, such as the *Torelli*, ran for Axis-held territories or neutral havens elsewhere.

The *Topazio* was less successful. For two days, she accompanied three other boats, the *Diaspro, Marea* and *Turchese*, all of them headed dutifully for Allied-held Bona on the Algerian coast. But during the night of the 10th, the *Topazio* slipped away, and Lieutenant Pier Vittorio Casarini hauled down the disgraceful flag of surrender. Two days later, his boat was twenty kilometers southwest of Sardinia's Cape Carbonara when it was attacked by a Sunderland. The *Topazio* sank almost at once, taking Lt. Casarini and his entire crew with her. By that time, all but forty-four of the Italian submarine service's original 172 boats had been lost, most of them after June 1942, when the Allies finally and completely broke all Axis military codes. In thirty-nine months of combat, Italian submarines sank thirteen warships, amounting to 24,554 tons. Their primary targets were, however, convoys or individual freighters, and they claimed 129 merchant vessels, an impressive 668,311 tons, up until the day of the Badoglio armistice.

Italians everywhere were flabbergasted by the dramatic turn of events. Mario Daneo was a *San Marco* guard on duty at Bordeaux's Italo-German submarine base when the news reached him. "Everyone was astounded and speechless," he remembered. "The following day, we were called into the square, and our commanding officer, along with the general commander in charge of the city, gave us a long speech in which he said that those of us who felt like it could continue with their assignment, as before. My friend, Precis Palesano, and I – he was a 3rd class Chief – looked at each other, and decided to stay. Of the 2,000 personnel from the Navy, the *San Marco* Battalion, *Carabinieri*, workers and specialists, more than 300 stayed. The others had to pack their suitcases and back-packs. At 16:30, five or six Germans came in and began loading all those who did not want to stay, and they were brought to a camp outside Bordeaux; whatever was not needed was taken away. More than one felt guilty and came back."[9]

A man who felt particularly guilty was Carlo Fecia di Cossato, among the most able of Italian submarine aces. Beginning on 15 April 1941, he commanded the *Tazzoli* in the western Atlantic, adding sixteen sunken ships to the boat's first two under the previous Captain Vittore Raccanelli for a total of 96,553 tons, plus another damaged ship of 5,000 tons. The Germans respected Di Cossato, and bestowed several awards on him, the most distinctive having been the Iron Cross First Class, presented in person by Admiral Dönitz. From his fellow countrymen, Di Cossato received the Gold Medal, the Italian Armed Forces' highest decoration, and two silver medals for military bravery. He was also a popular commander with fellow officers and enlisted men, who admired his intelligence and compassion.

On 2 February 1942, Di Cossato was given leave of absence, while the *Tazzoli* was placed under new command, stripped of armaments, and modified into a transport. As such, she departed Bordeaux for Japan with 165 tons of special cargo on 16 May, but was sunk the next day with all hands in a depth-charge attack carried out by the destroyer, U.S.N. *Mackenzie*. By then, her former commander had been transferred to the *Aliseo*, patrolling the Ligurian coast. It was while on station here that he learned of Badoglio's surrender, and received orders to attack German naval forces evacuating Corsica. There, he destroyed several German landing-craft outside Bastia, and went on to perform escort duty for Allied ships in the Adriatic throughout most of 1944.

But these operations weighed heavily on di Cossato, until he spoke openly of his deep disappointment with the post-Mussolini regime for the first time in mid-summer, and requested dismissal from active duty. When word spread to Taranto, crews at the naval base demonstrated angrily on his behalf, and the Gold Medal recipient was punished with a six-month suspension. Sometime thereafter, he received offers for a lucrative commission in the U.S. Navy. He turned it down without explanation.

Unable to join his family residing in Mussolini's Italian Social Republic up north, Di Cossato wrote to his mother on 21 August, about his "revolt toward the meanness of this period ... For the last nine months, I have reflected upon the extremely sad moral position in which I found myself, following the ignominious surrender of the navy to which I resigned myself only because it was presented to me as a direct order from the king ... You understand what is happening in Italy, and how we have been *unworthily betrayed*, and committed *an ignominious act* without any result. It is from this gloomy realization that I have developed a deep sadness, a disgust for what surrounds us. For months I have been thinking about my sailors of the *Tazzoli*, who are honorably on the bottom of the sea, and I think that my place is with them."[10]

Six days later, Captain di Cossato took his own life.

9

Hercules Spurned

It is my feeling that the Malta problem must be solved immediately.
General Erwin Rommel, March 1941[1]

With steady deterioration of relations between Italy and the Western Allies after 1938's Czech Crisis, Mussolini ordered the chiefs of his armed forces to consider their strategic options for a general European war. Among the criteria military analysts at the *Regia Marina* cited as essential for a prolonged confrontation with the French and British fleets was capture of Malta. Britain's island-fortress lay at the very heart of any struggle for control of the Central Mediterranean, and was particularly dangerous to Italy, whose southern territories were within striking range of air attacks.

Malta was an indispensible stop-over for Allied planes flying from Britain, via Gibraltar, to the Near East. All Italian movements came under observation from the centrally located island, from which a wide range of interdiction could be launched against Italy itself. Most importantly, each attempt at supplying Italian holdings in Libya had to run the gauntlet of bombers and warships stationed at Malta. Consequently, its early seizure was of paramount importance, and naval planners in Rome submitted their proposals for invasion.

Their British Admiralty counterparts, however, were no less cognizant of the island's pivotal significance in the event of a serious contest for domination of both North Africa and Southern Europe. During the years leading up to the Second World War, they bolstered its potential for both defensive and offensive operations aimed at the destruction of Italian sea power and assaults against the peninsula. Aware of Britain's on-going preparations to render Malta impregnable, *Commando Supremo* strategists knew its occupation could not be undertaken by the Navy alone, but required strong support from air power.

Almost as soon as the invasion scheme was presented to Mussolini for his approval, he knew it would not work. His Air Force commanders told him that they could spare, at most, only 100 warplanes, all of obsolete types, for any Maltese conquest until 1942, when modern aircraft production was supposed to be in full swing. If war came sooner, he planned to throw the bulk of the entire *Regia Aeronautica* at Malta in a temporary, massive, concerted assault sufficient to soften it up for the *Regia Marina* to put troops ashore. As a more realistic alternative to staking all his hopes on such a risky, uncertain operation, he suggested that Malta could be avoided entirely by re-routing supply convoys to French Tunisia, a far less formidable conquest. Italian North African forces already in place would require no outside assistance and greatly outnumber the French defenders.

These contingencies were sound, even admirable in the context of the times when they were discussed. But 1940's swift flow of events threw them all into a cocked hat. While the sudden fall of France reduced Italy's enemies by half, Hitler had meanwhile crafted a delicate accord with the French aimed at eventually winning them over as allies in his war against the British Empire. Hence, the *Führer* refrained from occupying most

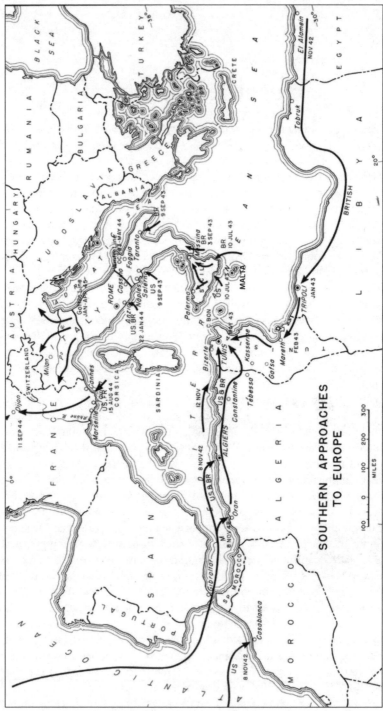

The southern approaches to Europe, conveying how the fronts in Africa,
Italy and location of Malta influenced strategy during the war

of France, proffered an unexpectedly generous armistice at Compiegne, arranged for the eventual return of all French prisoners-of-war, and kept his hands off the French Fleet. To court its voluntary participation required the good will of its commanders, so he was anxious not to offend Gallic sensibilities whenever possible. The seizure of French West Africa by Mussolini, his closest ideological ally, would ruin all diplomatic efforts to curry favor with Germany's traditional enemy.

Bowing to Hitler's *Realpolitik* was not difficult. Few military analysts believed the war could last very long, a reasonable supposition, given the era of the *Blitzkrieg*. Poland, Belgium, Holland, Denmark, Norway and France had each fallen in a matter of weeks. Britain, its forces already driven from the Continent, seemed next in line. To be sure, the Maltese sword was a dull weapon during the summer and early fall of 1940, when strong Italian convoys delivered troops and supplies to Libya with virtual impunity. But as the North African Campaign dragged on, the small island was heavily re-fortified, becoming a terrible menace to Italian fortunes in the Central Mediterranean. From late 1940, air and naval units operating out of Malta began to inflict evermore crippling losses on the *Regia Marina*, already handicapped by ULTRA code intercepts and its ignorance of radar.

However, the appearance of General Rommel's German *Afrika Korps*, together with the Italian *Ariete* and *Trento* Divisions in the Libyan Desert during February 1941, postponed the imminent collapse of Marshal Graziani's forces there. Something of a respite from Italy's long season of defeat afforded *Commando Supremo* strategists an opportunity to devise serious plans for the capture of Malta. The *Duce's* early emphasis on pulverizing air assaults against the island could be seriously reconsidered, now that increased bomber production made such large-scale raids possible, although both he and his commanders knew that Malta could not be subdued entirely by the *Regia Aeronautica*. Instead, concentrated air power was intended to stun the defenders long enough for naval units to land their troops.

Planners from supreme military headquarters in Rome and Berlin outlined all the details in Operation *Hercules*, for which they delegated three Italian parachute battalions, four Italian infantry divisions, and one German *Fallschirmjaeger* division. Their jump would be preceded by combined *Regia Aeronautica* and Luftwaffe raids carried out by 1,300 evenly divided Italian and German aircraft.

Soon after the first version of Operation *Hercules* was finalized, Kriegsmarine troop barges left over from Operation *Seeloewe*, or 'Sealion', 1940's aborted invasion of southern England, were to join an additional eighty Italian landing-craft, sixty-four smaller ferries, 725 launches and 225 motor-boats. These would be covered by virtually every warship in the *Regia Marina* to put ashore 32,000 German and Italian troops, plus an armored unit of captured Russian T-34 tanks. Wehrmacht and *Commando Supremo* strategists concurred that such a large-scale effort was dependent upon the Italian Navy's ability to achieve and maintain an acceptable measure of domination in the Central Mediterranean. Admirals at the *Regia Marina* agreed they needed more than a year to at least partially regain Italy's former ascendency at sea following the debacle at Taranto. Accordingly, Operation *Hercules* was set to begin on 10 July 1942.

A prelude to the bi-national attempt began auspiciously enough on 8 March 1941 when a flying armada of CANTs, *Cigognas*, *Sparvieros*, and Junkers Ju-88 medium-bombers blasted Malta as it had never been hit before, winning it the luckless sobriquet, "the most bombed real estate on earth". The island's infrastructure was shattered. Water and electricity were no longer available; most of its warships and all its aircraft were destroyed; the harbors badly damaged, and port facilities ruined. Barely able to provide for the survival of its inhabitants, let alone offer further resistance, Malta teetered on the brink of surrender.

And yet, the raid had only been a test. While it unquestionably caused widespread damage and chaos, *Commando Supremo* learned that the bombs dropped on Malta during this single attack were still insufficient to compel its capitulation. Reconnaissance photographs made after the aerial offensive convinced Axis planners that renewed air strikes combined with heavy mining operations in Maltese waters should make the enemy keep his head down long enough for the *Regia Marina* to pave the way for Operation *Hercules* in 1942. And, of course, it was essential to keep the island from being fortified.

The first step in separating Malta from the outside world had been taken the day after Italy's declaration of war. Beginning on the night of 11 June 1940, specialists aboard several small vessels of the *Orata* Group found and cut the first of seven deep-sea telegraph and telephone cables linking the island's military command with its Royal Navy headquarters at Gibraltar. These perilous operations were invariably conducted under cover of darkness, the unarmed group members' only protection. Their nerve-wracking work went on for more than two months without being detected before the last line was severed, plunging Malta into a communications black-out. So successful were the *Orata* men, they hauled up from the sea-bottom literally thousands of meters of enemy cable which were brought back to base for use by the frugal Italians then experiencing shortages, along with most other things, of such high-grade telegraph wire.

Meanwhile, mine production had gone into high gear, finally allowing the silent siege of Malta to begin on the night of 5 September. A destroyer *squadrilla*, the *Altair*, cautiously spread its first minefield over the roadstead to Valletta, the British naval base at Malta. During the next thirty months, *Altair* laid down just as many of the deadly carpets, which accounted for numerous Allied freighters and auxiliary vessels of all kinds, from tugs to mine-sweepers. Joining them on the bottom of the sea were three destroyers – *Jersey*, *Kujawjak* and *Southwold* – plus a submarine, the *Olympus*. More importantly, the far-flung minefields ham-strung all enemy traffic in Maltese waters throughout the Mediterranean Campaign.

Despite the formidable dangers presented by enemy mines, the British were desperate to reinforce Malta. On 21 July 1941, Admiral Cunningham dispatched six merchant ships and a troop transport to the vitally strategic island from Gibraltar. They were screened by the battleship *Nelson*, accompanied by heavy cruisers *Arethusa*, *Edinburgh* and *Manchester* in an operation appropriately known as 'Substance'. The crew of a CANT 'Heron' long-range reconnaissance plane spotted the convoy, but too late for its interception by Italian surface forces, so the British position was radioed to *Regia Aeronautica* headquarters. A flight of *Sparviero* bombers was scrambled, and they pressed their attack against the combined firepower of a dozen warships. H.M.S *Fearless* blazed up and sank, while another destroyer, *Firedrake*, holed beyond salvage, had to be scuttled, as the *Manchester*, severely damaged by torpedo hits, limped back to Gibraltar for lengthy repairs that kept her out of the fighting for months.

Although the 'Sparrowhawk's bloodied Cunningham's warships without loss to themselves, these targets were far less important than the freighters which arrived safely at Malta with enough supplies to fortify island resistance for the next few months. In the *Regia Marina's* last-ditch effort, a MAS torpedo-boat scored on the *Sydney Star*, but the Australian cargo vessel, despite being badly damaged, made Maltese port. The convoy's only non-warship loss had been the troopship *Leinster*, when she grounded early in the operation, and returned to Gibraltar for repairs. The success of 'Substance' was simultaneously enhanced by the escape from Malta of seven empty merchant vessels, which found their way back to Gibraltar without incident. Another such British operation would render Malta impregnable, and provide it with enough strength to initiate bolder offensive assaults by air and sea against Axis convoys and Sicily itself.

The Italians' continued failure to prevent the island from being so lavishly supplied forced them to undertake a radically unconventional operation. It aimed at nothing short of destroying the same convoy that had just arrived virtually intact at Valletta's Grand Harbour. After sundown, 25 July 1941, elite members of the *X Flottiglia MAS* left the Sicilian port of Augusta aboard an auxiliary ship, accompanied by a pair of torpedo-boats, *MAS* 451 and 452, for a surprise raid on the island-fortress. The *Diana* steamed into the night, while they readied their attack-craft: eight explosive motor-boats and a pair of *Maiale* 'Pig' human-torpedoes. As one of them attacked any enemy submarine it could find docked at Port Manoel, the other was supposed to blast a breech in Grand Harbour's defensive perimeter. Through it the explosive motor-boats and torpedo-boats would race to strike the anchored convoy. These maneuvers were to be preceded and covered by a diversionary air raid promised by the *Regia Aeronautica*.

Unfortunately for the operation, the squadron of *Sparvieros* arrived over Malta and concluded their bomb-run long before the *X Flottiglia MAS* was near enough to attack, leaving the defenders in a heightened sense of alert. But the crucial element of surprise was lost when enemy radar detected the *Diana* still twelve kilometers from Malta. Even so, she able to lower all her vessels into the water, while the British wondered precisely what the lone, stopped ship was doing out at sea in the middle of the night, beyond the reach of coastal batteries. They missed spotting the small, low-silhouetted attack-craft then quietly proceeding toward Grand Harbour, but knew something ominous was afoot in the inky darkness.

As planned, Chief Diver Pedretti steered his *Maiale* to the port's underwater barrier at Saint Elmo. Meanwhile, the other 'Pig' commanded by Major Tesseo Tesei placed its warhead at the harbor viaduct itself. Both detonated almost simultaneously, causing the entire port defenses to respond with machine-gun fire. The *X Flottiglia MAS* pressed the attack nonetheless. Its explosive motor-boats and torpedo-boats, brilliantly illuminated now in the blinding glare of searchlights, sped across the harbor at the immobile convoy. But before they could reach it, every one was knocked out by gunners of the Royal Malta Artillery. The torpedo-boats turned to escape, but were strafed by pursuing aircraft after first light. *MAS* 451 sank in flames with all hands, while all but two men aboard *MAS* 452 were killed. Pedretti, Tesei and their comrades all perished in the failed attempt.

They were revenged by their comrades in the 36th *Stormo* operating out of Deciomannu on 27 September, when the 12,427-ton freighter, *Imperial Star*, succumbed to a determined torpedo attack that also severely damaged the battleship *Nelson*. They were followed by the redoubtable *Aerosiluranti* anti-shipping specialists, who sank the 6,463-ton *Empire Pelican* and, near the Tunisian coast, the 5,649-ton *Empire Defender* in mid-November. *Regia Aeronautica* good luck rubbed off on the *Regia Marina* with less dramatic, more laborious efforts at sealing off Malta through the deployment of broad-spreading carpets of floating mines that decimated Force K.

This was Admiral Cunningham's flotilla assigned to protect the island and keep its supply routes open. On 18 December, Force K fell afoul of a minefield twelve kilometers east of Tripoli. As a heavy cruiser, the *Neptune*, slid beneath the waves, she was joined on the bottom by her own escort, the destroyer *Kandahar*. Two more cruisers were damaged, particularly the *Aurora*, which required extensive, lengthy repairs. Her ruined appearance beside the listing *Penelope* as they limped into Grand Harbour was a shock to Maltese morale.

All relief convoys to the island under siege were suspended, because they were now totally bereft of warship protection. Desperate to keep Malta alive, the British Admiralty tried sending single freighters to slip into Grand Harbour unescorted. But *Commando Supremo* kept a wary eye out for these lone vessels. Even before the destruction of Force K, too many big cargo carriers like the *Empire Guillemot*, *Empire Pelikan* and *Empire Defender* had been picked off by *Sparviero* torpedo-planes, transforming runs by individual merchant ships into suicidal voyages.

Now Malta was really in for a bad time. Almost isolated at sea, practically all that remained for its conquest was the destruction of remaining warplanes, land-based defenses and supplies. Meanwhile, the noose around its shipping routes grew ever tighter, as ships found passage through the Central Mediterranean increasingly hazardous. Still confident that air power was the deciding factor in modern warfare, Mussolini ordered prolonged aerial operations that would compel Malta's surrender or, at the very least, severely weaken its resistance to invasion. His iron ring had virtually cut off the beleaguered island from outside assistance by 17 November, when ten of the fourteen supply vessels dispatched from Gibraltar were sunk.

Regia Aeronautica crews had done much to keep Maltese heads down from Mussolini's June declaration of war to the end of 1940, dropping 550 tons of explosives on the island in 7,410 sorties for the loss of thirty-five aircraft against sixty-six of the defenders destroyed in combat. From January through May the following year, the Germans' X *Fliegerkorps* largely took over from their allies, losing fifty-nine Junkers bombers and Messerschmitt fighters. From June onward, however, the burden of attacking Malta was shared more equally by the Axis airmen. Commencing on 7 February 1942, combined squadrons of the Italian Air Force and Luftwaffe staged seventeen raids in twenty-four hours. Over the next week, they delivered 236 attacks. Worse was to come for Malta in the months that followed.

When numbers of Spitfires were hastily flown in to bolster the besieged island's defense, Italo-German bombers switched over to night-time raids, completing the last ninety of their 275 missions for March after dark. April was higher yet, with 6,782 tons of explosives dropped in 283 raids. Low-level sorties by Macchi *Saetta* fighters and *Stuka* dive-bombers against defensive positions were carried out in a methodical program to annihilate every manifestation of resistance, now that most Allied planes had been swept from the sky. On the 20th, as a special gift to Hitler for the *Führer's* 54th birthday, Mussolini's correctly reported that Malta's five RAF squadrons had only seven aircraft left between them. To help make up for these losses, on that same day a new American aircraft-carrier streamed to within flight range of Malta, then launched a spread of Spitfires toward the island.

Inside a week, every one was destroyed or rendered unserviceable. USS *Wasp* returned to the Pacific Theater, where she was promptly sunk by Japanese torpedo-bombers.

These were indeed evil times for the Allies. By spring, only a pair of surface warships – the destroyers *Kingston* and *Lance* – were left afloat at Malta. Now, they too rolled over on their moorings and sank, together with the submarines *Glafkos*, P-36 and P-39. Their loss was the final blow to Britain's undersea flotilla in the Central Mediterranean. Thereafter, surviving boats had to proceed individually toward Egypt, where they were absorbed by the Royal Navy at Alexandria. Meanwhile, Malta began to resemble the multi-cratered face of the moon in reconnaissance photographs. Intercepted transmissions from Valletta to the British Admiralty confessed that the situation was "almost desperate. Enemy operations might prove disastrous unless immediate steps are taken to counter them". Another month of similar punishment could force the island to run up the white flag.

For all its success, Mussolini's air offensive inadvertently sabotaged Operation *Hercules*. General Erwin Rommel, its early and enthusiastic supporter, now had his doubts. He wondered aloud to his Italian opposite, Ugo Cavallero, if a costly invasion that must drain resources from their own Libyan Desert campaign might be avoided, since the *Regia Marina* and Axis air forces appeared to have already won a *de facto* victory over Malta. But General Cavallero was seconded by Rommel's own Luftwaffe commander, Albert Kesselring, in demanding that the time-table for Operation *Hercules* be maintained at all costs. No one was sure Italian supremacy in the Central Mediterranean could be indefinitely maintained, they argued, especially now that America's 'arsenal of democracy' was beginning to make itself felt on North African battlefields and even at sea, where growing numbers of merchant ships attempting to supply Malta flew the Stars and Stripes.

"While we still control the area," Cavallero insisted, "we must take advantage of our favorable situation before the fortunes of war turn against us, as they did earlier. Such an opportunity may not come our way a second time."[2] Kesselring chimed in, "should things go badly for us here, we must be able to fall back on Malta. But if the enemy is still in possession of it, we'll be trapped in the desert with no way out."[3] Although Rommel was not deaf to their concerns, he was a gambler by nature, and somewhat under the spell of an elusive Egypt beckoning just over the eastern horizon. He had, after all, made his stellar reputation in combat across France and North Africa by taking chances. "There's no big victory without big risks," he was fond of repeating to others less confident in his future. "Stick with me! I'm bullet-proof!"[4]

It was precisely that kind of attitude which most endeared him to Adolf Hitler, who, above all human qualities, most admired, as Belgian SS General Leon Degrelle put it, 'guts', especially when majority opinion cautioned something less daring.[5] When the two extremist personalities met during late February 1942, at the *Führer's* headquarters in East Prussia, the Desert Fox enthusiastically depicted the effect of Mussolini's air offensive by claiming that Malta would soon become militarily insignificant. He conjured a verbal panorama of Panzers parading past the pyramids about the same time Operation *Hercules*, made redundant by the capture of Cairo, was supposed to take place in early July.

Hitler was easy to convince, chiefly because he was still stung by the fearsome sacrifice made by his *Fallschirmjaeger* less than a year earlier, when some 7,700 elite paratroopers had become casualties in their conquest of Crete. An airborne assault against heavier defenses at Malta would incur even greater losses the Wehrmacht could ill afford in its two-front war. Rommel dutifully repeated the warnings sounded by Cavallero (they both pegged him accurately as a self-serving mediocrity) and Kesselring, a highly regarded commander who was nonetheless "mistaken this time".[6]

The Maltese dilemma was a result of Hitler's failed Mediterranean strategy. In summer 1940, fresh from his stunning victories in Scandinavia, the Netherlands and France, his next objective had been Gibraltar. Its seizure would have allowed the *Regia Marina* access to the Atlantic Ocean, while limiting supplies to Malta to fewer, far more easily intercepted convoys from Suez, thereby helping to ensure Mussolini's victory in North Africa. Ideally, France, which was already close to declaring war on 'perfidious Albion' for attacks on its warships at Oran, would join with Germany and Italy in the Atlantic, thereby decidedly shifting the balance of power at sea against England. It was chiefly this hope that induced Hitler to keep hands off the French Fleet.

Accordingly, together with his chiefs-of-staff, he designed Operation *Felix* for the capture of Gibraltar. It called for two corps under the overall command of Field Marshal Walter von Reichenau to move into Spain during mid-January 1941. Protecting the flank of his assault against anticipated British intervention would be General Rudolf Schmidt's XXXIX Corps, including the 16th Motorized Division, 26th Panzer Division, and SS *Totenkopf* Division. The main invasion of Gibraltar was supposed to have been carried out by the XLIX Corps of General Ludwig Kuebler.

It comprised the *Grossdeutschland* Infantry Regiment, the 98th Regiment of the 1st *Gebirgsjaeger*, or 'Mountain' Division plus twenty-six medium and heavy artillery battalions, three observation battalions, three engineer battalions, two smoke battalions, and about 150 'Goliaths'. These were radio-controlled midget tanks armed with high explosives for the demolition of otherwise inaccessible enemy emplacements, such as pill-boxes. Junkers JU-88 medium-bombers, *Stuka* dive-bombers, Messerschmitt ME-110 ground-attack planes, and ME-109 fighters would cover Field Marshal von Reichenau's operation, while U-boats attacked Allied ships expected to flee the Rock.

His forces would have faced the 2nd King's and 2nd Somerset Light Infantry Regiments, together with the 4th Devonshire and 4th Black Watch. The 3rd Heavy Regiment, Royal Artillery, controlled 4th, 26th, and 27th Batteries, together with a pair of anti-aircraft batteries, the 9th and 19th, beside the 82nd Heavy Anti-Aircraft Regiment commanding three batteries – the156th, 193rd, and 256th. Although these were aided by the 3rd Searchlight Battery and radar, Gibraltar had no fighters or bombers of its own, guaranteeing air supremacy for the Luftwaffe.

Wehrmacht planners were unanimous in their conviction that an assault on Gibraltar would result in a quick victory with far-reaching implications for the future conduct of the war. All that was lacking in 1940 was French and Spanish cooperation, which appeared imminent. But while Adolf Hitler was entrained for his meetings with Vichy President Philipe Pétain and *Generalissimo* Francisco Franco, his own military intelligence chief was busy sabotaging plans for Operation *Felix*. In preparation of these high-level meetings, *Abwehr* head, Admiral Wilhelm Canaris, a dedicated anti-Nazi, convinced both leaders that Hitler intended to use the German operation as cover for seizing both Spain and Vichy France, and urged them to resist any request for co-ordinated activity with the duplicitous *Führer*.[7]

Previously disposed to joining the fight against Britain, Pétain now rebuffed Hitler's invitation to send the French Fleet into the Atlantic. Worse was to come at Hendaye, on Spain's frontier, where Franco refused to allow German forces on Iberian soil for the assault against Gibraltar, because its conquest by a foreign power would humiliate the Spanish people, who wanted to take the Rock by themselves. Unfortunately, they presently lacked sufficient materiel to undertake such an invasion. Hitler then offered to cancel Operation *Felix*, and supply Franco with all the aid he needed to carry out the attack himself. Again, the *Generalissimo* balked, arguing that Spain was still too weak from the ravages of its civil war to properly defend itself against British retribution.

Embittered by his lack of diplomatic success, Hitler returned to Berlin, confessing to his closest colleagues that he would have rather had his teeth pulled than endure such a frustrating meeting.[8] The *Führer* declared he should have never sent aid to such an ingrate as Franco, who begged for German help just five years earlier when Spain needed it most. Thanks to the behind-the-scenes' intrigue of Admiral Canaris, Operation *Felix* was canceled, and the Axis found itself increasingly bottled up inside the Mediterranean Sea between Gibraltar on the western end, Suez in the east, and Malta in the middle.

In 1942, there were very serious concerns about the strategically located island. Previously, the Allies had been virtually cut off from outside help. But now nothing stopped an abundance of supplies, arms, troops and equipment flowing from the American cornucopia into General Montgomery's Desert Army. The convoys which continued to bring this largesse steamed around the Horn of Africa, far beyond the reach of Axis planes or ships. Soon, the defenders of Malta would have enough reinforcements to resist any offensive thrown at them.

A window of opportunity for attack was still open, but it was closing with every U.S. freighter unloading supplies at Britain's Red Sea ports. Operation *Hercules* would divert forces, particularly much-needed aircraft, away from the seizure of Egypt, which would close the North African Campaign. Rommel's international prestige, even among Germany's enemies, combined with his persuasive arguments and risk-taking personality, prevailed upon Hitler to change his mind about invading Malta. "In any case," he said, "the island would be useless to Britain if the fighting in North Africa were to end."[9]

For obvious political, as well as less certain military considerations, the final decision had to lie with Mussolini and his *Commando Supremo*. The *Führer* concluded: "Make your case to them. I'll back you up, but we must abide by their decision."[10] Returning to Libya, Rommel asked the Italians to put off Operation *Hercules* until Tobruk had been captured and the Egyptian frontier crossed. To carry out his Nile Valley offensive he needed every Italian and German aircraft in the Mediterranean Theater, but only for a few weeks. After pushing the British back toward Alexandria, he would return the warplanes for the planned invasion of Malta.

More familiar with seasonal conditions in *Mare Nostro* than his German ally, Mussolini told him that a specific date had been carefully chosen by meteorologists, because late summer storms with high winds would seriously jeopardize the landings and interfere with air operations. Intrigued nevertheless by the bold plan to seize Tobruk and then storm into Egypt, the *Duce* wanted the best of both worlds, and was willing to risk rescheduling *Hercules* until the last week in July, if his own generals could be made to agree. They refused to consider any postponement. Malta was already almost on her knees, and the invasion build-up was nearing completion after nearly a year of preparations. Axis supremacy in the waters surrounding the island and the skies over it held firm, but American strength was building daily and might eventually tip the scales back into the Allies' favor if given enough time.

Rommel concurred with their argument, was conciliatory, and proposed a watered-down version of his demands. Now he wanted Italo-German air cover for just fifteen days, sufficient time to threaten Egypt's western frontier. That achieved, the warplanes would be returned in time for the invasion of Malta before the end of July. To this less radical proposal, *Commando Supremo*, after some hesitation, conceded a twenty-one-day extension of Operation *Hercules*, but only if Rommel endorsed a written statement to abide by his promise. His signature was small comfort to the Italian generals, who knew they were gambling with the future by granting even a few weeks grace to the dangerous little island. The invasion was nevertheless locked in for 30 July.

In fact, it had been compromised as early as 27 April, when Hitler reassigned most of his planes stationed in Sicily to the fighting in Russia. While the move was not at all the turning-point some historians describe, it did give Malta a breathing-space at a time when more than a few observers on both sides believed that the island could have been forced to surrender through air power alone, if the same large-scale raids had continued throughout spring. Be that as it may, the island was by no means saved by the departure of too many *Stuka*s to the Eastern Front. The *Regia Aeronautica* with its diminished German contingent continued, albeit on a smaller scale, to bomb the island's dwindling resources and prevented all but a bare minimum of essentials from getting to Valletta. These arrived almost entirely on aircraft dashing in by night and leaving before dawn, or aboard a few submarines acting as freighters.

But the quantities they carried were hardly sufficient to keep Malta alive, so five destroyers sailed at top speed on 11 May 1942 with goods for the besieged island. Confronted by superior Italian naval units south of Crete, the British warships doing double duty as merchant men turned about and raced for the sanctuary of Alexandria. The alert was out, however, and German Junkers 88 bombers flew out of Cyrenaica, sinking HMS *Kipling, Lively* and *Jackal*. Not only was the noose notched a bit closer around Malta, but the British could scarcely afford to loose any more surface vessels. Self-conscious of their shrinking presence in the Mediterranean, the cruiser *Charybdis* escorted by two destroyers on a supply mission from Gibraltar a week later returned without firing a shot when opposed by the *Regia Marina*'s 7th Cruiser Division.

A measure of the Royal Navy's low ebb in its history appeared during a pathetic attempt to disguise a target-ship with wooden gun turrets, fake barrels and canvas superstructure. Thus camouflaged, the ancient *Centurion* was supposed to fool the Italians into believing she was a new battleship. As Bragadin observed, "this stratagem revealed the seriousness of the period through which the British Navy was passing."[11] The transparent ruse elicited more derision than dread, however, and failed to save the convoy the phoney battleship was supposed to protect with her stage-prop armament.

On 15 May, the Italians showed they had come a long way from their years of uncoordinated operations. *Regia Aeronautica* bombers fended off air and naval attacks on *Regia Marina* cruisers and destroyers, enabling them to get on with the business of savaging a convoy. Of the five Malta-bound freighters, three went to the bottom, and another was severely damaged. The merchant vessels had been heavily protected by nine destroyers, two of them sunk, and five damaged by combined shells and aerial torpedoes. Other than a fire quickly extinguished on the veteran destroyer *Vivaldi*, the Italians suffered no damage.

Next month, a challenge arose that would determine Malta's ultimate fate in ways neither side could have anticipated. Determined to save the island at all costs, the Allies launched two powerful convoys simultaneously from east and west. They dredged up the last ounce of air and naval weaponry to ensure safe passage for at least a few merchant ships in the combined Operations *Harpoon* and *Vigorous*, the largest relief efforts of their kind ever mounted. Their sixteen freighters and single tanker were guarded by two aircraft-carriers, ten heavy cruisers, one mine-layer, assorted corvettes and torpedo-boats, with no less than thirty-six destroyers, most of them pulled from outside duty in the Atlantic and as far away as the Indian Ocean. These were among the last surface warships at the time remaining in service with the Royal Navy, all others still laid up for repairs or resting at the bottom of the sea.

On 14 June, the east-bound convoy from Gibraltar, *Harpoon*, was identified by Fiat RS-fourteen long-distance reconnaissance planes far from Malta, and its position radioed in time for interception to *Commando Supremo*. Admiral da Zara was notified aboard his flagship, the *Eugenio di Savoia*, which led the 7th Cruiser Division from its Sicilian harbor at Palermo screened by a flight of torpedo-bombers and several submarines. In well-coordinated attacks with the *Regia Aeronautica*, da Zara's force engaged the numerically superior warships, while *Sparviero* bombers went after the convoy.

Observing from the bridge of his flagship, the heavy cruiser *Kenya*, Admiral A.T.B. Curteis launched his carrier planes to break up the enemy. But concentrated anti-aircraft fire from the Italian warships was so intense no Fairey Swordfish could get near them. Focused entirely on annihilating his outnumbered opponents, Curteis neglected to dispatch any Spitfires for protection of the convoy, then being mauled by torpedo-bombers. Meanwhile, Admiral da Zara's skillful maneuvering of the 7th Division prevented the British from scoring any important hits on his cruisers, but he got in close enough to fire an accurate broadside at the destroyer *Bedouin*. As she slipped beneath the waves, he broke off action, satisfied that Operation *Harpoon* had been sufficiently diverted to allow for the convoy's destruction.

He was not far wrong. Surviving ships from the *Regia Aeronautica* onslaught struggled to reach port. In so doing, they strayed into one of Italy's numerous minefields, where another destroyer, HMS *Kujawiak*, was sunk, and a badly damaged freighter, the *Orari*, spilled most of her cargo into the sea. A lone mine-sweeper, the *Welshman*, and one merchant vessel, the *Troilus*, were the only ships to arrive at Grand Harbour in sound condition. Their few supplies did little, however, to relieve starvation beginning to spread throughout the long-suffering population of the island.

While the charred debris of Operation *Harpoon* drifted across the Western Mediterranean amid a vast oil slick, the other half of Britain's best attempt to save Malta approached from the east. *Regia Marina* commanders were no less determined to stop it. Their finest battleships, *Littorio* and *Vittorio Veneto*, repaired after surviving the Taranto raid, steamed out of Salerno at high speed, trailed by a pair of heavy cruisers, two light cruisers and a dozen destroyers under an aerial umbrella of torpedo-planes. Intimidated by this rapidly deployed show of strength, the heavily armed convoy turned back toward Alexandria with the *Littorio* and her company in hot pursuit. By the time they caught up with the fleeing enemy force, torpedo-planes had already slowed it down by damaging a number of units. During the fierce exchange of gun-fire that resulted, an Italian heavy cruiser was severely damaged and forced to withdraw. Later, she was scuttled by her own crew, who mostly survived to be rescued and brought back to Sicily.

But the men and ships of Operation *Vigorous* were not as fortunate. Between the attacking bombers and surface units, the British convoy lost eight freighters, four destroyers, and a torpedo-boat. Five more cruisers, three merchant vessels, another destroyer, plus two corvettes suffered serious damage. Appalling casualties aboard these ships sharply contrasted Italian losses, which, even including the scuttled cruiser, were minimal.

The *Regia Marina* emerged from its victory into undisputed, if temporary domination of the Central Mediterranean. So complete was the destruction of enemy opposition, the planned take-over of Malta seemed hardly more than an after-thought. With the sea-lanes wide open, supplies poured unhindered to the Axis armies in the Libyan Desert. Ten days after the defeat of the Allied convoys, Rommel captured Tobruk on 21 June, thanks also to the Italian and German planes diverted from attacking Malta. Its *raison d'être* appeared to have been rendered obsolete by air and naval actions that isolated the island and deprived it of any military value. Sealing it off was almost as effective and less costly than a full-fledged invasion, whose resources were obviously better employed in the ongoing conquest of North Africa.

Operation *Hercules*, deemed no longer necessary, was canceled. This decision seemed borne out over the following weeks, as Axis aircraft and ships came and went between Italy and Libya minus any interference from Malta, which fell into a dark silence. Doubtless, the island could have been occupied with relatively little effort from mid-June to mid-August 1942, but every man and weapon were needed for conquering the North African desert before the Americans arrived in force.

With a venerable reputation for stubbornness, the British had not given up on Malta, their only hope for cutting Rommel's supply-line. On 10 August, their ambitious attempt to relieve the island bastion passed into the Mediterranean as Operation *Pedestal*. This maximum effort mounted by the Royal Navy consisted of fourteen transports under the protection of battleships *Nelson* and *Rodney*, plus aircraft-carriers *Eagle, Indomitable* and *Victorious*, fielding a combined compliment of forty six Hawker Hurricane fighters, ten Martlet bombers, and sixteen Fulmar torpedo-planes. These powerful units sailed in tandem with anti-aircraft cruisers *Charybdis, Phoebe* and *Sirius*, together with fourteen destroyers. After the battleships escorted the convoy into the Western Mediterranean, they were relieved by a trio of heavy cruisers – *Kenya, Manchester* and *Nigeria* – the anti-aircraft cruiser, *Cairo*, and eleven more destroyers.

Laying in wait were 312 *Regia Aeronautica* warplanes at Sardinia and Sicily joined by Luftwaffe *Stuka*s and JU-88s, while the approaches to Malta crawled with Italian submarines and German U-boats.

A day after setting out from Gibraltar, Operation *Pedestal*'s formidable assembly of warships and transports was sighted by the *Uarsciek*, which sounded the alert after her torpedoes failed to find their targets. Another submarine, this time a German U-boat, came in closer to the convoy, skillfully dodging depth-charges thrown at her by numerous destroyers, to attack the lead aircraft-carrier. HMS *Eagle* shuddered under the blows of a torpedo salvo that left her dead in the water. Her crew tried desperately to save the ship's compliment of warplanes, but only four were launched in time to land a few minutes later on *Indomitable* and *Victorious*, before the other Hurricanes and Fulmars began sliding off her listing deck into the sea. The captain of U-73 peered through his periscope to watch the stricken aircraft-carrier haul over and disappear beneath the surface, taking more than 200 sailors with her.

At dusk, the British ships came within range of a Luftwaffe squadron stationed at Sardinia. Junkers 88 medium-bombers and Heinkel 111 torpedo-planes pressed their attack, but were unable to penetrate the heavy curtains of flak put up by *Charybdis, Phoebe* and *Sirius*, and returned, minus some of their comrades, without scoring a single hit.

The following day, Operation *Pedestal* afforded the Italians an opportunity to deploy two new weapons for the first time. During an afternoon engagement on 12 August, *Sparviero* torpedo-planes attacked with several *Motobomba*s. At more than 1,800 kilos apiece, they were intended to scatter a convoy by drifting down via parachutes into its center, where they detonated amid the closely guarded ships. Once the freighters were dispersed, they became more vulnerable. But intense fire from all three anti-aircraft cruisers forced the SM-79s to drop their *Motobomba*s at too great an altitude, and they exploded above the convoy with no effect, other than startling its crews with their terrific detonation.

The Italians then launched a remotely operated CANT seaplane packed with 1,900 kilos of ordnance at HMS *Indomitable*. A direct hit would have almost certainly disabled the veteran aircraft-carrier. But her good fortune held, as the flying-bomb refused to answer the commands of its radio control, willfully flying off on its own accord toward the south, harmlessly self-destructing in a thunderous fireball over the Libyan Desert, where the phenomenon panicked a camel caravan of nomads.

Less unorthodox weapons were equally ineffective. Between too many skillfully flown interceptors and thick walls of flak, forty *Sparviero*s attacking in concert were prevented from getting close enough to launch their torpedoes. The same ferocious opposition frustrated a wave of incoming *Stuka*s, but one of the German dive-bombers did penetrate the heavy defenses to unloose its single 1,700-kg bomb on Operation *Pedestal*'s second victim, the *Deucalion*. Unlike its mythological namesake, who survived the Great Flood, the freighter could not escape the waters that closed over her.

Bad luck continued to dog the Italians, however. A pair of new Reggiane 2000s sortied against HMS *Victorious*, whose gunners misidentified the enemy fighter-bombers as Hawker Hurricanes, which they somewhat resembled at a distance, and failed to fire a shot at the approaching planes. A near-miss erupted off the aircraft-carrier's port bow, but the other Reggiane's pilot scored a direct hit on the forward deck, where his 500-kilo bomb failed to explode.

After dark, *Regia Marina* commanders ordered a submarine 'wolf-pack' to engage the convoy. Anticipating such a move, Admiral Burrough in command of Operation *Pedestal* aggressively counter-attacked with depth-charges, sinking the *Ithuriel* and severely damaging the *Emo*, whose torpedoes had gone wide of their target. A destroyer rammed and sank the *Corzano*, later saving forty of her crew members, but eleven went down with her. All other Italian submarines were prevented from making contact with the enemy.

In their desperation to strike at the relatively unscarred convoy, *Stuka* pilots flew a few meters above the surface of the sea to avoid enemy radar and surprise HMS *Victorious*, damaging her flight deck so badly its planes had to be transferred to the *Indomitable*, already over-burdened with aircraft from the sunken *Eagle*. Blasted by three direct hits and struggling to contain a dangerous fire that threatened to engulf her, the *Indomitable*, limped back to Gibraltar in the company of another stricken warship, the torpedoed destroyer *Foresight*, which was subsequently abandoned and scuttled.

As the convoy entered the Skerki Channel after dark, it sailed into a trap set by Italian submarines. On the night of 13 August, Lieutenant Renato Ferrini, commanding the *Axum*, sighted Admiral Burrough's flagship, the *Nigeria*, accompanied by the dangerous anti-aircraft cruiser, *Cairo*. Ferrini launched his spread of torpedoes at the same moment another submarine, the *Dessie*, fired a salvo at the oncoming vessels. The *Nigeria* shuddered to a full stop, all power knocked out, after being struck amid ships. Suffering an explosion that blew off her screws, the *Cairo* stood on her stern before diving for the bottom, while the immobilized *Brisbane Star* and *Ohio* were left for dead by their escorts. Forced to abandon the *Nigeria* for a destroyer, the *Ashanti*, Admiral Burrough watched as his wounded flagship, whose crew had restored some power, returned at a greatly reduced speed toward Gibraltar.

Other torpedoes found the freighter *Empire Hope*, sending her beneath the surface in a matter of minutes. Not far from the scene of her demise, a mountain of fire arose from the surface of the sea to mark the end of a gasoline tanker that rolled over and disappeared in the midst of the conflagration after its bow had been blown off by the *Bronzo*. Lieutenant Puccini's *Alagi* then zeroed in on the *Kenya* and *Clan Ferguson*, hitting them both with two torpedoes apiece. While the heavy cruiser was able to remain afloat with severe damage, the merchant ship in her care keeled over and sank, leaving fifty three survivors to be picked up by Italian rescue ships after day-break.

By then, *Regia Aeronautica* bombers showed up to make their own contribution to the convoy's destruction. The carnage was joined by torpedo-boats roaring out of Ras Mustafa. Defying intense shelling from HMS *Manchester*, Ms.16 and Ms.22 sped to within perilously close range before launching their torpedoes. The cruiser's stern was literally shorn off, and the doomed ship slid to her deep grave the following day. Six more Italian, plus a pair of German torpedo-boats rushed in to dispose of the *Almeria Lykes*, *Glenorchy*, *Santa Elsa* and 3 other freighters in rapid succession. A final victim, the *Waimarama*, singled out by a Junkers 88, was actually lifted into the air by the force of a tremendous explosion just before dawn.

Morning revealed the wreckage of nine transports from Operation *Pedestal*'s original fourteen freighters scattered for hundreds of kilometers across the face of the sea. Of the four escorting cruisers that set out with them from Gibraltar, only one, the *Kenya*, was still afloat, but she was almost crippled. All the escaped transports had been damaged, most of them badly. The retrieved tanker, *Ohio*, was kept from sinking only by a pair of destroyers lashed on either side to keep her afloat. While the five surviving merchant vessels brought much-needed relief to the Maltese inhabitants, their invaluable supplies could do little more than prevent starvation, and did less to enhance the island's severely diminished military capabilities.

"For once," observes Hans Werner Neulen, "the cooperation between the U-boats and the German and Italian air forces was exceptionally successful, and the convoy was almost completely wiped out."[12] British warships had been literally driven from the Central Mediterranean. Not one Royal Navy vessel was to be seen there for the next three months. The Axis triumph was so sweeping, no one doubted that Malta had been successfully isolated without recourse to invasion, and Axis convoy routes were wide open.

At the end of the month, a successful British attack at Alam el Halfa Ridge had knocked out forty-nine tanks, seriously depleting Axis armor. But almost immediately thereafter, thanks to the defeat of Operation *Pedestal*, transports arrived in Tobruk with

234 Panzers, 251 M.3 tanks, seventy-two of the superb *Sahariana*s and another forty-seven German armored cars, 563 mixed pieces of field artillery, 350 Luftwaffe aircraft, and 427 warplanes from the *Regia Aeronautica*. To man the new weapons were sixty-seven fresh infantry battalions of German and Italian troops. Speedy arrival of these abundant resources was made possible by Italo-German victories at sea, so cancellation of Operation *Hercules* seemed justified.

Aerial reconnaissance revealed a disturbing picture, however. More than 150 new bombers and fighters were parked on Maltese air-strips. They were the very aircraft responsible for inflicting heavy losses on Italian convoys beginning after the middle of August, when a quarter of Axis supplies on their way to North Africa was sunk. Worse still was endured by the tankers, which lost a staggering forty-one per cent of the fuel oil dispatched. Allied strategists were confident they could avenge the recent fall of Tobruk by destroying its port, together with the other principle harbor at Benghazi. Neutralization of these two points of convoy embarkation would effectively sever Rommel's supply-lines, signaling the British 8th Army to begin its major offensive for which it had already been stockpiling arms and equipment over several weeks.

This abrupt and surprising reversal of fortune turned on the assassination of a single man. As head of the *Sicherheitsdienst* ('Security Service'), Reinhard Heydrich hunted down traitors and spies subverting the Third Reich. He was so adept in ferreting out sedition and espionage that even the Allies' partial penetration of Germany's 'Enigma' encryption device, through which Germany's entire military and diplomatic codes were transmitted, could not prevent Hitler's virtually unbroken series of victories for the first three years of the war. On 27 May 1942, the British Secret Service had Czech agents parachuted into Prague, where their thrown grenade exploded in Heydrich's car. The real turning-point of World War Two occurred precisely at 4:30 in the morning of 4 June when he died of his wounds. Mussolini was himself not far off the mark when he stated that "the wheel of fortune turned on 28 June 1942, when we halted before El Alamein."[13]

Henceforward, important traitors such as Wilhelm Canaris, chief of the *Abwehr*, Germany's own military intelligence, filled in the blanks for the so-called 'ULTRA Secret', British code-breakers now-perfected decryption of *Enigma* intercepts. Over the next few months, as they refined their penetration and the German turncoats supplied them with secret information, Allied strategists behind the front and officers in the field were provided with every Axis battle plan, time-table, sailing schedule, supply location, or troop strength in advance of operations. In short, virtually every Axis communication was now monitored by Churchill, Stalin and Roosevelt.

Neither Hitler nor Mussolini had any secrets from their enemies. After the war, Supreme Allied Commander, Dwight D. Eisenhower, characterized ULTRA as having been absolutely 'decisive' for the Allies' final victory.[14] Heydrich had stood between them and its effectiveness. His biographer, Robert Mikkelson, concluded, "Allied leaders in London and Moscow knew exactly what was at stake. Their murder of *SS-Obergruppenführer* Reinhard Heydrich guaranteed that the Third Reich would be crushed in the Allied pinchers of overwhelming numbers."[15]

But Germany was not the only victim of ULTRA. The entire Italian diplomatic and military structures were no less deeply compromised, encouraging British commanders to break the Italian armies in the Western Desert and put an end to the North African Campaign, beginning with retaking Tobruk and the assassination or capture of Rommel himself. They arranged for Spitfires flying in from Malta to catch Axis planes by surprise, then land at Allied-held bases in Libya, where they could refuel for flights back to the island. The heavy cruiser *Coventry*, six destroyers, sixteen motor gun-boats (MGBs) and twenty patrol-boats were to shield 900 demolition experts put ashore by dozens of landing-craft. After knocking out enemy airfields, communications, ammunition stores, fuel dumps, artillery positions and port installations, Axis ground forces would be isolated and annihilated at El Alamein.

The Tobruk operation began according to plan before daybreak on 13 September, when the destroyers *Sikh* and *Zulu* landed 400 demolition specialists without raising the alarm. The experts were spotted soon after, however, and held at bay by one company of mixed German and Italian sailors aided by a few *Caribinieri*. Meanwhile, a battalion of marines of the *San Marco* regiment stopped another 500 commandos simultaneously put ashore on the other side of the harbor. MGBs attempting to aid their comrades on the coast were blasted by a trio of Italian destroyer escorts and seventeen smaller craft. All the attacking vessels fled after suffering numerous hits, and one of their number was set ablaze. Caught in the first rays of dawn, they now came under the fire of shore batteries, whose gunners turned their attention to the two destroyers that landed the commandos, all of whom had either been killed or captured.

The *Sikh*, struck dead in the water, was abandoned by her crew, who saw their ship sink under another barrage from the vantage-point of bobbing life-boats. Heavy damage was similarly inflicted on the *Zulu*, which withdrew behind a smoke-screen, her upper decks trailing flames. She thereby escaped further punishment from coastal shelling, but became the special target of Italian warplanes. One 320-kilo bomb dropped by a single Macchi MC200 *Saetta* scored a direct hit on her foredeck, and the wounded destroyer capsized. The *Duce* could claim at least some credit for the 'Thunderbolt's' successful attack, because it was at his urging that this aircraft, originally intended solely as an interceptor, be hastily redesigned for the anti-shipping role.

Other Italian fighters appeared in such large numbers, Malta withdrew its proposed air-cover, leaving the routed surface vessels to fend for themselves. Newer Macchi *Folgore*s made low-level strafing runs against scattering naval units, sinking another MGB and ten patrol-boats. But the ordeal was not yet over for survivors of the foiled attack. While beating a swift retreat toward Alexandria, they were caught by warplanes of the Luftwaffe based at Crete. Junkers 88 torpedo-bombers converged on the *Coventry*, which went down by the bow after several direct hits. Keeping her company on the bottom was another MGB sunk by *Stuka*s.

The Tobruk assault achieved no results at a heavy cost the Royal Navy could ill afford. It also demonstrated the over-confidence British strategists placed in the ULTRA secret before it became fully operational. They did not have much longer to wait, however, before decipherment of Axis' codes was complete enough to make Field Marshal Montgomery's victory at El Alamein possible in late October.

Effects on the war at sea were no less deleterious. During November, 26% of supplies shipped to Libya were lost almost exclusively to air strikes directed from Malta, which received the benefits of a large convoy arriving intact on the 19th. The following month was still more catastrophic, with destruction of 52% of the freighters leaving Italy. A mere 4,093 tons of supplies and 2,058 tons of oil reached Rommel, who was swiftly running

Naval personnel form themselves into 'M' for 'Mussolini' during a pre-war display in Naples.

out of food to feed his men or gasoline to fuel his tanks. "In a man-to-man fight," he warned, "the winner has one more round in his magazine."[16]

Mussolini made a last, belated attempt to subdue Malta beginning 10 October by attacking with three bomber groups of CANTs and as many Macchi *Folgore* fighter groups, plus a *Stuka* dive-bomber group, and a fighter-bomber group of Re.2001s. The actual deployment of these forces was a fraction of the impression they gave, because attrition since the previous June had severely whittled down their numerical strength, until only eighteen CANTs and seven *Stuka*s remained.

For the first four months of 1943, ever-growing numbers of aircraft flying out of Malta obliterated the enemy's convoy system, as the *Duce*'s hopes for victory in North Africa steadily evaporated with every drop of oil earmarked for his desert armies spread on the surface of the sea. He was paying a steep price for cancelling Operation *Hercules*. Although Mussolini was not entirely to blame, responsibility before the Italian people was all his. And now he was hard pressed to explain to them not only the loss of their Empire, but the imminent invasion of their homeland. As other Caesars experienced before him, the barbarians would soon be knocking at the gates of Rome.

10

Unacknowledged Victory

One cannot help but admire the cold-blooded bravery and enterprise of these Italians.
Admiral Andrew Cunningham[1]

Admiral Cunningham's strategic triumph at Taranto was all out of proportion to its tactical effect. Incredibly, no ships were sunk. The *Littorio* had suffered more than enough damage to have wrecked practically any other battleship in the world, but was out of danger and towed to La Spezia for repairs after an unexploded magnetic torpedo was carefully extricated from her hull.

Just five months later, she re-entered service, a tremendous shock to Winston Churchill, who was sure at least three capital ships, she among them, had been completely destroyed by the November raid. At the time, he told the House of Commons that his Swordfish torpedo-bombers had "annihilated the Italian Fleet forever."[2] The reappearance of the torpedoed *Duilio* less than two months after the *Littorio* compounded the Prime Minister's consternation. In fact, only the *Cavour* was permanently knocked out of action; dry-dock workers were still putting her back into shape at the time of the 1943 armistice.

But the high objective of Admiral Cunningham's raid had been achieved. To push the enemy's capital ships even further away from his convoy routes, a large-scale bomber formation flying from bases on the island of Malta attacked Naples, where the Italians presumed their battleships and cruisers were beyond the range of RAF raiders. Typically, not a single *Regia Aeronautica* fighter was scrambled to intercept the intruders, but the harbor's anti-aircraft defenses were sufficiently intense to keep the Wellingtons and Whitleys at altitudes too high for bombing accuracy. On 14 December 1941, the cruiser *Pola* did receive some damage, however, and the Italian Admiralty ordered the fleet removed yet further to the west, thereby canceling out whatever threat the capital ships may have still posed to the Royal Navy. As they divided into two groups, sailing for Maddalena and Caglari, the Mediterranean seemed to have changed hands.

The *Regia Marina* was additionally compromised by a looming fuel crisis. The Navy had begun the war with approximately two million tons of oil, sufficient to keep all its vessels in operation, strategists calculated, for about eighteen months of combat. But by January 1941, 671,000 tons had already been used, while the Minister of Corporations requisitioned another quarter-million for industry and the *Regia Aeronautica*. Placed in tin containers which spoiled its allotment, the Air Force mistake was made good by 50,000 tons of gasoline *Supermarina* commanders were loathe to give up to the generally unhelpful flyers. Before year's end, the *Regia Marina* received 10,000 tons of low-grade fuel from increased domestic production and 15,000 tons from Rumania, but these quantities lagged far behind demand.

In planning for a short war, the *Duce* erred within the context of the times. If recent events were anything to go by, hostilities should not have lasted more than a few months or even weeks. It was, after all, the era of the *Blitzkrieg*. Campaigns in Poland, the Low

Countries, Scandinavia and France were intensely fought, though soon ended. A trend in modern warfare seemed to have been established. His own conquests of Ethiopia and Albania were brief affairs. Had Mussolini's reluctant Marshal in Libya kept the Italian offensive rolling forward, the same kind of 'lightning war' would have similarly brought the fighting in North Africa to a speedy, victorious conclusion. Having lost that initiative, Graziani presented Italy with an extended war she, in contrast to the British Empire, was not rich enough in natural resources to carry on for an extended period. Her only hope lay in forcing the enemy to a final decision as soon as possible, before the rapidly dwindling fuel supplies ran out.

To that end, just two weeks after the disaster at Taranto, the fleet was dispatched to hunt down the Royal Navy. On 27 November, it waylaid a convoy escorted by several cruisers. The Italians got in the first shots, scoring two heavy hits on the *Berwick*, forcing her to retire in the direction of Gibraltar. HMS *Renown* returned fire with a broadside of 32cm shells that left the destroyer *Lanciere* dead in the water, an action that misled Admiral Campioni in the belief that his forces were badly outnumbered. *Regia Aeronautica* reconnaissance, had there been any, would have convinced him otherwise.

His opposite, Admiral Somerville, was never without aircraft, and he sent eleven of them after the *Fiume* and *Vittorio Veneto*. But both cruiser and battleship skillfully eluded their torpedoes, then joined the rest of the fleet in opening fire again on the enemy vessels, which covered their rapid retreat behind a thick smoke-screen. Wrongly suspecting a numerically superior force lay just beyond the obscuring billows, Campioni recalled his ships and returned to Naples with the disabled *Lanciere* in tow.

Although Admiral Somerville was hauled before a board of enquiry into his speedy withdrawal from the battle, the Italians had not stopped the convoy from reaching its destination, and they missed a decisive encounter with the Royal Navy. Once again, lack of any aerial support was to blame, even though the action off Cape Teulada had taken place literally a few miles from Sardinia, where squadrons of *Regia Aeronautica* bombers and fighters sat idly by at their well-equipped airfield. Had but one reconnaissance plane been on hand to scout behind the smoke-screen laid down by Admiral Somerville, Campioni could have pursued his advantage with devastating consequences for the British warships and convoy.

The engagement had nevertheless given the lie to Churchill's boast that the Italian Fleet was dead. Its surprising reappearance in strength so soon after the carnage at Taranto left Admiral Cunningham nonplussed, and he ordered his ships to avoid all contact with enemy surface units for the rest of the year. Admiral Campioni had, therefore, somewhat minimized the worst effects of the 10 November raid. Now his carpet-mining in the Sicilian Channel, along the Italian coast and around Malta would be allowed to proceed unmolested. While less dramatic than fleet confrontations, the warships engaged in this tedious, dangerous work were planting the seeds of future British tragedies.

Moreover, *Regia Marina* crews were justifiably proud of the 197,742 tons of equipment, arms and fuel they transported to North Africa in just four months minus any losses during October and November 1940; only 7% of materiel was lost in December and January. But this abundance of supplies could not prevent the British Desert Army from investing Bardia and Tobruk. Even after both cities were entirely surrounded and under siege, the Italians received weapons, ammunition, food and fresh water by submarines arriving after dark, unloading their cargoes during the night, and slipping out unnoticed before dawn. The operations incurred no losses and sufficiently re-fortified the defenders, a success which so inspired observers of the Japanese Imperial Navy that they modeled a new class of submarines devoted exclusively to transport duties after the *Regia Marina* example.

Tobruk was a different story, however. *Supermarina* commanders could spare no surface ships for its defense, save the aged *San Giorgio*, a veteran of hostilities against Turkey in 1911, making her among the oldest ships still in service during World War Two. The ancient cruiser had been immobilized off shore and modified into a kind of floating anti-aircraft battery heaped with sandbags and enveloped in sub-surface steel-mesh netting. Incredibly, she survived everything the RAF threw at her, from repeated strafing runs to bombs and torpedoes. Her oft-machine-gunned decks awash with near-misses, gunners aboard the inert *San Giorgio* kept the attackers at bay for more than seven months, in the meantime downing numerous Swordfish and Fulmars.

Only after British land forces were able to bring up their artillery on the coast facing her was she doomed. But the Italians would not allow the old lady to be humbled by enemy landlubbers. Before they could zero in on the stationary target, the *San Giorgio* exploded and sank, scuttled by her own men, three of whom – the captain, an officer and torpedo specialist – chose to go down with their beloved ship. An unconscious Commander Pugliese was pulled from the water. Although badly wounded, he recovered.

But more than such heroics were needed to reverse the dire consequences of Taranto. Taking advantage of the Italian Fleet's withdrawal from the Central Mediterranean, a December convoy set out from Alexandria to Malta. By the time *Regia Aeronautica* reconnaissance planes reported the enemy's position, the moment had long since passed for interception by surface units. A lone submarine, the *Serpente*, happened to be on patrol in the area to sink the destroyer HMS *Hyperion* just southeast of Malta, where all the freighters offloaded their invaluable cargo without further incident. Stung by convoy success in slipping past virtually unnoticed, *Supermarina* commanders ordered all their capital ships returned to Naples for offensive operations, regardless of threats from RAF bombers, and redoubled the harbor's anti-aircraft defenses. They were soon put to the test.

On 8 January 1941, Italian military intelligence officers learned that the aircraft-carrier *Ark Royal*, escorted by cruisers and destroyers, had entered the western Mediterranean Sea, although the great warship's precise location was so far unknown. Soon thereafter, *Regia Aeronautica* spotter-planes lost track of its whereabouts, and *Supermarina* strategists assumed the British force had returned to Gibraltar. A few days later, however, carrier-launched bombers attacked Naples by surprise, scoring hits on the *Giulio Cesare* and knocking her out of commission. Since the Italian Fleet was now down to a single operational battleship, *Vittorio Veneto* accompanied the damaged *Cesare* to distant La Spezia for repairs.

Admiral Cunningham was not slow to make good use of their departure. The next day, he dispatched cruisers from Alexandria to escort a supply convoy bound for Malta, by now England's most important base in the Mediterranean Theater. All the Italians could muster was a pair of destroyer escorts. Hideously out-numbered and out-gunned, *Circe* and *Vega* boldly turned to confront HMS *Southampton* and *Bonaventure* accompanied by two destroyers, *Gallant* and *Hereward*, off Cape Bon, near the Italian island-fortress of Pantelleria. In the teeth of intense broadsides, the escorts kept up their own, over-matched return fire, and got off four torpedoes, which were adroitly side-stepped by their intended targets, then simultaneously circled away from each other to disengage from the action.

Although *Circe* escaped with only splinter damage, *Vega* took the brunt of a fatal salvo. Commander Fontana turned his listing ship back toward the enemy, eventually coming so close to the *Southampton* he was able to rake the cruiser with machine-gun fire. Although his ship was being furiously pummelled by the concentrated shelling of four superior warships, he kept firing to the very last moment. As she was finally going down, Commander Fontana gave his own life-jacket to an enlisted sailor, then disappeared with his ship into the sea. His sacrifice was not in vain. Distracted by the fight he put up, the *Gallant* wandered into a mine-field, where an explosion sheered off her bow. Barely able to stay afloat, the destroyer was towed to Malta, where her rusting carcass waited out the rest of the war.

The success of smaller vessels like the *Circe* and *Vega* contrasted dramatically in Mussolini's mind with the ponderous liability his capital ships had become after Taranto. Conscious, too, of Italy's rapidly dwindling fuel reserves, he concluded that a few, down-sized craft were not only more effective than the oil-guzzling battleships, but wasted far less of the precious black gold, the *Regia Marina*'s life-blood. Less was more, and he planned to replace the Fleet's major vessels with increased numbers of torpedo-boats, sub-chasers, submarines, mine-layers, destroyers, and destroyer escorts, together with some innovative designs, like explosive speed-boats, mini-subs and human torpedoes. The only new capital ships to be built would be aircraft-carriers, in view of the *Regia Aeronautica*'s failure to use the Italian peninsula as its own 'natural aircraft-carrier'.

The radical changes he proposed were predictably resisted by the House of Savoy's traditionalist naval strategists, who refused to admit that the days of their beloved battleships had been numbered by a handful of enemy aircraft. Over the conservatives' strenuous objections, the *Duce* got his way, and results were immediately forthcoming, when the Free French submarine, *Narval*, was sunk by the *Clio* torpedo-boat, off the coast of Tobruk.

The *Duce* had more reason to hope for a reversal of Italian fortunes at sea when a combination of German Luftwaffe and *Regia Aeronautica* reconnaissance aircraft identified enemy carrier-planes in the vicinity of the Balearic Islands on 8 February 1941. The enemy appeared to have come from the *Ark Royal*, so Admiral Campioni sortied with the *Veneto, Cesare* and *Doria* out of La Spezia. The last two had just completed repairs to their combat damage of only a few weeks before, unbeknownst to British pilots, who dropped mines at the entrance to La Spezia after Campioni had already left to intercept their own aircraft-carrier. He was joined by a trio of cruisers – the *Trieste, Trento* and *Bolzano* – along with a squadron of destroyers from Messina. But the *Ark Royal*, protected by battleships *Renown* and *Malaya*, the cruiser *Sheffield* and ten destroyers, had given him the slip, and were raiding Genoa.

When news reached Campioni of the bombardment, he swung his forces about and streamed at high speed to catch the enemy between them and Italian coastal defenses. These were striving unsuccessfully to hit back at the attacking warships hidden behind a thick fog that spread over the entire gulf. The shore batteries aimed blindly in the general direction of momentary muzzle flashes punctuating the dense layer of mist, without effect. This natural cover proved no hindrance to the British, whose pilots circling high overhead provided radio-directed fire on Genoese targets below. The city suffered extensive damage, and four cargo ships were sunk at their moorings, along with the *Garaventa*, an old training vessel set aside for children orphaned by the deaths of their fathers on duty in the *Regia Marina*. The main objective of the raid – destroying the *Duilio*, in Genoa for repairs of damage sustained at Taranto – was not, however, accomplished, because no shells hit the recuperating battleship.

After half-an-hour of unrelieved carnage, the enemy withdrew into the impenetrable fog still lying over the entire Ligurian Sea. Every available German and Italian aircraft was scrambled in a thorough search for the *Ark Royal* and her escorts, including an additional eighty bombers flying in from Sicily. But, invisible in the fog, luck was with the British again, and they returned to Gibraltar sight unseen. Although sorely frustrated and disappointed by this apparently lost opportunity to inflict a crushing blow on the enemy's surface forces, the Italians were getting their supply convoys to North Africa, the primary objective of the war at sea. Churchill sent urgent appeals to Cunningham, urging him to remove the Mediterranean fleet from Alexandria to Malta if necessary to stop the growing number of freighters getting through to Marshal Graziani's army in Libya.

"Every possible step must be taken by the Navy," he insisted, "to prevent supplies from reaching Libya. Failure by the Navy to concentrate on prevention of such movements will be considered as having let our side down."[3] He even suggested that the British battleship, *Barham*, be scuttled at Tripoli to bottle up the port entrance. But the Admiral dismissed his Prime Minister's suggestions as folly, and refused to budge from the relative safety of Egyptian waters until the arrival of additional naval and aerial reinforcements. Bowing under pressure from the Home Office, he reluctantly sent HMS *Valiant* and *Queen Elizabeth* to shell the harbor at Tripoli after it had been subjected to a ferocious, two-hour aerial bombardment. Convinced the raid would end in disaster, he was relieved to learn that the capital ships had been spared by the failure of *Regia Aeronautica* reconnaissance to locate them before, during, or after the attack. Thus unalerted, another opportunity for a decisive success slipped through the *Supermarina's* fingers.

Cunningham understood his battleships "had been incredibly fortunate, or perhaps the object again of Divine favour", and refused to ever again subject the Alexandrian Fleet to further "considerable and unjustified risks" on behalf of such negative results, as achieved in the raid on Tripoli.[4] While the city itself was almost reduced to ruin, the Admiral's only objective – the port – was not damaged, and the transfer of Axis supplies continued without a break. Churchill had been particularly irked by Cunningham's failure to prevent the appearance of General Erwin Rommel and his *Afrika Korps* in Libya, an event that would radically alter the entire Campaign. All 129,463 Germans arrived safely, except for a few individuals lost when an Italian transatlantic liner doubling as a troop-carrier, the *Conte Rosso*, was torpedoed and sunk by a submarine near Syracuse on 24 May. Otherwise, Rommel's men and their equipment had been transferred to North Africa intact, a singular achievement that won the *Regia Marina* high praise from Berlin.

In a Wehrmacht telegram, Mussolini was told, "Particularly gratifying is the fact that this operation could be carried out with so few losses, notwithstanding the great difficulties and the dangers of enemy action. We are convinced that it has been successful principally because of the prompt use of numerous naval units to escort the convoys, as well as the measures adopted by the Italian Navy's General Staff implementing the operational plans – plans which invariably were the right ones for meeting the situation."[5] German appreciation originated in part from the 79,183 tons of February supplies that reached North Africa on Italian vessels at a time when the Axis forces there required 70,000 tons per month. Losses amounted to just 1.5%. Although they rose to 9% in March, they declined to 6% over the following months.

Aware he had to do something to stem the flow of enemy equipment and arms, but still wary of risking his capital ships, Admiral Cunningham dispatched a quartet of destroyers from the 14th Flotilla to Malta in mid-April. From there, HMS *Janus, Jervis, Mohawk* and *Nubia* jumped a convoy spotted by their own reconnaissance planes near Kerkenah Banks. A direct hit struck the bridge of the lead Italian destroyer, *Luca Tarigo*. Commander Pietro De Cristofaro's leg was severed by a shell fragment, but he strapped up the ragged stump with his trouser's belt, and continued to direct return fire until he died from loss of blood.

HMS *Mohawk* moved in at high speed intent on delivering a *coup de grâce* to the listing warship, when an ensign ordered a spread of three torpedoes launched at close range. Explosions lifted the bow of the *Mohawk* out of the water, beneath which she plunged instantly afterward with all hands. Meanwhile, the doomed *Luca Tarigo*, her steering gear wrecked and deck-houses in flames, continued shooting at the three remaining British destroyers. Her aft gunners, among the last men still alive aboard the doomed warship, were still lobbing shells at the enemy as the seas broke over the decks.

The captain and all officers of another Italian destroyer were killed outright by an opening salvo which almost sank the *Baleno*. Surviving ship's hands managed to beach her on the Banks, where she lingered for another two days before slipping beneath the waves. The last surviving Italian destroyer did not abandon her convoy, but turned on the overwhelming enemy, unloosing torpedoes and firing all her guns. Riddled and sinking, with more than half her crew dead or wounded, the *Lampo* also ran aground on the Banks. Unlike the *Baleno*, however, five months later the ship was towed to Italy, where she was repaired and recommissioned.

Janus, Jervis and *Nubia* had all suffered damage, including numerous casualties, and were in no condition to continue pursuit of the convoy. Although three of its merchant ships were sunk during the course of close-quarters engagement, two others successfully beached themselves. The British, more interested in rescuing survivors of the vanished *Mohawk*, left them alone, and their cargos were eventually transferred to other Italian freighters bound for North Africa.

The encounter at Kerkenah Banks represented Cunningham's only serious attempt, and a costly one, that year to interfere with Axis convoys. The most supplies they delivered were a remarkable 125,076 tons in June. By then, 457,715 tons of equipment and fuel-oil had been off-loaded, with deleterious effects for British fortunes in the Libyan Desert. But the Admiral's lack of success was not confined to the Central Mediterranean. In late February, he ordered the seizure of Castelorizzo, a small island between Rhodes and Cyprus, from which to invade nearby Leros, where the Italians operated a strategically influential naval base in the Aegean Sea. Before dawn on the 25th, a landing ship escorted by an entire cruiser division put ashore 500 British commandos.

Castelorizzo was defended by a few dozen sailors and police, who radioed for assistance and held off the invaders for the rest of the day until help arrived. It came after dark in the form of Italian destroyers and torpedo-boats carrying 240 infantrymen from Rhodes. Despite the more than two-to-one odds against them, they managed to surround the British troops and force their surrender after only two days of fighting. Admiral Cunningham

The Italian heavy cruiser, *Zara*, led the *Regia Marina*'s great naval
parade in honor of Adolf Hitler's visit to Naples in May 1938.

complained to his superiors in London that the Italians "reacted with utmost vigour and
enterprise", making a "rotten business" of his attempted Castelorizzo take-over.[6]

But something more serious than anything he could muster began threatening the
Regia Marina after New Year's 1941. By the end of February, half its oil had been used up.
If the present rate of consumption continued, the entire Italian Fleet would be immobilized
by late summer. Henceforward, Germany and Rumania had to bear the burden of fueling
Mussolini's warships. Since Wehrmacht reserves were already stretched (and would be
considerably more distended after the invasion of Russia, in June), consignments to
Italy were limited. Her vessels required 200,000 tons of fuel-oil per month to perform
at maximum effectiveness. Yet, the Axis partners could only afford to send 50,000 tons
monthly, thereby severely restricting all Fleet operations. No longer at liberty to roam the
Mediterranean at will, Italian commanders only put to sea when forced by compelling
circumstances or prospects for success seemed particularly good. They did so appear on
27 March, when British convoys supplying Metaxas' forces in Greece had to be stopped.

Aboard his flag-ship *Vittorio Veneto*, Admiral Angelo Iachino led the heavy cruisers
Bolzano, *Trento* and *Trieste*, escorted by four destroyers, into the Aegean. East of Sicily,
they were joined by the heavy cruisers *Fiume*, *Pola* and *Zara*, plus two light cruisers
from Brindisi. Iachino had sortied only under the condition that he would be provided
sufficient air cover, but promised protection from both the *Regia Aeronautica* and Luftwaffe
never materialized. The British though, were made aware of Iachino's intentions through
intercepts of his *Enigma* messages. Thus alerted, Admiral Cunningham ordered an
aircraft-carrier accompanied by battleships *Barham*, *Valiant* and *Warspite*, together with
half-a-dozen destroyers, to intercept the Italians.

After sundown, Fairey Swordfish from the *Formidable* went after the *Vittorio Veneto*
and *Pola*, despite intense anti-aircraft fire that mostly spoiled their aim during the
twenty-minute action. Yet, several torpedoes struck the *Vittorio Veneto*, half her engines
were disabled, and she took on so much water her stern was almost awash. But the tough
battleship cranked up twenty knots again to resume leadership of the armada. One British

pilot made a suicide run into the glare of searchlights at the *Pola*, and was blasted out of the air, but not before dropping his torpedo. It scored a direct hit, knocking out all power and immobilizing the heavy cruiser. All the other Italian warships escaped damage.

Imperfect information radioed from *Supermarina* regarding the enemy's whereabouts convinced Admiral Iachino that only a small Royal Navy destroyer patrol was in the vicinity, so he ordered Admiral Cattaneo commanding the *Fiume* and *Zara*, along with the destroyers *Alfiere, Carducci, Gioberti* and *Oriani*, to aid the stricken *Pola*, about sixty kilometers southwest of Cape Matapan, while he proceeded with the main body of his force toward the Eastern Mediterranean in search of convoys bound for Greece. Meanwhile, Swordfish pilots mistakenly reported that their three torpedo hits on the *Vittorio Veneto* had all but sunk her. Accordingly, Admiral Cunningham dispatched a few destroyers, followed at some distance by a cruiser squadron, to finish off the assumed derelict. They mistook the inert *Pola* for Admiral Iachino's flagship, but refrained from attacking because of a mix-up in command orders, and steamed away to the north.

Eventually, their place was taken by the British cruisers, who likewise misidentified the *Pola* as the *Vittorio Veneto*, and were about to commence firing on the heavy cruiser, already dead in the water, when Admiral Cattaneo's six ships suddenly appeared. Only half of his crews were at battle stations, because they were preparing to rescue the *Pola* and had not been notified of any significant opposition in the area. In still another case of mistaken identity, her captain assumed the enemy warships were part of the rescue party sent to take her in tow, and sent up a red flare signal to show her precise position.

Suddenly, all the Italians were caught in the glare of a dozen searchlights like rabbits in the headlights of an on-coming car. British ordinance – from 31cm artillery to 7.7mm machine-guns – opened fire at point-blank range on their stunned victims. *Fiume* and *Zara* were instantly knocked out of action and burst into flames, their heavy turrets flying high into the air. When the *Zara* exploded, she took most of her crew, including Admiral Cattaneo, to the bottom. A badly damaged destroyer tried to counter-attack, but was listing so severely all her torpedoes went wide of their targets. Holed by enemy fire, the defiant *Alfieri* capsized, as her commander attended his wounded men.

Another destroyer, the *Carducci*, likewise sank in flames with her captain. Only two destroyers survived. Because it was last in formation, the *Gioberti* could have easily fled the carnage, but instead raced amid the enemy squadron, firing wildly in every direction with her relatively meager 13cm guns. Raked from stem to stern by innumerable hits, she turned away under a smoke-screen only after launching all her torpedoes, incredibly lucky to have escaped alive. Having fired all her torpedoes and most of her ammunition, the *Oriani* limped into Italian waters on one engine.

After the engagement, a destroyer, HMS *Jervis*, evacuated 258 survivors from the immobilized *Pola*, then sank her with a pair of torpedoes. The sea was littered with over-crowded life-rafts and men desperately clinging to wreckage. While the British were trying to save these unfortunates, Luftwaffe planes tardily appeared, and the rescue mission had to be aborted. To his great credit, Admiral Cunningham radioed the survivors' position to the *Supermarina*, which sent a large hospital-ship, the *Gradisca*, to the scene. It was the poignant end to a disastrous night, in which 2,400 Italian sailors were killed, missing or captured. British losses amounted to four men who perished aboard the only RAF bomber downed by the *Vittorio Veneto*'s anti-aircraft guns.

The lost Battle of Gaudo, as the Italians knew it, expelled them from the Eastern Mediterranean until the German victory at Crete. More immediately consequential, British supplies to their forces in North Africa could now resume uninterrupted. At the time, most military analysts, Axis and Allied alike, were convinced that the Battle of Cape Matapan broke the back of the *Regia Marina*. It was inconceivable that the fleet of any nation could have survived such a material and psychological blow, especially in view of Italy's worrying oil crisis. But for Mussolini, the 28 March catastrophe underscored in blood his decision to transform the Navy from a few capital ships, however splendid for their time, to many more smaller vessels that were cheaper to build and operate, more difficult to destroy, less individually important if lost, yet able to hit as hard as the broadside of a battleship. As even the anti-Fascist naval historian, Marc Antonio Bragadio, conceded, "the writer can state personally that at least in some cases, and at least during the first year of the war, Mussolini directly influenced the decisions of the *Supermarina* on the side of prudence."[7]

At the same time, the Royal Navy's undersea fleet in the Mediterranean was being hounded to annihilation by growing numbers of smaller warships. May Day certainly was that for HMS *Usk* when she sank under the guns of Italian destroyers near Sicily. Less than two weeks later, off the coast of Tripoli, another British submarine, *Undaunted*, was sunk by the torpedo-boat *Pleiadi*. On the last day of July, near Malta, HMS *Cachalot* was rammed and sunk by another torpedo-boat, the *Achille Papa*. Successes such as these stood in sharp contrast to the decimation of Mussolini's surface fleet, thereby helping him to over-ride the objections posed by conservative advocates of obsolete battleships.

The replacement process began with two transatlantic liners, the *Roma* and *Augustus*, requisitioned for the purpose of converting them into aircraft-carriers – the *Aquila*, or 'Eagle', and *Sparviero*, 'Sparrow Hawk'. Aware, too, of the *Regia Aeronautica's* consistent failure to scout for or protect the Fleet, Mussolini streamlined and simplified communications between the needs of ships at sea and participation of available aircraft. Close cooperation of the Luftwaffe with ground forces that made the *Blitzkrieg* so irresistible was held up as a model on which to build a new relationship between the *Regia Aeronautica* and *Regia Marina*. He also arranged with Hermann Goering for the manufacture in Italy of the *Stuka* dive-bomber under contract as the *Picchiatello*. Although neither the *Aquila* nor *Sparviero* were completed in time to be commissioned before the 1943 armistice, the reconnaissance skills and inter-service collaboration of Italian naval military aviation began to improve for the first time.

Mussolini additionally insisted on intensification of mining all waters the enemy was expected to sail, and stepped up the *Regia Marina's* already prodigious efforts in this direction. Again, results proved enlightening on 2 May, when an Allied convoy on its way to supply Malta was attacked by twenty *Regia Aeronautica* bombers and a trio of torpedo-planes, without effect. But as the vessels approached Cape Bon, the cargo-ship, *Paracombe*, exploded and immediately sank after hitting a mine. Soon after, a British destroyer, the *Jersey*, went down for the same cause. Less than a week later, Italian and German warplanes sortied against another convoy in the Bon area. Although they severely damaged the battleship *Renown*, the freighters scattered and strayed into one of the *Regia Marina's* far-flung minefields. Three merchant ships, including the large *Banfshire* and *Empire Song*, went to the bottom.

But running convoys was a hazardous business for both sides. On the night of 21 May 1941, cargo-ships trying to make their way to Axis forces fighting in the Aegean were overtaken by the cruisers *Ajax, Dido* and *Orion* in the company of four Royal Navy destroyers. The Italian vessels were protected by a single destroyer escort, the *Lupo*. Commander Mimbelli steamed rings around his convoy, enveloping it in a cloud of smoke, then came about to charge the overwhelming numbers and firepower of the enemy. He engaged a destroyer in an uneven artillery duel, then, to the astonishment of his opponents, pulled away sharply to launch a pair of torpedoes at the nearest cruiser from just 640 meters away.

While *Dido* put her helm hard over to avoid being hit, the emergency maneuver spoiled her gunners' aim, and the *Lupo* passed a few yards beneath *Orion*'s stern, spraying the heavy cruiser with concentrated machine-gun fire. But in so doing, Mimbelli had brought his destroyer escort directly between *Ajax* and *Orion*. In their enthusiastic determination to sink him, they over-shot their little target and fired on each other, causing appreciable damage on both sides. Peppered with eighteen 21cm-shell holes and riddled with lesser calibre hits from stem to stern, the *Lupo* miraculously escaped, although many men aboard her were killed and wounded. Mimbelli's courage and skill saved not only his ship, but three freighters from the convoy that was otherwise destroyed.

Several hours after this furious encounter, thirty Italian vessels in the Aegean were on an interception course with British surface units. *Sagittario*, Lieutenant Cigala Fulgosi's destroyer escort and the convoy's sole protection, laid down a concealing smoke-screen, then came about to singlehandedly engage five enemy heavy cruisers and two destroyers commanded by Admiral King. With their radar-directed guns, they opened fire from as far away as 12,000 meters. But Fulgosi had distracted them from concentrating on his troop ships overcrowded with Germany's elite *Gebirgsjaeger* soldiers bound for the fighting in Greece. Zig-zagging within 800 meters of the second cruiser in the lead, the *Sagittario* dodged one near-miss after another to launch a torpedo, which apparently exploded on contact, judging from the pall of black smoke that arose over the target. The other cruisers with their destroyers ceased firing and turned away. So then did Fulgosi, who went looking for the scattered troop ships, reassembled them, and steamed at full speed toward Greece.

When Admiral Cunningham learned that the important convoy had escaped, he dispatched another seven destroyers and two heavy cruisers, plus a pair of battleships to join up with King's force, then intercept and destroy the troop ships at any cost. Indeed, the price would be high. As the flotilla raced after its quarry, *Stuka* dive-bombers appeared overhead. They descended on the wildly maneuvering warships, sinking the destroyer *Greyhound*, along with the cruisers *Gloucester* and *Fiji*. These heavy losses were compounded by serious damage the battleships *Valiant* and *Warspite* incurred. Meanwhile, the *Sagittario* led its convoy to Pireaus, where the German troops carried Lieutenant Fulgosi on their shoulders in noisy triumph.

Less than a week after the *Sagittario*'s successful run against difficult odds, the experience of another convoy demonstrated that Mussolini's determination to establish a closer, working relationship between his navy and air force was at last congealing. On 27 May 1941, his freighters bound from Rhodes to the fighting in Crete, at Sitia, on the northeast coast, were detected by British surface units, which planned to ambush them in the narrow Casos Channel. In the past, Italian convoys were typically decimated during such circumstances. This time, however, *Regia Aeronautica* pilots spotted the warships in time, radioed their position directly to the *Supermarina*, and participated in a joint submarine attack that spoiled the enemy interdiction, allowing the convoy to proceed safely to Sitia. A *Sparviero* bomber claimed the Royal Navy destroyer, *Hereward*, which exploded and sank with a single torpedo hit. Continuing cooperation between aircraft and warships kept Italian attrition low during the conquest of Crete, so much so, the only casualties were two destroyer escorts, the *Curtatone* and *Carlo Mirabello*, and these were lost two days apart, on 20 and 21 May, not to British air or naval units, but to Greek mines.

In fact, it was during the Crete Campaign that innovative craft of the *Mezzi Navali d'Assalto*, or Naval Assault Teams, made their dramatic debut. These were not simply bomb-laden speedboats aimed at an enemy ship in the hope they might connect with their target. Even if they did, any explosion against an armored hull would produce little if any effect. The MNA unit actually required years of development as a complex secret weapon to fulfill the specialized task envisioned for it. A 300-kilo explosive warhead made up the entire fore section which sank to a predetermined depth just before impact. When this happened, water pressure triggered a detonation that caused a powerful sub-surface vacuum beneath the water-line of a targeted hull, breaking it. A gyro-compass kept the speed-boat on a straight-line course after the pilot locked his controls and jumped overboard clinging to the backrest doubling as a life-raft. Survivors were on their own, and could only hope they might be rescued by friendly forces.

Lieutenant Faggioni commanded the first six explosive motor speed-boats of the *Decima Flottiglia MAS* aboard the destroyers *Crispi* and *Sella* on the night of 25 May. Off the Cretan coast, they were lowered over the side twelve kilometers from the entrance to British-occupied Suda Bay. To reach the attack area, they had to navigate six kilometers of open water without being detected. Quieting their motors at low rpms, and keeping their fingers crossed, the MNA pilots cautiously proceeded in a long line across the still bay. They eventually came to the first of three, separate rows of defensive barriers protecting the anchorage. But the six-meter-long boats' shallow draft, combined with their ability to lift both screw and rudder out of the water, enabled them to clear all obstructions in perfect silence. Literally within hailing distance of a large freighter, Faggioni reassembled his team for final instructions.

As dawn began to reveal the silhouettes of several vessels, the Italian craft simultaneously fired up their engines, then accelerated toward their assigned targets at full throttle. Faggioni and another pilot aimed at HMS *York*, the enemy's largest capital ship stationed in Crete. He steered a collision course, set the gyro-compass, locked the rudder in place, grabbed the inflated back-rest, then hurled himself overboard only seventy five meters from the target. His nearby comrade followed suit, and both speed-boats crashed broadside at nearly thirty knots into the 10,000-ton cruiser before the alarm could be sounded. Convulsed by massive explosions, she began to go down, both of her engine rooms and boilers flooding, as a destroyer, the *Hasty*, towed the stricken cruiser toward shore, and grounded *York* to prevent her from sinking. Reduced to a twisted wreck, she was Britain's last heavy cruiser in the Mediterranean.

Other members of the *Decima Flottiglia MAS* sank one merchant ship, and damaged the 8,324-ton tanker *Pericles* so badly she spilled 500 tons of precious fuel. Three weeks later, while being towed to Alexandria, the crippled vessel sank in a storm. All six pilots were made prisoners of war, but their confinement did not last long. Lieutenant Faggioni's attack could not have come at a worse moment for Allied fortunes in the Aegean. With the loss of HMS *York* and vital oil from the *Pericles*, all hope for victory was lost. In fact, British forces surrendered on Crete one day after the ships were sunk.

Repercussions were far more serious. Gibraltar, Malta and Alexandria had become Britain's last bases in the Mediterranean, and they were too far distant from each other to effectively interfere any longer with Italian convoys bound for North Africa. Following the fall of Crete, an average of eighty freighters usually protected by thirty destroyer escorts, plus numerous torpedo-boats and mine-sweepers, and screened by long-range patrol aircraft and bombers of the *Regia Aeronautica*, crossed to Libyan ports without incurring significant losses.

The *Regia Marina* had demonstrated remarkable powers of recuperation after two major reverses, defeats which, in the words of Admiral Cunningham, "no navy in the world could have been expected to recover from in so remarkably short a period".[8] As though to underscore his observation, the *Littorio* and *Vittorio Veneto*, like ghost-ships from the disasters at Taranto and Cape Matapan, sallied forth to defend Sardinia from the British battleship *Nelson* and aircraft-carrier *Ark Royal* on 24 August. Additionally confronted by other veterans of past calamities, Admiral Cunningham's warships aborted their intended raid without firing a shot, and beat a swift retreat before the cruisers *Balzano, Gorizia, Trento* and *Trieste* came into firing range. Their position had been reported by *Regia Aeronautica* reconnaissance in a prompt fashion, alerting the surface units in time to protect Sardinia. Cooperation between Italian planes and ships had finally reached the degree of a working partnership approaching, if not yet equalling British levels.

Regia Marina resilience combined with Royal Navy attrition and defeat in the Aegean guaranteed the safe delivery of 4,327 men, 1,167 vehicles and 17,061 tons of equipment during the last half of 1941. In August alone, 37,201 tons of gasoline were transported, suffering a mere 1% loss, with dire consequences for the British Desert Army. Well supplied, Rommel seemed irrepressible now. The sole weapons apparently capable of severing his critical life-line were enemy submarines, but most of them had been sunk by Italian torpedo-boats or destroyers. Admiral Cunningham therefore ordered a new undersea flotilla into the Mediterranean during August. The new submarines achieved important success on the 20th, when the troop-ship, *Esperia*, went down with three torpedo hits. Because the sinking took place just a few miles from her destination in Tripoli, rescue efforts succeeded in saving virtually every man aboard.

The following month, an Italian convoy fell afoul of a British 'wolf pack' near Misurata. Although the *Vulcania* skillfully out-maneuvered a torpedo salvo aimed at her, others blasted two former transatlantic liners serving as troop-carriers. *Neptunia* and *Oceania* heeled over and sank with 384 men, most of them killed outright when the fatal torpedoes exploded. Their loss was relatively light, compared to the 6,500 souls on board both vessels. Many thousands of survivors owed their lives to the skillful rescue efforts of *Regia Marina* destroyer crews.

Aware that the new enemy submarines had passed through the Straits of Gibraltar, Mussolini was determined to strike the Royal Navy there at the earliest opportunity. His *Supermarina* commanders also realized that the upsurge in submarine attacks was part of an all-out effort aimed from the western Mediterranean, far beyond the Italian sphere of influence, to cut off Axis supply convoys. But Gibraltar was the best defended naval base on Earth, so something more than conventional strategy would be needed to destroy its protected anchorage. Strategists looked to a proposal made back in October 1935, when two sub-lieutenants outlined plans for a human-torpedo. The young men had been inspired by an innovative American Civil War craft that destroyed the frigate USS *Housatonic* during the naval blockade of Charleston, Virginia, in 1864. Although lost in the same engagement under mysterious circumstances, the CSA *Hunley* was the first submarine in history to sink an enemy vessel. Naval engineers at La Spezia were impressed with the sub-lieutenants' idea, and began serious work on the project the following January. Research and testing continued into the war, although the first operational models were not ready until late 1941.

Officially known as *siluro a lenta corsa*, or a 'slow running torpedo', the seven-meter-long SLC was a true submarine its two crewmen rode piggy-back into battle. Straddling the 54cm-wide vessel, they crouched behind its 'wind-screen' against the force of the water through which they passed at three knots. Electric pumps alternately filled or emptied tanks, allowing the vessel to rise and descend from sixty-meter depths. Storage batteries powering a small, 1.6 hp motor, quiet enough to avoid detection by sub-surface listening devices, drove the submersible over a six-kilometer operational range. The *Maiale*, or 'Pig', as it was affectionately nicknamed, often escaped the attention of sonar operators or look-outs, at least in the early days of its history, who sometimes mistook the manned torpedo for a passing shark.

It also featured a device that used compressed air to lift enough of the steel netting surrounding enemy ships, permitting the SLC to pass through. Occasionally, crews hand-snipped the protective wire-mesh with bolt-cutters. The *Maiale's* entire fore-section was a 230- to 260-kg explosive warhead that could be removed from the main body of the craft and secured beneath an enemy ship. Personnel armament consisted of 4.5-kg limpet mines fixed to the target's hull. They were not magnetically clamped, but either tied to bilge-pumps or floated up under the keel by an inflated bag. That accomplished, timers were set to detonate the *cimici* from one to six hours, enough time for a crewman, who carried five of the egg-shaped 'bugs' on his utility-belt, to clear the area.

The dare-devils who carried out these harrowing operations were known as 'gamma-men', from the 'g' in *guastatori*, assault engineers. Italy's pre-war lead in the development of self-contained breathing apparati – from compressed air tanks to regulators – made the military version of scuba-divers possible. Wearing face-masks and rubber body-suits, they belonged to an élite corps of rigorously trained volunteers, who were not expected to return once they left the mother-ship, under orders to depart, leaving the frogmen behind in enemy waters. Nearing the objective, crews ditched their *Maiale*, then swam toward the target with limpet mines at the ready. Once their mission was completed, they were given the option to either surrender or go into hiding, always a remote possibility, on shore. Only rarely did mother-ships plan to rendezvous with their *guastatori*. They were able, however, to vocally communicate with each other underwater via a thin metal sheet that vibrated inside their breathing mask.

Both g-men and their equipment were far ahead of their times, innovators of a whole new kind of warfare, the linear precursors of today's U.S. Navy SEALs. Italian SLCs could only attack stationary targets in port, but this limitation made the *Maiale* an ideal weapon for bold attacks on Gibraltar. Its roadstead was stealthily entered on the evening of 20 September by Captain Junio Valerio Borghese's submarine, *Scire*, which cruised on to launch three manned torpedoes near the mouth of Spain's Guadaranque River. The British had gotten wind of them, thanks to ULTRA intercepts of *Regia Marina* secret codes, and intensified base defenses with added patrol craft. They randomly dropped depth-charges throughout the Rock's immediate vicinity to make matters difficult for any unwanted submariners.

The *Maiale* crews were disappointed to find few warships, and minor ones, at anchor. They nonetheless proceeded to seek out their own victims. These included the tankers *Fionna Shell* and *Denbydale*, and, most spectacular of all, the *Durham*, an ammunition ship whose deafening explosion shattered the stillness of the night and preceded the dawn with a blinding fire-ball. After ditching their submersibles, the frogmen swam safely to the Spanish coast, and eventually made their way back to Italy. Half-a-dozen men with three disposable weapons destroyed 31,337 tons of enemy shipping at the world's premiere naval base in a single night. Their report concerning the absence of capital ships at Gibraltar was hardly less valuable. *Supermarina* now realized that the enemy's major surface units were concentrated not in the western Mediterranean, but at the Royal Navy's base in Alexandria. But to repeat a *Maiale* success at the opposite end of the Sea required careful, lengthy preparation.

Meanwhile, the British Admiralty determined that radar-guided night attacks by sea and air directed from Malta might yet grind the Axis convoys to a halt. The decision was the right one, because the *Regia Marina* was at a clear disadvantage during any operations after dark. Results were immediately forthcoming. In September 1942, 29% of Axis supplies bound for North Africa were sunk. Although losses declined the following month to 20%, such attrition was unacceptable.

Sure they had found the proper method for severing Rommel's lifeline, Royal Navy commanders were confident they could destroy two important convoys heading from Naples and Brindisi on 8 November. The larger of the two, referred to as the *Duisburg* after the lead freighter of seven merchant ships, was escorted by the heavy cruisers *Trieste* and *Trento*, plus a quartet of destroyers: the *Euro, Fulmine, Grecale* and *Mestrale*. Two Royal Navy cruisers, HMS *Aurora* and *Penelope*, accompanied by destroyers *Lively* and *Lance*, were led to ambush positions after dusk by a night-time reconnaissance plane, an aircraft without parallel in the *Regia Aeronautica*. The British waited until the escorts obliviously slid passed, bringing the exposed convoy to within point-blank range, then opened fire, sinking all seven freighters in rapid succession. It was a frightful massacre of confusion and dying ships amid garish sheets of flame. *Aurora, Penelope, Lively* and *Lance* turned for Malta, their mission accomplished.

Guided by the glare of their own burning convoy, the Italian destroyers came about to punish the attackers. But without radar, they had little chance of success in the darkness. *Euro*, commanded by the same Cigala Fulgosi of *Sagittario* fame, was blasted at close range. The destroyer survived, but too many of her crew had fallen.

Although shot through by numerous hits and in a perilous condition, *Fulmine* continued to oppose the superior enemy forces concentrating on her. Soon, the last operable gun fell silent when all its crew-members were killed. Lieutenant Garau manned it himself. He took orders from Lieutenant Commander Milano, who, despite the loss of his right arm in the battle, continued to shout firing directions. Both men went down with their ship, defiant to the end. Then the *Grecale* was straddled by an accurate salvo that left her dead in the water before she could launch torpedoes at the *Penelope*. By the time the Italian cruisers came about, the brief action was nearing its end. But the appearance of *Trieste* and *Trento* was enough to save the remaining destroyers by disengaging the British with a few salvoes. Even so, the entire convoy had been obliterated, with the loss of two destroyers.

The *Supermarina* was pressured between increasingly frantic calls for supplies to North Africa and the devastating onslaught of enemy night attacks. So, a desperate scheme was improvised to get at least one more convoy through before effective defensive measures could be put in place. The high-speed cruiser, *Cadorna*, faster than its British counterparts, departed Brindisi alone with tons of gasoline perilously stacked in cans littering her decks. At the same time, eight merchant ships left Naples, escorted by destroyers and two heavy cruisers, the *Trieste* and *Duca degli Abruzzi*. As soon as they were spotted by an RAF reconnaissance plane flying out of Malta, the convoy suddenly split into four sections.

Unsure which one to pursue, and distracted by the *Cadrona*'s simultaneous, inexplicably unescorted appearance, the British lost track of their quarry. In scattering, the freighters had given them the slip, however temporary, a dodge that allowed them precious time to get on with their voyage. They managed to race beyond the Strait of Messina, then reformed, but were soon after located again by aircraft surveillance. Fairey Swordfish came down on the convoy wrapped in a smoke-screen that would not stay put due to stiff sea breezes. The *Trieste*, trying to shield the supply ships in her charge, was hit with an exploding torpedo that knocked out her boiler section. As she slowed to full-stop, the bombers concentrated their attacks on her, ignoring the convoy, which slipped away unnoticed in the aerial frenzy to sink the heavy cruiser. *Trieste* fired back with everything she had, even her 21cm armament, while her crew worked feverishly to restore power. Having fended off every assault, she got under way again, as though by a miracle, and streamed slowly beyond the range of her pursuers, eventually making landfall in Messina.

Once more, radar found the missing convoy, illuminated now in the surreal glare of parachute flares descending over an inky, freezing sea. Bombers and torpedo-planes flew non-stop attacks against the supply ships, whose combined firepower, while formidable, was not impenetrable. The *Duca degli Abruzzi*'s stern practically lifted out of the water with a torpedo blast that blew away all her propellers, save one, which continued to keep her moving, however slowly. As before, the British pilots forgot about the convoy in their enthusiasm to sink a stricken heavy cruiser. Italian destroyers closed around her, adding their anti-aircraft defenses, and the Swordfish banked away. Like the *Trieste*, the *Duca degli Abruzzi* completed the voyage to Messina under her own power.

The virtually defenseless convoy was ordered to turn about and make for Taranto, because the *Supermarina* learned from deciphered Royal Navy communications that several cruisers had been dispatched from Malta to join the attack. The British once again lost track of the freighters, five of which returned to Italy. The other three and the speedy *Cadrona* finally arrived with their valuable cargos at Benghazi. The convoy operation was, therefore, partially successful, despite serious damage to two cruisers. More importantly, no ships had been lost, despite everything the enemy could throw at them. But the supplies they delivered were hardly enough to keep the Italo-German forces in North Africa alive. For lack of fuel and ammunition, Rommel's impetuous advance had been converted into a fight for bare survival. He radioed Rome and Berlin that he could not hold out much longer without replacement equipment, gasoline and food.

The *Supermarina* tried another ruse, sending a convoy along the Tunisian coast on 30 November. But the British were not easily deceived this time, and they attacked in force after midnight with the heavy cruisers *Ajax*, *Aurora*, *Neptune* and *Penelope*, accompanied by three destroyers. They were beaten to the interception position by Malta-based bombers, which torpedoed the *Mantovanni*. The four cruisers appeared while an Italian destroyer was engaged in rescuing survivors from the sinking tanker. Foregoing her opportunity to escape, the mightily out-gunned *Da Mosto* attacked the enemy head-on, loosing a spread of torpedoes at 900 meters, then disappeared behind her own smoke-screen in a reverse maneuver.

A few minutes later, she emerged, firing her relatively puny 13cm guns at the enemy warships. Her last torpedoes went off just 400 meters from the *Penelope*, whose broadside crashed into the destroyer's ammunition magazine. Immobilized, with most of her crew dead or wounded, the other cruisers closed in for the kill, but not too closely, because with her last breaths she spat out round after round from her only functioning gun, even as the seas spread over her decks. She disappeared with all hands.

The British sailors were awestruck, even deeply moved by such defiance. *Ajax, Aurora, Neptune* and *Penelope*, their crews turned out on deck for salute, passed gravely in tribute to the *Da Mosto* over the area where she went down, marked by floating wreckage and a spreading oil slick. It would be one of history's last acts of gallantry in a world of mutually intolerant ideologies, and underscored for many the war's tragic futility.

Inspired by the *Cadrona*'s dash from Brindisi to Benghazi, two more swift cruisers piled their decks as high as the bridge with cans of gasoline for the hard-pressed troops of General Rommel. *Da Barbiano* and *Da Giussano*, escorted by a single destroyer, the *Cigno*, steamed at full tilt out of Palermo, evaded enemy reconnaissance by circling far around the Egadi Islands, then made for Tripoli on 9 December. However, their superior speed, upon which they relied exclusively for success, was fatally compromised by high seas, and they aborted the run.

Unbeknownst to the Italians, they were being shadowed by a quartet of British destroyers, which concealed themselves behind the rocky promontory of Cape Bon. As the dangerously over-loaded cruisers passed, the destroyers launched several torpedo salvos at very short range. Within two minutes, both *Da Barbiano* and *Da Giussano* erupted into mountains of flame. Sheets of blazing gasoline widened across the water to engulf more than 900 lives, including an admiral and his entire staff. While trying to rescue survivors amid the hazardous conflagration, the *Cigno* was repeatedly attacked by enemy bombers, but managed to save herself and a few badly burned men.

Their ordeal climaxed more than a month of critical misfortune and catastrophe at sea. Equipment, arms and fuel totaling 79,208 tons left Italy for North Africa during November 1942, but only 29,843 tons arrived through the long gauntlet of Allied warships and bombers. Losses stood at 62%. Consequences for the entire Campaign were immediate and dire. By mid-December, Italo-German defenses crumbled before the well-supplied British 8th Army. Derna fell on the 19th, and Benghazi just four days later. Defeat, both in the Mediterranean and the Libyan Desert, seemed inevitable. But when general collapse appeared imminent, daring innovation and desperate measures would force the hand of the Goddess of Fortune.

Suicidal as such an attempt seemed, the *Supermarina* was planning another convoy run to North Africa before the wreckage of the last ill-fated attempt had been dissipated by the sea. The operation was a last-ditch, all-out effort to get supplies through to the remaining Libyan ports still in Axis hands while there was yet time. The existence of the *Regia Marina* was quite literally staked on the venture, which involved the Italian Navy's entire available combat strength. Four freighters of exceptionally large tonnage crammed with equipment, fuel, ammunition and food were escorted out of Naples on 16 December by the battleship *Duilio*, the heavy cruisers *Aosta, Attendolo*, and *Monteuccoli*, together with four destroyers. They were later joined by three more battleships, the *Cesare, Doria* and *Littorio*, the cruisers *Gorizia* and *Trento*, plus another ten destroyers. Their orders were simple: "Get the freighters through no matter what the cost!"

The heavily armed convoy was covered by an armada of *Regia Aeronautica* and Luftwaffe bombers, which identified a powerful enemy force of battleships and cruisers escorting a single freighter to Malta. British Admiral Vian was told to intercept the convoy after dark, as soon as the tanker had been safely delivered to Malta. But before sunset, his ships were attacked by Axis planes. Admiral Iachino, commanding the Italian flotilla, steamed toward the anti-aircraft activity in the distance and reached the enemy at dusk. There was just enough daylight left for the *Littorio* to open fire on them with her 39cm guns, followed by *Gorizia* and a destroyer, *Maestrale*. Admiral Vian immediately withdrew his units behind a billowing smoke-screen, refrained from carrying out any night attack, and the convoy proceeded on its way to North Africa. Malta-based aircraft stood down in the face of too many German and Italian planes in the area, so Admiral Vian dispatched part of his forces to Tripoli, where they were to ambush the four big freighters.

Some twenty-five kilometers from port, however, the warships strayed into one of the *Regia Marina*'s sprawling minefields. The heavy cruiser *Neptune* suffered a terrific explosion, followed soon after to the bottom by a destroyer. While the others were struggling to disengage themselves from the danger zone, damages inflicted on *Aurora* and *Penelope* knocked these heavy cruisers out of action for the next several months. Meanwhile, the Italian convoy docked without further incident at Tripoli to unload much-needed supplies. Its arrival, after more than a month of unrelieved loss, was nothing less than a triumph. Yet again, the Italians had bounced back over-night from persistent catastrophe to unexpected victory. No one understood at the time, but the First Battle of the Sirte, as it was later called, initiated a series of critical defeats that marked the end of British supremacy in the Mediterranean.

On the same evening *Littorio*'s guns were warding off a British naval squadron, an Italian submarine came to rest on the other side of the Mediterranean Sea at the edge of a forbidding minefield only a mile from the western entrance of the great Royal Navy base at Alexandria, Egypt. Three human torpedoes of the *X Flotilla MAS* quietly slipped away from the submarine *Scire* on a heading for the enemy's holy-of-holies, the fortified inner harbor where Admiral Cunningham's own flag-ship was moored in the company of other capital ships. British code-breakers, having penetrated *Commando Supremo* security, warned him of the forthcoming attack on his ships by aircraft, motor-boats or SLCs. He put Alexandria on high alert, and increased patrols of the harbor. But the Italians were not totally bereft of their own military intelligence.

Captain Borghese had been provided with detailed maps of the minefields around Alexandria captured from the British destroyer, *Mohawk*, sunk in shallow waters off the Tunisian coast nine months earlier. Thrilled by the operation's great potential for success, Mussolini himself had seen the crew off, shaking hands with the half-dozen gamma-men of Operation GA-3, the boldest assault ever made against Britain's Mediterranean Fleet. A few days later, in the early hours 19 December 1941, they were riding the porpoise-like submersibles like boys on dolphins, prepared to snip their way through steel wire-mesh netting surrounding the port of Alexandria. They were saved from such arduous, hazardous labor, however, by three incoming destroyers. As the protective gates were swung open to admit the unsuspecting warships, the *Maiali* followed along beneath their churning wakes, into the naval sanctorum. Soon inside, they split up to attack their own targets.

While manhandling his SLC between a pair of floats, Luigi Durand de la Penne ripped his dive-suit. His hands were so numbed by the freezing water he was unable to control the SLC, which struck the hull of HMS *Valiant*, and plunged fifteen meters before he could regain control. The unexpected dive had swept his comrade, Emilio Bianchi, away, and fouled the SLC's propeller in a cable. Alone, de la Penne literally dragged the immobilized torpedo uphill along in the mud until he reached the target. To avoid drowning in his flooded mask, he drank sea water, but was able to set the limpet mine about five meters below the keel, then activated the timer.

Both crewmen were captured soon after and warned Captain Morgan, commanding the *Valiant*, that his ship should be abandoned at once, because it was about to be sunk, but refused to divulge any particulars. He had them both locked in a hold far below decks, when a powerful explosion shook *Valiant* with great violence. The door of their captivity was jolted open, making possible their escape, but they were re-arrested on the deck of the shattered vessel. As it settled heavily to the floor of the harbor, a fully loaded 7,354-ton fleet-tanker several moorings away, the *Sagona*, erupted with a detonation potent enough to inflict serious damage on a neighboring destroyer, the *Jervis*. This was the same ship that sank the cruiser, *Pola*, the previous January. Pandemonium reigned amid the confused shouts of men and the shriek of alarm whistles. General chaos was punctuated by yet more rolling thunder coming from the direction of the *Queen Elizabeth*. In fifteen minutes, two battleships and a tanker had been knocked out of commission, along with a destroyer severely damaged. Notified of the attack, Churchill admitted that *Valiant* and *Queen Elizabeth* were reduced to "useless burdens".[8] Taranto had been avenged.

But the consequences for the Royal Navy were more serious. While all six *Maiali* crew members were made prisoners of war, their captivity was a small price to pay for such a heavy blow to British sea-power. It would not be the last and could not have come at a worse moment. Recently, Fritz Guggenberger, Lieutenant Commander of U-81, had sunk HMS *Ark Royal*, Britain's largest aircraft-carrier and responsible for so many deadly raids against Axis convoys, with a single torpedo about fifty kilometers east of Gibraltar. A few days later, Lieutenant Hans-Dietrich von Tiesenhausen's U-331 sank a 31,100-ton, state-of-the-art battleship in three minutes further west of the island. Contrasting the single fatality aboard *Ark Royal*, more than 800 men were lost when HMS *Barham*'s powder magazines detonated in a spectacular explosion.

Cunningham lamented, "Thus, our last two remaining battleships were put out of action. We are having shock after shock out here. The damage to the battleships at this time is a disaster."[9] Churchill concurred, "our naval power in the Mediterranean has been virtually destroyed by a series of disasters."[10]

Throughout November 1941, the *Regia Marina* had been relentlessly slaughtered by radar-guided night-attacks. Allied military analysts, keeping score of one Royal Navy victory after another, confidently predicted the demise of the Italian fleet with the subsequent collapse of Axis fortunes in North Africa by year's end. By mid-December, however, the tables had radically turned on the British. In his Christmas message to the nation, the *Duce* could truthfully boast, "after the most bitter suffering and against the best efforts of the most powerful navy on earth, through the unsurpassed courage and self-sacrifice of our sailors, Italy has regained mastery of the Mediterranean. Their victories have given us the right to refer to it, with greater justification than ever before, as *Mare Nostro*."[11]

The *Regia Marina's* triumph restored his confidence in ultimate victory, so much so he hesitated not a moment to join Germany against the United States when the time came on 7 December. Japan's Taranto-inspired raid on Oahu's naval base at Pearl Harbor in the Hawaiian Islands presented an optimum opportunity for going to war against a man, if not a people, he truly despised. More than a year before, during late April 1940, Franklin Roosevelt publicly cast the Italian leader in the role of aggressor by warning him of terrible repercussions in an extended conflict. F.D.R. stated that military ambitions directed at any of the Americas to seize its raw materials for war production would not be tolerated. Mussolini was particularly miffed, as he felt he had done everything conceivable to preserve the neutrality of his country against both German and Franco-British pressure for involvement on either side, thereby limiting the spread of hostilities. And hadn't he tried to prevent the outbreak of war at the very outset, offering to personally negotiate a settlement of the Polish problem the day Hitler attacked – an offer both the French and English turned down? What business did this Wall Street President have sticking his nose into Europe's internal difficulties, anyway? No one, save this man, had mentioned anything about threatening the other side of the Atlantic Ocean.

Containing his indignation, Mussolini had responded earlier in 1941, with ill-concealed outrage: "Italy's non-belligerency has effectively ensured peace for two hundred millions of men, but, notwithstanding, Italian merchant traffic is subjected to a constant surveillance that is vexatious and harmful. As far as I know, Germany is opposed to a further extension of the conflict, and Italy likewise. We must learn whether this is also the Franco-British aim. The only European nation that dominates a large part of the world and possesses a monopoly on many basic raw materials is Great Britain. Italy has no programs of that kind. As to the repercussions which an extension of the war fronts might have on the three Americas, I call attention to the fact that Italy has never concerned itself with the relations of the American republics, with each other, or with the United States – thereby respecting the Monroe Doctrine. And," he ended testily, "one might therefore ask for reciprocity in regard to European affairs."[12]

The "constant surveillance" by U.S. Navy warships of Italian merchant traffic Mussolini found so "vexatious and harmful" escalated to crisis proportions over the next nine months, culminating in February 1941, when Roosevelt ordered the seizure of all Italian vessels in American ports. Most of the ships were scuttled or sabotaged by their crews before the authorities could act, but Mussolini was infuriated. The U.S. was supposed to be a neutral nation, not at war with the Italian government, which was doing everything in its power to avoid hostilities with the most powerful industrial nation on Earth.

Some American voices were raised against the President's action, even in Congress, where he was accused of "playing craps for the destiny of our country", in the words of the first U.S. Congresswoman, Jeanette Rankin. "Many international acts of ours today," she said in reference to Roosevelt's seizure of the Italian freighters, "are acts of war", a sentiment echoed by popular opinion polls indicating 86% of American voters opposed entry into the European conflict.[13] Even leading democrats worried aloud that taking neutral Italian vessels had been illegal, a move clearly aimed at goading Italy into war.

The *Duce* lost his temper, crying out, "Illusion and lying are the basis of American interventionism – illusion that the United States is still a democracy, when instead it is a political and financial oligarchy dominated by Jews, through a personal form of dictatorship. The lie is that the Axis powers, after they finish Great Britain, want to attack America." His words were hardly meant to endear himself to Americans, who he genuinely liked and admired. "I understand how the American people, in their despair and confusion caused by the Depression, looked longingly to this man (Franklin Roosevelt) for help, because of all the attractive, if baseless promises he made. Now, the only way he knows to make good on those assurances is to spill the blood of innocent peoples on behalf of a war-stimulated economy."[14]

Mussolini strove to make a clear distinction between the Americans and their president. The *Duce*'s brief address in English for a 1930 Fox Movie-tone newsreel had epitomized his attitude throughout the decade:

"I am very glad to be able to express my friendly feelings toward the American nation. The friendship with which Italy regards the millions of citizens, who, from Alaska to Florida, from the Pacific to the Atlantic, live in the United States, is deeply rooted in our hearts. This feeling, created by mutual interests, contributed to the preparation of a new, happy era in the lives of both nations. I admire the wonderful energy of the American people, and I see and recognize among you that the love of your land is as deep as ours, my fellow citizens, who are working to make America great. I salute the great American people! I salute the Italians of America, who unite in a single love of both nations!"[15]

Even in late 1941, Mussolini still spoke publicly and privately of the pride he took in Italian contributions to American greatness, though he deplored "the plutocratic tyranny lurking beneath a sham-democracy" that actually ruled the United States. Its people were being fooled, he said, into believing that "the Jews' enemies were *their* enemies. As such, America is rapidly becoming the enemy of the world; the potential wrecking-ball of Western Civilization; the arsenal, not of 'democracy', but high finance."[16]

'Three peoples, one war', proclaims this Italian propaganda poster issued after Fascist Italy, the Third Reich and Imperial Japan declared war on the United States in December 1941.

Mussolini needed no urging to follow Japanese and German declarations of war with his own. The moment seemed propitious, because the Americans had been forced into a two-front war that would divide their resources and prevent them from concentrating everything against Europe. Inspired by the prospect of doing battle with "Roosevelt's duped minions", the *Duce* summoned military specialists to his headquarters in Rome for the purpose of attacking the United States' mainland at the earliest opportunity. Many daring plans were discussed – some credibly futuristic, others utterly fantastic – until a single proposal stood out from the rest: The same weapon that had just destroyed the pride of the British Fleet in Alexandria must be aimed at New York harbor.

11

Sunshine from Italy

Only the Italian Alpini *Corps is to be considered unbeaten on the Russian Front.*
Radio Moscow, 30 January 1943[1]

enito Mussolini did more than witness history's last grand display of cavalry. He ordered it. On 26 June 1941, more than 10,000 mounted troops, their bright sabers glinting in early morning sunlight, thundered across the vast parade grounds of northern Italy's garrison, where the *Duce* received their salute from a high reviewing pavilion. It took them nearly two hours to pass before his outstretched hand. As massed brass bands of the Savoia Household Cavalry blared forth familiar strains of traditional and Fascist march music, the horse regiments were followed by an additional 50,000 infantry, their officers resplendent in dress uniform, unit colors stirred by an early summer breeze.

The immense military pageant was not mere pomp and ceremony, but an official send-off to Italian armed forces committed just four days earlier in Operation *Barbarossa*. This was Germany's invasion of the Soviet Union, a campaign in which Mussolini was determined that his country would play an important role. He must come to Hitler's aid in Russia, just as the *Führer* had helped him in North Africa, a reciprocity necessary for the psychological cohesion of the Axis. Beyond such obvious and immediate political considerations, the *Duce* relished a military confrontation with Marxism.

"The unity sought by Europe since the fall of the Classical World has been an elusive ideal," he declared to the tens of thousands of officers and men assembled before the garrison. "You are the most privileged generation in the last sixteen centuries, because that longing will be fulfilled in the mission you are about to undertake. The greatest threat to civilization has generated the greatest social fusion our continent has known since the Roman Epoch, from which you are directly descended. Warriors from Scandinavia, the Germanic nations, the Latin, Slavic and Iberian peoples have put aside their local, relatively petty and self-destructive quarrels of yesterday in a single effort for their common survival. The campaign in Russia is a fundamental struggle for our existence and shared European identity. It is a fight of life or death against the dead-weight triumph of a debased sub-humanity, as exemplified in Marxism. We know this enemy of all mankind. Twenty years ago, we scoured him from our peninsula. Now we will purge him from the planet! Long live our continental civilization! Long live Italy!"[2]

Years before this oration, Mussolini often referred to Fascism as "the Third Alternative; the wave of the future", an ideological way of life more than a political system, that, in time, would be naturally adopted by other nations after democracy everywhere collapsed of its own myopic materialism and endemic corruption. He regarded Communism as essentially no different than liberalism, but rather a dynamic extreme of the same degenerate spirit and its logical development. It seemed to him a more dangerous phenomenon, however, because Marxism had been elevated to a kind of evangelical religion for fools, dilettanti, common criminals, and genetic inferiors by skillful propagandists, beginning with Lenin.

To Mussolini, democracy was a fading chimera, "the pimping little sister of bolshevism", which Stalin used to unite the masses of his people through an irresistible combination of emotional engineering and murderous terror.[3] The Soviets had shown their hand during the Spanish Civil War, and they were obviously waiting in the wings, off-stage in the east, for the optimum moment to take advantage of any perceived Axis weakness. Mussolini also shared Hitler's demographic dream of a radically reconstituted Russia, where European population pressures could be vented in a new kind of 'folkish colonialism'. Fascism's famous 'Battle for Wheat' in the early 1930s, when only emergency agricultural measures prevented Italy from experiencing severe food shortages, aroused in him special concern for the delicate balance between his country's available productive soil and its burgeoning population. Replacing the Soviet colossus with a Fascist New Order would at once expunge the perennial Eastern threat to Europe – from Genghis Kahn to Stalin – and provide vast expanses of 'living space' with new soil for the over-crowded continent.

While they concede his economic motives for invading Russia were not without worth, some critics of the *Duce's* decision to participate in Operation *Barbarossa* fault his timing, since the North African Campaign was far from won at the moment he unhesitatingly declared war on the USSR. They argue that the 62,000 troops and their equipment in the CSI (*Corpo di Spedizione Italiano*, the Italian armed forces fighting on the Eastern Front), would have been put to better use in the Libyan Desert, where such numbers might have prevailed against the battered but unvanquished British 8th Army.

Aside from the political impossibility of standing aside while Hitler's armies, together with volunteer forces from most other European countries, took the plunge into Russia, Mussolini believed that Stalin's swift defeat would deprive Churchill of his last hope for establishing a second front, and provide much needed mineral resources, particularly fuel-oil, for the under-supplied Axis war-machine. Moreover, Italy's situation in the Mediterranean had dramatically improved with the conquest of Crete just a month before, while Rommel, from all accounts, seemed well on the way to an inevitable triumph in North Africa.

Following Mussolini's garrison review, the CSI's eastward-bound cavalry and infantry traveled by troop-train from northern Italy into Rumania, where they began their long march through the Steppe Region. "These included three very sound and courageous divisions," he explained, "the *Torino*, the *Pasubio*, and the *Celere*, plus the Blackshirt formation."[4] By July, they reached the southern sector of Operation *Barbarossa's* advance into the Ukraine, where they wasted no time in taking several cities and towns, making "a favourable impression" on their German allies, according to Italian Army historian, Phillip Jowett.[5] The Axis juggernaut seemed unstoppable, and the Italians participated in countless engagements alongside *Panzergruppe Kleist* throughout middle and late summer.

On 26 August, Mussolini visited his troops in the Ukraine and met with their 57-year-old leader, Giovanni Messe, formerly a corps commander during the Greek campaign. Messe reported that morale was high, but some important shortages, especially in quality anti-tank rounds, were apparent. The *Duce* promised to send him improved ammunition, but was particularly struck by sympathy ordinary soldiers commonly expressed for the Russian people, "the first and most long-suffering victims of Communist despotism".[6]

Many individual Italians requisitioned Wehrmacht food and medical supplies for the suffering civilians. "The relations of the Italian soldiers with the local population were, as a rule, excellent," Neulen documented, "and, in some cases, exceptionally cordial, and no Italian thought of treating the Russians and the Ukrainians as 'second class' human beings, as the Germans did."[7] Through all the towns and villages they passed the Italians re-opened Christian churches closed for more than twenty years by the Soviet state, thereby winning widespread support from local people. Mussolini returned to Rome more convinced than ever that the war against Stalin was a 'holy crusade'.

In September 1941, his CSI rounded up 8,000 enemy troops during an encirclement undertaken in tandem with the Wehrmacht east of the Dneipr River. Crossing early the following month, the Italians pursued retreating Soviets into the big, strategic city of Stalino, which was first reached and occupied by two columns of the Savoia cavalry. Mussolini telegraphed Messe, "Convey my congratulations to the officers and men of the CSIR, also for the difficulties faced with Roman calm and Fascist fortitude."[8] The Marshall replied, "the victorious troops of the CSIR received your praise with pride and exultation, and showed their great joy by shouting after the fleeing enemy that name which for us is a symbol of victory – 'Duce!'"[9]

By year's end, a battalion of Black Shirt Fascist Militia was in the easternmost vanguard of Axis forces, celebrating Christmas Eve in the village of Krestovka, when they were driven from their stronghold by overwhelming numbers of infantry and waves of fighter-bombers. The Italian response was swift, however, and, after two days of counter-attacks launched by foot soldiers, with mounted artillery in support, Krestovka was recaptured, and the advance resumed.

As the Campaign progressed, the number of foreigners volunteering to fight for Italy swelled sufficiently to merit their own units. Among these were Cossacks of the *Gruppo Savoia*, identified by their white-blue-red chevrons of the old Imperial Russian tricolor. The Cossacks so distinguished themselves in battle they were permitted to wear a style a national dress known as the *tcherkesska*, a heel-length black coat, as part of their uniform. They were later transferred to lancers of the *Novaria* Regiment, and eventually joined German Cossack units, fighting to the very end of the war, after the Italians withdrew from Russia.

Other *Corpo* volunteers on the Eastern Front included Croats, who formed a mortar company, one anti-tank company, and an infantry battalion. Like their Cossack comrades, they were allowed to carry their national colors, in this case, a silver shield emblazoned with the Croatian red and white checker-board surmounted by the title, *Hrvatska*. While some Albanian units were not entirely reliable, the *Camicia nera*, First Albanian Legion MVSN, according to Jowett, "came out of the fighting with credit".[10]

The CSIR's air arm was originally composed of the 22nd *Gruppo Caccia* flying fifty-one Macchi 200s, and the 61st *Gruppo Osservazione Aerea* equipped with three squadrons of the versatile Caproni Ca.311, a twin-engine light-bomber additionally pressed into reconnaissance, patrol, ambulance, ground-attack, transport, trainer, and torpedo-bomber roles. From 27 August 1941, they operated from the small airfield of Krivoi-Rog, just south of the Dniepr River. Within days after their arrival, the Italian airmen shot down six Soviet SB-2 bombers and two I-16 fighters – the same types encountered in the Spanish Civil War – with no losses to themselves.

Three months later, following the Axis advance into Russia, all *squadriglie* relocated further east of the Dneipr to Saporoshje, from which they supported ground forces and escorted reconnaissance planes or bombers. Eastern Front markings for the *Saettas* were the most distinctive of their career: a broad fuselage band, wing-tip undersides, and cowling, all painted bright yellow, with white triangles on the wing's leading edge, and a white cross on the tail. Pilots in the 21st *Gruppo* would eventually be credited with seventy-four Soviet 'kills', losing fifteen of their own, and these mostly through accidents, rather than to the enemy. Among their outstanding flyers was Giuseppe Biron, who became an ace on the Eastern Front, thereafter returning to the defense of southern Italy in August 1943, when he shot down four more American aircraft – a B-17 *Flying Fortress* and three P-38 *Lightnings*.

Members of both Groups presented the Black Shirt Legion *Tagliamento* with a special Yuletide gift when they flew intensive, low-level bomb- and strafing-runs against Soviet hordes threatening Italian positions at Novo Orlovka in the Burlova sector. While Caproni crews slaughtered massed enemy formations on the ground, *Saetta* fighters downed five Russian aircraft, minus casualties.

"At Christmastime 1941," Mussolini recalled, "using forces and weapons far superior to the effective strength and material forces of the Italian divisions, the Russians launched a violent attack. They counted on taking the Italians by surprise, morally, at least. They thought they would find them in a moment of depression and homesickness, owing to the recurrence of the great feast of the Nativity, which the men of sunny Italy had to spend far from their family and country. But the Bolsheviks' calculations were shown to be false. In a bloody battle lasting a week, the Italian troops defeated the Bolshevik forces, and put them to flight."[11]

Three days later, the 369a *Squadriglia* destroyed six I-16 'Little Donkey' *Ishak*s along with three Red Air Force bombers in the Timofeyevka and Polskaya areas, again without loss to themselves. But the flying 'Rats' of Spanish Civil War infamy had their revenge on 29 December, when they overwhelmed a single pilot in a terribly lop-sided aerial combat. Captain Gorgio Iannicelli was the 369a *Squadriglia*'s 29-year-old commanding officer, falling against ten-to-one odds to posthumously receive Italy's highest decoration for bravery, the *Medaglia d'Oro*.

On 4 January 1942, the CSIR soldiers had their first real encounter with 'General Winter', when temperatures plummeted to minus 47 degrees Celsius. Winds and snowstorms were the worst in memory, and ground all operations to a halt. Freezing oil disabled machine-guns, vehicles and most artillery, whose shock absorbers on their carriers froze. Luckily for Axis soldiers, the Russians were no less immobilized by the extreme cold. Taking advantage of otherwise paralyzing conditions, Italian mechanics somehow got the 14-cylinder radial piston engines of their Macchi fighters to turn over for a surprise raid against the Red Air Force base at Krasnjy Liman. In low-level strafing runs, the *Saetta*s shredded twenty-one Soviet aircraft parked in the open, then shot down another five Yak-9 interceptors. On the 24th and 28th that same month, they surprised a flight of I-16 fighters, destroying four without loss to themselves. Another twenty-one aerial victories were scored by the Italians before March was over.

In spring, Mussolini responded to Commander Messe's pleas for additional aid. "No longer three," he later recalled, "but ten divisions were to take part. The glorious CSIR became part of the ARMIR – that is, the *Armata Italiana Russia*, the Italian Army in Russia."[12] Part of the expanded reorganization included combining *gruppi* into the *Comando Aeronautica Fronte Orientale*. It immediately moved further east, setting up headquarters at Stalino, then just south of the Donetz River, at Voroshilovgrad. From here, its air crews mostly carried out ground attacks against massed Soviet troops and armor, as the Red Air Force had been expunged from the sky, at least in the Italian sector, for most of 1942.

With the spring thaw appeared the first naval units of the *Regia Marina* in the Black Sea. They arrived in response to a request by Grand Admiral Erich Raeder, commander of the German Navy, on 14 January. He knew that the Wehrmacht's developing attempt to capture the southern coasts of the Crimean peninsula and the Azov Sea would be imperiled by the Red Navy's mighty Black Seas' fleet, against which his Kriegsmarine could offer no opposition. These enemy units included the battleship *Pariskaja Kommuna*, four heavy cruisers, and ten destroyers, together with numerous destroyer escorts, torpedo-boats, mine-sweepers, and gun-boats. Its twenty-nine submarines had already destroyed several Axis tankers transporting oil from Rumanian ports. Admiral Raeder had been particularly impressed by the spectacular successes won by Italian human-torpedoes at Alexandria, and hoped they might be able to achieve similar results in the Black Sea.

In response, the *Supermarina* dispatched an assault motor-boat group, or MAS, the 101st Flotilla, by rail from La Spezia across Eastern Europe to Simferopolis, where the craft made the rest of their long journey in trucks as far as Faos, which became the flotilla headquarters. Eventually, other bases were set up at Eupatoria, Yalta, Feodosia and Anapa, from which some 200 operations were carried out until May 1943. The Black Sea motor-boats had actually been preceded in April by six 35-ton CB pocket-submarines sent to Costanza via rail from the *Xth MAS*. They targeted enemy submersibles endangering Italian oil tankers with decisive success, sinking two of them in the first week of operations. After the Soviets lost S-32 and SHCH-306, the remaining Russian submarines were withdrawn. Italian CBs were still on duty into late summer 1943, claiming a final Red Navy submarine on 26 August.

The assault motor-boats made their debut by sinking a 5,000-ton steam-boat, followed forty-eight hours later with a crippled freighter finished off by a *Stuka* dive-bomber. In addition to their anti-submarine duties, the 16 motor-boats commonly attacked large barges jammed with Red Army troops, strafing them with machine-gun fire. A typical instance occurred on 18 June, when two assault motor-boats attacked an entire column of transport barges escorted by six gun-boats to Sevastopol. One barge was sunk, and all the others suffered such extensive damages and loss of life their relief operation was cancelled. The Italians suffered one fatality. During the battle for that city alone, the 101st Flotilla carried out 145 missions.

Between the Italian vessels and German bombers, the Soviets were reluctant to risk their powerful Black Seas' Fleet in open combat. The only such occasion took place in the night between 2 and 3 August 1942, as a heavy cruiser, the *Molotov*, and the *Kharkov*, a destroyer, attempted to intercept a German transport operation southwest of Kerch. They were attacked by three Italian motor-boats, but only one torpedo launched by Captain Legnani's MAS 568 found its target, crippling the *Molotov* with a nineteen-meter-long gash in her after-hull. The thunder of the direct hit had hardly died away when the speedy *Kharkov* bore down on the Italian motor-boat. 13cm shells began to fall in near-misses around MAS 568, which was able to neither out-maneuver nor out-run the destroyer, closing fast. In desperation, Legnani set all ten depth-charges at their minimal detonation times and depths, then dumped them over-board during a random series into the wake of his motor-boat. The *Kharkov* ran into a trio of exploding depth-charges that so badly damaged her she was no longer able to continue pursuit.

The 101st Flotilla lost a pair of torpedo-boats and one pocket-submarine, not in action, but at anchor, when their bases were damaged during air raids. The assault motor-boats were extremely busy, because they did not confine themselves to attacking other vessels, but supported numerous coastal operations, some of them the largest in the Campaign. These included forcing the passage at the Isthmus of Kerch; the victorious blockade of Sevastopol, among the Soviet Union's most important manufacturing centers; and conquest of the Crimea, for which they were singled out for high praise by German field commanders.

Frequent targets were enemy coastal installations, which were knocked out by demolition teams set ashore, or raked with heavy machine-gun fire. The 101st Flotilla also took part in the blockade of Leningrad, operating from the Finnish waters of Lake Ladoga, which lost its ice-cap for hardly more than two months each year. It was during this break that the besieged Russians sent out transport vessels. But their supply runs were called to a halt by the four torpedo-boats, which additionally accounted for a Bira class gun-boat, sunk by MAS 527. On 28 August 1942, a 1,000-ton *Manoa* troop-transport was sunk by MAS 528 with heavy loss of life.

On land, Axis forces continued to push the Soviets further east, depriving them of their most important industrial cities and harbors, while capturing mineral-rich regions of the Russian southwest. In March 1942, the AMIR was joined by another seven divisions, necessitating the reorganization of all Italian forces on the Eastern Front as the 8th Army, made up of the II and XXXV Army Corps. These reinforcements contributed significantly to an overall deeper advance into Soviet territory. In May, *Saetta* pilots of the 22nd *Gruppo Caccia* were singled out for special praise by the commander of the German 17th Army for having so effectively protected Luftwaffe bombers during the battle for Kharkov and their successful ground attacks against Red Army armor in the Slavyansk area.

The huge factory center of Rostov fell to Axis forces on 23 July, followed by another, Voroshilovsk, on 5 August, the Maikop oil fields four days later, and the strategic port of Novorossiysk on 6 September. By the time the Swastika banner was raised atop Mount Elbrus, the highest peak in the Caucasus Mountains, on 23 August, virtually all that was needed to end the Campaign was the capture of Stalingrad.

Sitting on the Volga, it played a pivotal role in arms' production and distribution, and was a vast collecting center and clearing house for raw materials. Without it, all that would be left to the Soviets was retreat to and long-term recuperation behind the distant Ural Mountains. As such, the city represented the last major obstacle to victory on the Eastern Front. For Hitler, the real goal of the campaign was taking the Baku oil fields in the Caucasus, as part of the Stalingrad operation. With their capture, much of the Red Army would grind to a halt.

Keenly aware of Stalingrad's vital role in the campaign, the Soviets threw massive resistance across the banks of the Don River, a last-ditch effort to protect the city, 186 kilometers away to the southeast. In early August, from the town of Serafirmovitch, they launched a surprise attack on Italian units at the very head of the enemy advance, intending not only to stop the invaders, but turn them back. The entire Axis offensive was suddenly in crisis. As the *Time-Life* historian, Henry Adams, writes, "The out-manned and out-gunned Italians were ordered to stand and fight to the death. And they did, beating back Soviet heavy tanks with the homemade incendiary bombs that the Russians (who also used them) called Molotov cocktails. In the fighting at Serafirmovitch, the Italians lost 1,700 men, but they captured 1,600 prisoners and a huge cache of Soviet arms".[13]

As described by the Italian historical writer, Salvatore Vasta, "On the night of the 23rd (August), the most forward position of the AMIR, led by Colonel Lombardi and held by *Val Tagliamento*, 18th *Battaglione/*3rd *Bersaglieri*, a horse artillery group of 75/27s, and a Savoia cavalry squadron, received the order to get ready to hold positions against an impending attack to the last man. The vital importance of the AMIR's position was underscored by the fact that failing to hold would allow the Russians to break into the Ukraine and behind the Germans. During the 'Christmas Battle', under extreme weather conditions, and against determined Russian forces, the Italian line held."[14]

Three days later, the 3rd Cavalry Division *Amedeo Duca d'Aosta*, comprising 600 horse-soldiers, together with a few German units, charged 2,000 Soviets defending themselves with mortars and artillery on the Isbuschenski Steppe. The lead squadron achieved complete surprise by attacking head-on, while the other, armed with sabers, rode down the Reds from behind their positions. These were overrun in history's last significant cavalry charge. It destroyed two Soviet battalions, forcing another battalion to withdraw, while capturing 500 prisoners, four heavy artillery pieces, ten mortars and fifty machine-guns.

"During this counterattack," Vasta continues, "the *Tagliamento* advanced furthest, to Woroshilowa, which was a Russian supply depot taken and held against repeated enemy counterattacks. It is said that when the survivors of the Legion marched back past Iwanoka, a German major ordered his detachment to present arms, commenting to Consul Nicchiarelli that 'a new term should be invented to describe the legionnaires of Woroshilowa: *Panzer Soldaten*'."[15]

In the midst of the related battle of Krassny-Lutsk, Messe telegraphed excitedly to Mussolini, "For twelve days these same troops, deployed on the Don in contact with the German 6th Army, have been fighting heroically and bloodily to bar the way against the Bolshevik hordes which, to the tune of three divisions of twenty-seven battalions, have hurled themselves savagely on the sector held by only one of our divisions, of six battalions, seriously threatening the supply lines of the 6th Army itself, extending towards Stalingrad. But they have not broken through! And they shall not! The extremely fierce battle is still in progress, but it will end inevitably with a new and splendid Italian achievement."[16]

The Axis offensive was saved, and the last obstacle before Stalingrad collapsed. By this time, Russian soldiers found the Western Allied portrayal of their Italian opponents as inept cowards increasingly difficult to accept. Even the Soviets' redoubtable T-34 and fearsome KV-1 tanks, which had run rough-shod over the Italians for practically the first year of the Campaign, were being knocked out at an alarming rate.

By the end of April 1942, the first examples of a 90/53 flak-gun mounted on an armored carriage arrived at the Eastern Front from Italy. It fired *Effecto Pronto*, or 'HEAT rounds' which could pierce 70mm armor plating at an incredible kill-range of 2,200 meters. Anti-tank gunners became so highly skilled, Red Army tankers were advised by their commanders to avoid anything which so much as resembled an Italian *Semovente*. Albano Castelletto, a gunner assigned to the elite *Voloire* cavalry, recalled that his regiment operated "with the German infantry, where our mounted battery so distinguished itself with its promptness and accuracy that the German commander exclaimed to me that 'Italian artillery is fantastic!'"[17]

The Soviets' surprise Don offensive struck the Italian Eighth Army on 16 December, seizing the *Comando Aeronautica Fronte Orientale*'s airfield at Kanamirovka two days later, and surrounded 11,000 Italians at Scertkovo. Enrico Pezzi, the C.A.F.O. commander, personally flew into the pocket where his besieged troops were grateful for the provisions and medical supplies brought in a Savoia-Marchetti *Pipistrello* from the 246a *Squadriglia Transporto*. For the return flight, his capacious tri-motor was filled with some of the most seriously wounded servicemen and carried to hospital facilities at Voroshilovgrad, but the aircraft vanished *en route*, a victim, like five other SM.81s, of compromised Axis codes.

Wehrmacht forces led by General Erich von Manstein attempted a breakthrough to Axis troops trapped at Stalingrad. Aimed at crushing the relief effort, an immense Soviet counter-blow fell on the 8th Army occupying positions northwest side of the city, near the Chir River. The *Voloire* was overwhelmed, and two fellow officers took their own lives, rather than surrender. Suicide was often preferable to being taken by an enemy for whom torturing prisoners of war was standard policy. Castelletto was among the wounded artillerymen taken by regular Red Army troops before being handed over to partisans, then force-marched toward a detention center. During the three-day ordeal, he and his comrades received no food, while some of them were stripped naked in the sub-zero temperatures, then doused with freezing water for the amusement of the camp and left behind.[18] Among the Russians' booty were crates of oranges inscribed with the words, "Sunshine from Italy. Benito Mussolini."

Pilots of the 21st *Gruppo Autonomo* C.T.'s last twenty-five *Saetta*s flew their final missions on 17 January, blasting Soviet armor and strafing Red Army infantry to support German troops in the Millerovo area. They also successfully defended Junkers Ju.52 transports ferrying wounded veterans of the fighting at Stalingrad to the rear against overwhelming numbers of Soviet interceptors. The Macchi fighters were now impossibly outnumbered by hordes of Red Air Force warplanes.

On the ground, the situation was no less desperate for Italian foot-soldiers. Just before reaching internment and at the end of his strength, Castelletto, together with other *Voloire* survivors, was rescued in an attack launched by the *Alpini* Corps. In so doing, however, its men had risked their own annihilation, and found themselves trapped near Nikolayevka. The Germans, also in headlong retreat, could offer no assistance, so the *Alpini* fought a series of ferocious engagements with the outnumbering enemy, eventually punching through encirclement on 26 January. Four days later, Axis forces at Stalingrad surrendered, and Radio Moscow announced, "only the Italian *Alpini* Corps is to be considered unbeaten on the Russian Front."

On the 22nd, remnants of the *Comando Aeronautica Fronte Orientale* fell back to their former base at Stalino, where its crews abandoned fifteen *Saetta*s damaged beyond repair before evacuating with the rest of the *Armata Italiana in Russia*. Its soldiers had fought well on the Eastern Front, as borne out by their staggering losses. 229,000 Italians marched into Russia, leaving behind 85,000 dead, and retreated with 30,000 wounded. Material losses were likewise disastrous. Of the *Corpo*'s 22,000 trucks, armored vehicles and tanks, only 3,800 escaped destruction. Casualties in artillery were even more severe, with 1,200 field pieces lost from an original 1,340.

With the loss of North Africa in spring and an Allied invasion threatening southern Europe, Hitler agreed with the *Duce* that AMIR survivors should be returned to Italy for the defense of their homeland. But the *Führer* was not entirely conciliatory. On 6 April 1943, while General Messe's East Front veterans were being re-stationed throughout the Italian peninsula, Mussolini convened with the *Führer* in Austria to discuss the possibility of a separate peace with Russia. Just before their meeting, members of the *Esercito*'s high command, led by General Ambrosio, urged the *Duce* to argue Italy's inability to defend herself without German assistance. The Axis should extricate its forces from the East and concentrate them in the Mediterranean, where the future of the whole war would be determined.

But Hitler had by then already written off North Africa as untenable. Far from being decisive, the entire Mediterranean World, including Italy, was useful only in so far as the fighting there continued to delay the Allies, waste their resources, and sidetrack them from interfering with "this war's center of gravity in the East".[19] Hitler reminded Mussolini of the "catastrophic losses" incurred by the Soviets since the beginning of Operation *Barbarossa*, while the Wehrmacht was gearing up with an array of futuristic arms that would utterly out-class anything dreamt of by Stalin, who had, after all, sued for a secret peace behind Anglo-American backs, and would doubtless do so again, once the Axis resumed the offensive. "For now," he confidently assured the *Duce*, "all we have to do is hold out long enough to allow an opportunity for our reconstituted armies and new weapons technologies to be brought into the field."[20]

His friend's self-assurance was infectious, and Mussolini returned to Rome bubbling with fresh plans for a future that included victory in the East, as well as in the Mediterranean. But after he informed the Italian high command that the war against Russia would go on, General Ambrosia discretely assigned his top aides with discovering ways and means of overthrowing the *Duce*.

12

Middle Age Crisis

*The Fascist Age embodies the will of the Duce in whom all
the mysterious forces of our race converge.*

Encyclopedia Italiana, 1932

Although concealed by war-time Allied propagandists and since ignored by mainstream historians, "the steady, hard-fought projection of British power in the Mediterranean," writes historians Greene and Massignani, "had suddenly come unraveled in a matter of weeks. ... The balance of power in the Mediterranean Sea had shifted."[1] For an extended period from December 1941 to August 1942, British sea-power collapsed between Gibraltar and Alexandria, where her capital ship force had been virtually annihilated. While the *Regia Marina* likewise greatly suffered in the struggle, it, no longer the Royal Navy, ruled the waves. Admiral Cunningham conceded the failure of his fleet in a dismal communiqué to Churchill, when he glumly suggested that "some other means, perhaps aircraft, may be more successful in wrestling control from the enemy".[2]

There were simply not enough warships still afloat to oppose the Axis convoys which now streamed virtually unhindered to North Africa. The Italian victory was clear, but unpublicized, and remains generally unknown even today. A turning point had been reached during mid-December 1941. Supplies flooded into Libyan ports, allowing Rommel to run roughshod over their Allied opponents. He received an unprecedented 150,389 tons of supplies, along with 86,031 tons of gasoline; less than 1% of the material that left Italy was lost. Consequences for the desert campaign were dramatic, as the Italo-German forces switched back over to the offensive. On 21 January 1942, they threw the British 8th Army out of Agedabia and Beda Fomm. A week later, they retook Benghazi, capturing 1,300 trucks in the process. The British were pushed back to Gazala on 6 February with the loss of forty tanks and as many pieces of field artillery. More than 1,400 Allied troops surrendered.

All Admiral Cunningham had left to oppose the Italian convoys were submarines, which he hoped might reassert control of the Mediterranean. Thus began a new contest between his underwater fleet and the *Regia Marina*. To begin, the Italian tanker, *Lucania*, was sunk on 12 February after a British submarine attack. A larger prize was won when HMS *Urge* torpedoed and sank the *Giovanni Della Bande Nere* near Stromboli on 1 April. The heavy cruiser had been on her way from Messina to La Spezia for repairs when she went down with half her crew. British submarines scored again on 29 May off the coast of Libya, where a destroyer, the *Emmanuelle Pessagno*, was dispatched by the *Turbulent*. Another destroyer, the *Giovanni De Verazzano*, was lost in the waters near Tripoli after being attacked by HMS *Unbending* on 19 October. But these successes could not seriously challenge Italian naval supremacy, and were not achieved with impunity.

On 13 February, the *Circe* depth-charged HMS *Tempest* for six hours before forcing the British submarine to the surface. As her crew jumped overboard, she was captured by the Italian destroyer, but sank under tow because of damage sustained in the hunt before reaching Taranto. Another British submarine, P38, succumbed to the depth-charges of Italian destroyers a week later off the coast of Tunisia. Not far from the Libyan coast, the *Pegaso* sank HMS *Urge* a few weeks after she claimed the *Giovanni Della Bande Nere*. On 6 August, again in the perilous waters off Tobruk, the same torpedo-boat destroyed HMS *Thorn*, one of three submarines accounted for by *Pegaso* in 122 days. That month, two more British submarines, *Olympus* and *Triumph*, were lost to Italian mines. The British underwater offensive went down with P48, torpedoed by the *Ardente* near Tunisia on Christmas Day.

Months before, Admiral Cunningham realized the futility of trying to recapture the initiative with his undersea fleet alone. But more threatening than British submarines was the *Regia Marina*'s ongoing oil crisis. On 10 January 1942, reserves were down to 90,000 tons, sufficient for about another month of operations before its ships would have to shut down. Germany responded with enough fuel to keep them in combat until the end of April, when 50,000 tons began to arrive from Rumania on a monthly basis, but this amount was barely adequate to keep the Navy alive. Some cruiser activities, such as escort duty and mining missions, were suspended to reduce consumption, a move that enabled the capital ships a free hand to deal with the Allies in an emergency. The situation improved during summer, when the Germans contributed an additional 10,000 tons in July and 23,000 tons in September. As part of Mussolini's downsizing initiative, the venerable battleships *Giulio Cesare*, *Duilio* and *Doria* were decommissioned at the end of December, their crews transferred to newer, smaller, faster units requiring much less fuel.

By then, reserves were down to 70,000 tons, enough for just one sortie undertaken by the whole fleet. During the previous year-and-a-half, Italian convoys supporting Axis troops in North Africa were invariably menaced by enemy flotillas. Now, it was the Royal Navy's turn, under similar conditions, to supply Malta, the only Allied bastion in the Central Mediterranean. With most of their last available warships, the British assembled a convoy bound for the relief of that besieged island. Before the operation could get under way, however, one of its most important capital ships, the heavy cruiser *Naiad*, was lost to the torpedoes of a German U-boat. Despite this setback, four freighters departed Alexandria on 20 March in the company of an anti-aircraft cruiser, the *Carlisle*, and six destroyers.

A few hours later, after sundown, four more destroyers, together with the cruisers *Cleopatra*, *Dido* and *Eurylaus* steamed out behind them at a wary distance. To divert all potential *Regia Aeronautica* and Luftwaffe reconnaissance away from the convoy, two aircraft-carriers allowed themselves to be sighted south of the Balearic Islands, and the British 8th Army in Libya staged a feint that distracted Italian and German planes from their usual Mediterranean patrols. Additional efforts at deception included a pair of torpedo-boats north of Tunis, where they called too much attention to themselves and were attacked by Italian fighter-planes, which sank one of the vessels. The other was driven ashore at Cape Bon, where it surrendered.

These elaborate measures to prevent the Alexandria convoy from being detected by the *Regia Marina* were in vain. The ships were reported on 21 March by the submarines *Onice* and *Platino* on station in the eastern Mediterranean. The alarm went out, and the battleship *Littorio*, in company with the heavy cruisers *Bande Nere*, *Gorizia* and *Trento*, escorted by eight destroyers, steamed at full speed from their bases at Messina and Taranto. The Italian 3rd Division was commanded by Admiral Iachino, who relished the opportunity of intercepting the enemy force. But his two cruisers and eight destroyers would be up against five cruisers and eighteen destroyers. Hopefully, his renowned battleship would make up for any numerical deficiencies. This disparity would worsen when the destroyer *Grecale* returned to Italy with engine trouble brought about by a massive storm that escalated to hurricane proportions.

Both opposing squadrons sighted each other through the deteriorating weather conditions, and Admiral Vian, commanding the convoy, immediately hid his ships behind billowing smoke. *Gorizia* and *Trento* turned away, a maneuver that encouraged the British warships to leave the concealment of their smoke-screen. As soon as they emerged, every gun of the Italian 3rd Division opened fire on them, and Admiral Vian ordered additional smoke laid down for *Carlisle, Cleopatra, Dido* and *Eurylaus*.

Admiral Iachino brought his force to within less than 10,000 meters of the enemy, shortening the range and maintaining fire as effectively as possible in consideration of the hellish storm that ravaged his ships. The destroyers *Kingston, Lance, Legion* and *Lively* made a surprise run out of the smoke-screen to fire several torpedo spreads at the *Littorio*. But the battleship outmaneuvered them all, and her 39cm guns sent the destroyers packing back into the security of their smoke-screen. All had been severely damaged, especially the *Kingston*, which burst into flames.

With night falling, Admiral Iachino's radar-unequipped ships broke off action, made all the more impossible by winds, rain and waves of biblical proportions. In view of these adverse weather conditions, Italian gunfire had been exceptionally accurate. The after turrets of Admiral Vian's flagship, *Cleopatra*, were demolished with heavy casualties, while the destroyer *Havock* was left dead in the water. Crews of another destroyer, the *Sikh*, were so preoccupied with putting out several on-board fires she disengaged from the fighting and randomly discharged all her torpedoes into the open sea to avoid self-destruction.

Although the Allied convoy escaped through the typhoon, the battle had delayed its timetable by four, critical hours. The quartet of heavily laden merchant ships was supposed to have docked at Malta during the dead of night and unloaded its cargoes

The *Bande Nere* turns to fire at HMS *Carlisle*.

before sunrise, thereby avoiding an anticipated Axis air-raid. Instead, dawn found them still at sea, south of the besieged island, where they were spotted by *Regia Aeronautica* and Luftwaffe pilots. *Sparviero* torpedo-bombers and *Stuka* dive-bombers sent the *Clan Campbell* to the bottom, then inflicted so much damage on the *Breconshire* she was driven aground. While trying to extricate her, the destroyer *Southwold* collided with a mine and sank. Soon after, the *Breconshire* succumbed to concerted bomber attacks, which additionally claimed a destroyer, HMS *Legion*, that had attacked the *Littorio*. Another veteran of Admiral Vian's flotilla, the *Havock*, fled from Malta, but was torpedoed on the run by an Italian submarine, the *Aradam*. After running herself aground, the destroyer was blown up by her own crew.

The surviving merchant ships, *Pampas* and *Talabot*, arrived safely in Malta, but were almost immediately thereafter destroyed during an air-raid before they could unload much of their cargoes. From the convoy's original 25,900 tons, just 5,000 had been delivered. The Second Battle of the Sirte, as it came to be known, demonstrated the unshaken naval supremacy of the *Regia Marina* in the Central Mediterranean. It set in motion the destruction of four enemy freighters and three destroyers, with serious damage to four other warships. The Italians suffered no losses, and their own convoys flooded North African ports with supplies. It would be another three months before the British attempted to supply Malta again.

Another large convoy successfully defended itself from combined air strikes from *Regia Aeronautica* and Luftwaffe bombers on 14 June 1942, but turned back for Alexandria when Admiral Vian in command of the formation learned that a powerful interception force was under way. The batttleships *Littorio* and *Vittorio Veneto* in the company of cruisers *Aosta, Garibaldi, Gorizia* and *Trento*, plus a quartet of destroyers, were steaming at high speed from Taranto.

Four separate and concerted aerial attacks on the warships succeeded in leaving the *Trento* immobilized and on fire with a torpedo hit, and three destroyers separated to attend the stricken cruiser. Assuming the Italians had been stopped, Admiral Vian turned his vessels about again to resume their original heading for Malta. In truth, the main body of Italian warships continued to close on the convoy.

Once more, Fairey Swordfish and Fulmars tried to at least slow them down, but all assaults were spoiled by intense anti-aircraft fire. U.S. B-24 *Liberator*s made their debut in the Mediterranean with high-altitude bombing runs against the defenseless Italian ships. But the Americans' aim was poor, and, for all the hundreds of bombs dropped, only one exploded on contact with the *Littorio*'s forward turret, without effect. None of the attacking bomber-pilots bothered to notify Vian that they failed to deter the Italian surface fleet still heading his way. The Allies' usually exemplary inter-service cooperation had broken down.

Admiral Vian was shocked to learn from his own aerial reconnaissance that the enemy was rapidly approaching, then immediately ordered his formation to come about once more and make for the east with all speed. The Italians pursued him until they were satisfied he would not attempt another run to Malta.

Action in the wake of these events escalated to some particularly violent confrontations. The drifting *Trento* was a sitting duck for the torpedoes of a British submarine. In just a few minutes after they exploded, the heavy cruiser vanished beneath the waves with nearly half her crew. Then Fairey Swordfish swarmed over the *Littorio* on her homeward voyage.

Despite a torpedo hit forward, the doughty battleship continued on her way without loss of speed. Admiral Vian's brutalized convoy was harassed by *Regia Aeronautica* and Luftwaffe aircraft all the way back to Alexandria.

The British cruisers *Arethusa* and *Birmingham* suffered extensive damage, while the destroyers *Airedale* and *Nestor* went down under the torpedoes and bombs of *Sparviero*s and *Stuka*s. U-boats and German torpedo boats operating out of Crete joined in the melee to sink another destroyer, HMS *Hasty*, the merchant ship *Buthan*, even a cruiser, HMS *Hermione*. Against these losses, the Italians prevented yet another important convoy from reaching its destination at the cost of a single cruiser.

A simultaneous success was scored during the so-called Battle of Pantelleria, when a convoy from Gibraltar was attacked by the cruisers *Eugenio di Savoia* and *Montecuccoli*, together with the destroyers *Ascari, Malocello, Oriani, Premuda* and *Vivaldi*. As dawn broke on 15 June near the island of Pantelleria, the Italian warships distracted Royal Navy escorts, allowing Luftwaffe and *Regia Aeronautica* bombers to attack the freighters, which blundered into one of the *Regia Marina*'s numerous minefields. Seven merchant vessels were sunk, including a pair of British destroyers.

Victory at sea meant corresponding success on land. Just three days after these strikes against Allied convoys, on 18 June, Rommel launched a powerful offensive that shattered the Allied line in Libya. Only seventy-two hours later, he rolled into Tobruk, the city that had defied capture for the previous year-and-a-half. Huge stocks of materiel with a horde of prisoners fell into his hands. Thus abundantly supplied, the Desert Fox routed his enemies from Salum to Sidi Barrani, and made them give up their best stronghold at Marsa Matruk. By month's end, he was about twenty-five kilometers from Alexandria. The seizure of that city, the Royal Navy's Eastern Mediterranean headquarters, would mean an effective end to the fighting in North Africa. Axis strategists were even now planning the next campaign, envisioning an invasion through the Near East to link up with Wehrmacht forces in Odessa.

But as the Italo-German armies were about to cross the Egyptian frontier, they began to out-run their supplies. Freighters landing at the captured ports of Tobruk and Marsa Matruk were invariably attacked by strong formations of enemy bombers. Allied interception was uncanny, because warplanes often appeared just as the merchant ships were trying to unload their cargoes. Luftwaffe technical specialists wrongly concluded the RAF operated an improved radar with greater distance-search capabilities. They never suspected that the assassination of Reinhard Heydrich on 4 June literally turned over all Axis codes to British intelligence. Months were still needed to fine-tune the ULTRA secret, but it was already helping to stem Rommel's offensive by pinching off his supplies. They had fallen to record lows during June, with only 41,519 tons reaching Rommel's forces. This already meager amount was further depleted by the 8,000 tons of material and 1,192 tons of gasoline lost to torpedo-bomber attacks.

Mussolini realized the critical necessity of maintaining the initiative and was determined to reassert his compromised supply-lines. In robbing Peter to pay Paul, he temporarily stripped the Italian peninsula of its air defense, sending virtually every available warplane to protect North African ports and provide an aerial umbrella for the convoys. Since the arrival of the *Afrika Korps* in the Libyan Desert, he had been reluctant to take a hand in the Campaign, deferring to General Rommel's admirable flare for mobile warfare. But this latest crisis afforded *Il Duce* opportunity to exercise his preference for radical solutions.

Denuding Italy of air-cover, he jeopardized the homeland by exposing it to unopposed raids by American B-24 Liberators. High civilian casualties would have dangerously undercut his political base at a time when popular criticism of his policies was on the rise, to say nothing of significant damage factories within range of the long-range bombers might have incurred. But luck had not yet deserted him, and the unguarded, midsummer skies over Italy were not darkened by a single enemy aircraft. His risk paid off, as the convoys enjoyed a marked resurgence, delivering 91,491 tons of arms, ammunition, equipment, food and gasoline. By the end of July, losses had dropped to barely 6%, allowing Rommel to make good his gains, fortify his positions and prepare for a renewed offensive that must put an end to the Campaign with the seizure of Egypt. The Royal Navy evacuated Alexandria, where port authorities prepared to blow up the harbors at a moment's notice. In Cairo, British Army headquarters staff burned classified papers, and prepared for a retreat into Palestine.

On 29 June, Mussolini landed in Tripoli to witness this apparently inevitable triumph on the day Marsa Matruh fell. But he did more than wait to attend a victory parade through the Egyptian capital. For more than three weeks, he toured the front, visiting every Italian Army and *Afrika Korps* unit, where he sought to encourage individual soldiers and whole companies alike with his redoubtable charisma. He returned to Rome on the 21st, disappointed by Rommel's reluctance to conquer the Nile Valley, but confident in the ultimate triumph of his forces.

Mussolini's use of almost the entire *Regia Aeronautica* to protect Libyan ports had ensured the successful offloading of his freighters, but he did not have enough aircraft to provide the same kind of cover for all Italian convoys. They were nonetheless able to deliver 51,655 tons of materiel to North Africa in August, although 41% of the gasoline and a quarter of the supplies were lost to enemy bombers. The following month saw an improvement with 20% of the 77,526 tons lost, and October witnessed the arrival of 33,390 tons of supplies, plus 12,308 tons of fuel. Despite losses of up to 26%, the *Regia Marina* struggled through to deliver a remarkable 94,045 tons of supplies to Rommel's forces in November. Whatever damage Italy's military reputation may have suffered early in the North African Campaign was more than made up for by the ferocious sacrifices consistently endured by men aboard the convoys running the deadly gauntlet of Allied aircraft to Libyan ports, month after month.

This phase in the struggle for the Mediterranean seemed strange – almost eerie – to Mussolini for the almost complete absence of the Royal Navy. In truth, all its capital ships and most of its smaller units had been either sunk or damaged. The *Duce*'s fleet had temporarily won the war at sea, but now opposition came entirely from the air. Ongoing refinement of the ULTRA secret ultimately broke the Axis codes so effectively anti-shipping bomber pilots were literally directed to their targets when the Italians were most disadvantaged. At least their fuel crisis was overcome for some time on 27 November, when, in consequence of the Anglo-American landings at French Morocco and Algeria, German forces occupied the naval base at Toulon.

As an important indication of the high esteem in which he held the *Regia Marina*, Hitler allocated 60,000 of the 80,000 tons of French oil turned over to the Italians. This windfall made it possible for them to reactivate five battleships, together with heavy cruisers of the 7th and 8th Divisions. The mere reappearance of these capital ships was enough to crimp British convoy runs to Malta, forcing the freighters and their escorts to risk dangerous passage near the ubiquitous minefields laid down by the *Regia Marina*.

In December, 1942, however, cooperation between Allied code-breakers and aircraft finally began to deprive Rommel of victory in North Africa. Of the 12,981 tons of supplies sent to Tripolitania, just 4,093 tons of equipment and 2,058 tons of fuel-oil succeeded in reaching him.

Typical was the fate of two convoys on 2 December. Accompanied by the destroyers *Camicia Nera*, *De Recco* and *Folgore*, together with the destroyer escorts *Clio* and *Procione*, the freighters *Aspromonte*, *Aventino*, *K.T. 1* and *Puccini* carried troops, armored vehicles and munitions bound for Tunisia. Two other merchant ships protected by a destroyer escort, the *Lupo*, sailed for the island fortress of Pantelleria. Before sundown, German reconnaissance aircraft alerted the first formation to an enemy cruiser with destroyers on an interception heading.

Since neither the Luftwaffe nor *Regia Aeronautica* would be able to operate over the sea after dark, the British refrained from attacking until nightfall, when they could bring their radar-directed ordinance to bear. Their first salvos missed, however, as the merchant vessels hid behind a smoke-screen laid down by destroyer escorts, while the trio of Italian destroyers turned on the superior foe. HMS *Argonaut* was one of the few Royal Navy cruisers still serviceable. Her 21cm guns sank the *Folgore* in short order, then blasted the *De Recco*, leaving the Italian destroyer dead in the water.

But the *Camicia Nera* got in close enough to fire a spread of torpedoes before successfully turning away. A pair simultaneously hit the *Argonaut* fore and aft, blowing away her bow and sheering off most her bridge, together with two of her four propeller screws and almost the whole rudder assembly. Suffering heavy casualties amid the blacked-out hulk, the crew struggled to keep her from sinking. Later, she was towed to Gibraltar, then to a United States shipyard, for repairs too extensive for completion. Meanwhile, after launching her devastating torpedo salvo, the *Camicia Nera* rushed to rejoin the convoy, but she was too late to save it from total destruction. After making radar contact, Fairey Swordfish attacked the smaller convoy bound for Pantelleria in the garish light of parachute flares, torpedoing the freighter *Veloce*. As the *Lupo* came to her assistance, she was surprised by four enemy destroyers, which sent her and the *Veloce* to the bottom in a matter of minutes.

The other Italian merchant ship escaped to land at Pantelleria, a lone survivor of the night's slaughter. Luftwaffe bombers appeared over the scene of battle at first light, but by then four freighters of the Tunisia-bound convoy had disappeared beneath the waves with heavy loss of life. The German pilots did pick up the trail of the British destroyers, however, and sank one of them, the *Quentin*, before she could reach Malta.

Two days later, the *Regia Marina* suffered another tragedy when its entire 7th Division was knocked out of action by the high-altitude precision bombing of USAAF B-17 Flying Fortresses in their raid on the naval headquarters at Naples. A capital ship, the *Attendolo*, was sunk, and extensive damage was incurred by the *Montecuccoli* and *Eugenio*, along with four destroyers. To place the rest of the fleet out of harm's way, *Commando Supremo* transferred it further north to La Spezzia on 6 December.

The warships' withdrawal was somewhat offset by the appearance of a new battleship, *Roma*. She gave the British Admiralty so much cause for alarm the Royal Navy maintained its low profile in the Mediterranean well into the New Year. More compensation arrived in the next five days, when three human-torpedoes were launched from the submarine *Ambra* at Algiers' harbor. Led by 'gamma-man' Mario Arillo – his head, masked in seaweed, poking just above the surface of the water – his *Maiali* sank a transport, the *Berto*. The freighters *Armattan*, *Empire Centaur*, and *Ocean Vanquisher* were all disabled with severe damage that knocked them out of the war. These losses amounted to 22,000 tons of Allied shipping – not bad for three little 'pigs'.

But with 52% losses such as those inflicted on the convoys during 4 December, sending surface ships across the open sea to North Africa was rapidly becoming suicidal. Instead, Italian submarines were ordered to resume the role of underwater merchant ships. Beginning again in January 1943, they ran supplies from Italy to Libya, completing forty-seven such missions with the loss of only two boats, the *Santarosa* and *Sciesa*. While the quantities of supplies they carried were naturally far less than cargoes freighted by purpose-built surface vessels, they at least kept the Italo-German armies in North Africa alive. Rommel often expressed his deep gratitude to the crews by personally welcoming them on their arrival.

Not all Italian submarines had abrogated their true nature as hunters that month. On the 29th, the *Platino* attacked a large convoy headed for Alexandria. Lieutenant Vittorio Patrelli Campagnano fired a spread of torpedoes, sinking two destroyers and damaging a merchant ship, then eluded pursuing escort vessels by diving his boat beneath the full length of the convoy. Emerging at its opposite end, he fired twice more from the *Platino*'s stern tubes to send a large freighter to the bottom. After New Year's 1943, submarines were about the *Regia Marina*'s only operable warships due to their relatively modest fuel requirements. The entire Italian surface fleet of capital ships had been immobilized from January for lack of oil. The following month, a mere 3,000 tons went to the *Regia Marina*. By April, in addition to the submarines, destroyers of the 9th and 7th Divisions on escort duty to and from the dwindling Axis bridgehead in Tunisia were the Navy's only surviving warships still in service.

Right up until the last day of the North African Campaign, Italian convoys, both on and under the sea, continued to challenge increasingly difficult odds. Typical was the night action of 15 April 1943, when two destroyer-escorts sailing ahead of four freighters engaged a flotilla of enemy destroyers. One of the escorts, the *Cigno*, went down in flames, but took a British destroyer, the *Pakenham*, with her. Individual exploits such as these, however, could not remove the Allied stranglehold from Axis lifelines of supply.

In February, 23% of all goods leaving Italy were lost before they could reach North Africa. USAAF and RAF interception grew ferocious over the following months, with 41% destroyed during March and April. Ferrying troops to Libyan battlefields was substantially more successful, because the *Regia Marina* employed its fastest warships. They landed 52,000 men on Tunisian shores, losing a dozen destroyers and eleven destroyer-escorts in 155 round-trips, with the official loss of 3,400 lives, or more than 7% of the individuals on board. Actual losses were substantially lower, because many of the men thrown into the water were picked up by air-sea rescue units.

Between November 1942 and May 1943, 67,498 out of 72,616 troops arrived safely in North Africa, and of the 5,118 casualties, many were saved. An effort to not only relieve Allied pressure but divert at least some enemy forces from attacking the North African-bound convoys was undertaken on the evening of 7 May, when three manned torpedoes sailed against the Rock. Before the knocked-out cargo vessels could sink, *Camerata*, *Mahsud* and *Pat Harrison* were towed to shore, where they remained disabled wrecks for the remainder of the war. The sudden loss of 19,375 tons in the bold attack at Gibraltar, according to historians Greene and Massignani, "did succeed in diverting British men and materials to defending the port."[4] But not enough to sway the course of fate.

That same month witnessed the almost complete annihilation of the Italian convoy system, when 77% of its supplies were sent to the bottom. As a consequence, Axis-occupied Cyrenaica, Tripolitania, Bengasi and Tripoli were evacuated. By then, Rommel and his troops had been pushed into the northwestern corner of Tunisia by the combined British 8th Army and U.S. 5th Army. In a last ditch effort to shore up their difficult position, a trio of destroyers carrying reinforcements raced at full speed from Sicily. But before they were within sight of land, the warships were pounced by a squadron of B-25 Mitchell medium-bombers. All three were sunk with the loss of 900 soldiers on board.

The end of Mussolini's War in North Africa was near. Completely cut off by a relentless enemy air force, his desert army and German allies were trapped on a shrinking Tunisian bridgehead from which there was no escape. The sea that brought them to this impasse would not carry them away. Nearly 250,000 bedraggled, heartbroken men grimly awaited the inevitable.

13

North African Finale

I know I haven't offered you much; sand, heat, scorpions, but we've shared them together. One more last push, and it's Cairo. And if we fail, well, we tried ... together.
Field Marshal Erwin Rommel[1]

Since spring 1941, the Italo-German forces seemed to represent an unbeatable combination. Self-confident and supplied with improved weapons, Axis commanders vowed to switch from the wily defensive strategies that had frustrated their enemies. In 1942, they resolved to go over on the offensive with the capture of key cities like Tobruk, Alexandria and, finally, Cairo itself. Rommel informed his superiors in Berlin that they could expect a successful conclusion of the North African Campaign anytime from mid- to late summer.

"In that event," Hitler told him excitedly, "you will march through Syria, Iraq and Iran, then cross the Armenian border into Russia. There, the Soviets will be caught between our army group presently moving downward through the Caucasus and your forces coming up from the south."[2] Syria was still controlled by the Vichy French, who could be counted upon to allow German passage through their territories, and both Iraq and Iran, although officially neutral, did not disguise their pro-Reich feelings.

Rommel's prospects were even brighter after America's entry into the war. Previously, that country's aid to Britain had been inviolable under the protection of U.S. neutrality, allowing millions of tons of supplies to reach the Empire's forces in North Africa. With the Japanese attack on Pearl Harbor, however, American ships were now fair game for U-boats, which accounted for more than 500 U.S. freighters sunk from January to June 1942. British re-supply fell off drastically, while advanced weapons began reaching the *Afrika Korps* and Italian Desert Army in quantity.

Among the most important was the self-propelled *Semovente* 75/18 gun firing a shell specially designed to penetrate the 70mm armor of the Allies' leading tanks. The *Effetto Pronto*, or 'Quick Effect' round took its toll of the new Shermans and Grants beginning to make their appearance on North African battlefields, just as it had on the Eastern Front against Soviet armour. Unlike the diesel-powered Panzers, American tanks used gasoline, and the Grants were known as 'Coffins for Seven Brothers' by Russian crews who used the vehicles in their unsuccessful defense of the Don. *Semovente* gunners found them no less inflammable.

Arriving, too, was the *Cannone-Mitragliera Da 20/65 Modello 35*, known more simply as 'the Breda'. This 20mm anti-aircraft gun was among the best of its kind, and much feared by RAF pilots whenever they made low-level attacks against ground targets. With improved weapons and better supplied than during 1941, the Italo-German forces began their year of offensive operations by taking Agedabia and Beda on 21 January. A week later, they recaptured Benghazi in a lightning attack that netted them 1,300 trucks before the valuable vehicles could be evacuated or destroyed. Early next month, the British put

Afrika Korps *Sonderführer* Kurt Caesar's illustration of Italian
troops during an armoured attack in the Libyan Desert.

up a particularly fierce defense before Gazala, because its loss would stretch to the limit the already tenuous convoy route from Malta. In the vicious battle that followed on 6 February, the loss of 1,400 Commonwealth troops, forty tanks, and as many pieces of field artillery could not prevent the fall of this strategic port-city. Henceforward, Allied ships trying to reinforce the beleaguered island would be forced to run a hazardous gauntlet between Italian airfields in Benghazi and German bases on Crete.

The British Desert Army continued to dwindle throughout winter, as its supplies were increasingly chocked off and Rommel's combined attacks steadily undermined its ability to resist. No sooner had the 56th Division entered the battlefield against Italian forces on 29 April then the British were forced to withdraw after suffering too many heavy casualties. Less than a month later, the renowned *Ariete* Division decimated the 3rd Indian Motor Brigade, as Rommel beat back the British 8th Army. An immense minefield prevented the *Trieste* Division from joining the battle, until a path through the explosive obstacle course was cleared by the Italian XX Corps. Its artillery then blasted enemy positions near Sidra Ridge, where the British 2nd and 22nd Armoured Brigades were likewise shelled with devastating effect by the *Ariete* Division.

Seizing the moment, Rommel spearheaded an attack through the first line of Commonwealth defense at Gazala that knocked out 100 Crusader, Matilda and Sherman tanks, and captured 3,000 POWs. Alarmed that the entire campaign might be in jeopardy, the British launched a desperate counter-offensive, *Aberdeen*, on 5 June, surrounding the German 15th Brigade, and threatening it with annihilation. Storming to the rescue was the Italian X Corps, which held up Commonwealth troops in the north, while French forces at Bir Hacheim were contained by the *Trieste* Division and German 90th Light Division. The 15th and 21st Panzer Divisions then hooked up with the *Ariete* Division to confront the 42nd and 7th Royal Tank Regiments, the 2nd, 4th and 22nd Armoured, 9th and 10th Indian, and 201st Guards Brigades. After an armoured assault was broken by Italian anti-tank guns at the Sidra and Aslagh ridges, the 22nd Armoured and 201st Guards Brigades were shot to pieces, as Bir Hacheim finally fell to the *Trieste* Division on 11 June. The *Ariete* Division then wheeled around in company with the 21st Panzer Division to drive off the badly battered 4th Armoured Brigade, and the *Aberdeen* counter-offensive fizzled. Now, the British had nothing left to stop Axis forces from going after Tobruk.

On 20 June, the rescued *Deutsche Afrika Korps* and Italian XX Corps engaged the city defenders in savage fighting that developed into hand-to-hand combat. The next day, *Regia Aeronautica* Capronis and Luftwaffe *Stukas* launched a massive aerial bombardment that brought Tobruk to its knees. Among the booty were thirty tanks, 2,000 vehicles, 400 artillery, 33,000 prisoners, and several thousand gallons of precious fuel. Thus re-equipped, the Italo-German armies drove at Alexandria. They overran the original British defenses at Marsa Matruh standing guard at the Egyptian frontier, then found themselves unexpectedly deadlocked with Commonwealth forces at El Alamein.

But something had changed. The British seemed to be able to read Rommel's mind. Wherever he turned his Panzers, enemy anti-tank guns were waiting for them. He was no longer able to surprise his opponents, who seemed to anticipate his every move. Although he could not have known that enemy intelligence officers were reading all his orders and strategic plans, he did suspect either spies in the *Afrika Korps* or Italian turncoats were somehow getting sensitive information to the other side. The traitors, however, were not Italian, but German.

The effects of betrayal were soon in coming. Less than thirty days after Reinhard Heydrich's assassination, the hitherto victorious *Ariete* Division was savaged by the combined forces of Britain's 1st and 7th Armoured Brigades and the New Zealand Division. A week later, on 11 July, the 382nd German Regiment, together with part of the Italian *Trieste* and *Sabrantha* Divisions, was overrun. Mussolini dispatched additional *Semovente* anti-tank guns manned by an elite parachute division, the *Folgore*, the 'Lightning'. Also known as the 18th *Cacciatori d'Africa*, 'The Hunters of Africa', they were ordered to take up positions between Deir el Munassib and the Qaret el Himeimat heights to cover Axis forces while recuperating from recent reverses at El Alamein.

Allied crypographers had yet to entirely fine-tune their so-called 'ULTRA Secret', however. They often lagged behind the rapid change of events which characterized desert warfare. While the *Afrika Korps* was still too weak for action, the *Ariete, Brecia* and *Trento* Divisions captured the Siwa oasis on 21 July. A British attack the next day failed to dislodge the Italians, who knocked out 146 tanks and took 1,400 Commonwealth prisoners.

Undeterred by these losses, the 9th Australian and 1st Armored Brigades overran the *Trento*'s 61st Battalion and the German 361st Regiment. Axis commanders counter-attacked with a *Trento* artillery barrage that blasted twenty-seven tanks, along with thirty armoured cars and trucks. A thousand Commonwealth troops surrendered. Furious shelling by the Italian XX Corps forced New Zealanders of the 22nd Armoured Brigade into a minefield, where ninety-seven *Valentine* tanks and 120 anti-tank guns were blown to bits. Shortly thereafter, the British tried to break through the area held by Italian paratroopers

Italian troops in desperate combat with the British 12th Armoured
Brigade. Illustration by DAK *Sonderführer* Kurt Caesar.

at Deir el Munassib. The 18th *Cacciatori d'Africa* repulsed the attacks with heavy losses
to Commonwealth forces in men and armoured cars.

By late August, London code-breakers had improved their ability to read enemy
communiqués in advance of major engagements. Their expertise was put to good use on
the 30th, when Rommel tried to take the Alam el Halfa ridge. The British were waiting
for him, and knew his plans in advance. Four days later, he was beaten back with forty-
nine tanks and fifty artillery destroyed, plus 2,450 casualties. These losses were especially
painful, because only dwindling numbers of Italian freighters were now able to successfully
elude ULTRA-guided anti-shipping aircraft and naval units. For the rest of September
and most of October, Rommel carefully husbanded his forces for a final showdown that
might yet turn the tables on the Allies, as he had done so often in the recent past. He
was a mortal human being, however, and an over-long tour of duty began to tell on his
nerves. The stress of eighteen months non-stop combat was effecting his health. On 23
September, he was flown to several hospitals in Europe, suffering from acute liver problems
and high blood pressure.

While he was hospitalized on leave in Austria, ULTRA cryptographers flashed the
news to the Commander of the British 8th Army, General Bernard Montgomery, who
used Rommel's absence to launch the second Battle of El Alamein on the night of 23
October. It opened with a barrage of 900 artillery pieces, virtually all of them U.S.-made.
By then, the Eighth Army's shot-up British equipment had been more than amply replaced
by American stockpiles of armour and ammunition, without which Operation *Lightfoot*
would not have been possible. Since the previous June, Axis supplies to North Africa had
been steadily pinched off, as *Regia Marina* convoys were slaughtered by Allied bombers

and warships. The arrival of desperately needed oil and ammunition was reduced to a trickle. Meanwhile, stores of arms and equipment accumulated at Montgomery's disposal.

A comparison of forces arrayed against each other prior to the battle demonstrates the scope of the numerical advantage he possessed. His 230,000 Commonwealth troops faced 80,000 German and Italians. Some 700 Axis aircraft participated, but of this number only 180 dive-bombers and 150 fighters were confronted by more than 1,000 British ground-attack planes and interceptors. Rommel's 1,468 guns contrasted with 2,311 enemy artillery pieces, and he was down to just 210 Panzers, plus another 280 inferior Italian light tanks. These faced off 1,230 Shermans, Grants, Lees, Crusaders, Valentines and Matildas. As though this numerical disparity on Montgomery's side was not enough to ensure him a complete triumph, he had advance copies of all German and Italian intentions, supplies, dispositions, and movements on his desk days before the first shot was fired, thanks to ULTRA intercepts.

Not surprisingly, Operation *Lightfoot* began as planned, but it soon ran into a defensive barrier prepared in advance by military engineers of the *Folgore* Parachute Division. Their 15-kilometer-long strip comprised a thick minefield overseen by 3,500 paratroopers and 1,000 infantry of the *Guastatori d'Africa* manning eighty field cannons and five Panzers. Bracing for action near Naqb Rala on 24 October, they were outnumbered by the enemy five to one in guns, thirteen to one in men, and seventy to one in tanks. Despite these apparently impossible odds, the British were thrown back in four different assaults in as many days with severe losses.

By then, the *Afrika Korps* and other Italian forces had been badly mauled in separate fighting, but skillfully disengaged from the annihilation Montgomery planned for them on 4 November. Only the *Folgore* paratroopers, with 1,100 dead, wounded or missing, still held out, and Rommel ordered them to join his retreat through the desert. He left behind in El Alamein 32,000 men, 1,000 artillery pieces and 450 tanks. Only 35 Panzers and less than 100 Italian tanks escaped the carnage, an amazing achievement in view of the disproportionate numbers they fought.

But the British paid dearly for Operation *Lightfoot*. About 13,560 of their best troops were casualties. The élite 9th Australian Division alone was drained by more than 3,000 casualties, and losses in armour were high. Although the Axis had been badly bloodied, Montgomery's chief goal had been to end the North African Campaign with their capture or obliteration. Aware that the Panzers were desperately low on fuel, he tried to cut them off at Fuqa, but failed. His enervated army was still too weak from sacrifices at El Alamein. Then he tried to pin down the outnumbered, under-equipped Germans at Mersa Matruh, but they escaped him again. For all his efforts to capture the *Afrika Korps*, it continued to elude his grasp.

Neither, however, was Rommel strong enough to counter-attack. His only hope lay in surviving long enough for fresh supplies to reach him from Europe. The *Regia Marina* and Luftwaffe must regain the initiative in the Mediterranean, he insisted to Mussolini and Hermann Goering, or North Africa would be lost. Additional squadrons of *Stukas* and Junker Ju.88 medium-bombers were hurriedly withdrawn from the Eastern Front to escort Italian freighters, while the *Duce* ordered all available warships into convoy duty, regardless of the *Regia Marina*'s fuel crisis.

Just weeks after the debacle at El Alamein, first specimens of the Messerschmitt Me.323 *Gigant* landed near Tunis. With a range of 1,300 kilometers, the six-engine transport could carry a 10,000-kg. cargo of arms, ammunition and spare parts. It less often ferried 120 fully equipped troops with additional room for sixty stretcher patients and medical personnel. The 'Giants' typically flew in large groups at a time, accompanied by smaller Junkers Ju.52s, veterans of the Spanish Civil War and a half-dozen campaigns since. Provided fighter escort by long-range Messerschmitt Me.109 and Macchi MC.202 *Folgore* fighters, the transports played a major role in saving the Italo-German forces from destruction in 1942.

The monstrous Messerschmitts touched down in Tunisia, where Rommel had diverted his armies to prevent himself from being outflanked by 107,000 U.S. troops landing at Casablanca, Oran and Algiers on 8 November. But the Americans posed less of a threat than he anticipated. In their first confrontation with the Germans, a U.S. infantry battalion relieving the British 1st Guards Brigade at Longstop Hill was brushed aside with little effort. The Guards retook Longstop, but another German counter-attack soon forced them off, too.

The British suffered a far more serious defeat that December. *Panzerabteilung* 501, supported by *Stuka* dive-bombers, captured Tebourba, near Tunis, destroying 134 of 182 enemy tanks engaged in the furious battle. The extent of British demoralization was demonstrated two days later, on the 6th, when the mere appearance of three *Tiger* and four Pz III tanks traveling from Dscheideida to El Bathan routed the remaining forty-eight Churchills and Matildas without firing a shot.

Signs of Axis revival continued into 1943, when, on 10 January, teams of nine and ten troopers from the Italian *Arditi* Regiment parachuted behind enemy lines in Algeria, Libya and Tunisia to demolish bridges at Beni Mansour, Bonira and Uadi Bouduvaou. After three years of virtually incessant combat, however, Rommel was ill with an ulcer condition, his willpower drained, and hitherto unrivaled decision-making ability impaired. Instead of riding herd on the panicked Americans all the way back to Casablanca after thrashing them at the Kasserine Pass, he turned around to face the British 8th Army still pursuing him since El Alamein. General Montgomery had been forewarned by ULTRA of every aspect of Rommel's intended attack. At the Battle of Medenine, 6 March, German armour was thoroughly repulsed with heavy losses. But the Axis capacity for swift recuperation continued to frustrate Allied commanders.

Montgomery's pursuit was stopped during late March at the Mareth Line, where his 56th Division was badly shot up by Italian artillery. At the same moment, U.S. General Patton's thrust to the Eastern Dorsal hit a dead end defended by the *Afrika Korps* in front of Fonduk and Faid. Beginning 7 April and for the next two days, repeated attempts by the 34th American Infantry Division to take Kairouan met with such fierce counter-attacks the G.I.s refused to leave their fox-holes when ordered to counter-attack. But attrition suffered by Italo-German forces could no longer be made good. During early spring 1943, the Allied edge in military intelligence and espionage was bolstered by a superfluity of weapons spilling from America's industrial cornucopia.

In mid-April, RAF fighters intercepted a flight of German transports winging their way across the Mediterranean Sea toward Tunisia. Each Me.323 was formidably defended by two 20mm MG 151 cannons in wing-turrets; two 13mm MG 131 machine-guns protruding from the nose-doors, with five additional 13mm's firing from behind the flight deck and positions along the beam. Although some British pilots paid with their lives for close passes on the well-armed *Gigant*, a low cruising speed of only 225 km/hr, plus its

55-meter wing-span, prevented the huge aircraft from executing evasive maneuvers. Out of the sixteen attacked in the April formation, just two *Gigants* survived the encounter.

These losses were compounded with renewed sinkings incurred by Italian convoys, their escorts overwhelmed by five-to-one odds. Of the 60,000 tons of supplies shipped to Rommel in March, he received only about 8,000. Tonnage declined even more steeply the following month. Although the *Afrika Korps* and Italian desert forces operated on strictly husbanded equipment – much of it worn out almost beyond use – and materials captured from their enemies, they continued to inflict severe reverses on the British and Americans until the last day of the campaign. On 20 April, the *Folgore* attacked Takrouna, an important British stronghold. Deemed unassailable because of its position atop a high, sheer-sided hill impossible to climb, it was nonetheless taken by the Division's last 200 surviving paratroopers. They held out for two days against overwhelming opposition, fighting to the last man. That same day, 30 Macchi *Lightnings* and *Greyhounds* of the 1st *Stormo* clashed with twice as many Spitfires over the Straits of Sicily, where the British lost seventeen fighters to the Italians' two.

From 19 to the 29 April, for all his efforts, Montgomery failed to dislodge the 1st Italian Army from Enfidaville. His 56th Division, still licking its wounds from an unpleasant encounter with Italian artillery at the Mareth Line a few weeks before, suffered additional heavy losses. The Italians, horrendously outnumbered and down to their last ammunition in a hopeless situation, set an incomparable standard for personal heroism. But theirs was the final hurrah of the Axis in North Africa. On 8 May, Tunisia fell. Nearly a quarter-million prisoners were taken at the Cape Bon peninsula five days later. With the destruction of all convoy systems and air traffic, any and all means to evacuate them no longer existed. "Owing to the enemy's complete sea and air command of the Sicilian Channel," Mussolini explained, "only very few soldiers and officers escaped capture. A few boat-loads of intrepid navigators left the shores of Cape Bon, and succeeded in reaching the western coast of Sicily."[3]

The Campaign had been decided by its lack of supplies. As Marc' Antonio Bragadin, Commander (R), *Regia Marina*, observed, "The enemy understood that to win in Africa it was necessary only to strangle the Italian supply line. Therefore, the British concentrated their efforts to that end. The Italian Navy in its turn was forced to devote practically its entire energy to meeting this increasingly pressing problem. From the violent collision of these two determined programs, a long period of warfare resulted."[4]

Mussolini knew that victory had been possible in North Africa during 1942 only "if the flow of troops and supplies to the Axis had been on a scale enabling them not only to resist, but attack, particularly in the initial period, when American forces had not yet reached the size they subsequently attained ... as to supplies, these were hindered on a growing and almost prohibitive scale by the English naval and air forces which had command even of the shortest crossing, i.e., the Sicilian Channel, which might well be called the graveyard of the Italian merchant marine."[5]

General Montgomery, for his part, owed the British Desert Army's crucial victories largely to a deadly brew of ULTRA intercepts and U.S. materiel. Not even the genius of Erwin Rommel nor the devotion unto death of the men under his command could succeed against such a combination.

14

Mussolini Island

The English were not so far wrong when, after conquering it, they christened it 'Mussolini Island'.

Benito Mussolini[1]

The collapse of the North African Campaign in May 1943 came as a shock to the Italian people. They knew that their armed forces had suffered reverses in the desert, but total defeat seemed beyond the realm of possibility. They seemed to be clearly winning the war – with some important reverses – from June 1940 to July 1942. How could such a reversal of fortunes have occurred? How could the domination of *Mare Nostro* have slipped away from the *Regia Marina* without its magnificent fleet being defeated in a major battle?

Mussolini himself would have difficulty answering such questions. Incredibly perhaps, his popularity suffered little with the loss of his empire. Secret polls conducted separately by the Fascist Party and the hostile House of Savoy, whose pro-British aristocrats were looking for an end to both the *Duce* and hostilities, both agreed that the majority of Italians were more inclined to blame the ineptitude of his generals (a not entirely unfounded accusation) than his own leadership. *Mussolini ha siempre raggione!* – "Mussolini is always right!" – still held sway. Appalled as they were by the surrender in North Africa, an enemy invasion of the homeland was out of the question, because popular confidence in national defense rested chiefly on Pantelleria.

Lying between Tunisia and Sicily, the tiny island was universally regarded as the 'Italian Gibraltar', a fortified outpost bristling with huge artillery and hundreds of lesser guns manned by companies of elite troops; a sheltered harbor protecting flotillas of torpedo-boats; and a squadron of the *Regia Aeronautica*'s finest pilots and planes. Military propaganda had for years depicted Pantelleria, less than half the size of Malta, as an unassailable bastion shielding the entire Central Mediterranean from regional contingencies, such as the fall of North Africa. The image of an anchored, unsinkable super-battleship was applied to the island.

This characterization, while over-stated for mass-consumption, may have been at least partially accurate until the first year of the war, when Pantelleria's supplies of arms and ammunition were steadily raided by *Commando Supremo* procurement officials to make up for accumulating losses in Libya and Tunisia. By late 1942, the island had been mostly stripped of its defenses, reduced to a fraction of their former capabilities. This 'floating fortress' upon which the Italian people based their faith in ultimate victory, or, at any rate, in a stalemate that would stave off invasion, was no longer able to protect itself, let alone southern Europe.

But the Allies were likewise deceived. They too, believed in Pantelleria's formidable reputation, and were certain the whole Mediterranean Theater hinged on its seizure. A major air-sea operation was designed to limit casualties, which were expected to be high, regardless of any precautions. Several USAAF bomber squadrons were prepared for large-scale raids against the island, accompanied by a naval blockade. Landings would take place only after resistance had been impaired, but high losses were officially anticipated.

"The Italians did not fight with much enthusiasm in North Africa", General Dwight Eisenhower, commanding U.S. troops in newly conquered Tunisia, told his military colleagues on the eve of the assault."[2] But they can be expected to resist fiercely, once their homelands are threatened." British Field Marshal Montgomery observed in an aside to French General Marcel, "if they behave as the Yanks did at the Kasserine Pass, we should have no difficulty taking Pantelleria."[3] The barb was one of numerous taunts typifying ill will among U.S. and British commanders throughout the war, and referred to 30,000 American troops routed by the *Afrika Korps* just three months earlier in Tunisia.

In truth, conditions for the 7,000 poorly armed soldiers and 10,000 impoverished civilians of Pantelleria were dire. Neither food nor supplies of any kind had reached them since January, and drinking water had become so scarce, military and civilian personnel alike relied mostly on the central island's three natural wells to relieve their thirst. Defenses were down to an insufficient number of anti-aircraft weapons and handful of large guns incapable of covering the entire coast. Against these less than formidable odds, beginning 18 May, the Americans launched 100 heavy and medium bombers in two to four raids every twenty-four hours over the next ten days.

Virtually all defenses were knocked out in short order, save the island's few, remaining, largest artillery pieces which had been emplaced under natural rock shelters several meters thick. The only three surviving wells were destroyed, and growing numbers of panicked women and children began crowding into caves or underground ammunition storage bunkers, as their sole protection against the murderous onslaught from the sky. With their homes and all public services obliterated, they huddled, starving and ravaged by thirst, amid stacks of live shells they prayed would not explode.

Roads linking defensive positions were rendered impassable by numerous bomb craters, so emergency crews toiled all through the night to repair them, because workers would have been otherwise machine-gunned during daylight hours by enemy fighters flying low-level strafing missions and shooting at anything that moved. Even these after-dark repairs became impossible following the 29th, when American aircraft illuminated the entire island in the brilliance of descending parachute flares. They were thus enabled to commence the round-the-clock, indiscriminate saturation bombing of Pantelleria.

The carnage was bolstered by salvo after salvo fired from destroyers laying off shore. With the roads no longer passable and most telephone wires cut, communication between outposts had to be carried out on foot by couriers who risked their lives venturing beyond the shelter of caves. Unable to sleep or fight back, all the inhabitants could do was to keep their heads down. Their misery was compounded by the destruction of all hospital facilities for the burgeoning cases of wounded, who were cared for by under-equipped field clinics short on medical supplies of all kinds.

Both German and Italian aircraft made serious, persistent attempts to interdict the U.S. bombers. A communiqué sent from the fighting at Pantelleria to Rome reported that the garrison "has been facing the ceaseless enemy air attacks with unflinching courage, and yesterday destroyed six airplanes." A later radio message cited "eleven more enemy planes" brought down.[4] But five-to-one odds prevented all save a handful of Junkers or

Macchi transports and fighters, usually carrying a few medical or food supplies, from making precarious landings on Pantelleria's holed runways.

Some 250 Luftwaffe and *Regia Aeronautica* interceptors fought their way into the skies over Pantelleria during the last eleven days of its merciless siege, shooting down forty-three USAAF and RAF aircraft, while losing fifty-seven of their own. These casualties were prohibitively high, and forced the cancellation of all further assistance by air. Ordinarily effective motor torpedo-boats sortied together against the naval siege, but, minus air cover, they were strafed by hordes of Allied fighters which prevented them from coming within firing range of any targets.

A final, self-sacrificial effort on the part of both *Regia Marina* sailors and *Regia Aeronautica* pilots succeeded, however, in punching through the U.S. blockade long enough to allow the passage of a single water-tanker. The ship also carried a vitally needed water purification and distilling plant. Tragically for the thirsty islanders, their port had been so devastated by air-raids, the *Arno* was unable to deliver this invaluable equipment or a single drop of water, and forced to return to Trepani. On board were 1,000 German troops originally stationed on Pantelleria. Their departure added to the defenders' demoralization, yet they still refused to surrender.

They had a reputation for incredible toughness going back many centuries. Thirteen centuries before, the entire Christian population had been butchered by Arab invaders, who were pushed into the sea by Roger II leading Italian forces from Sicily during 1123 A.D. 430 years later, Pantelleria was sacked again, this time by the Turks. These historic parallels made some islanders hope that Mussolini would similarly come to their aid from Sicily, and expel these 20th Century versions of 8th Century invaders. But conditions were so awful during the spring of 1943, residents may have felt more like dispossessed persons exiled by the Caesars, who used Pantelleria as a place of banishment during Imperial Roman times.

Sure no one could endure such intense punishment meted out for eighteen consecutive days, the Americans demanded an unconditional surrender from Pantelleria's governor, Admiral Gino Pavesi. As he explained in a communiqué sent to Rome, "throughout yesterday, 10 June, and last night, heavy enemy bomber and fighter formations followed one another uninterruptedly over Pantelleria, whose garrison, though battered by the onslaught of some 1,000 enemy machines, has proudly left unanswered a fresh demand to surrender."[5] His refusal to respond prompted the most severe beating yet inflicted on the island. At its eastern end alone, B-24 Liberators dropped in excess of 5,000 tons of high explosives, more than twice the amount that fell on Malta in a single month at the height of Axis air activity in 1942.

On 9 June, as a consequence of this concerted air assault, all of Pantelleria's fifty-two square kilometers suddenly vanished for the next two days under an immense pall of dust, through which gunners could not sight their field artillery, most of it destroyed, in any case. Just a single pair of anti-aircraft artillery were still operable, but rendered useless by their position high atop Magna Grande, the island's 837-meter-high volcano.

In the clear, blue skies above this unnatural inferno, *Regia Aeronautica* pilots, oblivious to the numerical odds against them, fought with unmatched ferocity. In an uneven melee that pitted fourteen *Folgores* and four Italian-flown Messerschmitt-109s against fifty RAF Spitfires and American P-38s, eight Spitfires were shot down for the loss of three Macchi 202s.

Admiral Pavesi sent a personal telegram to Mussolini, informing him that all further resistance was futile, and, in the name of the civilian population, appealed for permission to surrender. As soon as the *Duce* granted his request, a white flag was hoisted from the antenna of the island's only radio station building. Over its microphone Pavesi informed the Allies of his willingness to capitulate.

Allied propagandists juxtaposed his surrender broadcast with the story of Malta, whose stalwart defenders survived more than two years of air-raids, while Pantelleria held out for less than a month. The analogy was used to reaffirm Italian cowardice and general lack of enthusiasm for 'Mussolini's war'. Such comparisons were not entirely applicable, however, because Malta suffered only a fraction of the bomb tonnage dropped on much smaller Pantelleria. Even so, the *Duce* later learned to his chagrin that the actual condition of the beleaguered island contrasted with its dramatic appearance under fire. During the entire siege, the garrison lost just "fifty-six dead and 116 wounded, almost all of them Blackshirts in the anti-aircraft defenses," he discovered. "The civil population and troops barricaded in the underground hangers had suffered only insignificant losses. The entire garrison of 12,000 men was taken prisoner almost intact ... The hangars, dug out of the rock, had nullified the effects of the enemy bombs. The 2,000 tons of bombs certainly did fall on the island, but on rock, not men! ... Admiral Pavesi had lied; today we may say that he betrayed us. Not even the underground hangars were demolished, and the airfield was left almost intact."[6]

While it is true that the garrison, having been cut off from all outside aid, was in no position to have held out indefinitely, the island could have delayed the inevitable, thereby affording valuable time for fortifying Sicily. Pavesi's imperfect defense, however brief, was not in vain, and resulted in important repercussions for the entire Mediterranean Campaign. Pantelleria had never been a danger to the Allies, who could have sailed past it with impunity toward their invasion of Sicily. By wasting nearly a month in an entirely avoidable expenditure of effort, they provided the Italians with much-needed time to beef-up their Sicilian defenses, which had been no less neglected than those left on Pantelleria. Consequently, Anglo-American troops would pay dearly on the plains of Sicily for this previous diversion to the smaller island.

"It was this damnably stupid 'island-hopping' mentality that gave our enemies the luxury of time," complained General Omar Bradley, "and that needlessly cost so many American soldiers their lives in the Mediterranean. The same misguided strategy was applied in the Pacific, where most islands we took with such heavy losses should have been bypassed, so we could have gone after real objectives to end the war sooner by two years and thousands of less dead G.I.s"[7]

Despite General Bradley's condemnation of 'island-hopping' against both Italy and Japan, Eisenhower granted Mussolini another grace period in yet one more useless operation against an even more insignificant island. For all its virtually non-existent fortifications, the Americans still needed an entire week of massive air raids and naval gunfire to take Lampedusa. With more than a month to prepare for the invasion of southern Europe, Italian troops, accompanied by the *Hermann Goering* Armored Division, took up their positions in Sicily.

To divert public attention from the apparent calamity at Pantelleria and restore morale, Mussolini ordered a suicidal mission far behind enemy lines, just as Italian defenders of the island capitulated. On 12 June, a lone, long-range bomber flew undetected to North

Africa. Since the conclusion of the Desert Campaign in May and subsequent concentration of activity in the Central Mediterranean at Pantelleria, Allied security had gone slack in liberated Libya. Counting on American complacency, the tri-motor CANT *Alcione* was mistaken by ground observers for a B-17, as it approached Benghazi.

They did not, however, notice two parachutes pop from the aircraft and float to earth. They belonged to a pair of volunteer commandos, who stealthily made their way to the Benina North Airport. Slipping past USAAF guards, Franco Cargnel and Vito Procida ran unopposed among the large collection of Flying Fortresses, Liberators, Marauders, and Mitchells. As the Italian demolition experts dashed unseen from the enemy air base, it suddenly erupted into thunderous chaos amid pyres of flames. Twenty American bombers were reduced to heaps of twisted, melted metal, and a dozen more warplanes damaged.

While the dramatic raid achieved its propaganda purposes, it could not conceal the looming presence of the Allies at Italy's southern doorstep. But propaganda is a double-edged sword. While the Americans were duped into imagining that Pantelleria had been a required objective in their conquest of the Peninsula, Italians no less regarded this Central Mediterranean 'Gibraltar' as an impregnable bulwark against invasion. Its capture after less than a month of resistance came as a greater shock to them than the loss of North Africa, and national morale was badly shaken.

"The fall of the island burst on the Italians like a shock of cold water," according to Mussolini himself. "One may say that the real war began with the loss of Pantelleria. The peripheral war on the African coast was intended to avert or frustrate such an eventuality."[8] Remaining hopes were pinned to successful resistance on the much larger, but nearer island, although now the possibility of enemy forces setting foot on the homeland itself was considered for the first time. "With the fall of Pantelleria," he said, "the curtain went up on the drama of Sicily."[9]

Privately, however, he was realistically pessimistic, if hopeful – not for Sicily – but for the outcome of a broader strategy. He considered Sicilian resistance ultimately untenable. The island, thanks to enemy air supremacy, was almost as difficult to supply as Pantelleria had been, and the topography did not lend itself to defense. He nevertheless wanted Axis forces to put up a vigorous fight for Sicily, but only to waste the Allies' time and resources. "There is an Italian proverb," he told his commanders, "that he who defends himself is lost. A passive defense would certainly result in that conclusion. An active defense can, on the contrary, wear out the enemy forces and convince him of the futility of his efforts ... We can still keep the situation under control, provided we have a plan and the will and capacity to apply it, as well as the necessary resources. Briefly, the plan can only be this: resist on land at all costs; hold up enemy supplies by the extensive use of our sea and air forces."[10]

Decisive battles could be fought later, in Italy itself, where the invaders would find themselves greatly disadvantaged by its mountainous interior. Twenty two centuries earlier, Carthaginian armies ravaged the Peninsula. Despite a series of humiliating defeats, the Romans never gave up, and eventually expelled the invaders. In the process, the Roman people grew tough, ultimately creating the greatest empire in history. Mussolini wanted the same for 20th Century Italians, whose reputation for frivolity he considered too well deserved. The inevitable loss of Sicily and Allied landings in southern Italy would be necessary to set the stage for a real contest of arms to take place in the interior.

"In 1917, some provinces of the Veneto were lost, but no one spoke of 'surrender'. Then, they spoke of moving the government to Sicily. Today, if we must, we shall move it to the Po Valley. There, we shall fight the enemy on our terms, not his," he confided to Field Marshal Graziani, forgiven and reinstated after his 1940 failures in the Libyan Desert. "And in an environment strange to him, but known to us like the back of our hand."[11] Fascist propaganda, Mussolini stressed, must make at least something of this strategy clear to the Italian masses, who could otherwise despair when confronted by so many apparent failures to stop the Allied occupation of their country.

"Believe me," Mussolini fatalistically enthused to Marshal Graziani, as Allied landing-craft were about to hit the Sicilian beach-heads, "invasion will have a winnowing effect on our people! It will separate the wheat from the chaff among Italians. In a life-or-death struggle, a people either courageously confronts it and rises to greatness, or knuckles under and disappears. A fifth of the population may stand against us, but almost as many will rally to the *fasces*, more radicalized than ever before, and with them we'll regain the upper hand. The innocuous majority, motivated always by self-interest, will sit it out on the sidelines to applaud whomever wins. We'll have the Revolution all over again! For the time being, it's important the enemy is delayed and wasted out of his supplies as much as possible at Sicily and, soon after, in southern Italy itself, thereby allowing us time to prepare for the real fight in the mountains."[12]

Mussolini was keenly aware of the drastic disparity between Axis and Allied forces for the upcoming invasion. Hence, his dream of luring the Anglo-Americans into Italy's rugged interior, where he would deal with them in the same way Roman legions crushed the occupying Carthaginians more than twenty centuries before.

"At the end of June," he wrote, "a thousand omens went to show that the landings in Sicily would take place in the first half of July."[13] To oppose them, his Navy operated a dozen submarines, half as many motor torpedo-boats, five heavy and light cruisers, and only two battleships – the stalwart *Littorio* and the new *Roma*. Also new was the Italian Air Force's Reggiane Re.2002, the *Ariete*, or 'Ram', and Macchi's MC205, the redoubtable *Veltro*. But less than 100 *Greyhound*s and only fifty *Ariete*s were on hand to confront an Allied air armada of more than 3,000 warplanes flying toward Sicilian beach-heads from bases in Malta.

The invasion had been preceded by a number of attacks carried out by USAAF heavy bombers against Italy's naval bases on 28 June. American strategists were not sure how many enemy warships still survived, and, all too aware that the *Regia Marina* had risen from the dead more than once to wreck havoc on Allied operations, ordered the aerial destruction of the Italian Fleet. In a massive raid against Livorno, the *Bari*, a heavy cruiser, was sunk, the only casualty of its kind. Other capital ships were either too well protected or camouflaged, and U.S. reconnaissance photographs could not account for additional vessels Allied commanders knew still existed. The unknown whereabouts of these missing enemy warships were to keep the Americans looking over their shoulders throughout the campaign, not without reason, as events confirmed.

Allied operations against Sicily began officially just before daybreak, 9 July, when 500 Allied landing-craft carrying 100,000 troops in ten divisions with 800 tanks and other armoured vehicles set out for the beaches at Avola, twenty-nine kilometers south of Syracuse. A massive air-drop by thousands more U.S. paratroopers got under way at the same time. The operation went virtually unopposed, until British commandos arriving in gliders near Syracuse during the pre-dawn hours seized a key bridge over the Anapo. Two companies of hastily assembled Italian naval personnel armed with bolt-action *Carcano* rifles pushed them back to the other side of the river after intense fighting. But as the *Regia Marina* sailors tried to retake the bridge, they were caught in automatic weapons' crossfire that virtually annihilated them.

Odds against the *Regia Marina*'s two battleships, eight destroyers and three dozen other serviceable warships of all kinds were not much better than those confronting their comrades in the air. Between them, the Allies operated six battleships, seven aircraft carriers, seven battle-cruisers, three heavy cruisers, five light cruisers, approximately 100 destroyers, and literally hundreds more destroyer-escorts, torpedo-boats, anti-aircraft cruisers, mine-sweepers, submarines, and corvettes.

Against an Allied air armada of 3,680 machines, combined Axis forces could muster more than 2,000 of their own, but only as much as sixty per cent, or as few as forty per cent of Italian aircraft were operational. The dauntless pilots of these available mounts nonetheless rushed to the defense of Sicily with a dawn raid on 10 July. Thirteen unescorted *Alcione* bombers flying out of Perugia skimmed just above the waves beneath radar detection. The old tri-motors surprised the invaders to score hits on a number of ships and sink several landing craft, though at the price of four *Kingfisher*s lost.

Their costly success heralded a day of ferocious fighting, during which Italian airmen flew no less than 500 sorties in the first twenty-four hours of the Campaign, inflicting damage on Anglo-American forces, but suffering terrible casualties of their own. From 1 July to the 10th, Mussolini closely followed the action: "Enemy losses in planes were also considerable. No fewer than 312 machines were shot down by the Axis fighters and A.A. artillery."[14] In truth, Italian pilots alone destroyed 375 U.S. and British aircraft by that time.[15] Axis losses were almost as high, although the majority of Luftwaffe and *Regia Aeronautica* planes were destroyed on the ground, not in aerial combat.

But as the massive invasion gathered momentum, operations became virtually suicidal. On the 13th, all but one of eight *Picchiatello*s – Italian-flown *Stuka*s from the 121st *Gruppo Tuffatori* attacking the invaders at Augusta – were brought down. The following week, five of sixteen *Ariete* bombers belonging to the 5th *Stormo d'Assalto* were destroyed, even though they were vigorously protected by twenty *Folgore*s and Messerschmitts. *Regia Aeronautica* fighter pilots were to fly an additional 152 sorties throughout July until 17 August, when Sicily fell. During the two-month campaign, some 800 Italian and 586 German aircraft were destroyed. Allied losses in the air approached 2,000.[16]

While waves of assault troops washed ashore, engulfing all defensive installations around Syracuse, troops of the Italian XVI Corps rushed to relieve the outnumbered defenders, but were blocked by four-to-one odds on the ground. Even so, stiff resistance in southeastern Sicily threw the operation schedule off by three days, allowing Italo-German forces enough time to take up their pre-arranged positions. From these, they launched a series of counter offensives that threatened to hurl the invaders back into the sea, something more than Mussolini dared hoped for. As the British Second World War chronicler, Charles Messenger, observed, the Sicilian Campaign "proved to be much harder and longer than originally expected by the Allies".[17]

American troops landed in the southwest near the town of Gela situated atop a commanding hilltop, overcoming local opposition and digging in along a row of hills just south of Mount Castellucio, where they awaited the arrival of additional supplies before pushing further inland. The Italian 3rd Battalion, 34th Infantry Regiment was detached from the *Livorno* (sometimes known as the *Napoli*) Division, stationed a day's march away, to participate in a three-pronged operation aimed at expelling the invaders before their necessary resources could be put ashore. The *Hermann Goering* Panzer Division and Italian 33rd Infantry Regiment were supposed to attack from left and right, respectively, as the 3rd Battalion pinned down the enemy and pushed him into the arms of the pinchers.

While the Battalion column commanded by Lieutenant Colonel D.U. Leonardi was on the march, it was strafed by P-51 Mustangs just before sundown on 11 July. However, training for the aborted invasion of Malta kept losses down to just two soldiers killed, twenty wounded, and five trucks damaged. This low-level attack represented the only attempted interdiction by U.S. warplanes throughout the Gela phase of the invasion, because most Allied aircraft were diverted from the ground fighting on stand-by to oppose the momentarily expected appearance of the Italian Fleet. As events unfolded over the next few days, American infantry were made to keenly feel this absence of air cover.

On the morning of 11 July, the Axis pincer movement began with Leonardi's officers and men storming across a flat, barren terrain offering little natural shelter, save for a few, widely scattered ditches. Intense and instantaneous American artillery fire dueled with the Battalion's mortars and 75mm field guns, as casualties among the charging infantry soared. Helping to account for the carnage and responsible for slowing down the advance were eight American sharpshooters and a pair of machine-gunners firing from a small house on the battlefield. Hand-grenades lobbed through the window silenced them, and the attack surged forward. The Americans suddenly beat a quick withdrawal, during which Leonardi's 3rd Battalion seized their positions, taking a number of weapons and prisoners from the U.S. 26th Infantry Regiment. *Livorno* heavy artillery arrived just then to blast the entire enemy line, from which the Yanks stampeded into the arms of the *Hermann Goering* Division and 33rd Infantry Regiment.

Responding to the G.I.s' desperate pleas for help, Allied capital ships lying off shore opened up on the enemy's pincer movement with a concentrated barrage unprecedented for its ferocity. Seasoned German infantry broke and ran for their lives, as the Italian regiment ground to a halt. Only 3rd Battalion infantrymen continued to move forward, although at an awful cost in human life. But in hand-to-hand combat, they eventually overran the new U.S. positions to take more prisoners and abandoned equipment. Colonel C. Martini, the Regiment commander, radioed the Battalion, praising its "superb behavior in battle," and "the brilliant result attained".[18]

As the Yanks pulled away in a precipitous retreat resembling a rout, the shelling suddenly stopped, and the Italians sent out a reconnaissance platoon to determine the whereabouts of the invaders. Its leader, Lieutenant Baldassare, found "no traces of Americans in the area we patrolled. They are still falling back to Gela. Patrol stands near the Gela roadblock. Waiting for orders."[19]

"On Monday, the 12th, at 1 p.m.," Mussolini proudly recalled, "all Rome and all the nation hung over the wireless with keen ears and eager hearts. Crowds gathered round the loudspeakers. Late that Sunday evening, it had been announced that Augusta had been retaken, and that following a counter-attack by the *Napoli* and *Goering* divisions, an enemy smokescreen in the Bay of Gela gave grounds for thinking that he might be re-embarking his men and material. Communiqué No. 1143 seemed to confirm these reports. It said, 'In Sicily, the struggle continued bitterly and without pause throughout yesterday, during which the enemy tried vainly to extend the slight depth of the coastal

Soldiers of the Italian 3rd Battalion, 34th Infantry Regiment, lob mortar shells at American troops during the Sicilian invasion near Gela.

strip occupied. The Italian and German troops after counter-attacking decisively have defeated enemy units at several points, compelling them in one sector to withdraw'."[20]

Leonardi hoped to seize the opportunity afforded by the foe's disappearance from the battlefield in an immediate assault against Gela, using the momentum of 3rd Battalion's advance to storm the town and push the Yanks back into the sea. His troops had just reached the Gela roadblock and were digging in for the attack, when Allied naval gunfire rained down 21cm and 39cm shells on them. Their numerical strength had been reduced to just 400 men, not enough to take the town, so reinforcements were urgently requested from the 34th Regiment. Leonardi was disappointed when relief came only in the form of a mortar company.

By the time it arrived, however, the enemy battleship barrage had been replaced by salvos of heavy artillery directed from troops of the U.S. 26th Infantry Regiment regrouped in and around Gela, where they anticipated a siege. Return fire rained down from 81mm mortars set up by the Italians on Colle Frumento, a hillock overlooking the town, and American casualties began to mount. After this softening-up bombardment, Leonardi planned to storm the town, from which the foe could be expelled from at least this part of Sicily. But his hopes were frustrated when he was informed that the 34th Regiment had itself suffered too many losses in men and equipment to spare him any reinforcements.

While the main body of his troops withdrew under cover of darkness, the Americans left Gela to reclaim unopposed the vacated ground they lost during the day, and outflanked the Battalion's 9th Company. Its members escaped, however, joining armed motorcyclists of the substantially reduced 155th *Bersaglieri* atop Mount Castelluccio. There, several hundred men from both groups improvised a defensive position around the Battalion headquarters.

Just before sunrise on 12 July, they were shelled by a brief but massive barrage hurled at them from the combined ordinance of field artillery and naval guns, followed by waves of U.S. infantry advancing in a frontal attack. The hopelessly outnumbered defenders, still shaken from their drubbing meted out in the pre-dawn bombardment, continued to fight with desperate fanaticism, so much so, it took the G.I.s two hours of fierce combat before finally overwhelming Mount Castelluccio. But only a handful of *Bersaglieri* and their 9th Company comrades were captured. By then, 70% of the 3rd Battalion's men were killed, wounded or missing.

A glum Mussolini told Admiral Franco Maugeri, one of his captors after the Badoglio coup, "If the *Goering* Division had resisted more strongly, the Americans would have been thrown back into the sea at Gela, and that might have changed a lot of things."[21]

The waters around Sicily were no less hotly contested, although prodigious numerical superiority possessed by the Allies at sea and in the air made Italian sorties of any kind perilous in the extreme. They nonetheless took place. The *Supermarina* dispatched its dozen submarines available for the campaign to attack the Anglo-American armada off the southeastern coast of Sicily, where four were sunk within the first three days of the invasion.

Typical was the *Piero Micca*, among the *Regia Marina*'s most successful veterans in continuous service from the day Italy declared war. According to Jackson, "she was a good, maneuverable seaboat", which, under Commander Meneghini, laid a barrage of forty mines outside the Royal Navy base at Alexandria. She alternated her mine-laying duties with transporting fuel and supplies to Tobruk, Leros and Cyrenaica, eluding the enemy until 29 July 1943, when another submarine, HMS *Trooper*, torpedoed her in the Straits of Otranto.[22]

Such losses were compounded by the destruction of Italy's latest undersea craft, large vessels built to serve as both attack boats and transports, with cargo capacities of 200 tons. Built for long-range missions, they featured numerous improvements over earlier designs, better living conditions for crew members, and foreshadowed today's huge, world-cruising submersibles found in the Russian and U.S. Navies. Among the first of these, the *Remo* was making a high-speed, after-dark surface-run from the Ionian to Tyrhennian Seas. As she approached the straits, she was torpedoed and sunk by another submarine, a British boat, on 15 July. American bombers sank her sister ship, the *Romolo*, while she was on patrol in the same area, just three days later.

The *Remo*'s fate was somewhat offset two nights later by the *Scipione*, christened after Mussolini's favorite Roman commander. The dangerously unescorted light cruiser steamed at high speed through the Strait of Messina, where she was beset by four British torpedo-boats. As they pressed their attack, the accuracy of her gunnery was such that the two leading torpedo-boats were sunk almost at once, and a third set ablaze and adrift. With that, the fourth MTB turned away at full throttle. The *Scipione* would survive the Sicilian Campaign to keep the Allies guessing when she would strike again.

Regia Marina motor torpedo-boats, even smaller in number than its submarines, fared better, when MAS 31 and 73 encountered two enemy destroyers off Cape Spartivento, just before dawn on 15 August. Defying intense deck-gun fire from the British vessels, the Italians closed for the kill. MAS 31 scored a hit on one of the warships, knocking it out of action, and the two motor torpedo-boats retired unscathed. With the Allied capture of airstrips on Sicily, however, further Italian naval operations opposing the invasion had to be terminated. Enemy air supremacy over the battlefield was complete, allowing USAAF and RAF bombers to range at will, attacking all enemy ships with impunity. But the

Italian Navy's part in the Sicilian Campaign was by no means over. In fact, it played the key role in Mussolini's broader strategy.

On 3 August, stiff resistance on the Catania plain, where the island's last defenses had been gathered, could no longer be expected to hold out against the combined weight of the American 5th and British 8th Armies about to trap Axis forces at Messina. In what General Eisenhower assumed would be hardly more than a formality, he was surprised to find all attempts at closing the gap there firmly rebuffed.

While German and Italian units held the Allies at bay, a veritable fleet of small, auxiliary vessels that had been kept in reserve for the present contingency steamed at high speed from Calabria on the Italian mainland toward Sicily's northwest coast. They comprised motley flotillas of mine-sweepers, tugs, motorized barges, fishing boats, yachts, schooners, excursion vessels, ferries, and almost anything that could float. These disparate units were covered by the last specimens of Reggiane *Ariete* and Macchi *Veltro* fighters, which gave Mustang and Spitfire pilots a run for their money, despite Allied numerical supremacy.

Word spread that the redoubtable *Littorio* and *Roma* battleships, accompanied by the *Scipione*, together with every other surviving Italian warship, were on their way to clear the Messina Channel in a suicide run. Although untrue, U.S. naval authorities and British Admiralty commanders, unprepared for such an imaginary confrontation, quickly withdrew most of their surface units from around northern Sicily, allowing the masses of auxiliary vessels to pass largely unmolested, at least at sea. Most destruction came from the sky, but Italy's odd assortment of ships and boats continued to evacuate troops and supplies amid a torrent of falling bombs.

The rescue operation continued non-stop for nearly two weeks, despite all opposition by Anglo-American forces. They were gradually taking ground, although at the highest attrition rate of the entire campaign. On 16 August, the last ferry carrying men and materiel away from Sicily steamed out of Messina, just as British troops entered the other end of the city. Its port facilities were being blown to bits under the falling bombs of an American air-raid, while Italian demolition experts sabotaged permanent installations. Despite losses among the odd assortment of vessels participating in the evacuation, they saved more than 70,000 German and Italian soldiers, including 10,000 tanks, armored cars, trucks and various military vehicles. In excess of 17,000 tons of ammunition arrived safely in Calabria.

From Mussolini's point of view, the Sicilian Campaign concluded in Italy's favor. "It was a success," he stressed, "not a victory. That will come later, because the men and resources that can make it happen escaped to fight another day, on our terms, not the enemy's." Ironically, this optimism was voiced while he was under arrest after the fall of his Fascist regime. "The British escaped annihilation at Dunkirk," he told his sympathetic captors, "and look where they are now! If they could do it, so can we. We did it at Sicily, and we shall triumph in the end!"[23]

15

The Ordeal of Blood

*There is only one way to redeem our disgrace, to re-establish the equilibrium,
and that is by the sternest of all ordeals – the ordeal of blood. Only
through this ordeal shall we be able to answer another and no less grievous
question: Are we faced with an eclipse or with a final sunset?*
Mussolini[1]

Observers on the ground at a training field near Pisa gasped in horror, as a four-engined heavy bomber only a few hundred meters overhead seemed to hang in mid-air a moment before losing control in a precipitous stall. The thirty-three-ton aircraft nosed down to plummet in an explosive crash that killed every man on board. Among them was Bruno Mussolini. The accident may have similarly marked the beginning of the end of the young man's father, who never fully recovered emotionally from the loss of his son. "There was a Mussolini before Bruno's death," Vittorio, the *Duce*'s son, remembered, "and a Mussolini after it. I'm not saying that prior to 7 August 1941, our father smiled often, but despair was not part of his emotional range. The tragedy turned him into a different man, whose lost stare, at times, provoked pity."[2]

The many thousands of letters and telegrams expressing sympathy from surviving family members who lost their own children in the war may have created a new, personal bond between the Italian people and their *Duce*, but they were little compensation to him. In *I Speak With Bruno* published shortly after his son's accident, he wrote with a sad mixture of guilt and pride, "My 'live dangerously' was fulfilled in your life."[3]

Bruno's death did not seem to impair Benito Mussolini's decision-making powers, although it did mark the onset of gastric problems which grew more intense over the years to come. Recurring bouts of stomach pain were sometimes so severe, he occasionally removed himself from the direction of the war.

Close associates also noticed an air of fatalism bordering on resignation that infrequently clouded his spirits. But he invariably roused himself with renewed enthusiasm by delving into some new plan. During autumn 1942, his suffering seems to have become especially acute, but doctors were helpless to do much for him, because they understood that his condition resulted from the heavy burden of anxiety imposed on him by the war, a stress exacerbated by extended mourning for the premature death of his son.

On 11 October, he was visited by *Reichsführer SS* Heinrich Himmler, widely regarded as among the most amiable of all the Nazi élite, even by British and American pre-war visitors to Germany, despite his horrendous reputation. The two men were old friends, and the *Duce* was always made to feel at ease in his presence. Himmler had ostensibly stopped by for an informal lunch, during which the conversation turned to their mutual health concerns. The *Reichsführer* had come to Rome, he said, in search of treatment for similar gastric ailments, and Mussolini was happy to oblige him with a few medical contacts.

In reality, Himmler had been personally dispatched by Hitler to assess the condition of Fascism in Italy and, specifically, the *Duce's* health.

Returning to Berlin, Himmler reported that so long as Mussolini lived, Fascism would remain the popular phenomenon it had become and continue to stand by the German alliance. True, there was evidence of growing discontent with the progress of the war in some major cities, but it appeared to be mostly aimed at the *Duce's* underlings, not at the man himself. His health was not as vigorous as it should be, but he still seemed physically competent to withstand the rigors of office, at least for the next few years. Even so, Himmler emphasized, Mussolini would do well to find someone with whom he could partially share his heavy responsibilities. Unfortunately, no man approached the *Duce's* leadership stature. If he died suddenly or were overthrown, Italy would almost certainly disintegrate into national chaos and withdraw from the war, possibly even turn against Germany.

Less than two weeks after the *Reichsführer's* visit, Axis forces in North Africa were severely mauled in the Battle of El Alamein, and Mussolini began to lose faith in winning a two-front war. His suspicions were confirmed in early winter 1942, when a tidal-wave of Soviet troops and materiel overwhelmed Axis positions along the frozen Don River, setting the stage for the debacle at Stalingrad. On 16 December, his foreign minister, Count Ciano, met with Hitler to sound him out on the possibility of coming so some kind of terms with Stalin for an end of the fighting on the Eastern Front. Italo-German forces would then be free to concentrate their combined might on deciding the North African Campaign, where the war would be finally won.

The *Führer* would have none of it. Russia was at the end of her rope, he insisted. By spring, the Caucasus would fall, closing down the Soviets' major manufacturing capabilities. Then support could be diverted from the East to Rommel's conquest of Egypt. "All we need are a few more months to stabilize the situation on the Don," he said, "before we can bring all our strength to bear in the Libyan Desert."[4]

Ciano was unimpressed. He confided to Mussolini that Italy must extricate herself from the war before she was made to pay too high a penalty for her association with the Third Reich. "I do not see how that is possible," the *Duce* confessed, "unless you are suggesting a separate peace with the Allies. If so, I hardly need remind you of the German consequences of such an act. Still, we must consider all options where the survival of our country is concerned. Let's give Hitler a chance. He's been right before, when everyone else thought he was wrong. We can certainly hang on in North Africa through early spring. Besides, a final decision on this matter is not demanded just now."[5]

Ciano agreed, but put out feelers to certain members of the Fascist Grand Council who would be interested in deposing Mussolini as soon as possible. On 8 January 1943, he conspired with two of them – Giuseppe Bottai, a university professor, and Minister of State, Roberto Farinacci – to put forward the inept Field Marshal Ugo Cavallero or opportunistic Field Marshal Pietro Badoglio as candidates for the *Duce's* replacement. At his retreat in La Rocca della Caminate, where Mussolini was recovering from a flare up of his gastric disorder, he learned of the covert meeting through OVRA, the *Organizzazione Vigilanza Repressione Antifascismo*, his secret police.

Realizing that the use of drastic measures in wartime would only undermine the nation's already shaky morale, he drew up a list of loyal Fascists he intended to take the positions of unreliable government men. His first move came on 31 January, when he

THE ORDEAL OF BLOOD   179

replaced the armed forces Chief-of-Staff, Cavallero, with the non-Fascist but apparently patriotic General Vittorio Ambrosio. A few days later, Ciano was relieved of his responsibilities but left unmolested, while OVRA agents watched his every move.

Although Mussolini seemed to have scotched mutiny in the ranks of his own government, he was powerless to suppress it elsewhere. On 5 March, the unthinkable happened when the Fiat Aviation plant in Turin went on strike, the first ever since the *Duce* took office in 1922. He was appalled and ordered the Fascist militia to put down the work stoppage by compulsion if necessary, stating that wartime necessity justified such action. More incredibly, the militia openly disobeyed him, refusing to force the workers back to the plant. The strike spread to neighboring northern cities, threatening to do serious damage to Italy's military production. It was no coincidence that Turin, where the strikes originated, had been the center of *Giustiziae e Liberta* ten years before. Although the underground movement appeared to have been successfully crushed by the onset of the Ethiopian War, a few 'sleeper cells' waited in patient dormancy for the right moment to strike again.

Then, just as quickly as the labor unrest flared up, it died out. Before month's end, the Fiat factory was operating again at full capacity, and the remainder of Mussolini's reign was unplagued by work stoppages. He owed the quick solution of this potentially incendiary situation not to the rubber truncheons of strike-breaking police, but unknown workers still loyal to him. They convinced their fellow assembly-line laborers that shutting down Italy's means of arms production would be a dishonorable betrayal of soldiers at the front. In countless, unofficial meetings and extempore speeches from factory benches, the strike leaders were shouted down, and order restored. The *Duce* was a lucky man, and he knew it.

With renewed confidence in the support of his people, he traveled by train to meet Hitler in Austria on 6 April. By now, the situation at the Don was supposed to have turned in favor of the Axis, with forces from the Eastern Front diverted to North Africa for the final victory there. Instead, 110,000 German, Rumanian and Croatian troops had fallen at Stalingrad and another 91,000 made prisoner the previous January. Meanwhile, Rommel's situation in Tunisia was becoming daily less tenable. He could not be expected to hold out much longer.

With the imminent loss of North Africa, the Anglo-Americans would be in a position to assault Sicily and the Italian mainland. To save Europe from eventual invasion, Mussolini believed, a peace must be made with Stalin, who had already demonstrated his willingness to conclude a strictly Russian-Axis armistice behind the backs of his Western partners. That done, Germany and Italy could get on with winning the war against the British and Americans while there was still time.

Hitler had some fast talking to do if he did not want to lose his Italian ally. He flattered him by disclosing all his secret plans for Operation *Citadel*, an enormous counter-offensive set to regain the initiative in the East at Kursk in early July. True, the Allies might take North Africa by then, but winning the Russian Campaign would more than compensate such a loss, if only because the Axis could then devote all their energies to defeating the enemy in the Mediterranean. He spoke, too, of Germany's secret weapons' program based on technological advances far beyond anything envisaged by the Anglo-Americans with their propeller-driven warplanes and conventional explosives.

"In Germany," Mussolini told his teenage son, Romano, "Hitler himself took me to the factories manufacturing the arms that will turn the war around. What's important

Rendering of Adolf Hitler's own sketch for a proposed monument to Benito Mussolini. Scheduled to be set up in Berlin, its construction was halted by the Second World War.

is not to lose faith. The rest will come on its own."[6] It was on this tour that he learned for the first time about the jet aircraft, cruise missiles, ballistic rockets, and, most secret of all, an atomic bomb under development in the Reich. The prospect of fielding this futuristic military technology caught fire in the *Duce*'s imagination. He now believed with the *Führer* that all the Axis forces needed do was to hold out, delay the Allies long enough – even at the expense of otherwise vital territories – for the inevitable deployment of these 'wonder weapons'.

But his enthusiasm for continuing the war did not spread to his new Chief-of-Staff. After leaning of Mussolini's new resolve to fight to the bitter end, General Ambrosio initiated his own plan for removing him from power. Meanwhile, the war went from bad to worse. On 10 April, the Italian cruiser, *Trento*, was sunk by American heavy bombers near La Maddalena. From 20 to 21 April, the *Folgore* Parachute Division fought to the last man defending the Takrouna stronghold. But Tunisia finally fell to the Allies on 8 May, followed on the 13th by the surrender of 275,000 German and Italian troops at the Cape Bon peninsula. Italians regarded Pantelleria as the rock on which any Anglo-American invasion of Italy would shatter.

But with the surrender of the fortress-island on 12 June, the country was faced with the gravest crisis in its history. Four days later, Mussolini met in council with fifteen cabinet members, who suggested that he relinquish at least some of his responsibilities, although his continued position as the nation's supreme authority was really at issue. To their surprise, he readily agreed to bring the matter to the attention of the next Grand Council meeting scheduled for the following week, and promised to abide by its majority decision, whatever the outcome.

The next several days were filled with momentous incident. On 17 July, after months of virtually unrelieved defeat at sea, the Italian cruiser, *Scipione Africano*, won a stunning naval action against a squad of British motor torpedo-boats off Messina, as described earlier. The success was important to Mussolini, because it gave him some measure of confidence when he met just two days later with Hitler in the northern Italian town of Feltre. The *Duce*'s entourage urged him to ask the *Führer* for assistance in extracting Italy from the war before the Anglo-Americans invaded the peninsula. But Mussolini knew such a request would fall on deaf ears, and instead arranged for direct military assistance.

The arrival of German troops and arms on Italian soil would be a joint effort with the *Esercito* to defend Italy, but under direct Wehrmacht control. Although critics portrayed the stationing of Hitler's forces in Italy as his most recent conquest, it was, in fact, fulfillment of the Axis Pact, drawn up four years earlier, when first Germany and Italy, then Japan, Rumania, Bulgaria and several other mostly Eastern European nations pledged to aid one another in the event of attack or invasion.

While the two men were conferring, American B-24 Liberators were carrying out the first heavy bombing of Rome. The attack came as a terrible shock to both the Italian people and their leaders. Rome was regarded as a *citta sacra*, a 'sacred city', undefended for lack of any strategic targets. USAAF commanders had nevertheless deemed the Eternal City's government offices worthy of annihilation, and hoped the raid might help bring the Italians to their senses. Pope Pius XII rushed into the streets, administering last rites to the dead and the dying, his robes soaked with their blood. 1,400 mostly non-combatant men, women and children – including numbers of priests and nuns attending the wounded at Rome's General Hospital – perished in the attack. Another 6,000 were injured.

"One more illusion had vanished in smoke," Mussolini sadly declared, "namely, that Rome, the Holy City, would never be raided; that the best anti-aircraft artillery was the Vatican itself; that Myron Taylor (a U.S. businessman and Freemason, he was Franklin Roosevelt's personal emissary to the Holy See) had brought the Pope a guarantee to that effect from the American President, and other things of that nature – hopes, desires – all of that had been wiped out by a brutal bombardment which had lasted nearly three hours, had caused thousands of victims, and destroyed whole quarters of the city."[7]

In their efforts to break Italian morale, Allied air ministers ordered the additional 'carpet bombing' of Genoa, La Spezia, Milan, Naples, and Turin. Until now, RAF and USAAF air raids killed 64,000 civilians, injuring tens of thousands more. In a spirited response, *Regia Aeronautica* interceptors were credited with shooting down 275 U.S. and British bombers over Italy from spring until 8 September 1943, although the actual tally was substantially higher. It was during this desperate period that some of Italy's best fighter pilots became aces by destroying five or more enemy aircraft. On 27 August, for example, the 3rd *Stormo* C.T.'s Luigi Gorrini, flying a Macchi *Veltro*, shot down two Boeing B-17 Flying Fortresses and a Lockheed P-38 Lightning over Latium in central Italy during a single engagement. At the time of the armistice a few days later, his score would rise to twenty-one 'kills'.

But on 24 July, the shadow of Rome's first air raid hung over the Grand Council when its members convened to consider the fate of their *Duce*. Leader of the opposition was Dino Grandi, President of the Chamber of *Fasci* and Corporations, who despised Germans and Italy's alliance with them. According to Romano Mussolini, "my father still allowed Grandi to present his order of the day, knowing full well that it would mean his ruin. Despite the fact that *Il Duce* had the militia on his side, as Galbati and other loyal Fascist leaders had repeatedly assured him, he didn't try to react. It would have been very easy for him to block Grandi's initiative on the no-confidence vote. He could have done so right up to the last moment of that interminable meeting, by having the militia enter the room after deactivating the door-blocking device. The door control was in front of him – a small push-button apparatus attached to the underside of the long U-shaped table around which the voters seated. All *Il Duce* had to do was press a button to put an end to the conspirators, and many others in the room would have certainly denounced them as well."[8]

As promised, Mussolini subjected his personal future to a roll-call of cabinet members. The vote went against him, nineteen to seven, with two abstentions. The next day, again according to protocol, he personally reported the Grand Council's confirmation to King Victor Emmanuelle. The monarch despised such political popularity contests, and contemptuously brushed aside its majority vote as vulgar, whichever way it had gone. All that mattered, he insisted, was that Italy get out of the war which had made the *Duce* the most hated person in his own country.

"At this moment," Mussolini replied, "I am certainly the most intensely disliked, or, rather, loathed man in Italy, which is only natural on the part of the ignorant, suffering, victimized, under-nourished masses subjected to the terrible physical and moral burden of the 'Liberator' raids, and to the suggestions of enemy propaganda. Political and military circles aim their sharpest criticisms at those who bear the responsibility for the military conduct of the war."[9]

With that, he tendered his resignation. Victor Emmanuelle seemed compassionate, offering an armed escort of his own palace guards to convey Mussolini home. In fact, the disingenuous monarch had been conspiring for weeks with Duke Pietro Acquarone, Minister of the Royal Household, who, as Klibansky noted, "played a leading part in the *coup d'état* of July 1943, acting as the King's chief advisor and go-between, and coordinating the actions of the generals with those of the Court."[10] The palace guards Victor Emmanuelle assured Mussolini were for his protection instead placed him under arrest. Sixty years later, his son, Romano, asked rhetorically, "Is it true that Hitler, whom my father met at Feltre on 19 July 1943, six days prior to the king arresting my father and subsequently confining him at Gran Sasso, wanted to have a detachment of the SS protect him --- a development that would have changed the course of events?"[11]

The day of Mussolini's arrest, Pietro Badoglio, dismissed and disgraced for his failed campaigns in Libya and Greece, proclaimed himself as new prime minister in such evasive language Italians everywhere were unsure the *Duce* had voluntarily retired or been overthrown, especially after the Marshal told them that the war would continue at Germany's side. According to historians Greene and Massignani, "Most of the officers and men of the Italian armed forces were caught completely by surprise."[12]

The King's own nephew, the Duke of Aosta, was no less astounded, and dismissed the radio announcement as 'enemy propaganda'. Confusion combined with domestic wartime conditions to facilitate Mussolini's effortless overthrow. "Over a million Fascists were under arms," he explained, "from the Var to Rhodes, from Ajaccio to Athens. Only a few members of the Party remained in Italy, and they had dedicated themselves almost exclusively to social service."[13]

Having publicly pledged his loyalty to Germany, Badoglio at the same moment undertook secret surrender negotiations with the Allies through the Vatican. They specified that Italy should be allowed the protection of a formal armistice in exchange for declaring war on the Third Reich. The Allied Supreme Commander hesitated to accept, because Anglo-American policy called for Italy's unconditional surrender. Amid general uncertainty and growing confusion, chaos began to spread outward from Rome like shock waves from a seismic epicenter.

In an effort to win over General Eisenhower, Badoglio indiscriminately rounded up several hundred loyal Fascists and had them shot to death on the spot without trial, then disclosed the positions, strengths and weaknesses of all German troop placements throughout the peninsula. It was not enough. Eisenhower responded that the Marshal had just forty-eight hours to have the Italian military stand down, free all captured prisoners, turn over the country's arsenals, and accept the establishment of an Allied military government. Badoglio balked. He had offered friendship to the Allies, but they were treating him like the powerless spokesman of an already vanquished nation.

On 17 August, Sicily fell, followed a fortnight later by two British divisions landing at Reggio di Calabria. Unsure Italian resistance continued, because Badoglio had been in the grip of indecision for more than a month before he finally repudiated the Allies' draconian terms. His procrastination continued to cost the lives of soldiers on both sides. Ignoring the turncoat Marshal, Eisenhower broadcast Italy's surrender on 8 September. Badoglio was compelled to either accept it, or run the risk of being caught simultaneously between the Anglo-Americans and the Germans. That same day, he informed his fellow countrymen that the cost of peace with the Allies was war with Hitler. The announcement plunged Italy into civil war, as pro-Fascists sought protection with the Wehrmacht invading from the north, and anti-Fascists embraced the Allied invasion from the south.

While the two camps began to define their territories and square off, the fate of the Italian Fleet was in serious doubt. Part of Eisenhower's surrender terms included "the immediate transfer of the Italian Fleet and its aircraft to those places that will be designated by the Allied Command with the details of their disarmament."[14] In other words, they were to be spoils of war, contrary to earlier assurances that the Fleet would be merely deactivated. As Admiral (ret.) Bragadine observed, "It is true that later the Italian Navy was treated quite differently from what it was led to expect by the promises and pledges of the Allies."[15]

Several battleships, a number of cruisers and auxiliary vessels were still serviceable, and the Anglo-Americans wanted them for their proposed invasion of southern France. The *Supermarina's* plan to either scuttle its remaining ships or suicide them against the enemy in the event of a national surrender had been set aside by Eisenhower's terms, which called for the mobilization of all Italian resources against Germany.

Shame ran deep and widespread throughout all ranks of the *Regia Marina*, as the same warships that had only a year before virtually scoured the British from the Central Mediterranean were now led in pitiful procession by Admiral Cunningham aboard his Royal Navy flagship into the service of their enemies. His prize catch was the *Roma*, a new, state-of-the-art battleship, which set out independently under orders to intern herself in Malta. From her bridge, Admiral Carlo Bergamini, as the Naval High Commander, led the line of other Italian vessels into captivity. Details of the humiliating surrender terms had been deliberately withheld from him by Badoglio to avoid losing the Fleet in its proposed last sortie against the enemy.

Bergamini had fired up the *Roma's* boilers after learning of the Allied landings at Salerno, which he anticipated opposing in coordination with the Luftwaffe. Only after he was safely out at sea was he notified of Italy's altered position on 9 September, a day following the armistice. His battleship joined up with two others, the *Vittorio Veneto* and *Littorio* (renamed the more politically correct *Italia* after Mussolini's arrest), together with the cruisers *Eugenio di Savoia, Montecuccoli* and *Regolo*, and eight destroyers.

As this remnant of the Italian Fleet steamed through the Gulf of Asinara into the Straits of Bonifacio, morale plummeted, and a rash of suicides broke out on all the ships. Some officers urged Admiral Bergamini to make for neutral, Axis-friendly Spain, which he appeared to do when he led the ships through the Bocche di Bonifacto, a strait between Corsica and Sardinia, turning away from the course to Malta laid out for him by Admiral Cunningham.

Luftwaffe reconnaissance located the *Roma*, but the Germans drew the wrong conclusion. Admiral M. Bohlken, the Wehrmacht commander at La Spezia, was by then aware of Badoglio's agreement with the Allies, and notified Berlin at once: "The Italian Fleet has departed during the night to surrender itself to the enemy."[16] Orders arrived at the Luftwaffe's 3rd Squadron in Marseilles, and fifteen Dornier-217 medium-bombers took off to intercept the apparently turncoat ships. As they steamed twenty-three kilometers southwest of Sardinia's Cape Testa, one of the German planes released a weapon making its debut in the Mediterranean Theater. The one-meter-long FX-1400 was remotely controlled and featured a small assist rocket motor. Also known as the 'Fritz X', it was specifically designed to carry an anti-shipping warhead.

The first guided bomb fell on the *Roma*'s stern, where its lengthy control wires got caught in the rudder but failed to detonate the missile's warhead. Another *Fritz* struck the bow, piercing it clear through before exploding in the sea on the opposite side. Five minutes later, however, the magazines took a direct hit, causing a serious fire. For the next twenty minutes, the crew fought desperately to contain it, until a terrific explosion erupted in a column of flame and smoke, as the 1,500-ton number-two turret was blown overboard. The battleship listed heavily to starboard before breaking in half and disappearing into the sea.

Lost with her were two admirals, including Bergamini, eighty-six officers, and 1,264 sailors. Allied strategists were shocked by the *Roma*'s sudden end, as some indication of the price they would have to pay for invading southern France. Abandoning all immediate plans for such an invasion was important collateral the Germans collected from their destruction of the Italian flagship.

Mussolini was kept ignorant of these tragic events. Badoglio wanted him alive as part of the booty he intended paying the Allies for their willingness to put aside the harsh terms of unconditional surrender. The *Duce*'s royal captors had moved him from one secret location to another, as much to save him from falling into Allied clutches, as to foil any attempt by his followers to free him. He passed his 60th birthday alone on Ponza, a tiny island where Roman Caesars two millennia before him exiled troublesome relatives.

When throughout the 1920s and '30s, congratulations had showered him from around the globe, now "nobody gave me a thought on July 29th, with one exception." He was handed a telegram that read in part, "The feelings I express to you today of complete solidarity and brotherly friendship are all the more cordial. Your work as a statesman will live in the history of our two nations, destined as they are to march towards a common fate. I should like to tell you that our thoughts are constantly with you … I once more sign myself with invincible faith. Yours, Goering."[17]

The *Reichsmarshal* was not the only German leader closely following events in Italy. Since the *Duce's* arrest on 25 July, Adolf Hitler ordered his intelligence agents in Italy to determine Mussolini's precise whereabouts, and entrusted the commando expert, *SS-Sturmbannführer* Otto Skorzeny, with abducting him, no matter how extreme the circumstances of his confinement. They were difficult, indeed. In early September, the *Duce* was transferred to the Albert Rifugio hotel on Gran Sasso, high in the remote Abruzzi Mountains. The steep, lofty terrain prevented any kind of frontal assault, and rendered a parachute drop impractical. The base of the mountain was guarded by stationed troops who could be quickly reinforced if necessary by a direct rail line.

Intercepted radio messages alerted the Germans to the probability of Mussolini's location atop the Gran Sasso, a suspicion confirmed by aerial reconnaissance, and photographs clearly revealed the unique challenges of the operation. Skorzeny's solution was to use the world's first mass-produced heliocopter. With its twin, twelve-meter-wide rotors, the 12.25-meter-long Focke Achgelis Fa 223 could carry eight soldiers over 700 kilometers up to 2,400 meters, landing vertically directly in front of Mussolini's hotel door if necessary. A single *Drache*, or 'Dragon', was all the Wehrmacht could spare from the Eastern Front, where the innovative aircraft were busily engaged in med-evac operations. Even so, Skorzeny was willing to attempt his assignment with just seven other commandos. Fortunately for him, perhaps, the helicopter broke down *en route*, and he was forced to consider an alternate strategy.

Luftwaffe General Kurt Student believed a glider assault could carry it off. A similar operation he engineered on 10 May 1940 had overpowered Holland's Eben-Emael, a great fortress deemed 'impregnable' by military experts. Now, he designed an equally daring mission that would likewise depend upon the element of surprise to succeed. Hitler gave the order, and a squad of DFS 230 assault gliders towed by Junkers-52 transport planes in the company of several Fieseler *Storch*, or 'Storks', rose from the Practica di Mare airfield shortly after noon on 12 September. The Fieseler Fi.156 was a remarkable STOL ('short take-off and landing') aircraft, able to get airborne after only sixty meters or less, and land in a third of that distance. Otto Skorzeny and ninety paratroopers huddled aboard the little armada of soldiers and *Stork*s headed toward the Abruzzi Mountains.

They flew at a collective airspeed of just 180 km/hr, as set by the gliders. But as the planes swooped down toward the summit of Gran Sasso, their pilots were horrified to see that what they had been led to believe was a meadow by reconnaissance photographs was actually a short piece of very steep ground terminating suddenly in a sheer drop hundreds of metres to the valley floor. A *Stork* piloted by Walter Gerlach touched down within twenty metres of the precipice. With great skill, every glider landed atop the Gran Sasso, although one crashed, injuring every man on board. Skorzeny's glider came to rest only a few meters from the main entrance of the hotel Albert Rifugio. He kicked down its front door, then machine-gunned a radio transmitter and its operator, the operation's lone fatality. Having observed the landing from his second story room, Mussolini ran downstairs into the lobby, where he was confronted by the tall *SS-Sturmbannführer*: "Duce, I have come to rescue you!"[18]

As they ran outside to a waiting Fieseler *Storch*, the same men who had until just minutes earlier been his captors stood to bid him farewell with the Fascist salute. Personally entrusted by Hitler with Mussolini's safety, Skorzeny insisted on joining him, even though his extra presence aboard the ordinarily three-seat Fi.156 made it dangerously overloaded.

In addition to the *Duce*, it was already crowded with a pilot and navigator. Gerlach pushed the 240-hp, 8-cylinder engine to maximum rpms, as paratroopers shoved the light airplane forward to assist its lift. There was a long, breathless moment, as the *Storch* literally fell over the drop-off and plummeted in a steep dive, until Gerlach finally regained control. He flew it back to the Practica di Mare airdrome, where the *Duce* was bundled into a waiting Junkers trimotor. A few hours later, Mussolini landed at the *Führer*'s headquarters in Rastenburg. Hitler was on hand to greet him personally, as the older man stepped from the plane – unshaven, haggard from his ordeal, but smiling wearily.

Word of his dramatic escape dominated war news around the world, and even enemy commentators could scarcely conceal their admiration for the daring German commandos who successfully executed it. The rescue amounted to a propaganda coup that got Mussolini's new political life off to a strong start, and his reputation as one of the grand, extraordinary characters of history in the Italian style of Benvenuto Cellini gained renewed popularity.

After a few days rest in Germany, the *Duce* flew back to his resort at La Rocca delle Caminate, in northern Italy, near Salo, a small village on the shores of Lake Garda, soon to become the headquarters of his new national capital. Six days later, a powerful transmission from Radio Munich was broadcast across Italy and around the world. Of the innumerable public speeches Mussolini delivered during the previous twenty-five years, none was so widely heard, nor elicited such strong, contrary emotions. "Blackshirts, men and women of Italy," he began. "After a long silence, my voice calls out to you, and I am sure you recognize it. It is the voice that has been with you in difficult times, and in the triumphant days of our patriotism."[19]

Following a description of his underhanded arrest by the King, peripatetic detention, and liberating abduction, Mussolini spoke knowingly of harsh conditions imposed by the Allies, thanks to German intelligence reports. He was therefore able to knowingly contrast events between 1940 and 1943 in words closely paralleling his memoirs the following year: "When one compares the Italy of 1940 with what it is today, now that it has been reduced to an unconditional surrender such as no nation worthy of the name would have ever greeted with outbursts of rejoicing like those after September 8th, it must be admitted that the comparison is heart-rending. Then, Italy was an empire. Today, she is not even a state. Her flag flew from Tripoli to Mogadishu, from Bastia to Rhodes and Tirana. Today, it has been hauled down everywhere. Enemy flags are flying over our home territory. Italians used to be in Addis Ababa. Today, Africans bivouac in Rome."

"The unconditional surrender of September 1943 was the greatest material and moral catastrophe in the 3,000 years of our history. From that fatal month onwards, the sufferings of the Italian people have been indescribable and surpass anything human to enter the realms of imagination. Never did nation climb a more dolorous Mount Calvary! Many millions of Italians today and tomorrow will have to experience in their own bodies and souls what defeat and dishonor mean, what it means to be completely disarmed. The bitter cup will have to be drained to the dregs. Only by reaching the depths can one rise once more to the stars. Only the fury at suffering too great humiliation will give Italians strength for victory."

He added somewhat cryptically, "There is a Mussolini who embodies the Mussolini of yesterday, even as the one of yesterday embodied the one of today, and this Mussolini,

though no longer living at the Palazzo Venezia, but at the Villa delle Orsoline, has put his shoulder to the wheel with his usual determination."[20]

Despite overthrow and imprisonment, he was still the same *Duce*. His broadcast elicited rage and despair among growing numbers of Italian partisans, but encouraged popular resistance to the already resented occupation authorities. More immediately significant, from every part of the northern peninsula, volunteers by the thousands flocked to Mussolini's phoenix-like reappearance. Thus encouraged, he was hailed on 23 September as the leader of the Italian Social Republic (RSI), a reborn Fascist regime purged of concessions to the monarchy and the church, and officially recognized as an independent state with its own embassies and ambassadors by Bulgaria, Slovakia, Croatia, Rumania, Hungary, Japan, Thailand, Japan, Manchuria, and the Third Reich.

Contrary to Allied critics, the Salo Republic was not a puppet-state manipulated by the Germans, although, of course, it was indebted to them for its existence. Hitler knew that any attempt to manipulate a Fascist resurgence would appear transparently artificial. Far better to allow his ideologically kindred friend to mostly have his own way. For his part, Mussolini relished the opportunity of radicalizing his movement; to purge it of its conservative tendencies, and attract young blood into its ranks by reviving the old revolutionary appeal it early possessed when struggling for power. But there were new influences to be embraced. In addition to the Roman salute, RSI followers greeted each other with the three middle fingers of the right hand, palm inward, to signify the Republic's motto: *Onore, Corragio, Fedel*: 'Honor, Courage, Loyalty.'

A broad streak of mysticism ran through the Salo Republic, due in part to *Anthroposofia*, an occult movement emphasizing the spiritual, prehistoric origins of the Aryan race. In reaction to Christianity, condemned by some radicals as a form of religious bolshevism, the tri-finger salute's esoteric significance stood for *Wollen-Wissen-Koennen* – 'Will-Wisdom-Understanding' – inscribed over Wewelsburg Castle, in Germany, where Italian volunteers in the *Waffen-SS* were in training. A collar patch of the RSI's *Vendetta* Battalion similarly featured the image of three arrows united by a yoke, not unlike the symbol of Jose Antonio de Rivier's *Falange* in the Spanish Civil War. But a more obvious change was the Italian flag. Its central House of Savoy coat of arms was replaced by a Roman eagle grasping the *fasces*.

Mussolini felt reinvigorated and freed from compromising with a fossilized Catholicism and a stifling monarchy by the radicalism electrifying his new ideological life. "Our battle is an ungrateful one," he declared, "yet it is a beautiful battle, since it compels us to count only upon our own forces. Revealed truths we have torn to shreds, dogmas we have spat upon. We have rejected all theories of paradise. We have baffled charlatans – white [conservative], red [Marxist], and black [Catholic] charlatans, who placed miraculous drugs on the market to give their form of felicity to mankind. We do not believe in programs, in plans, in saints or apostles. Above all, we do not believe in their kind of happiness, in their 'salvation', in any 'Promised Land'."[21]

Some loyal, though moderate Fascists and patriotic nationalists were put off by the radical tone of Mussolini's reform. "I who have dictated this doctrine," he told them, "am the first to realize that the modest tables of our laws and program – the theoretical and practical guidance of Fascism – should be revised, corrected, enlarged, developed, because already in part they have suffered injury at the hand of time." He brushed aside warnings that such extremism would deter, not encourage recruitment by arguing that radical measures were the most popular in times such as these: "You admit the people into the citadel of the State, and the people will defend it. If you close them out, they will assault it."[22]

He was right. More than 200,000 volunteers stepped forth before the end of 1943 to flesh out four new divisions trained in Germany by Wehrmacht instructors in Heuberg, Sennenlager (Wuttemberg), Munzingen (Baden), and Grafenwoer. These became, respectively, the *Italia, Littorio, Monterosa*, and *San Marco*. As some indication of the popular support enjoyed by the Salo Republic, another two full divisions were added before war's end. Outfitted with modern equipment and weapons mostly superior to anything they knew in the old Italian Royal Army, the volunteers' level of training and morale were high.

When Mussolini visited them during April and again in July 1944, his spirits were greatly uplifted. "With so many young men such as we have just seen," he told his party secretary, Alessadro Pavolini, "one gets the impression that most of Italy is on our side, even if those compatriots presently trapped behind the enemy lines of occupation are physically prevented from speaking and acting freely."[23]

His recruitment efforts were aided at least in part by the Allies themselves. Welcomed as peace-makers by war-weary Italians in the days immediately following his arrest, Anglo-American demands for 'supplementary rations', such as liquor, cigarettes, private cars, or any other luxury goods were taking a heavy toll on the Italians. The purchasing power of both the British pound and U.S. dollar became so inflated that even black market prices soared beyond the reach of ordinary people. Food costs rose by 700%, as the average Italian worker earned three slices of crusty bread per twelve-hour work-day. Death through malnutrition spread throughout the Allied-occupied areas, while theft and prostitution reached epidemic proportions. These conditions melded with the ensuing civil war to drastically inflate the numbers of persons killed. As Greene and Massignani report, "It is probable that more Italians died in World War II after September 8, 1943 than before, at least if one discounts casualties from high-altitude Allied bombing."[24] The countryside itself was populated by millions of impoverished, ailing people.

To assist the Allies in their conquest of Italy, Roosevelt government officials cut deals with Mafia leaders deported to the U.S. by Mussolini two decades before, reinstalling them throughout Sicily and southern Italy. In his brief history of organized crime as the Americans' own secret weapon to further their Italian policy, King Orry tells how "Lucky Luciano, head of Murder Inc. and *Capo di Tutti Capi*, arranged Mafia support for the invasion; he did this from his prison cell in New York State for a few business and personal concessions, of course. So, Lucky was released and flown back to his homeland to 'facilitate the invasion', and, on the side, to re-set the Mafia's power structure and establish its new narcotics empire."

"Vito Genovese, well-known New York hoodlum wanted for murder and numerous other crimes, turned up in uniform in Sicily as a liaison officer attached to the U.S. Army. The U.S. also resuscitated another convicted *Mafiosi*, Don Cali Vizzini, and placed him in control of the island's civil administration with complete authority, military vehicles and supplies at his disposal. Through threats, bribes and skill, these grafters soon out-maneuvered the do-gooding military government of occupied territory to the degree that it was estimated that of all military supplies landed at Naples for the Allied armies, at least a third was stolen from the port."

"So, for the last sixty-odd years, America has suffered from this act of stupidity, and Italy far worse. For what Italian Prime Minister has been able to govern without Mafia connections and support?"[25]

Economic misery and moral decline combined with street crime, disease, squalor, and political chaos. Anglo-American popularity was not helped by publication of a U.S. scheme to dissolve Italy as a nation by carving up the entire peninsula among the Allies, with the northeast of the country parceled out to the despised Yugoslavs. Its better-known counterpart, the so-called 'Morganthau Plan' – the brain-child of the U.S. Secretary of the Treasury, Henry Morganthau – similarly outlined the partitioning of postwar Germany. Mussolini had warned that "capitulation would be the end of Italy, not only as a great power, but as a power at all."[26] And now the words, "*Duce*, return to us!", were daubed on ruined walls across Italy south of Rome, as General Eisenhower's advisors warned him that the dictator's reputation was undergoing a popular upswing.

Life under the liberators was becoming so intolerable even many of the Grand Council members who voted against Mussolini in July now regretted their decision. Dino Alfieri, the Fascist Minister for Press and Propaganda, and Giuseppe Bastianini, the Under-Secretary for Foreign Affairs, pleaded forgiveness from their refuge in Switzlerland, as did the President of the National Fascist Confederation of Agricultural Workers, Annio Bignardi, and the Minister of Corporations, Tullio Cianetti. Giacomo Suardo explained that he abstained from voting one way or the other, due to his position as President of the Senate, and applied for membership in the Republican Fascist Party. But the *Duce* would have none of it. "If these gentlemen had voted differently back then," he said, "the situation would not have developed as it has for them, for me, and, more importantly, for our country."[27] All, save Cianetti, who was sentenced to thirty years imprisonment, were condemned to death *in absentia* by Verona's Fascist Republican Tribunal. The high-profile Minister of Foreign Affairs, Count Galeazzo Ciano, and four others who cast their negative votes, were executed by firing squad on 1 November 1944.

A day after founding the Salo Republic, Mussolini met with Himmler for the creation of an Italian SS. Its purpose was to build an élite fighting corps that would set high standards for the rest of the RSI armed forces to emulate. In early October, 3,000 signed up. But Eastern Front veterans of the *Corpo di Spedizione Italiano*, who had fought beside the Germans in Russia, were quick to join the SS after King Victor Emmanuel declared war against Germany on the 13th. Eventually, more than 15,000 volunteers served in the various Italian SS formations.

Insignia patch of the Italian SS.

Their baptism of fire came in January 1944, opposing the American landings at Anzio. Members of the 2nd Battalion, 1st Italian SS Infantry Regiment, led by a former Blackshirt lieutenant-colonel, Delgi Oddi, distinguished themselves in capturing a number of prisoners, together with a much-needed haul of Thompson sub-machine-guns. A determined effort by the U.S. 3rd Infantry Division to break the Italian line shattered, saving the entire Italo-German position, while continuing to trap the Americans at the Anzio beachhead. Of the 650 Italian SS men who participated, just forty-six survived. Dead and living had raised the high criteria Mussolini demanded of them. "They set a great example of faith and love of our homeland," he said as he awarded Italy's Silver Medal to the 2nd Battalion's banner. "They resisted with indomitable tenacity and bravery in combat for many days, making an oath with the blood of 70% of their soldiers, and writing one of the most beautiful pages of glory in the highest traditions of the *real* Italy."[28]

Himmler added, "Because of the demonstration of courage and sense of duty displayed by the volunteers of the Italian SS, they are henceforward designated as units of the Waffen-SS, with all the duties and rights that implies."[29]

In August 1944, the 29th SS Division, supported by the renowned *Folgore* parachute regiment and several Blackshirt formations, mounted a successful anti-partisan sweep throughout northern Italy. Beginning with about 20,000 anti-Fascist militants in May 1944, their numbers reached ten times that number by war's end. As early as 1943, they were a serious threat to the Salo Republic and its ally. Their destruction of an important ammunition train on its way to the fighting at Monte Cassino on 20 December additionally killed 500 German troops. By year's end, some 2,200 partisan sorties had been carried out. On 4 June 1944, they were strong enough to get Badoglio fired and depose King Victor Emmanuelle, who fled into exile.

Accordingly, the Italian SS devoted much of its time to battling the underground movement, eventually accounting for the deaths of more than 35,000 partisans. Another operation aimed at them was undertaken in October, 1944 against the insurgent Vinadio fortress, near Turin, by the *SS Italiana* in conjunction with the *Brigate Nere*. Equivalent to the German Volkssturm, it was made up mostly of older men and teenage civilians, one of numerous auxiliary formations fighting parallel to the RSI's *forze armate*. "The origin of the partisan movement which is scourging Italy," Mussolini explained, "dates back to 8 September, when hordes of soldiers could not regain their homes, and so joined the anti-Fascist fugitives, escaped convicts, and those set free from concentration camps. Besides the war between the armies, civil war has thus broken out, with episodes of savagery such as, until yesterday, would have been thought impossible on Italian soil."[30]

Italy's regular 'armed forces' were divided over the split between the Anglo-American south and the Fascist north. The *Esercito* had fallen directly under the control of Marshal

Recruitment poster for the Italian SS.

Badoglio, who put its 100,000 men, about 50,000 less than Mussolini's Salo Republic, at the disposal of the Allies. But most did not join out of any affection for their new superiors. Rather, service in the army was for many the only source for food and shelter. Hence, the quality of Badoglio's divisions was not invariably first-rate, and desertions were commonplace.

The partisans represented far more of an obstacle to Mussolini's *Esercito Nazionale Republicano*. He did attract many regular army units, among the most valuable having been the X *Arditi* Regiment of commando experts. Just a year before, they fought beside Hitler's Panzer armies on the Eastern Front at Zhitomir, Kiev, Novocobiscoia, Kirovgrad, and numerous other battles. Still in possession of their reconnaissance vehicles, the *Arditi* commandos became part of the 2nd *Fallschirmjäger*, a parachute division. Once again with their German allies, they participated in the fighting around the Dutch towns of Eindhoven and Arnhem, where General Montgomery's Operation *Market Garden* was so thoroughly shot up. Other Russian Campaign veterans to side with the *Duce* belonged to the Blackshirted *Camicie Nere* 'M' Assault Legion, thrown in reckless counter-attacks against the Anzio beachhead, performing there with great valor, as attested by the high attrition their ranks suffered.

By mid-1944, the morale of Allied troops in Italy was so low, a mutiny was just narrowly prevented at Anzio. The Americans not only failed to break out of their virtual encirclement, but were still trapped on the beaches they occupied months before. A bitterly popular barracks' ballad of the period was 'The D-Day Dodgers', taken from a public statement made by Lady Astor from the safety of her English country estate, where she contemptuously compared heroic Allied servicemen fighting in the Normandy invasion with 'lowly' British infantry ('D-Day dodgers' she called them), mired in Italy. The song's sarcastic words were underscored by the melody to which they were set: an internationally famous German popular song of the period, *Lily Marlene*. This disaffection for the war was expressed in action by the British 46th Infantry Division, which particularly suffered from severe problems with soldiers going AWOL.

The *Regia Marina* likewise largely fell under the control of Marshal Badoglio, who saw to the internment of all its surviving capital ships in Allied hands. A few unserviceable cruisers, destroyers and submarines still in port after the armistice were usually scuttled or sabotaged by their crews, in defiance of King Victor Emmanuelle's orders to the contrary. By contrast, the only 'fleet' Mussolini had at his disposal comprised four torpedo-boats, two anti-submarine vessels, and a small number of patrol craft the Germans were able to confiscate from Italy's western coast harbors after the armistice of 8 September. Five submarines were stationed at Betasom, and another five in the Black Sea. Other Italian warships on station in various oceans of the world were divided in their loyalties.

As many vessels as possible were drafted into the RSI Navy, the *Marina Nazionale Republicana*, or *Divisione Decima*, by Junio Borghese, the so-called 'Black Prince', commander of the renowned *X MAS Flotilla* human-torpedoes. Before the Badoglio coup, they had destroyed 265,000 tons of Allied shipping, "compelling the enemy to commit disproportionate resources to defend against a relative few," according to Greene and Massignani.[31] It was an historic achievement for a tiny handful of special operations experts Borghese hoped could be repeated on behalf of the *Marina Nazionale Republicana*. After tireless recruitment, he gathered together enough naval personnel to build a division-strength organization, about 50,000 men, enough for him to spare 5,000 volunteers for training in Germany, where they were to form the basis for an élite marine unit.

Throughout the last months of 1943, *Marina Nazionale Republicana* commanders had high hopes of building the small but efficient fleet into a valuable fighting force to oppose anticipated enemy landings along the western coasts of the peninsula. The flotilla even operated an underseas unit of midget submarines led by the full-sized *Aradam*, scuttled in Genoa harbor when word came of the armistice, but since relocated by the Black Prince, and ready to sail in January 1944, loaded with human-torpedoes.

Unlike the *Regia Marina*, the *Regia Aeronautica* went over almost in its entirety to the Salo Republic, where it became the *Aeronautica Nazionale Republicana* (ANR). The 8th *Gruppo* alone obeyed Badoglio's order to join his *Aeronautica Co-Belligerante*. All other units either disbanded or flew north. Typical was the Italian Air Force's finest fighter in mass-production, the Macchi MC.205, *Veltro*: Out of sixty-six *Greyhounds* still in service when the turncoat Marshal proclaimed his Co-Belligerent Air Force, only six remained behind in the south. More tellingly, of the *Regia Aeronautica*'s 12,000 officers and 167,000 NCOs, less than 200 heeded his call join him. Until the Badoglio armistice, 12,748

Many Italian pilots joined Mussolini's *Aeronautica Nazionale Republicana*, because they were disaffected by the murder of their legendary airman, Ettore Muti.

Italian SS recruiting poster in honor of Ettore Muti.

Italian airmen perished in the various campaigns, including 1,806 officers. Thousands more were to join them in the civil war that followed.

Along with ancient Fiat biplanes – the *Falco* and even older CR.32 – the ANR possessed one of the Second World War's finest interceptors, the Fiat G.55 *Centauro*. Although the *Centaur* first saw action with the 353rd *Squadriglia* defending Rome in summer 1943, its operations were mostly conducted in three *squadriglie* forming the 2nd *Gruppo Caccia Terrestre*, flying out of Veneria Real. Able to climb to a ceiling of 6,000 meters in seven minutes, twelve seconds, the fighter's 1,475-hp, 12-cylinder inverted-Vee piston engine gave it a maximum speed of just under 645 km/hr. Its sterling performance made the *Centauro* the equal, at least, of the best Allied fighters, and enjoyed a solid reputation as an ideal bomber-destroyer afforded by its three 20mm cannons mounted in the engine and wings, plus two 12.7mm machine-guns in the fuselage. Unfortunately for the defense of Italy, just 274 of the G.55s had been produced to contend with literally thousands of American P-47 Thunderbolts and P-51 Mustangs.

Meanwhile, fellow Italians in the Allied-approved Co-Belligerent Air Force were soon disillusioned with their new Allies, who ordered them to transport supplies for Tito's Communist partisans in Yugoslavia – a shameful assignment that sparked the first defections. Eventually, the once-proud *Regia Aeronautica* was entirely absorbed into something called the 'Allied Balkan Air Force'. Those pilots who stayed on were further denigrated by being given only worn-out, second-hand aircraft to fly. By then, according to Neulen, they "despised the politicians whose slogans no longer meant anything to them."[32]

As early as October 1943, Ernesto Botto, the legendary 'Iron Leg' of Spanish Civil War fame, worked with *Generalfeldmarschall* Wolfram von Richthofen, the Luftwaffe commander in Italy, to build the *Aeronautica Republicana*, as it was first known, with German assistance. As soon as he became its Undersecretary, Botto began making frequent radio transmissions, appealing for support. In just three months, almost 7,000 recruits responded to his broadcasts, among them, top aces of the defunct *Regia Aeronautica*, including Adriano Visconti, now Commander of the 1st *Gruppo Caccia*. He traveled to Germany with a number of fellow officers who underwent conversion training in the Messerschmitt Me.109G.

As members of the expanded *Aeronautica Nazionale Republicana*, they returned to the skies over Turin, flying not only Messerschmitts, but Macchi *Greyhounds*, to shoot down more enemy aircraft accounted for than by any other Italian unit its size. Visconti was himself credited at this time with downing two P-38 Lightnings and a pair of P-47 Thunderbolts, bringing his total number of 'kills' to ten. Promoted to *Maggiore*, he was given command of the entire 1st *Gruppo 'Asso di Bastoni'*. It made its debut on 3 January 1944 with the destruction of four P-38 Lightnings, minus casualties. Before March, Visconti and his men claimed 26 'kills', mostly American, for the loss of nine comrades.

On the 11th of that month alone they scored a dozen victories, losing three Italians. After Lt. Boscutti baled out of a stricken *Veltro* and was hanging defenseless in his parachute harness, he was deliberately machine-gunned to death by a U.S. pilot. Another A.N.R. officer was identically shot a week later, when thirty Macchi *Greyhounds* were joined by sixty Messerschmitt *Gustavs* of JG.77 to intercept 450 Allied bombers and dozens more Lockheed Lightnings, P-51 Mustangs and Spitfires. That the Axis airmen were able to bring down four of the enemy against such odds, for the loss of just one of their own, was remarkable. Like Lt. Boscutti, Corp. Zaccaria was shot to death while suspended under his parachute by a P-38 pilot. According to Neulen, "Allegedly, there was an RAF order that authorized the shooting of Axis pilots hanging from parachutes."[33]

Attrition of Italian and German machines was high, less from aerial combat than during ground attacks by outnumbering squadrons of USAAF fighter-bombers. But throughout most of 1944, these loses were made good by efficient factory production and successful cash collections provided by the civilian population. While virtually every Italian warplane was represented in the *Aeronautica Nazionale Republicana*, its effectiveness was increasingly compromised by lack of sufficient replacement parts and aviation fuel, especially by early winter 1944.

The A.N.R.'s final operations were undertaken by ten S.M.79s combined in an anti-shipping group at Ghedi beginning in October. They celebrated Christmas Day by attacking an Allied convoy near Ancona, torpedoing a 7,000-ton freighter. Responding to the unexpected sortie within twenty-four hours, P-47 Thunderbolts descended on the airfield to shoot up the venerable bombers parked in the open at the Lonate Pozzolo airfield. The survivors' parting shot came on 5 January 1945, when a last pair of *Sparvieros* sank a 5,000-ton transport off the Dalmatian coast.

Following the final collapse of the RSI in late April, 1945, *Maggiore* Visconti negotiated a surrender with Communist partisans in Milan, guaranteeing full military honors and protection for his men of the 1st *Gruppo*. A few hours later, he and his flight adjutant, *Sottotenente* Stefanini, were found murdered, shot in the back.

16

Day of the Lion

Better to live one day like a lion than the lifetime of a sheep!
Mussolini[1]

History came full-circle on 29 October 1944, when Benito Mussolini made his last public speech in Milan. Exactly twenty-two years before, he had set out from this same city in the 'March on Rome' that brought him to power. That early triumph had been preceded by a period of violent struggle, just as years of difficult warfare seemed to culminate somehow in the 1944 mass-rally. The outpouring of popular support it generated for him inspired his sometimes flagging spirits, while stiffening the backbone of the Salo Republic under an increasingly heavy siege from the air. His words were broadcast from the Lyric Theater around the world, and commentators everywhere observed that, despite all the reverses he had experienced in the previous year, the *Duce* seemed to lack none of his fiery rhetoric.

He could not help comparing Italy's present international crisis to the national challenge presented to her in 1922: "From this city, a new energy went out to save our country from decline and create an epoch of self-determination whose spiritual achievements will outlast every one of its merely material manifestations. So too, that same, ever-young dynamic paces forth from this same place to rescue our invaded land from total destruction, and instead spark restoration of those eternal ideals that made us great!"[2]

Milanese acclaim for Mussolini was not generated solely by celebration of Fascism's most important anniversary. That same month, shortly before his commemorative speech, volunteer soldiers of the RSI's *Monterosa* Division smashed an advance undertaken by superior numbers of Brazilian forces. The Italians followed up their successful defense with a counter-attack of their own that routed the South Americans. More than two years before, President Getulio Vargas had striven to maintain Brazil's neutrality, but came under increasing pressure from U.S. President Franklin Roosevelt to enter the war against Italy, even though neither country felt itself aggrieved by each other. While the majority of Brazil's military, in the army, was inclined toward Fascism, its small navy and smaller air force favored alliance with the Western Allies.

According to historian, James P. Duffy, "Vargas walked a tight-rope between his pro-Axis and pro-Allied military factions so well that American diplomats themselves were never sure what his true feelings were. A State Department recommendation that he request the assistance of U.S. troops to bolster his defenses was politely turned down. Instead, Brazil requested weapons for its army to use in its own defense (against Argentina, not Germany or Italy. Joseph) U.S. military officials were reluctant to send arms for fear that they would be used against American forces should the day come that the United States had to take up the defense of the Brazilian bulge against a German threat."[3]

Vargas's lack of enthusiasm for joining the Allies so alarmed Roosevelt, he had his military advisors draw up a 'Joint Basic Plan for the Occupation of Northeastern Brazil'.[4]

F.D.R., who publicly decried Hitler's invasion of neutral countries, was about to undertake the same measures in South America. On 21 December 1940, he approved Operation *Rubber Plan*, designed to open with the unannounced naval bombardment of Brazilian shore installations as a prelude to an amphibious landing of Marines.

"Earmarked for action were the 1st and 3rd Battalions of the 5th Marines," writes Duffy, "supported by a fleet centered on the battleship USS *Texas*, the aircraft carrier USS *Ranger*, and twelve troop transports. Once the beachhead was secured by the Marines, the 9th Army Division Reinforced was to relieve the Marines and become the occupying force, holding as many strategic locations as possible, with special attention to the airports. Should additional forces be required, the 45th Army Infantry Division was to be in ready reserve. These forces, which were involved in amphibious landing exercises were to be prepared to sail to Brazil on ten days' notice from the President."[5]

When Vargas got wind of Operation *Rubber Plan* in January 1942, he was so horrified, he immediately broke diplomatic ties with Italy, and allowed 150 U.S. Marines to be stationed at several Brazilian airfields. These actions could not quell F.D.R.'s suspicions, however, and it was not until May, when Vargas signed the Brazilian-American Defense Agreement drawn up for his endorsement by Roosevelt's men in Washington, that "the planned assault and occupation were dropped."[6]

Despite Yankee intimidation, the Brazilian President tried to keep his country from being dragged into the fighting. More than eight months after the Japanese attack at Pearl Harbor, he held back from committing his armed forces in any way, until finally caving in to U.S. pressure, reluctantly issuing a declaration of war against the Axis. The expeditionary force he very gradually assembled was not deployed until July 1944, when it joined the Allies in northern Italy, and was subsequently mauled by the *Monterosa* Division. This early October victory regained not only territory, but morale, shifting the RSI's center of power to Milan, where Mussolini relocated his offices from Salo on 18 December.

While he was being cheered through the streets of Milan, the U.S. 5th Army, still bogged down in the mountains south of Bologna and hampered by the headlong flight of their Brazilian allies, was forced to call off its latest offensive. German and Italian SS defending the city beat back all attacks. In just six days, the Americans there suffered 15,700 casualties, beyond anything with which the replacement system could keep up. Mussolini and Marshal Graziani sought to exploit this defensive victory with a fresh offensive, *Winterstorm*. While German forces were thrusting through France again at the Battle of the Bulge, the Italian *Monterosa* Division and German 148th Infantry Division simultaneously struck against the American line in the Apennine Mountains. Allied intelligence had dismissed the morale of the *Monterose* as 'very low', and planned to move against it after Christmas. But the Italo-German offensive beat them by twenty-four hours.

In the pre-dawn darkness of 27 December, two German assault battalions rushed the Sommocolonia garrison defended by the U.S. F Company, 2nd Battalion, 366th Regiment supplemented with Communist partisans. Only eighteen of the defenders survived to run for their lives. But the heavy weight of Operation *Winterstorm* was directed against the 92nd Buffalo Infantry Division, made up entirely of Afro-American troops led by white officers, Major-General Edward M. Almond and Colonel Raymond G. Sherman.

Although eighty medium and heavy field-guns, together with some first-rate German artillery batteries, equipped Operation *Winterstorm*, its soldiers attacked without tanks or air-cover, all of which the enemy possessed in abundance. Even so, one town after another fell in rapid succession. As a standard precaution against just such an enemy assault, Almond and Sherman had rigged high explosives at vital bridges, but the surprised troops forgot to detonate them. The attackers were rich in mortars, and these they used in concentrated groups to maximize their fire effect. Townspeople in Gallicano, located just outside the battle-zone, reported that U.S. F Company exhibited every sign of panic, fleeting resistance, and general chaos. By nightfall, all attacks were suspended, because the entire American line had crumbled.

The next day, 28 December, the offensive was resumed without resistance. A German assault column literally walked into Pian di Coreglia, its objective, without having to fire a shot. Patrols sent forward as far as the distant village of Calavorno reported that the Buffalo Division appeared to be still in full retreat. Indeed, it had withdrawn from combat in headlong flight. Less than 100 prisoners were taken, because the rest of their comrades were more fleet-footed. But the Axis soldiers netted numerous Browning 12.7 mm machine-guns, bazookas, mortars, and ammunition, together with stocks of much-needed food.

Over the next four days, U.S. warplanes attacked the Axis ground troops trying to defend themselves with a few 20mm and 88mm anti-aircraft guns. American pilots shot up everything in sight, including the Camporgiano hospital, where Germans and Italians were casualties, along with a number of captured G.I.s also being treated for wounds. By New Year's Day, the murderous air strikes had been called off. Nothing could dislodge the gains made by Operation *Winterstorm*. These comprised a conquered wedge twenty kilometers wide and nine kilometers deep which stood largely intact throughout the rest of the war. In fact, its defenders continued fighting for days after Mussolini's death the following year.

According to historian Richard Lamb, "Graziani's Italian troops were no match for fierce, battle-hardened Gurkhas" of the British 8th Indian Division, which was supposed to have immediately counter-attacked after the Buffalo soldiers pulled back, recapturing Barga.[7] In reality, the town had already been evacuated as unnecessary before the Gurkhas arrived. They encountered no opposition, other than a trio of stragglers – two Italians and a single German soldier – taken later in the vicinity. This only was the 8th Indian Division's 'fierce counter-attack'.

In reports to their superiors, the Buffalo Division's white commanding officers, Almond and Sherman, blamed its failure to contain the Axis offensive on the allegedly poor fighting quality of their black troops. But both German and Italian veterans of the fighting claimed that Afro-American soldiers often resisted with resolute determination. They were routed because of the Operation's complete surprise, which might have similarly affected any defenders informed by their own leadership that no such attack was expected or even possible.

The propaganda value of *Winterstorm* was considerable. It discouraged the anti-Fascist partisans, many of whom had already lost stomach for civil war. Even before the Offensive began, the Communist *Garibaldi* units disbanded and gave up their weapons to German forces from late November to early December. *Winterstorm* further depressed the Americans' already low morale following the bloody collapse of their October operations. At the close of the previous month, Fascist militia units seized the so-called 'Free Republic of Alba', the first Communist outpost in northern Italy. Simultaneously, the outnumbered, under-equipped men of the RSI's *Monterosa* Division and Germany's 148th Infantry Division drew an influx of new volunteers. The Axis had stood the test of combat at its worst and could still conquer, even at this late hour in the war. Among the high mountains of his homeland, Graziani had redeemed his reputation among Mussolini's followers as a competent, loyal general.

Operation *Winterstorm* was the last hurrah of the Axis in Italy, however. Although the gains it won and subsequent attacks carried out by the Italian SS mostly held the enemy at bay throughout the first quarter of 1945, by late March, the RSI's supply problems had become hopelessly acute. A 200,000-strong partisan army was rising like an irrepressible tidal-wave to swamp the RSI, which had already lost total domination of the skies to American fighter-bombers. In early April, its headquarters at Lake Garda could no longer be defended, and Mussolini was faced with the final, major decision of his life: Establish a last-ditch effort with 5,000 of his closest followers before Valtellina, still controlled by the Waffen-SS, or make a break for the Swiss border.

Incredibly, RSI morale remained mostly high until the last day of hostilities, even among the *Volontari de Francia*, attached to the *Fulmine* Battalion of the *X Decima MAS* 2nd regiment. As late as April 1945, its French volunteers were still able to pull off some stunning successes against overwhelming odds, such as their firefight in the 162nd German Division's sector, where they closed a gap opened by British commandos. Four months earlier, just 214 men of the *Fulmine* successfully defended the Tarnova della Selva outpost from an attack by 1,300 Yugoslav partisans. A week later, on 26 January, two companies of the *Barbarigo* battalion routed Tito's forces at the Bainsizza plateau, as part of the RSI's ongoing success in the face of enormous opposition. These, however, were the only bright spots in an otherwise darkening reality.

"Everything was falling apart," his son, Romano, remembered, "and yet, even in February of 1945, *Il Duce* refused to give up hope." Along with the *Volontari de Francia* and *Fulmine*, thousands of other volunteers swore to make a last stand for and with Mussolini. "He planned to reach Valtellina with a group of his most loyal followers. He was assured there would be at least 30,000 troops with whom he could lead the final resistance against the Allies' invasion. For him, this last battle would have represented a sort of purifying sacrifice. 'This will be the Thermopylae of Fascism,' he used to say. 'Like Leonidas and his heroes, I will sacrifice myself to block the enemy's way.'"[8]

Throughout March, Mussolini enthusiastically busied himself with preparations for a showdown with the enemy at his own 'Fiery Gates'. For years, Allied leaders vowed to stand him in front of an international tribunal for crimes against humanity. "I can already see the trial they will stage for me at Madison Square Garden," he laughed, "with people in the stands looking at me as if I were a caged beast. No, it is better to die with weapons raised. Only this can be an end worthy of my existence."[9]

But early the next month, he inexplicably and irrevocably changed his mind. "These comrades willing to join me at Valtellina will be of more use to their country rebuilding it in the hard times to come," he told Renato Ricci, head of the RSI militia.[10] In fact, they went on to make a final stand of their own for Fascism without the *Duce*. Led by Italian SS leader, Major Mario Carita, they were finally surrounded by U.S. forces on 20 May, refused to lay down their arms, and perished to the last man in a massive artillery barrage.

Even with the end approaching, Mussolini could not help envisioning the future beyond his own death. "The present war will produce an alteration in order of rank. Great Britain, for instance, is destined to become a second-class power, in view of disclosure of Russian and American strength ... In a short time, Fascism will once more shine on the horizon. First of all, because of the persecution to which the Liberals will subject it, showing that liberty is something to reserve to oneself and refuse to others. And, secondly, because of a nostalgia for 'the good old days' that little by little will gnaw at the Italian heart. All those who fought in the European and, especially, the African wars will suffer particularly badly from this nostalgia. Time will pass, and the days of Fascism will be missed."[11]

He was rudely snapped back into present reality on 23 April when Marshal Graziani reported that the Wehrmacht in Italy was about to surrender. That evening, Mussolini decided to make for Switzerland, because he believed only there would he have an opportunity to publicize a collection of original documents that would, in his mind, justify his past conduct before world history. Both the German military authorities and Fascist die-hards strenuously urged him to forego any attempt to reach Switzerland, because the entire countryside, they warned, swarmed with partisans. His subordinates had already prepared, without his authorization, several means of escape. There was a CANT seaplane or a *Sparviero* tri-motor to take him to Franco's Spain, a four-motor Piaggio air-ambulance capable of reaching the Canary Islands, and a long-range Savoia-Marchetti *Marsupiale* standing by for a transatlantic flight all the way to what would soon become Juan Peron's Argentina.

Hermann Goering, who certainly had enough of his own problems at the time, offered a Junkers-52, its Luftwaffe insignia and swastikas replaced by deceptive Croatian insignia, to take Claretta Petacci, along with her parents and sister, Myriam, to Barcelona. But the *Duce*'s mistress preferred to remain by the side of her lover. His son, Vittorio, pleaded with him to hide from the blood-crazed partisans in a Milan apartment at least until the Anglo-Americans arrived. Mussolini shunned all these avenues of escape, even unto the last possible moment. "I don't want to beg for salvation," he stated emphatically, "while the finest men are sacrificing themselves for me and for Italy's dignity!"[12]

Undeterred by warnings of local partisan activity and not tempted by offers of refuge, he set out in a German SS motor column that included a small truck carrying his precious papers. "If I advance," he had always said, "follow me. If I retreat, kill me. If they kill me, vindicate me."[13]

Wearing a Wehrmacht helmet and army greatcoat, he sat in anonymous silence among the war-weary soldiers heading slowly back to their shattered Reich. At the outskirts of Dongo, a small town thirty-three kilometers from the Swiss border, the column was stopped by guerrilla fighters. Scanning the rows of seated SS men, a partisan was astounded to find Benito Mussolini among them. He was arrested and taken to improvised quarters at Lake Como, on 28 April 1945. Shortly thereafter, a local committee of the Communist Party decreed he must die, and ordered a fellow partisan, Walter Audisio, to carry out the order. Just eleven years before, the *Duce* had granted clemency and a pardon to this same man formerly convicted of actively trying to overthrow the state.

Of the innumerable attempts on Mussolini's life since he became Italian Premiere in 1922, one assassin escaped, another was deported, and two sentenced to thirty years imprisonment, both eventually freed after serving a relatively short term. "I am a man who is 'hard to kill,'" he once said. "At the hospital in Ronchi, in March 1917, with my body riddled with splinters, they thought I would die, or, at best, have my right leg amputated." Referring to "my Panzer-like head," he related that "on my return from the

Fascist Congress held in Florence in 1920, a formidable smash which splintered the bars of a level crossing outside Faenza only gave me a slight concussion, as my shock-proof skull had brilliantly neutralized the blow. Less innocent perhaps and incredibly tedious were the attempts made on my life in 1925 and 1926 – a couple of bombs, a series of revolver shots, both masculine and feminine, native and British, besides a few other attempts, the origin of which remains obscure. Nothing out of the way."[14]

Lightheartedly relating these events in a casual conversation with Hitler before the war, the *Führer* gravely turned to him and said with deep sincerity, "*Duce,* you're too good to be a dictator!"[15]

Aware now his life had come to an end, Mussolini tore open his shirt and demanded that he be executed at once. Fumbling nervously, Audisio obliged by trying to shoot him with an Italian automatic rifle, but it would not fire. Twenty two years earlier, just after the Fascists had come to power, an elderly Catholic nun had prophesied from her death-bed in Rome that no weapon in all Italy would ever be found to kill Benito Mussolini. The trembling Audisio tried again, this time with an Italian pistol. It, too, refused to function. The *Duce* stood calmly waiting, while a French hand-gun was loaded, then aimed point-blank at his bared breast. The MAS 7.65mm pistol fired, and he fell, among the last of the 410,000 Italians to die in Mussolini's War.

During its final months and those immediately thereafter, partisans killed an additional 300,000 of his followers in the paroxysm of bloodshed that seized all Italy.

17

An Unlikely Pen-Pal

History shall be kind to me, because I intend to write it.

Winston S. Churchill[1]

Although still a popular controversy in Italy and, to a lesser degree, Britain and the U.S., personal correspondence Winston Churchill carried on with Benito Mussolini before and during the Second World War is virtually unknown to the rest of the outside world. While such communication between two international statesmen who, publicly at any rate, were deadly enemies may not seem all that significant or even extraordinary, the supposed content of their letters makes them potentially significant in the extreme.

The letters are said to have revealed in part that during May 1940, shortly after he became Prime Minister, Churchill tried to buy Italy's co-belligerence against Hitler by bribing her with the territories of other peoples, some of whom – like France and Greece – were already allied with Great Britain. The following October, he allegedly wrote to Mussolini requesting personal protection from Axis leaders in the event of Britain's surrender. Before year's end, Churchill proposed in another letter to the *Duce* that Britain and Italy conclude an armistice in North Africa, then join Finland for an invasion of the Soviet Union.

Of all allegations made for the contents of Mussolini's papers, Churchill's suggestion that Britain and Italy conclude a peace for the specific purpose of jointly invading Russia is at once the most outrageous and best documented. It was verified by a number of observers and participants, including an officer in the élite *Decima MAS*, Sergio Nesi; his superior, Valerio Borghese, the 'Black Prince' himself; Pietro Carradori, the *Duce's* orderly; and other, credible eyewitnesses. They testified that the Second World War's strangest and most secret gathering took place on 16 November 1944, at Montorfano, the *Decima Flottiglia MAS* base near the shores of Lombardy's beautiful Lake Iseo, not far from the city of Bergamo.

Inside the headquarters building surrounded and secured by a unit of heavily armed *Decima* sailors, Commander Borghese chaired a meeting attended by representatives of the R.S.I. Government (Francesco Maria Barracu), Army (General Giuseppe Violante), and Ministry of the Navy (Captain Fausto Sestini). The German ambassador to Italy, Rudolf Rahn, appeared with *Obergruppenführer der SS* Karl Wolff, in charge of all German forces in Italy and a close confidant of Hitler himself. Across the table from these high-ranking Axis leaders sat plenipotentiaries for United States President Franklin D. Roosevelt and head of the Allied Expeditionary Forces, General Dwight David Eisenhower. Beside them were senior British Army officers representing Marshal Bernard Montgomery and Prime Minister Winston S. Churchill, who had called the covert meeting to discuss his four-point proposal: Official British-U.S. recognition of the R.S.I. and an immediate armistice between all Axis and Allied states; participation of the U.S Fifth Army and

British Eighth Army on the Eastern Front against the Soviet Union; the cooperation of Wehrmacht troops in Italy transferring Allied forces to the fighting in Russia; inclusion of the Italian divisions *Littorio, Monterose, San Marco* and *Italia*, together with the *Decima MAS*, in the Russian Campaign.

After having heard the proposal translated, Commander Borghese asked the Allied representatives why Italy's Co-Belligerent Government of the south had been left out of the proposal. The British replied that the post-Badoglio cabinet was itself largely Communist, and composed of untrustworthy schemers more interested in plunder and bloody vendettas than civil order. All four R.S.I. officers welcomed a unified defense of Western Civilization, as did the Germans, who promised they would urge the *Führer* to seriously examine the plan put forth by the Prime Minister. The Americans, on the contrary, refused to even consider Churchill's suggestions, which were categorically spurned by both U.S. representatives. Their unalterable rejection caused the meeting to be broken up without any further discussion of an Anglo-American alliance with the Axis powers against the USSR.

Churchill arranged another, almost identical meeting with different and, hopefully, less adamantine plenipotentiaries for Roosevelt and Eisenhower at Porto Ceresio, a small commune or 'municipality' on Lake Lugano bordering Switzerland. Results were identical to the Lake Iseo conference, however, and no further attempts were made to forge an alliance of enemies against Stalin.

During a telephone conversation between Mussolini and his German ally late in the war, Hitler wondered about the British, "Aren't they aware of the Russian colossus?"

"Actually," the *Duce* replied, "Churchill had forecasted that danger many years ago. But, *Führer*, you are aware of this."

"Yes, I know," Hitler said dejectedly. "I know all the details."[2]

What were they? 'Details' of Lake Iseo's meeting that came to nothing just six days before their telephone conversation of 22 November? In any case, Mussolini make a direct reference to Churchill's Allies-Axis proposals when he wrote to Marshal Graziani on 9 January 1945. "At this time, I feel it is extremely important to put these papers in a safe place," referring to his high-level correspondence, "first of all, the exchange of letters and the *agreements* [author's italics] with Churchill."[3]

The renowned American historian, Peter Tompkins, who was an agent of the U.S. Office of Strategic Services in Rome during the war, wondered "why must an agreement between Churchill and Mussolini, which had been reached during the meetings at Porto Ceresio and on Lake Iseo, be so radically erased as to require the killings of Mussolini and Claretta Petacci? Churchill's reputation would have been seriously damaged had it become known that he was plotting with the *Duce* of Fascism and a few Nazi generals in Italy in order to have Italian and German forces join the Western Allies to fight the USSR together ..."[4] Churchill was, after all, to stand for re-election in 1951.

Mussolini supposedly preserved additional correspondence with Churchill's predecessor, Neville Chamberlain, who is believed to have written similar sentiments he expressed to U.S. Ambassador, Joseph P. Kennedy, in early 1941, to the effect that Britain would have never gone to war against Germany "without the urging of William C. Bullitt", Franklin D. Roosevelt's representative in Europe immediately prior to the start of World War Two, "and the American Jews". In fact, Chamberlain's statement was quoted by James Forrestal in his memoirs as the U.S. Secretary of the Navy.[5]

Two or three letters from Roosevelt himself allegedly described the American President's desire to have the British Empire in Africa replaced "by Italy's more humane form of imperialism".[6] Other topics discussed in the correspondence, mostly by Churchill, included 1938's Munich Crisis, Italy's entry into the war, and her 1940 invasion of Greece – all portrayed in language radically at odds with official Allied positions publically taken on these historical events.

Additional and, in Mussolini's view, yet more damaging disclosures appeared in the letters. "Churchill knows I have ammunition," he told his Armed Forces Chief of Staff, General Rudolfo Graziani, in February 1945, and referred to the Prime Minister's October 1940 letter as "one he would regret. This correspondence is from heads of states, representing delicate and explosive documents." Two months later, he stated that "these documents are worth even more than if we had won the war."[7] If so, it is difficult to believe that a few political indiscretions on Churchill's part could have been so valuable.

The letters and documents must have contained something more 'explosive', and Mussolini did tell his closest confidants that they featured certain 'agreements' he made with the Allies that would prove immensely surprising to a world audience. Their contents have never been disclosed, but only surmised, based on hardly more than a few hints from Mussolini and a few other sources. Moreover, no references to his end of the correspondence survives. How he might have responded to the alleged letters from Churchill, Chamberlain and Roosevelt is unknown.

Was the *Duce* only bluffing, as part of a vain effort to buoy up the flagging morale of his followers in the last days of the RSI? Or did he actually possess highly incriminating evidence with drastic repercussions for the post-war world? Mainstream historians insist Churchill wrote to Mussolini on only one occasion, in a public telegram just before the start of hostilities, pleading with him to turn away from war. As the price for Italy's alliance against Germany, as supposedly cited in Mussolini's secret documents, Churchill was willing not only willing to give up Malta and Gibraltar, but to sell off the territories of foreign peoples, even those of his own allies, with or without their consent; specifically, France's Savoy, Tunisia and Nice, plus Yugoslavia and Greece, as part of the bargain.

In Churchill's own published memoirs, no mention is made of any friendly correspondence with the Italian dictator, portrayed instead as the evil antithesis of everything decent and civilized. Yet, Churchill was an outspoken admirer of his alleged nemesis since 1922, after the Fascists came to power in their 'March on Rome'. He was quoted by all leading British newspapers at the time as having said, "If I were an Italian, I would proudly wear a black shirt. I am all for Fascism in Italy."[8]

Shortly thereafter, he prepared excerpts from his World War One history for publication in Mussolini's own newspaper, *Il Popolo di Italia*, which ran sixteen installments throughout 1927. Even after the Ethiopian War, Churchill continued to publicly refer to Mussolini as "a Roman genius".[9]

There is no doubt that correspondence between the two men did indeed go on throughout the war. A German report for 25 September 1943 stated that Gestapo agents recovered literally dozens of Churchill's communications with Mussolini, even long after the war began, all of them expressing admiration for Italian Fascism, and hopes for cooperation with the British Empire. Such correspondence no doubt did exist, because Mussolini showed it to virtually everyone in his immediate circle – literally, hundreds of persons – including his wife, Rachele. She responded to questioning by British historian,

David Irving, that she saw the files containing the Churchill letters, but refused to comment on their contents.[10]

For his 1994 book on the controversy, *Careggio segreto*, 'The Secret Correspondence', investigator Fabio Andriola traced thirty persons who personally saw the communications from Churchill, some of them dated as late as the winter of 1944-45.[11] Among those eyewitnesses was C.A. Biggin, the Salo Republic's Minister of Education, and General Graziani, both of whom testified to the documents' existence after the war. Andriola's investigation was preceded by a number of Italy's leading historical researchers, among them, Giorgio Cavalleri, whose *Ombre sul Lago*, or 'Shadows on the Lake', reproduced the *Duce*'s printed command to the head of the Republic's film department, ordering him to photocopy "certain letters of top priority".[12] As part of his order, he asked if the film-maker had anyone in his agency who was fluent in the English language. But Mussolini really needed more than a translator, because he wanted someone with connections in the British government.

In January 1945, he secretly summoned John Amery to join him at his Milan headquarters. Until then, the thirty-three-year-old ex-patriot was busy organizing the British Free Corps, a unit of fellow countrymen recruited from German prisoner-of-war camps to fight as volunteers under the Waffen SS on the Eastern Front against the Soviets. Previously, Amery made a series of broadcasts on Berlin Radio condemning the Western Allies for supporting Communist Russia, earlier serving the Nationalist cause in the Spanish Civil War, when he was awarded a medal of honor by the Italians.

More important to Mussolini at the moment, John was the son of Leopold Charles Maurice Stennett Amery, then a high-ranking member in Churchill's cabinet and one of the most influential politicians in Britain. Father and son were not estranged, despite their polar opposite destinies and ideologies, and it was through John that Mussolini hoped to personally liaison with Leopold and the British government, either for the presentation of his "explosive documents", or the guarantee of a public trial.

While he endeavored to contact the British authorities under the very noses of the German SS, John Amery made public speeches and radio broadcasts for the *Duce* until the end of the war. How successful Mussolini was in these covert efforts is not known, but the fate of his young go-between indicates perhaps something about them. After the RSI's collapse, John Amery was arrested by Communist partisans, who turned him over to the British. Arraigned on charges of treason, he was condemned to death in record time – eight minutes after appearing in front of the bench in what seems to have been an official attempt at permanently silencing him before he could give testimony potentially embarrassing or even harmful to the powers that be.

But John Amery was not the only person aware of Mussolini's papers to have been promptly silenced. Robert L. Miller, in his foreword to *Mussolini, The Secrets of His Death*, writes that more than 500 northern Italians who knew at least something about the documents in various ways were killed at war's end.[13] Among the victims was Claretta Petacci herself, shot to death by a British agent, according to the local partisan commander in charge of her and Mussolini after their arrest, Bruno Giovanni Lonati.

In April 1945, Mussolini summoned a carpenter to make three watertight cabinets specifically for storing photocopies of the Churchill letters and other documents he considered so valuable. One set was presented to his wife, Rachele, and another sent ahead to Switzerland, where a British government contact he knew near Basel awaited their delivery. He kept one set, along with the originals, next to his own person. In addition to these cabinets filled with sensitive correspondence was another, separate collection of related documents kept in large leather bags and transported in an Alfa-Romeo truck, as part of Mussolini's small convoy heading for the Swiss border.

Better than making a last stand for Fascism and going out in a blaze of glory might be his exposure of the Churchill correspondence, which, he deeply believed, would vindicate himself before history. Retreating SS officers warned him repeatedly against his change of plans, arguing that he would never make it to Switzerland, because of widespread partisan activity in northern Italy. They nevertheless provided him with a small escort, after he proved obdurate to their pleas for reason. Before getting under way, he collared Franz Spogeler, an SS captain and personal friend, to whom he entrusted a last letter, written on 23 April, to Churchill: "Can I count on you to get this to him?"

"All I can promise is that I shall try," and Spogeler made his way to the British occupation forces in southern Germany with the confidential missive. In it, Mussolini requested an opportunity to defend himself in an international court of law, to which he would voluntarily entrust his fate, and ended with a pointed but non-specific reference to "documents you will be no doubt find interesting and useful".[14]

In 1944, after learning of the Allies' determination to put the Axis leaders on trial for 'crimes against humanity', he stated publicly, "I declare that I, and I alone, assume the political, moral and historical responsibility for all that has happened. If Fascism has been a criminal association, the responsibility has been mine."[15] This same sentiment, if not these exact words, were part of the missive he had dispatched to Churchill.

However, Spogeler was arrested shortly after crossing the Bavarian frontier, where British authorities confiscated the letter, which subsequently disappeared. Likewise vanished was the set of photocopied documents sent ahead to the British government contact in Switzerland. Precisely who this official may have been is not known, but Mussolini trusted him enough with the valuable correspondence. He apparently believed these and related documents were so crucially important he was willing to stake his life on them. But it seems precisely because of their explosive nature that the British were determined he would never be allowed to present them anywhere, under any conditions.

When Mussolini was arrested outside the northern Italian town of Dongo, four bags of correspondence and the Alfa-Romeo carrying additional documents were seized by the partisans. They sold the vehicle's contents, except the leather bags, to the British Foreign Office, whose London headquarters disclosed the sale in a paper trail open to public scrutiny. The Neville Chamberlain and Franklin Roosevelt letters were supposedly 'pruned and combed' out of the collection; i.e., destroyed, per orders from the BFO's head, as stated in the public record.

Urbano Lazaro, the partisan who arrested Mussolini, had the four bags of documents placed in the safekeeping of a local bank at Da Maso. He recalled later that a fellow Communist, code-named 'Renzo', went through the third bag, in which he found a number of files headed 'Churchill'. After Communist Party leader, Dante Goreri, arrived to order Mussolini's execution, he photocopied the contents of the four bags. The original documents were sold to a pair of British agents from the Field Security Service, and have since vanished. The photocopies were entrusted to another Resistance member with the code-name of 'Cavalieri', who refuses to make them public until a specified period after his death. At the time of writing, 'Cavalieri' is still alive, although his family has expressed reluctance to disclose them at any time in the future.

Whether or not Churchill read the *Duce*'s April 23rd request for a fair trial is not known. In any case, the Prime Minister never entertained any intention of allowing Mussolini a public forum in a court of law, and relished the thought, as he expressed himself to President Roosevelt during their Casablanca Conference in 1943, of having the Italian leader strangled to death in the Roman forum as soon as he was captured. That sentiment was underscored by Italy's most acclaimed postwar historian, Renzo de Felice, in his 1995 book about the last year of the war, *Red and Black*.[16] He was able to trace an agency in the British government, the Special Operations Executive, headed by Max Salvadore, commissioned to assassinate the *Duce* on-sight. This secret order contravened the terms of the Italian armistice, signed by Badoglio in Sicily on 3 September 1943, which specified that Mussolini must be taken alive and turned over the U.S. XV Army Group Command headed by General Mark Clark.

By the time Salvadore caught up with the founder of Fascism in April 1945, Mussolini had already been arrested by Communist partisans, who were holding him for the arrival of their local leader, Dante Goreri. Judging it more politically expedient for Italians to do the killing than a foreign invader, Salvadore returned to the SPE only after having seen Mussolini's mutilated corpse strung up by its heels in Milan's public square. De Felice's reconstruction of events has been substantiated by veteran partisans who witnessed Mussolini's last days. "The documents in my possession lead me to draw one conclusion," he stated. "Mussolini was killed by a group of partisans from Milan upon the request of the British secret services. ... Their national interest was at stake, tied to the explosive compromises in the correspondence that the British Prime Minister was thought to have exchanged with Mussolini before and during the war."[17]

Thereafter, Churchill apparently set himself a three-part agenda for 1945: Win the war, win re-election, and find every scrap of his incriminating correspondence with the dead *Duce*. Victory in Europe was not followed by success at the polls, however, and, in their first opportunity to elect Churchill, British voters turned him out of office during July. Pursued by the 'black dogs' of depression, he traveled to northern Italy's Lake Como, ostensibly to paint and forget his disappointment. He had long admired the tactic of hiding in plain sight; to conceal one's real intentions under some public diversion. While newsreels showed him peacefully daubing his canvasses at the sea-side, he was out and about from 1 to 17 September, visiting all the places where the late Italian dictator spent his final days. He sought out and met with the carpenter ordered by Mussolini to build the three cabinets for the photocopied documents and letters. The carpenter told Churchill he did not know anything about the documents themselves, nor what became of them.

Later, Churchill 'had tea' with Romano Tebezi, director of the Da Maso Bank, at the same local branch in which the partisans Urbano Lazaro and 'Renzo' deposited the four bags of correspondence, one with files marked 'Churchill', they took from Mussolini when they arrested him. During a summer 1945 visit to Lake Como, Churchill stayed at the British Secret Service headquarters, located in the former villa of Guido Donegan, once a prominent industrialist and close friend of the *Duce*.

Imprisoned immediately after the war, Donegan told a fellow prisoner, once a high-ranking Fascist Party functionary, about the Churchill correspondence. Unbeknownst to either of them, their conversations were monitored, and Donegan was whisked out of his confinement by a pair of British soldiers, who took him away in a jeep. To his astonishment, he was soon being interrogated by none other than Winston Churchill "about some missing letters". Donegan was kept in solitary confinement until his mysterious death the following year.[18]

Despite Churchill's efforts to conceal his true intentions, they aroused the suspicions of several Swiss newspaper reporters, who published various accounts of his strange behavior. The prominent Basel daily, *Voix Ouvrieve*, headlined, '*Les documents de Mussolini disaparissent el M. Churchill apparait*' on 18 September 1945. Editor Leon Nicole wrote that Churchill was observed by his reporters burning large stacks of official-looking documents in a fire behind the Donegan villa.[19]

During early April 1945, Mussolini had entrusted one set of his photocopies to a lifelong friend, Tomasso David, chief of R.S.I. intelligence and leader of the 'Silver Foxes', professional saboteurs. Throughout the immediate postwar years, David was unable to find employment due to his past involvement in the Fascist National Party and, later, the Salo Republic. He was arrested during 1951 for illegally trying to change his identity and, in view of his political record, given a lengthy prison sentence. While incarcerated, David contacted the Italian Premiere, Di Gaspari, offering to barter the Mussolini documents in exchange for an early release.

Less than two years later, Churchill was in New York City for a highly publicized visit to the birthplace of his mother, Jenny Jerome, at 462 Henry Street. Like his sojourn to Lake Como in September 1945, his American appearance served as cover for an ulterior motive. In March 1953, he was hosted by Mayor Vincent Impalleteri, who had extensive ties with the Italian government, including Premiere Di Gaspari, from whom he received Tomasso David's collection of Mussolini documents. Once these were handed over to Churchill, who satisfied himself as to their authenticity, David was not only acquitted and freed from prison, but awarded Italy's highest military honor, the Republican Gold Medal, which included a life-long pension. For a former enemy leader, close confidant of the *Duce* and convicted criminal to have experienced such a dramatic reversal of fortunes seems inexplicable, given the anti-Fascist fervor of postwar Italy, unless he possessed some particularly persuasive material.

In his last days, the *Duce* may also have been trying to leave Italy with more than sensational documents, but rather something the Swiss, he hoped, would find especially interesting: sixty-five kilos of gold bullion, worth today about five billion U.S. dollars. This hoard represented all the valuables taken from native and foreign Jews in Italy before their removal to German concentration camps until 1945. When Mussolini was arrested by partisans in April, they turned it over to their superiors in the Italian Communist Party, who used the unexpected windfall to achieve political power during the postwar period. None of the 'Dongo treasure', as it was popularly known, ever found its way back to its rightful owners.

Along with gold bullion, the Italian Communist Party would have also received the Mussolini papers. A partisan known only as 'Gugliemo' took possession of all the *Duce*'s effects and dutifully handed them over to his superiors. They knew that Stalin wanted his Italian comrades purged, as he had high-ranking Party functionaries everywhere, so, to curry favor with the West, they gladly handed over the compromising documents to Churchill. Having thus easily obtained the originals, he spent the rest of his time in Italy hunting for any and all facsimiles. Aware that he was trying to track down every scrap of the missing records, agents in the British Foreign Office notified him during 1954 that copies of his wartime correspondence with Mussolini were still circulating in Italy.

He scribbled over the report, "They are all forgeries", and returned it to the BFO. His choice of words was revealing.[20] "Forgeries" signify bogus copies of originally genuine documents. If the whole lot was fake, he might have described the controversy as 'fraudulent'. In any case, he seems to have satisfied himself that by the mid-1950s all his self-incriminating letters had been accounted for and destroyed. He would appear to have done a very though job of it, and the only copies which may still survive are allegedly in the possession of the Cavalieri family, whose members refuse to disclose them.

Churchill undoubtedly sent communications to his Italian nemesis long before and during the Second World War. Less clear was the specific nature of their contents. Mussolini hinted at various 'agreements' concluded between the two statesmen. Surely something more than a few political indiscretions would have been needed to so utterly persuade Mussolini that the documents he possessed could alter his fate and that of the postwar world, while sending Churchill on a long, personal quest to gather up every trace of their existence.

The enigma of Mussolini's documents boils down to a pair of alternative conclusions: Either they never existed – at least in the sense that they were paradigm-shattering materials – or Churchill succeeded in recovering and destroying all of them, including their copies. That the *Duce* possessed at least some records he deemed uniquely important is beyond question. What precisely they contained, however, cannot yet be established with absolute certainty until either authenticated reproductions or the documents themselves come to light. Until then, the letters exchanged between both men remain one of the unanswered questions of World War Two.

18

The Italian Atomic Bomb

*Me ne frego! – 'I don't give a damn!' – the proud motto of the Squadristi, scrawled by
a wounded man on his bandages, is not only an act of philosophic stoicism. It sums up a
doctrine which is not merely political. It is evidence of a fighting spirit which accepts all risks.*
Benito Mussolini[1]

F or most of the 20th Century following the end of the Second World War, military
historians affirmed that the American nuclear program was far in advance of similar
research undertaken anywhere else in the world, particularly by German scientists,
who never came close to developing, let alone deploying an atomic weapon of their own.
But the continuing release of hitherto neglected documents and eyewitness accounts from
the final years of that conflict are beginning to reveal some altogether different conclusions.

It now appears certain that the Axis powers, including Italy, outstripped the Allies'
nuclear research in almost all respects. For example, Italian nuclear physicists were ahead
of their foreign colleagues in the years immediately prior to World War Two. By 1936,
Enrico Fermi and Franco Rosetti belonged to Europe's foremost atomic research program.
Their team, however, was divided with the anti-Semitic legislation that became law in
Italy two years later, because some of the scientists, including Fermi, had Jewish wives.[2]

They relocated to the United States, where their work led to America's atomic bomb,
which further divided their ranks, because men like Rosetti staunchly opposed the
application of nuclear power for military purposes. Addressing Fermi and the others, he
told them unequivocally, "you have disgraced your profession and stained your hands
with blood no amount of time can cleanse". Rosetti was so appalled by their "betrayal of
humanitarian science" in building an atomic bomb, he turned his back on nuclear physics
to embrace an entirely different science: paleontology.[3]

His colleagues who remained behind in Italy, however, had no such moral misgivings.
On the eve of hostilities, in 1939, scientists at the University of Milan issued the first
international patent for an atomic reactor. Its potential for the creation of an explosive
device without destructive parallel was immediately recognized, given the war-fever of the
times, and state allocations were provided for expanding practical laboratory investigation
into a potentially new arms technology. Fermi and the others who had migrated to America
did not take all University results with them. They knew as much or less about creating
a nuclear bomb than their colleagues back in Milan before the reactor patent was issued.

Atomic research in Italy proceeded slowly, if deliberately for months after Mussolini's
declaration of war against the Western Allies in June 1940, but virtually came to a standstill by year's end, due to severe shortages in essential resources requisitioned by the
Esercito and *Regia Marina* for conventional weapons' production. The University of Milan
physicists were further compromised by that venerable institution's inadequate facilities
and out-dated equipment. Their complaints did not go unheard, however, because they
found in the *Duce* an ardent admirer of their research. During May 1942, he transferred

the lot of them to the Third Reich, where some of its superior, state-of-the-art laboratories had already been set aside for that nation's own nuclear development.

The Italians found conditions entirely satisfactory, and enthusiastically shared their own atomic reactor information with German colleagues. Moving the physicists to the Reich proved inadvertently fortuitous after the Allied invasion of southern Italy made relocating men and material to Mussolini's Salo Republic, in the north, increasingly difficult from mid-1944 onwards. By then, however, all nuclear research, of which the Italians were part, had come under the purview of the SS, primarily for reasons of security. Little is known about the Italian contribution at this time, although several high-ranking officers in the *Duce*'s new armed forces allegedly witnessed German atomic testing, suggesting they were involved in its development at the highest levels of security.

Occasionally, Mussolini himself implied the deployment of nuclear weapons in the near future. As his situation in northern Italy became more desperate, he dropped hints with greater frequency, always in an air of self-confidence. As late as 21 April 1945, he told his Chief of Staff, General Graziani, "It is necessary to resist for another month. I have enough in my hand to win the peace."[4]

There is no doubt he was referring specifically to the impending availability of atom bombs, because the very next day he wrote in his Political Testament, "The wonder weapons are our hope. It is laughable and senseless for us to threaten anybody at this moment without a basis in reality for these threats. The well-known mass-destruction bombs are nearly ready. In only a few days, with the utmost meticulous intelligence, Hitler will probably execute this fearful blow, because he will have full confidence. It appears that there are three bombs, and each has an astonishing operation. The construction of each unit is fearfully complex, and of a lengthy time of completion."[5] Conventional historians claim he had been duped by Hitler's promises. Yet, Mussolini's statements fit perfectly into the context of the times.

Seven months before, a Luftwaffe flak rocket expert flying "from Ludwigslust (south of Luebeck), about twelve to fifteen kilometers from an atomic bomb test station ... noticed a strong, bright illumination of the whole atmosphere, lasting about two seconds. The clearly visible pressure wave escaped the approaching and following cloud formed by the explosion. This wave had a diameter of about one kilometer when it became visible and the color of the cloud changed frequently ... The diameter of the still-visible pressure wave was at least 9,000 meters while remaining visible for at least fifteen seconds. The combustion was lightly felt from my observation plane in the form of pulling and pushing. About one hour later, I started with an He 111 from the A/D24 at Ludwigslust and flew in an easterly direction. Shortly after the start, I passed through the almost complete overcast (between 3,000-4,000-meter altitude). A cloud shaped like a mushroom with turbulent, billowing sections (at about 7,000-meter altitude) stood, without any seeming connections, over the spot where the explosion took place."

"Strong electrical disturbances and the impossibility to continue radio communication as by lightning, turned up. Because of the P-38s operating in the area Wittenberg-Mersburg, I had to turn to the north, but observed a better visibility at the bottom of the cloud where the explosion occurred (sic)."[6]

Doubtless, the pilot saw the explosion of history's first atomic bomb. Among its better known witnesses was Dr. Josef Goebbels. Immediately after the early October 1944 blast, the Reich Propaganda Minister reported in a national broadcast that he had just seen a test of Germany's latest military technology, "the awesome power of which made me catch my breath and stopped my heartbeat."[7] Such "weapons of mass-destruction", he assured his listeners, were far beyond anything imagined by the enemy, and capable of annihilation on an unprecedented scale. Historians assume he was referring exclusively to V-2 rockets then being mass-produced in Germany's underground factories. But the ballistic missiles had already been raining on London for more than a month by the time Dr. Goebbels made his radio appearance. Moreover, it was only at this same moment that Hitler finally authorized production of an atomic bomb. Hitherto, he had been unwilling to allocate military spending on an expensive, unproven theory. But the successful Luebeck experiment changed his mind. Almost immediately after receiving the *Führer's* authorization, his scientists proceeded with a second nuclear test during the night of 11 October at Ruegen, Germany's largest island in the Baltic. This event is particularly cogent to our discussion, because the only foreigner allowed to witness it was an Italian Army officer. His attendance was all the more remarkable, in that security was so tight, only a handful of select observers from the Wehrmacht and Nazi Party was given clearance. Indeed, even any knowledge of the experiment had been restricted to just a dozen individuals outside the physicists. One of those privileged persons was Benito Mussolini.

Hitler had notified him the previous month of the upcoming test. It was then that 27-year-old Luigi Romersa was summoned to the *Duce* residing at his Salo headquarters. "I want to know more about these weapons," he told the veteran Italian Army officer, now a war-correspondent for Milan's *Corriere della Sera*. "I asked Hitler about them, but he was less than forthcoming."[8] Armed with letters of introduction to both Dr. Goebbels and the *Führer* himself, Mussolini's personal envoy flew non-stop to Berlin, where he was immediately taken in charge by SS guards. The following night, they drove him for two hours through a constant downpour to the coast of northern Germany. There, they accompanied Romersa aboard a swift motorboat that took them to the shores of the Baltic island of Ruegen.

On 12 October 1944, he and a few other men – high-ranking members of the German Army, SS and Nazi Party – were conducted by several physicists to a model village of ordinary dwellings surrounded by tall trees and populated exclusively by sheep. After a cursory inspection, the guests walked about one kilometer away to a concrete bunker fitted with a few, small observation ports of very thick glass. Even so, Romersa and company were instructed to wear darkly tinted goggles for what an official described would be "a test of the disintegration bomb. It is the most powerful explosive that has yet been developed. Nothing can withstand it."[9] A series of warning sirens and flashing, red lights announced the imminent detonation, which occurred as "a sudden, blinding flash" followed by "a thick cloud of smoke" that "took the shape of a column, and then that of a big flower," as a tremor went through the concrete bunker.[10] No one was allowed to leave for several hours, until the lingering effects of the explosion had dissipated.

"The bomb gives off deathly rays of utmost toxicity," they were told. Before being allowed to leave the bunker, scientists and guests had to don white, coarse, fibrous cloaks of asbestos with thick, glass eye-holes. Thus covered, they returned to the blast site, and were appalled at what they saw. The grass was now the color of leather, and "trees around had been turned to carbon. No leaves. Nothing alive." The sheep were "burnt to cinders." The sturdy houses visited just a few hours earlier "had disappeared, broken into little pebbles of debris."[11]

Romersa returned at once to Italy, where he briefed Mussolini on his experience. The *Duce* reacted, not with joy, but dark concern, saying nothing more than sternly warning the Milan journalist to regard his visit to Ruegen as a state secret of the utmost priority. True to this command, he said nothing of the October 1944 nuclear test until two years after the war, in a newspaper article. But when "everyone said I was mad", Romersa published a fuller account in *Oggi* magazine, during the 1950s.[12]

What Romersa left out of his account was nonetheless obvious enough; namely, that he was one of the very few observers allowed to witness the Ruegen exercise only because Italian physicists were an integral part of atomic research. Had they not been vital to the supremely classified Axis program, the SS would have never cleared a foreign newspaper correspondent (of all people!), no matter how politically impressive the source of his credentials, to Germany's most clandestine weapon, especially so late in the war, when the Third Reich's options for victory were rapidly diminishing. Romersa's chief task was to report on progress made by the Italo-German scientific team and to inform Mussolini that he could expect an operational nuclear device by spring the following year. This only explains the *Duce*'s statements in late April 1945, regarding the imminent availability of a 'disintegration bomb' and the need 'to resist for another month'.

Like Mussolini, Hitler initially evinced a similar lack of enthusiasm for atomic weaponry. As far back as 1941, when Carl von Weizsäcker, one of the leaders of Germany's nuclear research team, filed a draft patent application for a plutonium bomb, the *Führer* expressed his skepticism in a private conversation with Otto Skorzeny. He was the same SS commando-leader who, two years later, would rescue the *Duce* from Gran Sasso. "This device, if their description of it proves to be correct," Hitler concluded, "will have very little tactical value, because rarely are enemy concentrations large and dense enough, either on land or at sea, to be effectively targeted in a 1.5 kilometer blast-radius, except for industrial cities, which conventional air-strikes are presently quite capable of destroying, as this war has already shown.

"Their atomic bomb is actually a strategic weapon designed to kill large numbers of civilian populations confined in urban centers, thereby brow-beating a people into surrender. As such, it has less military utility than propaganda value as an instrument of terror. By the very nature of its destructiveness, it has an automatic, built-in circuit-breaker: If we were to cause a plutonium explosion over London, it would only be a matter of time before the British did the same thing to Berlin.

"Identical reasoning has prevented the use by all sides, even the Soviets, of poison gas in this conflict. Everyone knows the consequences. Von Weizsäcker and his colleagues should nevertheless continue their research. How wonderful if they could come up with an atomic-powered U-boat or transport-plane! Those I would gladly fund. But they will not get many *Reichsmarks* from me for a weapon whose only efficacy, so far, is the propagandistically detrimental, militarily useless incineration of non-combatants."[13]

While his armies were victorious on every front, Hitler could afford such views. But as hundreds of thousands of German civilians were being consumed in the flames of Anglo-American carpet-bombing, he reversed his original disdain for an atomic bomb, especially after the Allied landings at Normandy, in June 1944. The paired nuclear test five months later, although successful, was a relatively small affair, and a final experiment with a substantially larger discharge was necessary before military application could take place.

This occurred at the troop parade ground and barracks at Orhdruf, in south-central Thuringia, when two uranium devices were detonated on 4 March 1945. Both were observed by Soviet spies, who radioed the Kremlin that the Orhdruf explosions produced a "highly radioactive effect."[14] As part of their experiment, the SS officers, who supervised the dual test, confined captured Red Army commissars from the nearby Buchenwald concentration camp to barracks at the center of the blast.

"In many cases, their bodies were completely destroyed," according to the spies, who added that such a weapon could "slow down our offensive".[15] Kremlin officials deemed their report so important, Josef Stalin himself received one of the four copies stamped 'Urgent Priority'. But if he was alarmed, Hitler was overjoyed. On 9 March, Dr. Goebbels told a large audience at Goerlitz, "Just the day before yesterday [three days after Thuringia's two nuclear bombs were successfully detonated], he told me, 'I believe so firmly that we will master this crisis, and I believe so firmly that when we throw our armies into the new offensive, we will beat the enemy and drive him back, and I believe so firmly that we will someday add victory to our banners, as firmly as I have ever believed anything in my life'."[16]

The *Führer*'s late-hour elation was remarkably similar in tone to Mussolini's April 21st statement that he had enough in his hand "to win the peace", because both leaders hoped that Hitler's *Siegeswaffe* would be ready to turn the tables on the Allies "one minute before midnight". But by the time the SS completed final nuclear testing at Orhdruf, the military situation had surpassed even the power of an atomic bomb to reverse.

Preparations for deployment of nuclear arms may have begun in Italy almost a year before the Luebeck blast witnessed by Hans Zinsser, when a specimen of the *Regia Aeronautica*'s only four-engine heavy bomber appears to have been specifically modified to accommodate such a weapon. The Piaggio P.133 was an advanced version of the P.108B, unique not only because a single example was produced, but due to its unusual streamlining. The standard crew of ten men was reduced to just two – pilot and navigator/bombardier – while both its armor-plating and defensive machine-guns were stripped to afford a heavier payload.

The quartet of 1,500-hp Piaggio P.XIIRC.35 eighteen-cylinder radial engines was upgraded for improved power, and the bomb-bay enlarged. Although the lone P.133 was never officially designated an 'atomic bomber', extraordinarily high security surrounding its manufacture, together with the suggestive features of its design alterations, left some post-war historians wondering if the big Piaggio was intended to drop a nuclear bomb amid the Allied fleets massing for the invasion of the Italian mainland after the fall of Sicily. The P.133 might have been ready to participate in such a mission, but, clearly, no such device was yet available.

The Piaggio had to be modified for its unique task by Mussolini's air force technicians, because Italy's only purpose-built nuclear bomber fell into Allied hands after the Badoglio armistice of September 1943. Although officially known as a 'transport', the Savoia-Marchetti S.M.95 was ordered by the *Regia Aeronautica* at a period in the war when such a model was not needed, even senseless, which alone casts serious doubts on the real intention of its designers. Powered by four Alfa Romeo engines, it was twenty-three meters long, with a thirty-five-meter-wing span, which afforded it a tremendous lifting capacity. But the monster's outstanding feature was its prodigious range of 12,005 kilometers. The S.M.95's ability to carry a heavy payload over great distances suggest to some aviation historians that the 'transport' was actually intended to deliver a heavy bomb to cities along America's Eastern Seaboard.

The idea for an aerial assault on New York originated with Piaggio's chief test pilot, Nicolo Lana, in April 1942. He volunteered to fly a stripped-down P.23R, a tri-motor that had established several long-distance records before the war, dropping a single 1,000-kg. bomb on the city center, then ditching near the Nantucket Lighthouse, where he and his flight engineer would be picked up by a waiting submarine. His simple scheme offered every prospect of success. U.S. coastal defenses during the first half of 1942, when German U-boats prowling off America's eastern shores scored some of their greatest successes, were appallingly weak. Unfortunately for Lana's plan, the only P.23R in existence was destroyed in a landing accident near Albenga, and no other Italian plane had the Piaggio's outstanding range.

Had the mission been carried out, damage to New York would have been inconsequential, but the effect on Allied morale at a time when the war was not going well for the Western powers would have made a powerful impact, resulting in a triumph for Axis propaganda. Strategically, the consequences could have been no less significant, as the Americans would have doubtlessly diverted much-needed resources and manpower to protecting North America from further attack.

Despite the P.23R's mishap, Air Staff commanders had been intrigued by Lana's proposal, but realized the *Regia Aeronautica* did not possess another plane that could fly the distance to New York without stopping *en route* for refuelling by a submarine-tanker, an overly complex operation made all the more hazardous by increasingly effective Allied counter-measures. A new aircraft conceived specifically for such a mission needed to be designed and built. Hence, the Savoia-Marchetti S.M.95. Under cover as a 'transport', its first prototype flew on 8 May 1943. Performance was very good, military modifications were made, and flight-testing began on 2 September. Six days later, the Badoglio government switched sides, and the imminent mission was scrubbed. When the lone SM.95 was seized by Badoglio's government authorities, RSI planners were forced to modify the conventional Piaggio for the same purpose supposed to have been fulfilled by the four-engined Savoia-Marchetti.

Underscoring the probability of *Regia Marina* preparations for a specially redesigned aircraft able to carry an atomic bomb was the German Luftwaffe's simultaneous modification of its own heavy bomber, the Heinkel He. 177 *Greif*, or 'Vulture'. According to military air historian, David Mondey, work on a *Greif* at the Letov plant, in Prague, was intended "to provide an enlarged bomb-bay to accommodate the planned German atomic bomb".[17] The conversion began in late 1943, just when the Piaggio was being redressed in Italy. Not coincidentally, some of the German nuclear research was at that time being carried out in Czechoslovakia, where the Heinkel bomber was also converted to carry an atomic device. It would appear then, that both German and Italian Air Force officials anticipated the availability of atomic bombs sometime in late 1943.

One may only surmise that the contemporary political upheaval and *de facto* civil war that afflicted Italy with the arrest of Mussolini and subsequent turmoil in the wake of Badoglio's September armistice prevented transportation of the delicate, top secret, fissionable materials and valuable equipment from reaching the Piaggio's airstrip. The bomb intended for its sortie against the Allied invasion fleet may have been, moreover, a hastily packaged contingency than a real finished product, and the Italo-German physicists welcomed Italy's temporarily stabilized military situation as a necessary breathing-space to properly finalize their many years of work in the creation and deployment of a true weapon less encumbered by the potentially disastrous uncertainties inherent in incomplete research.

While tactical use of a nuclear weapon against the Anglo-American invasion of Italy may have been the most practical option envisioned for it by the *Commando Supremo*, the propaganda value of such a device would not have been missed by Mussolini or men like Julio Valerio Borghese. Borghese was Commander of the X Light Flotilla, whose human-torpedoes had scored spectacular successes against British ships at Alexandria and Gibraltar. With America's entry into the war on 9 December 1941, he believed these unconventional submersibles represented Italy's best hope for striking the U.S. mainland. Borghese recalled later, "the psychological effect on the Americans, who had not yet undergone any war offensive on their own soil, would, in our opinion, far outweigh the material damage which might be inflicted. And ours was the only practical plan, so far as I am aware, ever made to carry the war into the United States."[18]

Beyond its obvious propaganda value, such an attack would sink several valuable freighters, and New York's important harbor might be sufficiently damaged, as was the port of Alexandria, to close it for lengthy repairs. Far more significantly, following the attack, the Americans could be counted upon to divert substantial effort, materials and weapons from their war effort for the reinforced defense of not only New York, but the entire eastern seaboard, just as the Japanese withdrew many of their forces to protect Tokyo after it had received unimportant damage from 1942's Doolittle raid. German V-1 missile attacks against London two years later prompted a similar reaction from the British. As the Doolittle raid raised American morale after months of uninterrupted bad news, Borghese's New York operation would have an identical impact on Italian spirits. Potential repercussions – strategically, economically and psychologically – would certainly pay high military dividends on a meager investment in men and materiel.

The *Duce* and *Commando Supremo* heartily approved the scheme in late January 1942, and Borghese got to work on it immediately. The operation was set to take place in mid-December, when daylight would have been minimal and the extended darkness allowed his crews maximum time to carry out the operation. After dark, their vessel was to be delivered into the waters off Fort Hamilton. From there, it would cruise up the Hudson River to the merchant shipping docks along West Street, where 'frogmen' in scuba-gear would attach explosive charges to five or six freighters. After scuttling their submersible, the crews could choose to either surrender or go into hiding. Several thousand U.S. dollars were, in fact, provided each man, in the event he chose to avoid capture.

Due to the limited range of the *Maiale* human-torpedoes which attacked the British Fleet at Alexandria, Borghese envisioned using one of the *Regia Marina*'s pocket-submarines then operating with good success in the Black Sea against the Soviet Navy. But these 'midgets' were still too large for accommodation aboard a standard ocean-going submarine on a transatlantic mission from Europe to North America. Instead, he resurrected an earlier two-man submersible known as the Goeta-Caproni Project (after the inventor, Vincenzo Goeta, and its parent company), inaugurated in 1936.

Following extensive redesign, especially for silent running, two examples of the craft, which had been stored and almost forgotten for the previous six years, were tested under conditions of extreme secrecy in secluded Lake Iseo, later the site of another top secret undertaking, Churchill's alleged Allied-Axis alliance against the Soviet Union. One of the submersibles sank irretrievably to the bottom of the lake, but the other achieved an operational range of 113 kilometers while cruising beneath the surface at six knots, performing admirably at forty-five-meter depths.

Renamed CA 2, it was ready for action by mid-summer 1942, when Borghese contacted Admiral Karl Dönitz. The commander of the German U-boat arm was intrigued by the project's innovative audacity, but expressed his regret that he simply could not spare a single *Milchkuh*, or 'Milk Cow' submarine-refueller as a carrier for the CA-2 until late fall. Borghese knew that would not leave him enough time to make the necessary modifications, install the submersible, or test and train with it, so he visited the Italians' Atlantic submarine headquarters at Bordeaux. Rear-Admiral Romolo Polacchini, the base commander, was enthusiastically taken with the proposal, for which only the *Regia Marina*'s best submarine was good enough, in his opinion.

Lieutenant Gianfranco Priaroggia's *Leonardo Da Vinci* had just returned on 1 July after sinking 20,000 tons of Allied merchant shipping in the course of a single patrol, and both commander and submarine seemed ideally suited for the New York operation. The capacious Marconi class vessel could easily accommodate the CA 2, after its forward deck-gun and mounting were replaced by a cradle between the resistant hull and superstructure. Two large cranes on either side of the cradle lifted the pocket-submarine in or out of its cradle in which it rested, its upper one-forth exposed above decks. Both cranes folded away automatically into their own watertight compartments. "The operation against New York," Borghese stated, "had passed out of the planning stage into that of practical operation."[19]

The complicated remodeling went under way with thorough but unusual haste, allowing extensive sea trials to begin on 9 September. The equipment and procedures required some adjustments, but the CA 2 with its two crew members was consistently released and recovered without difficulty, even in somewhat rough seas. Before month's end, Lieutenant Priaroggia announced both his *Leonardo Da Vinci* and the midget-submersible were ready to undertake their mission. Borghese proudly notified his superiors in Rome, informing them that he would sail for New York on 19 December. The attack was scheduled to commence during the Winter Solstice. But too his shock and dismay, the *Supermarina* responded that the mission must be postponed for another year.

"New technological developments" then still in the making would render the operation far more effective than if it were attempted in 1942. Since such a surprise attack was a singular undertaking that could not be repeated, its maximum destructive potential had to be assured. No further explanation was given, although Borghese agreed that if the CA 2 could be eventually provided with more powerful explosive charges, as implied in the *Supermarina* communication, the long wait would be worthwhile. In the meantime, he pulled military strings to have additional pocket-submarines built and tested.

The *Leonardo Da Vinci* had her deck-gun restored after the CA 2 was removed, but all other modifications for the submersible were undisturbed in preparation for the rescheduled 1943 mission, as Priaroggia was promoted to Lieutenant Commander "for outstanding service in war" on 6 May. But seventeen days later, his submarine was depth-charged by the British frigate, *Ness*, and a destroyer, HMS *Active*, just off Cape Finestrelle. There were no survivors. By this time, the war in the Atlantic had drastically shifted against all Axis vessels, both under and on the sea, but Borghese was undeterred in his determination to hold the *Supermarina* to its word: New York must be attacked during the next Winter Solstice.

He turned from submarines to aircraft as the alternative delivery system for his CA 2. The specimen he chose was one of the outstanding airplanes of the war, a maritime reconnaissance model with exceptional flight characteristics. The CANT 511 was originally designed in September 1937, as the world's largest double-pontoon hydroplane, intended for civilian flights carrying mail, cargo and sixteen passengers between Rome and Latin America. The thirty-four-ton aircraft was powered to a cruising speed of 405 km/hr by four 1,350-hp Piaggio PXII C. 35 radial engines. At the time of its maiden flight, in October 1940, five months after Italy's entry into the war, the 511 was converted into a military role. Final testing took place between late February and early March 1942, when test pilot Mario Stoppani succeeded in taking off and landing the fully loaded CANT in rough seas with three-meter waves and winds gusting between fifty and sixty-five km/hr.

This extraordinarily rugged stability and the hydroplane's exceptional range of 5,000 kilometers seemed ideally suited for special, unconventional missions, including plans to free fifty Italian pilots and soldiers imprisoned in far-off Jeddah with a commando raid. Using the CANT to bomb Bathumi and Poti, Soviet Black Sea ports, or Baku, on the Caspian Sea, and the Persian Gulf's oil facilities at Bahrain, were seriously considered. But Borghese laid claim to the only pair of 511s before these schemes could be sanctioned, and had the machines transported to Lake Treviso for modification.

Seating arrangements and cargo areas were torn out to make room for a pair of human-torpedoes. Ezo Grossi, who had since replaced Rear-Admiral Romolo Polacchini as the Italian base commander at Bordeaux, provided a large, ocean-going submarine-tanker to rendezvous at prearranged coordinates with the giant hydro-planes on two separate occasions – once coming and going across the Atlantic Ocean – to refuel the sea-planes *en route* to the target.

While such air-sea refuelling stops had been undertaken by Italian crews earlier in the war, none, of course, were conducted over such immense distances made especially perilous by Allied supremacy at and over the sea. Even so, renovation of the 511 began in June 1943, and proceeded with determination until the air frame suffered some damage during a low-level run by USAAF fighters. Repairs commenced at once, but before they could be completed the Italian armistice was announced on 8 September, and the project abandoned. At sixty tons, however, the CA 2 was too heavy to be carried by any aircraft, so Borghese returned to the *Maiale* for his New York attack.

As intriguing as the operation itself was its sudden postponement in late 1942, when men and equipment were ready to carry out their mission. The suspension occurred just as Piaggio's alleged 'atomic bomber' was waiting for a nuclear device to be installed in its specially modified bomb-bay. Did the *Supermarina* delay the New York attack by twelve months because Mussolini expected to have an atomic bomb at his disposal by late fall or early winter 1943? His overthrow in mid-summer of that year rendered that project mute, at least until he could assert his new political base in Salo. Certainly, by April 1945, he talked as though such a weapon were about to fall into his hands.

Whatever documentation may have specified an Italian nuclear device must, of necessity, have been highly restricted. If such documentation did exist, it may still lie buried in the undisclosed archives of British intelligence. Naturally, such information would have been classified as the most secret of all and restricted to only very few supreme officials on a strictly need-to-know basis. The paper trail left by a weapon with the potential to reverse the course of history must have been necessarily scant and thoroughly covered up by the authorities. Abundant, if circumstantial evidence nonetheless suggests that the Italians were on their way to building an atomic bomb in the late 1930s. From 1942, they combined their efforts with German physicists in a joint attempt to deliver an operable device in time to win the war for the Axis. Hence, the *Duce*'s urgent appeal to his forces to "hold out for another month".

As early as fall 1942, his scientists may have informed him that the bomb would be ready by late the following year, when the singular Piaggio P.133 stood by to receive its unique payload, and Borghese's human-torpedoes would have been ready to attack New York with something more than a few explosive charges magnetically fixed to the hulls of freighters tied up at the West Street dock. Political upheavals, however, intervened to prevent the deployment of such advanced weaponry.

Someday future investigators probing the declassified files of British intelligence may find wartime documents outlining the extent of nuclear research undertaken by Fascist Italy and Nazi Germany. Perhaps when such important papers come to light they could reveal that New York City missed becoming history's first victim of a nuclear holocaust by margins too narrow to contemplate.

19

Could Mussolini Have Won His War?

History takes no account of hypothetical events which do not come to pass.
Benito Mussolini, 1943[1]

To even pose such a question as asked by this chapter seems preposterous, given standard portrayals of the *Duce*'s military incompetence and all-around inferiority of his armed forces. But these conventional assessments are deeply flawed. There were, in truth, several crucial moments during the Second World War when he could have radically altered its outcome, perhaps in his own favor.

Mussolini was confronted by the earliest of those turning-points in March 1940, after learning from his chiefs of staff that more than 3,000 warplanes screening thoroughly mechanized ground forces ready for action were at his disposal. Had he been able to see behind this deception to the real condition of his forces, he would have certainly avoided war with the Western Allies at that time, regardless of any provocations, and put the modernization of Italy's military machine into full gear for later involvement.

Although its renovation would not have been complete by June 1941, when Germany invaded Russia, he was ideologically bound to participate in Operation *Barbarossa*. Italian contribution to the fighting on the Eastern Front could have been substantially more significant than it was, had he obtained from the conflict until then, and might have tipped the scales against Stalin, who was already pressed to the navel by Hitler's Wehrmacht. By then, the *Regia Aeronautica* would have been well on the way to replacing its obsolete biplane fighters and tri-motor bombers with the high performance interceptors and long-range aircraft which were eventually produced. These warplanes would have been more than a match for anything flown by the Red Air Force and at least equal contenders against British Spitfires and American Mustangs.

There were other, technical developments, which, if better nurtured, might have significantly changed the course of events. The most obvious of these was failure to carry forward advances in radar, invented by a fellow Italian, the famous Marconi, who gave his country a head-start in its application. Inability to take it further was to cost the *Regia Marina* not only many ships and more lives, but also early victory in the Mediterranean. The Germans were quite generous with their own radar technology, offering the navy and civil defense commanders examples of the latest *Freya* instrument, and inviting Italian technicians to study the military application of state-of-the-art electronics in the Third Reich.

Italy's most controversial technological innovation was the atomic bomb being constructed in concert with German nuclear physicists. While the whole story of its development is still far from full disclosure, it seems likely that such a device was about ready for deployment in late 1943. Evidence suggests the bomb would have been available by early summer, as reflected in efforts of both Mussolini and Hitler to give their 'Victory Weapon' time for deployment by delaying the Allied advance as long as possible. It was probably this consideration that convinced *Commando Supremo* strategists to enigmatically postpone Prince Borghese's midget-submarine attack on New York City.

By fall 1942, training and trials for the operation had been successfully completed. The time was ripe for a North Atlantic passage, because German U-boats still largely dominated most of the sea-lanes. Nothing would have prevented the 'Black Prince' from carrying out against the United States the same kind of mission that paralyzed Britain's Royal Navy at Gibraltar and Alexandria. Had the New York raid gone ahead as planned and succeeded with conventional explosives, its ramifications would have far exceeded their prodigious propaganda effect.

The single most decisive factor in the defeat of the Axis powers was the so-called 'ULTRA secret' which allowed Allied commanders to learn the battle strategies, troop strengths and dispositions, and orders of the German, Italian and Japanese general staffs in advance of their execution, especially after June 1942. These military intelligence considerations are rarely if ever cited by mainstream historians as possible causes for Italy's fate in World War Two. More often, they point to Malta as the key to Allied victory. From this strategically located base, British ships and planes attacked Italian convoys trying to supply their troops in North Africa, and later used it as a springboard for the invasion of the peninsula itself. Mussolini's chief error, therefore, was his failure to seize Malta.

But we have learned that his air and naval forces, importantly aided by the German Luftwaffe, had effectively neutralized the island by spring 1942, without recourse to a costly invasion. He, along with with every other Axis strategist, did not doubt that the island could be contained for as long as necessary. They had no way of knowing that Allied cryptographers would so thoroughly penetrate the highest levels of their military security by June, after the last obstacle to their decipherment had been eliminated with the assassination of Reinhard Heydrich. Henceforward, Malta began to reassert itself as a supremely lethal threat to Italian domination of the Central Mediterranean.

Most students of modern history may find it strange that among World War Two's most crucial turning-points and possibly Mussolini's greatest strategic success was his October 1940 attack on Greece. In creating a successful diversion, he undoubtedly saved his men in Libya. If Churchill had not depleted Britain's Western Desert Army by aiding the Greeks, General Wavell's forces would have undoubtedly steamrolled the Italians, expelling them from North Africa months before Rommel could have arrived to save them. It was also Graziani's last chance to regain the offensive, which would have no less decisively ended the campaign, but in an Italian victory, with drastic consequences for the rest of the war.

Hitler, for his part, was particularly annoyed by the necessity of Wehrmacht involvement in the Balkans, just as he was preparing to invade Russia. His conquest of Yugoslavia and Greece delayed the launch of Operation *Barbarossa* from mid-spring to early summer 1941. But if German forces had gotten under way when he planned, in early May, they would have found themselves bogged down by the most ferocious torrential rains ever experienced throughout Eastern Europe. The Luftwaffe would have been grounded, the artillery and Panzers mired in mud, and the infantry halted by swollen rivers. The nearly two-month postponement afforded Hitler by campaigning in Yugoslavia and Greece guaranteed a good start for his attack against the Soviets.

Fasces emblem on Chicago's Columbus Memorial.

On the contrary, had Operation *Hercules* been allowed to proceed as intended, in July 1942, it probably would have succeeded, despite the Allies' intelligence edge, because the British were still too low on men and equipment. The island's 25,000 defenders would have nonetheless cost the Axis invaders dear, just as Hitler anticipated. Italian occupation of Malta at this time would have unquestionably prolonged the fighting in the Mediterranean and North African theaters, but not necessarily won them for Mussolini. The Americans were becoming adept at island-hopping, and could have just as surely taken Malta, as they did Pantelleria.

Even so, Italian forces could have seized Malta with ease if they invaded when it was deeply understrength during early summer 1940. Some *Commando Supremo* strategists had, in fact, insisted upon the island's early capture as a precondition for Mediterranean victory. To be sure, Malta's occupation before it was properly fortified would have guaranteed safe passage of Italian convoys, the life-blood of Axis forces in North Africa, throughout the desert campaign. The poor performance of Italian arms in France at this time, however, suggests an invasion of Malta would not have succeeded.

Before the decoding intercepts of ULTRA finally sealed Mussolini's doom, the most decisive moment for Italian fortunes came in Libya during September 1940, when Graziani refused to maintain the momentum of his offensive. He may have been right to pause for resupply, but missed his best chance for success by waiting for the British to re-take the initiative. Had the Marshal resumed his attack in October, his men would have found General Wavell's forces far more unready for battle than suspected. By year's end, the Italians would have likely been in Alexandria, and driven their enemies from Egypt.

Commando Supremo could then have focused on Gibraltar in early 1941. Its capture or neutralization would have allowed *Regia Marina* surface ships access to the Atlantic Ocean, where the Royal Navy would have been hard-pressed between the Italian High Seas Fleet and the German Kriegsmarine. Great Britain could have been strangled into defeat before America's official entry into the war after 7 December. With North Africa in Axis hands, the *Regia Aeronautica* and *Esercito* would have been free to devote the bulk of their forces to fighting the Soviets, who might have cracked under the added pressure of Italian planes and troops.

These speculations are by no means far-fetched. Although some are closer to the realm of probability than others, any one of them might have drastically altered the final outcome of Mussolini's War. But winning it for him was not everything. He believed in a kind of parallel world, the flip-side of Earthly existence, where Fascism lived on undiminished by transitory military outcome.

"We have created our own myth," he declared in 1935. "This myth is a faith, it is passion. It is not necessary that it shall be a reality. It is a reality by the fact that it is good, a hope, a faith, that it is courage."[2]

Hope he never lost, and courage his soldiers never lacked.

Notes

Introduction: The First Casualty of War
1. Cassels, Alan, *Fascism*, NY: Thomas Y. Crowell, 1975.
2. Hayward, James, *Myths and Legends of the Second World War*, Stroud: Sutton Publishing, 2005.
3. Bradford, Ernle, *Siege: Malta, 1940-1943*, Barnsley: Pen and Sword Military Classics, 2003.
4. Haining, Peter, *The Chianti Raiders: The Extraordinary Story Of The Italian Air Force In The Battle Of Britain*, London: Anova Books, 2005.
5. Deakin, F.W., *Brutal Friendship: Mussolini, Hitler and the Fall of Italian Fascism*, London: Phoenix Press, 2000.

1   Crossing a 20th Century Rubicon
1. Gregor, James A., *Young Mussolini and the Intellectual Origins of Fascism*, Berkeley CA: University of California Press, 1979.
2. Payne, Stanley G., *Fascism: Comparison and Definition*, Milwaukee WI: University of Wisconsin Press, 1980.
3. Biagi, Enzo, editor, *Storia del Fascismo*, Florence: Sadea-Della Volpe, 1964.
4. Waldman, Victor, *Mussolini*, Chicago IL: Hollingsdale Press, 1949.
5. Mussolini, Benito, *Mussolini Memoirs*, 1942-1943, London: Phoenix Press, 2000.
6. Elson, Robert T., *Prelude to War, World War II*, Alexandria VA: Time-Life Books, 1977.
7. Troege, Walter, *European Front*, NE: Preuss, 2008.
8. Gregor, James A., *Italian Fascism and Developmental Dictatorship*, Princeton NJ: Princeton University Press, 1979.
9. Haining, Peter, *The Chianti Raiders: The Extraordinary Story Of The Italian Air Force In The Battle Of Britain*, London: Anova Books, 2005.
10. Mussolini, Benito, *Mussolini Memoirs*, 1942-1943, London: Phoenix Press, 2000.
11. Smith, Dennis Mack, *Mussolini*, London: Weidenfeld & Nicolson, 1981.
12. Waldman, Victor, *Mussolini*, Chicago IL: Hollingsdale Press, 1949.
13. *Encyclopedia Britannica*, Macropedia Volume 12, Chicago IL: The University of Chicago, Encyclopedia Britannica, Inc., 1981.
14. Del Valle, P.A., *Roman Eagles over Ethiopia*, Harrisburg PA: Military Service Publishing Company, 1940.
15. Baer, George W., *The Coming of the Italian-Ethiopian War*, Cambridge MA: Harvard University Press, 1967.
16. Barker, A.J., *The Italo-Ethiopian War, 1935-36*, London: Cassell, 1968.
17. Coffey, T.M., *Lion By The Tail: The Story of the Italian-Ethiopian War*, London: Hamish Hamilton, 1974.
18. De Bono, Marshal, *Anno XIII: The Conquest of an Empire*, London: Cresset Press, 1937.

19. Bosworth, R.J.B., *Mussolini*, NY: Hodder Arnold, 2002.
20. Waldman, Victor, *Mussolini*, Chicago IL: Hollingsdale Press, 1949.
21. Arnold, A.C., "Italo-Abyssinian Campaign", *Royal United Services Institution Journal*, February 1937, pp 71-88.
22. Del Boca, Angelo, *The Ethiopian War*, Chicago IL: University of Chicago Press, 1969.
23. Pinza, Ezio, *Ezio Pinza: An Autobiography*, NY: Ayer Co Pub, 1977.
24. Boddy, Kasia, *Boxing: A Cultural History*, NY: Reaktion Books, 2009.
25. Baker, Jean-Claude, *Josephine Baker: The Hungry Heart*, NY: Cooper Square Press, 2001.
26. Smith, Dennis Mack, *Mussolini*, London: Weidenfeld & Nicolson, 1981.
27. Bosworth, R.J.B., *Mussolini*, NY: Hodder Arnold, 2002.
28. Nicolle, David, *The Italian Invasion of Abyssinia 1935-36*, Oxford: Osprey Publishing, 1997.
29. Ibid.
30. Parducci, A., "Askaris: The Story of Italian Colonial Troops", Rome: *Coorte*, Vol. 1, Issue 9, 1999.
31. Polson Newman, E.W., *Italy's Conquest of Abyssinia*, London: Thornton Butterworth, 1937.
32. Schwab, Peter, editor, *Ethiopia and Haile Selassie*, NY: Facts On File, Inc., 1972.
33. Barker, A.J., *The Italo-Ethiopian War, 1935-36*, London: Cassell, 1968.
34. De Bono, Marshal, *Anno XIII: The Conquest of an Empire*, London: Cresset Press, 1937.
35. Starace, A., *La marcia su Gondar*, Milan: A. Mondadori, 1937.
36. Pedriali, Ferdinando, *Stato Maggiore Aeronautica – Ufficio Storico, L'aeronautica Italiana nelle guerre coloniali – Guerra Etiopica 1935 – 1936* (*Italian Aviation in the colonial wars – Ethiopian War 1935 – 1936*), Rome : Stato Maggiore Aeronautica – Ufficio Storico, 1997.
37. Polson Newman, E.W., *Italy's Conquest of Abyssinia*, London: Thornton Butterworth, 1937.
38. De Bono, Marshal, *Anno XIII: The Conquest of an Empire*, London: Cresset Press, 1937.
39. *Il Duce! Songs of Italian Fascism 1922-1943*, Oakleaf Records, U.S. (NJ), #OAK-CD-302-01.
40. Smith, Dennis Mack, *Mussolini*, London: Weidenfeld & Nicolson, 1981.
41. Mockler, Anthony, *Haile Selassie's War*, NY: Signal Books, 2003.

2 Flying Rats

1. Waldman, Victor, *Mussolini*, Chicago IL: Hollingsdale Press, 1949.
2. Ibid.
3. Hitler, Adolf, *Hitler's Table Talk 1941-1944*, NY: Enigma Books, 2002.
4. Smith, Dennis Mack, *Mussolini*, London: Weidenfeld & Nicolson, 1981.
5. Waldman, Victor, *Mussolini*, Chicago IL: Hollingsdale Press, 1949.
6. Mussolini, Benito, *Mussolini Memoirs*, 1942-1943, London: Phoenix Press, 2000.
7. Peers, E. Allison, *The Spanish Tragedy*, Oxford: Oxford University Press, 1936.

8.   Mondey, David, *A Concise Guide to Axis Aircraft of World War II*, Middlesex: Temple Press, 1984.
9.   Gooch, John, *Mussolini and his Generals: The Armed Forces and Fascist Foreign Policy, 1922-1940*, Cambridge: Cambridge Military Histories, Cambridge University Press, 2007.
10. Edwards, Jerome E., *Foreign Policy of Col. McCormick's Tribune 1929-1941*, Reno NV: University of Nevada Press, 1971.

3   A Modern Gallic War
1.   Waldman, Victor, *Mussolini*, Chicago IL: Hollingsdale Press, 1949.
2.   *Encyclopedia Britannica*, Macropedia Volume 12, U.S. (IL): The University of Chicago, Encyclopedia Britannica, Inc., 1981.
3.   Mussolini, Benito, *Mussolini Memoirs*, 1942-1943, London: Phoenix Press, 2000.
4.   Fox Movie-tone Newsreel, 'Special', 6 July, 1930.
5.   Mussolini, Benito, *Mussolini Memoirs*, 1942-1943, London: Phoenix Press, 2000.
6.   Ibid.
7.   Buchanan, Patrick J., *Churchill, Hitler, and "The Unnecessary War": How Britain Lost Its Empire and the West Lost the World*, NY: Three Rivers Press; Reprint edition, 2009.
8.   Mussolini, Benito, *Mussolini Memoirs*, 1942-1943, London: Phoenix Press, 2000.
9.   Ibid.
10. Ibid.
11. Tomes, Jason Hunter, *King Zog of Albania*, NY: NY University Press, 2003.
12. Ibid.
13. Ibid.
14. Ibid.
15. Ibid.
16. Edwards, Jerome E., *Foreign Policy of Col. McCormick's Tribune 1929-1941*, Reno NV: University of Nevada Press, 1971.
17. Mussolini, Benito, *Mussolini Memoirs*, 1942-1943, London: Phoenix Press, 2000.
18. Ibid.
19. Ibid.
20. Baker, Nicholson, *Human Smoke, The Beginnings of World War II, the End of Civilization*, NY: Simon & Schuster, 2008.
21. Ibid.
22. Mussolini, Benito, *Mussolini Memoirs*, 1942-1943, London: Phoenix Press, 2000.
23. Ibid.
24. *The Marshall Cavendish Illustrated Encyclopedia of World War Two*, Volume 2, NY: Marshall Cavendish, 1985.
25. Mussolini, Benito, *Mussolini Memoirs*, 1942-1943, London: Phoenix Press, 2000.
26. Brinkley, Doug, *An American Sees the New Germany*, NE: Preuss, 2001.
27. Ciano, Galeazzo, *Diary*, 1937 to 1943, London: Heinemann, 1958.
28. Mussolini, Romano, *My Father, Il Duce*, NY: Random House, 2006.
29. Mussolini, Benito, *Mussolini Memoirs*, 1942-1943, London: Phoenix Press, 2000.
30. Gibson, Alexander, *The Roots of World War Two*, CA: Trundle Press, 1955.
31. Farrell, Nicholas, *Mussolini: A New Life*, London: Phoenix, 2005.

32. Ibid.
33. Smith, Jean Edward, *FDR*, NY: Random House Trade Paperbacks, 2008.
34. Baker, Nicholson, *Human Smoke, The Beginnings of World War II, the End of Civilization*, NY: Simon & Schuster, 2008.
35. Ibid.
36. Jackson, Robert, *Air War Over France*, London: Ian Allan, 1974.
37. Ciano, Galeazzo, *Diary*, 1937 to 1943, London: Heinemann, 1958.
38. Klibansky, Raymond, editor, *Mussolini Memoirs*, London: Orion Publishing Group, Ltd., 2000 reprint of the 1949 original released by Weidenfeld & Nicolson (London).

4 King Of Beasts By The Tail

1. Mallett, Robert, *Mussolini and the Origins of the Second World War, 1933 -1940*, Basingstoke: Palgrave Macmillan, 2003.
2. Finaldi, Giuseppe, *Mussolini and Italian Fascism*, NY: Longman, 2008.
3. Kesselring, Albert, *The Memoirs of Field-Marshal Kesselring*, London: Greenhill Books, 2007.
4. Haining, Peter, *The Chianti Raiders: The Extraordinary Story Of The Italian Air Force In The Battle Of Britain*, London: Anova Books, 2005.
5. Ibid.
6. Dunning, Chris, *Courage Alone: The Italian Air Force, 1940-1943*, Aldershot: Hikoki, 1998.
7. Vergnano, P., *Fiat Fighters, 1930-1945*, Genoa: Intyrama, 1969.
8. Shores, Christopher, *Regia Aeronautica: A Pictorial History of the Italian Air Force, 1940-1943*, Warren MI: Squadron Signal, 1976.
9. Haining, Peter, *The Chianti Raiders: The Extraordinary Story Of The Italian Air Force In The Battle Of Britain*, London: Anova Books, 2005.
10. Sgarlato, N., *Italian Aircraft in World War Two*, NY: Delta, 1979.
11. Apostolo, Giorgio, and Massimello, *Italian Aces of World War 2* (Osprey Aircraft of the Aces No 34), Oxford: Osprey, 2004.
12. Thompson, Jonathan W., *Italian Civil and Military Aircraft, 1930-1945*, NY: Aero Publishers, 1963.
13. Haining, Peter, *The Chianti Raiders: The Extraordinary Story Of The Italian Air Force In The Battle Of Britain*, London: Anova Books, 2005.
14. Ibid.

5   Snatching Defeat from the Jaws of Victory

1. Hart, B.H. Liddell, *Scipio Africanus, Greater Than Napoleon*, NY: Da Capo Press,1994.
2. Farrell, Nicholas, *Mussolini: A New Life*, London: Phoenix, 2005.
3. Trye, Rex, *Mussolini's Afrika Korps: The Italian Army in North Africa, 1940-1943*, NY: Axis Europa Books, 1992.
4. Mussolini, Benito, *Mussolini Memoirs*, 1942-1943, London: Phoenix Press, 2000.
5. Ibid.

6. Klibansky, Raymond, editor, *Mussolini Memoirs*, London: The Orion Publishing Group, Ltd., 2000 reprint of the 1949 original released by Weidenfeld & Nicolson (London).

7. Mussolini, Benito, *Mussolini Memoirs*, 1942-1943, London: Phoenix Press, 2000.

8. Ibid.

9. Deakin, Friedrich W., *The Brutal Friendship: Mussolini, Hitler and the Fall of Italian Fascism*, NY: Harper & Row, 1962.

10. Ridley, Jasper, *Mussolini: A Biography*, NY: Cooper Square Press, 2000.

11. Mussolini, Benito, *Mussolini Memoirs*, 1942-1943, London: Phoenix Press, 2000.

12. Trye, Rex, *Mussolini's Afrika Korps: The Italian Army in North Africa, 1940-1943*, NY: Axis Europa Books, 1992.

13. Knox, McGregor, *Hitler's Italian Allies: Royal Armed Forces, Fascist Regime, and the War of 1940-1943*, Cambridge: Cambridge University Press, 2000.

14. Walker, Ian, *Iron Hulls Iron Hearts: Mussolini's Elite Armoured Divisions in North Africa*, Marlborough: The Crowood Press, 2006.

15. Madej, W. Victor, *Italian Army Order of Battle: 1940-1944*, Allentown PA: Valor Publishing Company, 1987.

16. Neulen, Hans Werner, *In the Skies of Europe, Air Forces allied to the Luftwaffe, 1939-1945*, Marlborough: The Crowood Press, 2005.

17. Trye, Rex, *Mussolini's Afrika Korps: The Italian Army in North Africa, 1940-1943*, NY: Axis Europa Books, 1992.

18. Jowett, Philip S., *The Italian Army, 1940-45*, Oxford: Osprey Publishing, 2000.

19. Mussolini, Romano, *My Father, Il Duce*, NY: Random House, 2006.

20. Author's personal correspondence

21. Vasta, Salvatore, "'M' Battalions: the *Duce*'s Own", Rome, *Coorte*, Vol. 1, Issue 7, 2000.

22. Burgwyn, James H., *Empire on the Adriatic, Mussolini's Conquest of Yugoslavia 1941–1943*, NY: Enigma Books, 2005.

6 Desert Fox In A Henhouse

1. Pitt, Barrie, *History of the Second World War – Rommel: The Desert Fox* (Part 13), NY: Marshall Cavendish USA Ltd., 1973.

2. Neulen, Hans Werner, *In the Skies of Europe, Air Forces allied to the Luftwaffe, 1939-1945*, Marlborough: The Crowood Press, 2005.

3. Generalkommando des Deutschen Afrikakorps, editors, *Marsch und Kampf des Deutschen Afrikakorps*, Band I, Munich: Carl Röhrig Verlag, 1941.

4. Kitchen, Martin, *Rommel's Desert War: Waging World War II in North Africa, 1941-1943*, Cambridge: Cambridge University Press, 2009.

5. Apostolo, Giorgio, and Massimello, *Italian Aces of World War 2* (Osprey Aircraft of the Aces No 34), Oxford: Osprey, 2004.

6. Mussolini, Benito, *Mussolini Memoirs*, 1942-1943, London: Phoenix Press, 2000.

7. Churchill, Winston S., *The Churchill War Papers: The Ever Widening War*, Volume 3: 1941, NY: W.W. Norton & Co., 2001.

8. Irving, David, *Churchill's War Volume II: Triumph in Adversity*, London: Focal Point Publications, 2001.

7   Mare Nostro

1. Bragadin, Marc' Antonio, Commander (R), Italian Navy, *The Italian Navy in World War II*, translated by Gale Hoffman, Annapolis MD: United States Naval Institute, 1957.
2. www.regiamarina.com.
3. Churchill, Winston S., *The Churchill War Papers: The Ever Widening War*, Volume 3: 1941, NY: W.W. Norton & Co., 2001.
4. Horsley, Terrence, *Find, Fix and Strike*, London: Eyre and Spottiswoode, 1943.

8   The *Duce*'s Dolphins

1. Legnani, Admiral Antonio, http://www.regiamarina.net/subs/documents/subs_1941/1941_us.htm.
2. Jackson, Robert, *Submarines of the World*, London: Amber Books, 2000.
3. Legnani, Admiral Antonio, http://www.regiamarina.net/subs/documents/subs_1941/1941_us.htm.
4. Jackson, Robert, *Submarines of the World*, London: Amber Books, 2000.
5. Sanzio, Raffaele, http://www.regiamarina.net/subs/people/stories/sanzio_us.htm
6. Jackson, Robert, *Submarines of the World*, London: Amber Books, 2000.
7. http://www.valoratsea.com/subwar.htm.
8. http://www.2worldwar2.com/submarines.htm.
9. Daneo, Mario, http://www.regiamarina.net/subs/people/stories/daneo_us.htm
10. http://www.regiamarina.net/subs/people/commanders/feciadicossato/feciadicossato_us.htm

9   Hercules Spurned

1. Bragadin, Marc' Antonio, Commander (R), Italian Navy, *The Italian Navy in World War II*, translated by Gale Hoffman, Annapolis MD: United States Naval Institute, 1957.
2. Trye, Rex, *Mussolini's Afrika Korps: The Italian Army in North Africa, 1940-1943*, NY: Axis Europa Books, 1992.
3. Kesselring, Albert, *The Memoirs of Field-Marshal Kesselring*, London: Greenhill Books, 2007.
4. Sadkovich, James J., "Of Myths and Men: Rommel and the Italians in North Africa, 1940-1942", *The International History Review*, XIII, May 1991.
5. Degrelle, Leon, *Epic: The Story of the Waffen SS*, Costa Mesa CA: Institute for Historical Review, 1983.
6. Pitt, Barrie, *History of the Second World War – Rommel: The Desert Fox* (Part 13), NY: Marshall Cavendish USA Ltd., 1973.
7. Manvell, Roger and Fraenkel, Heinrich, *The Canaris Conspiracy, The Secret Resistance to Hitler in the German Army*, NY: Pinnacle Books, 1969.
8. Boyar, Jane, *Hitler Stopped By Franco*, NY: Marbella House, 2001.
9. Hitler, Adolf, *Hitler's Table Talk 1941-1944*, NY: Enigma Books, 2002.
10. Sadkovich, James J., "Of Myths and Men: Rommel and the Italians in North Africa, 1940-1942", *The International History Review*, XIII, May 1991.

11. Bragadin, Marc' Antonio, Commander (R), Italian Navy, *The Italian Navy in World War II*, translated by Gale Hoffman, Annapolis MD: United States Naval Institute, 1957.
12. Neulen, Hans Werner, *In the Skies of Europe, Air Forces allied to the Luftwaffe, 1939-1945*, Marlborough: The Crowood Press, 2005.
13. Mussolini, Benito, *Mussolini Memoirs*, 1942-1943, London: Phoenix Press, 2000.
14. Singh, Simon, *The Code Book, The Science of Secrecy from Ancient Egypt to Quantum Cryptography*, NY: Anchor Books, Random House, 1999.
15. Mikkelson, Robert, *Reinhard Heydrich*, NE: Preuss Press, 1995.
16. Pitt, Barrie, *History of the Second World War – Rommel: The Desert Fox* (Part 13), NY: Marshall Cavendish USA Ltd., 1973.

10 Unacknowledged Victory

1. Bragadin, Marc' Antonio, Commander (R), Italian Navy, *The Italian Navy in World War II*, translated by Gale Hoffman, Annapolis MD: United States Naval Institute, 1957.
2. Thompson, Robert, *The Struggle for the Mediterranean*, 1940-1944, OH: Campbell Publishers, 1950.
3. Bragadin, Marc' Antonio, Commander (R), Italian Navy, *The Italian Navy in World War II*, translated by Gale Hoffman, Annapolis MD: United States Naval Institute, 1957.
4. Ibid.
5. www.regiamarina.com.
6. Thompson, Robert, *The Struggle for the Mediterranean*, 1940-1944, OH: Campbell Publishers, 1950.
7. Ibid.
8. Ibid.
9. www.regiamarina.com.
10. Ibid.
11. Waldman, Victor, *Mussolini*, Chicago IL: Hollingsdale Press, 1949.
12. Ibid.
13. Woelfle, Gretchen, *Jeannette Rankin: Political Pioneer*, Honesdale PA: Calkins Creek Books, 2007.
14. Waldman, Victor, *Mussolini*, Chicago IL: Hollingsdale Press, 1949.
15. Fox movie-tone news, 'Special', 19 April 1930.
16. Ibid.

11 Sunshine from Italy

1. Chuikov, Vasili I., *Battle for Stalingrad*, NY: Ballantine Books , 1968.
2. Waldman, Victor, *Mussolini*, Chicago IL: Hollingsdale Press, 1949.
3. Ibid.
4. Mussolini, Benito, *Mussolini Memoirs*, 1942-1943, London: Phoenix Press, 2000.
5. Jowett, Philip S., *The Italian Army, 1940-45*, Oxford: Osprey Publishing, 2000.
6. Mussolini, Benito, *Mussolini Memoirs*, 1942-1943, London: Phoenix Press, 2000.
7. Neulen, Hans Werner, *In the Skies of Europe, Air Forces allied to the Luftwaffe, 1939-1945*, Marlborough: The Crowood Press, 2005.

8. Mussolini, Benito, *Mussolini Memoirs*, 1942-1943, London: Phoenix Press, 2000.
9. Ibid.
10. Jowett, Philip S., *The Italian Army, 1940-45*, Oxford: Osprey Publishing, 2000.
11. Mussolini, Benito, *Mussolini Memoirs*, 1942-1943, London: Phoenix Press, 2000.
12. Ibid.
13. Adams, Henry, *World War Two: Italy at War*, Alexandria VA: Time-Life, Inc., 1982.
14. Vasta, Salvatore, "'M' Battalions: the *Duce*'s Own", Rome, *Coorte*, Vol. 1, Issue 7, 2000.
15. Ibid.
16. Mussolini, Benito, *Mussolini Memoirs*, 1942-1943, London: Phoenix Press, 2000.
17. Hoyt, Edwin P., *199 Days: The Battle for Stalingrad*, NY: Forge Books, 1999.
18. Chuikov, Vasili I., *Battle for Stalingrad*, NY: Ballantine Books , 1968.
19. Coraja, Santi, translated by R.L. Miller, *Hitler and Mussolini,* NY: Enigma Books, 1985.
20. Ibid.

12 Middle Age Crisis
1. Greene, Jack and Massignani, Alessandro, *The Black Prince and the Sea Devils*, NY: DaCapo Press, 2004.
2. Bragadin, Marc' Antonio, Commander (R), Italian Navy, *The Italian Navy in World War II*, translated by Gale Hoffman, Annapolis MD: United States Naval Institute, 1957.

13 North African Finale
1. Sadkovich, James J., "Of Myths and Men: Rommel and the Italians in North Africa, 1940-1942", *The International History Review*, XIII, May, 1991.
2. Ibid.
3. Mussolini, Benito, *Mussolini Memoirs*, 1942-1943, London: Phoenix Press, 2000.
4. Bragadin, Marc' Antonio, Commander (R), Italian Navy, *The Italian Navy in World War II*, translated by Gale Hoffman, Annapolis MD: United States Naval Institute, 1957.
5. Mussolini, Benito, *Mussolini Memoirs*, 1942-1943, London: Phoenix Press, 2000.

14 Mussolini Island
1. Mussolini, Benito, *Mussolini Memoirs*, 1942-1943, London: Phoenix Press, 2000.
2. Eisenhower, Gen. Dwight David, *Crusade in Europe*, NY: Doubleday, Inc., 1963.
3. Irving, David, *The War Between the Generals Inside the Allied High Command*, NY: Congdon & Weed, 1981.
4. Mussolini, Benito, *Mussolini Memoirs*, 1942-1943, London: Phoenix Press, 2000.
5. Klibansky, Raymond, editor, *Mussolini Memoirs*, London: The Orion Publishing Group, Ltd., 2000 reprint of the 1949 original released by Weidenfeld & Nicolson (London).
6. Mussolini, Benito, *Mussolini Memoirs*, 1942-1943, London: Phoenix Press, 2000.

7. Reeder, Red, *Omar Nelson Bradley: the Soldiers' General*, NY: Garrard Pub. Co., 1969.
8. Mussolini, Benito, *Mussolini Memoirs*, 1942-1943, London: Phoenix Press, 2000.
9. Ibid.
10. Ibid.
11. Ibid.
12. Waldman, Victor, *Mussolini*, Chicago IL: Hollingsdale Press, 1949.
13. Mussolini, Benito, *Mussolini Memoirs*, 1942-1943, London: Phoenix Press, 2000.
14. Ibid.
15. Apostolo, Giorgio, and Massimello, *Italian Aces of World War 2* (Osprey Aircraft of the Aces No 34), Oxford: Osprey, 2004.
16. Dunning, Chris, *Courage Alone: The Italian Air Force, 1940-1943*, Aldershot: Hikoki Publications, 1998.
17. Messenger, Charles, *A World War Two Chronicle*, London: Arcadia House, 1995.
18. Madej, W. Victor, *Italian Army Order of Battle: 1940-1944*, Allentown PA: Valor Publishing Company, 1987.
19. Follain, John, *Mussolini's Island: The Untold Story of the Invasion of Sicily*, NY: Hodder & Stoughton, 2007.
20. Mussolini, Benito, *Mussolini Memoirs*, 1942-1943, London: Phoenix Press, 2000.
21. Klibansky, Raymond, editor, *Mussolini Memoirs*, London: The Orion Publishing Group, Ltd., 2000 reprint of the 1949 original released by Weidenfeld & Nicolson (London).
22. Bragadin, Marc' Antonio, Commander (R), Italian Navy, *The Italian Navy in World War II*, translated by Gale Hoffman, Annapolis MD: United States Naval Institute, 1957.
23. Waldman, Victor, *Mussolini*, Chicago IL: Hollingsdale Press, 1949.

15 The Ordeal of Blood

1. Waldman, Victor, *Mussolini*, Chicago IL: Hollingsdale Press, 1949.
2. Mussolini, Romano, *My Father, Il Duce*, NY: Random House, 2006.
3. Smith, Dennis Mack, *Mussolini*, London: Weidenfeld & Nicolson, 1981.
4. Coraja, Santi, translated by R.L. Miller, *Hitler and Mussolini,* NY: Enigma Books, 1985.
5. Moseley, Ray, *Mussolini's Shadow: The Double Life of Count Galeazzo Ciano*, New Haven CT: Yale University Press, 2000.
6. Mussolini, Romano, *My Father, Il Duce*, NY: Random House, 2006.
7. Mussolini, Benito, *Mussolini Memoirs*, 1942-1943, London: Phoenix Press, 2000.
8. Mussolini, Romano, *My Father, Il Duce*, NY: Random House, 2006.
9. Mussolini, Benito, *Mussolini Memoirs*, 1942-1943, London: Phoenix Press, 2000.
10. Klibansky, Raymond, editor, *Mussolini Memoirs*, London: The Orion Publishing Group, Ltd., 2000 reprint of the 1949 original released by Weidenfeld & Nicolson (London).
11. Mussolini, Romano, *My Father, Il Duce*, NY: Random House, 2006.
12. Greene, Jack and Massignani, Alessandro, *The Black Prince and the Sea Devils*, NY: DaCapo Press, 2004.
13. Mussolini, Benito, *My Autobiography*, NY: Scribner's, 1928.

14. Eisenhower, Gen. Dwight David, *Crusade in Europe*, NY: Doubleday, Inc., 1963.
15. Bragadin, Marc' Antonio, Commander (R), Italian Navy, *The Italian Navy in World War II*, translated by Gale Hoffman, Annapolis MD: United States Naval Institute, 1957.
16. Sadkovich, James J., *The Italian Navy in World War II*, Westport CT: Greenwood Press, 1994.
17. Mussolini, Benito, *Mussolini Memoirs*, 1942-1943, London: Phoenix Press, 2000.
18. Annussek, Greg, *Hitler's Raid to Save Mussolini: The Most Infamous Commando Operation of World War II*, NY: Da Capo Press, 2006.
19. Waldman, Victor, *Mussolini*, Chicago IL: Hollingsdale Press, 1949.
20. Mussolini, Benito, *Mussolini Memoirs*, 1942-1943, London: Phoenix Press, 2000.
21. Ibid.
22. Waldman, Victor, *Mussolini*, Chicago IL: Hollingsdale Press, 1949.
23. Ibid.
24. Greene, Jack and Massignani, Alessandro, *The Black Prince and the Sea Devils*, NY: DaCapo Press, 2004.
25. Orry, King, http://www.321gold.com/editorials/orry/orry082108.html
26. Mussolini, Benito, *Mussolini Memoirs*, 1942-1943, London: Phoenix Press, 2000.
27. Waldman, Victor, *Mussolini*, Chicago IL: Hollingsdale Press, 1949.
28. Mussolini, Benito, *Mussolini Memoirs*, 1942-1943, London: Phoenix Press, 2000.
29. Landwehr, Richard, *Italian Volunteers of the Waffen-SS*, Brookings OR: Siegrunen, 1987.
30. Mussolini, Benito, *Mussolini Memoirs*, 1942-1943, London: Phoenix Press, 2000.
31. Greene, Jack and Massignani, Alessandro, *The Black Prince and the Sea Devils*, NY: DaCapo Press, 2004.
32. Neulen, Hans Werner, *In the Skies of Europe, Air Forces allied to the Luftwaffe, 1939-1945*, Marlborough: The Crowood Press, 2005.
33. Ibid.

16 Day of the Lion

1. Mussolini, Benito, *My Autobiography*, NY: Scribner's, 1928.
2. Waldman, Victor, *Mussolini*, Chicago IL: Hollingsdale Press, 1949.
3. Duffy, James P., *Target: America, Hitler's Plan to Attack the United States*, Westport CT: Praeger, 2004.
4. Ibid.
5. Ibid.
6. Ibid.
7. Lamb, Richard, *War in Italy, 1943 to 1945, A Brutal Story*, London: Collier, 1965.
8. Mussolini, Romano, *My Father, Il Duce*, NY: Random House, 2006.
9. Mussolini, Benito, *Mussolini Memoirs*, 1942-1943, London: Phoenix Press, 2000.
10. Mussolini, Romano, *My Father, Il Duce*, NY: Random House, 2006.
11. Mussolini, Benito, *Mussolini Memoirs*, 1942-1943, London: Phoenix Press, 2000.
12. Mussolini, Romano, *My Father, Il Duce*, NY: Random House, 2006.
13. Moseley, Ray, *Mussolini: The Last 600 Days of IL Duce*, NY: Taylor Trade Publishing, 2004.
14. Mussolini, Benito, *Mussolini Memoirs*, 1942-1943, London: Phoenix Press, 2000.

15. Coraja, Santi, translated by R.L. Miller, *Hitler and Mussolini*, NY: Enigma Books, 1985.

17 An Unlikely Pen-Pal

1. Langworth, Richard (editor), *Churchill by Himself: The Definitive Collection of Quotations*, NY: PublicAffairs, 2008.
2. Coraja, Santi, translated by R.L. Miller, *Hitler and Mussolini*, NY: Enigma Books, 1985.
3. Mastrorocco, Allessandro, *The Mysterious Murder of Benito Mussolini Documents from US Strengthen the British Theory and Churchill's Role* http://ww2history. suite101.com/article.cfm/the_mysterious_murder_of_benito_mussolini.
4. Tompkins, Peter, *Mussolini, the Final Truth*, DVD documentary.
5. Forrestal, James V., *The Forrestal Diaries*, edited by Walter Millis, NY: The Viking Press, 1951.
6. Irving, David, *Churchill's War Volume II: Triumph in Adversity*, London: Focal Point Publications, 2001.
7. Garibaldi, Luciano, *Mussolini, The Secrets of His Death*, NY: Enigma Books, 2005.
8. Ibid.
9. Ibid.
10. Cavalleri, Giorgio, *Ombre sul Lago*, Rome: Rienzi Editoriale, 1989.
11. Andriola, Fabio, *Carreggio segreto*, Milan: Piemme, 1991.
12. Cavalleri, Giorgio, *Ombre sul Lago*, Rome: Rienzi Editoriale, 1989.
13. Garibaldi, Luciano, *Mussolini, The Secrets of His Death*, NY: Enigma Books, 2005.
14. Popham, Peter, "Churchill 'ordered killing of Mussolini'," *The Independent*, http://www.independent.co.uk/news/world/europe/churchill-ordered-killing-of-mussolini-558130.html.
15. Mussolini, Benito, *Mussolini Memoirs*, 1942-1943, London: Phoenix Press, 2000.
16. de Felice, Renzo, *Red and Black.*, London: Chessman Publishers, Ltd., 1995.
17. Ibid.
18. Tompkins, Peter, *Mussolini, the Final Truth*, DVD documentary.
19. de Felice, Renzo, *Red and Black.*, London: Chessman Publishers, Ltd., 1995.
20. Cavalleri, Giorgio, *Ombre sul Lago*, Rome: Rienzi Editoriale, 1989.

18 The Italian Atomic Bomb

1. Mussolini, Benito, *Mussolini Memoirs*, 1942-1943, London: Phoenix Press, 2000.
2. Fermi, Laura, *Mussolini*, Chicago IL: University of Chicago Press, 1961.
3. Segre, Emilio, *Enrico Fermi, Physicist*, Chicago IL: University of Chicago Press, 1970.
4. Tompkins, Peter, *Mussolini, the Final Truth*, DVD documentary.
5. Mussolini, Romano, *My Father, Il Duce*, NY: Random House, 2006.
6. Hans Zinsser affidavit, U.S. military intelligence report, 19 August 1945, roll number A1007, National Archives.
7. Manvell, Roger and Heinrich Fraenkel, *Doctor Goebbels: His Life & Death*, London: Greenhill Books, 2006.
8. Mussolini, Romano, *My Father, Il Duce*, NY: Random House, 2006.
9. Romersa, Luigi, *Le armi segrete di Hitler*, Milan: Ugo Mursia Editore, 1999.

10. Hooper, John, "Author fuels row over Hitler's bomb; Germany 'came close to nuclear device in 1944'; Last living witness saw Baltic test explosion", London: *The Guardian,* 30 September 2005, http://www.guardian.co.uk/world/2005/sep/30/books.italy.
11. http://greyfalcon.us/Hitler%20abomb.htm.
12. http://en.wikipedia.org/wiki/Luigi_Romersa.
13. http://greyfalcon.us/Hitler%20abomb.htm.
14. Farrell, Joseph, *Black Sun: Nazi Germany's Attempt to Develop an Atomic Bomb,* Kempton IL: Adventures Unlimited Press, 2004.
15. Ibid.
16. Manvell, Roger and Heinrich Fraenkel, *Doctor Goebbels: His Life & Death,* London: Greenhill Books, 2006.
17. Mondey, David, *Concise Guide to Axis Aircraft of World War II,* Middlesex: Temple Press, 1984.
18. Greene, Jack and Massignani, Alessandro, *The Black Prince and the Sea Devils,* NY: DaCapo Press, 2004.
19. Ibid.

19 Could Mussolini Have Won His War?

1. Mussolini, Benito, *Mussolini Memoirs,* 1942-1943, London: Phoenix Press, 2000.
2. Smith, Dennis Mack, *Mussolini,* London: Weidenfeld & Nicolson, 1981.

Selected Bibliography

See the Notes for details of additional sources used.

Abshagen, Karl Heinz, *Canaris, Patriot und Weltbuerger*, Stuttgart: Union Verlag, 1949.

Bagnasco, Erminio, *Submarines of World War Two*, Annapolis MD: Naval Institute Press, 1977.

Bird, Vivian, "An Examination of British War Crimes During World War Two", Washington D.C.: *The Barnes Review*, vol.VI, no.6, November/December 2000.

Bishop, Chris, *Encyclopedia of Weapons of World War II*, NY: Barnes & Noble, 1998.

Bosworth, R.J.B., *Mussolini*, NY: Hodder Arnold, 2002.

Cowdery, Ray R., *Reinhard Heydrich: Assassination!*, Lakeville MN: Northstar Commemoratives Inc., 1998.

Finaldi, Giuseppe, *Mussolini and Italian Fascism*, NY: Longman, 2008.

Gooch, John, "Decisive Campaigns of the Second World War", *Journal of Strategic Studies*, Volume 13, March 1990.

Gosling, John, *The Ghost Squad*, London: W.H. Allen, 1959.

Greene, Jack and Massignani, Alessandro, *The Naval War in the Mediterranean, 1940-1943*, London: Chatham, 2002.

Henshall, Phillip, *Vengeance, Hitler's Nuclear Weapon: Fact or Fiction?*, Stroud: Alan Sutton Publishing Ltd., 1995.

Hibbert, Christopher, *Mussolini: The Rise and Fall of Il Duce*, Basingstoke: Palgrave Macmillan, 2008.

Hitler, Adolf, *Hitler's War Directives, 1939-1945*, edited by H.R. Trevor-Roper, London: Pan Books, 1983.

Jameson, Fredric, *Fables of Aggression: Wyndham Lewis, The Modernist as Fascist*, Berkeley CA: University of California Press, 1979.

Joes, James, *Mussolini*, NY: Franklin Watts, 1982.

Kemp, Paul, *Underwater Warriors*, London: Arms & Armour, 1996.

Kinsey, Gordon, Bawdsey, *Birth of the Beam*, London: Dalton, 1983.

Ludwig, Emil, *Talks With Mussolini*, London: Allen & Unwin, 1932.

Lundari, Giuseppe & Compagni, Pietro, *I Paracadutisti Italiani 1937-45*, Milan: Editrice Militare Italiano-Serie De Bello', 1999.

Mallett, Robert, *The Italian Navy and Fascist Expansionism, 1935-1940*, London: Frank Cass, 1998.

Manvell, Roger & Fraenkel, Heinrich, *The Canaris Conspiracy, The Secret Resistance to Hitler in the German Army*, NY: Pinnacle Books, 1969.

Mattioli, Guido, *Mussolini Aviatore*, Milan: Editoriale Penne, 1935.

Mehner, Thomas, *Hitler und die 'Bombe': Welchen Stand erreichte die deutsche Atomforschung und Geheimwaffenentwicklung wirklich?* Rottenburg: Kopp Verlag, 2002.

Molinari, Andrea, *Desert Raiders: Axis and Allied Special Forces, 1940-43*, Oxford: Osprey Publishing, 2007.

Morgan, Philip, *The Fall of Mussolini: Italy, the Italians, and the Second World War*, NY: Oxford University Press, USA, 2008.

Munoz, Antonio J., *Slovenian Axis Forces in World War II, 1941-1945*, NY: Axis Europa Books, 1995.

von Plehwe, Friedrich-Karl, *The End of an Alliance, Rome's Defection from the Axis*, Oxford: Oxford University Press, 1971.

von Plehwe, Friedrich-Karl, *Als die Aesche zerbrach*, Berlin: Limes Verlag, 1980.

Puzzo, Dante A., *Spain and the Great Powers*, NY: Columbia University Press, 1962.

Ragnarrsson, Ragnar J., *US Navy PBY Catalina Units of the Atlantic War*, Oxford: Osprey Publishing, 2006.

Ridley, Jasper, *Mussolini: A Biography*, NY: Cooper Square Press, 2000.

Rowher, J., *Axis Submarine Successes of World War Two*, London: Greenhill Books, 1999.

Sadkovich, James J., "Of Myths and Men: Rommel and the Italians in North Africa, 1940-1942", *The International History Review*, XIII, May, 1991.

Santoro, General G., *Stralcio dell'Opera Aeronautica Italiana nella Seconda Guerra Mondiale*, Milan: Mondadori, 1953.

Walker, Ian, *Iron Hulls Iron Hearts: Mussolini's Elite Armoured Divisions in North Africa*, Marlborough: The Crowood Press, 2006.

Web Sites
http://missilegate.com/rfz/swaz/chapter1.htm
http://service.spiegel.de/cache/international/spiegel/0,1518,346293,00.html
http://www.commandosupremo.com
http://www.guardian.co.uk/italy/story/0,12576,1581690,00.html
http://www.history.navy.mil/library/online/sublosses/sublosses_scamp.htm
http://www.marina.difesa.it/storia/movm/Parte06/MOVM6063.htm http://www.regiamarina.com
http://www.regiamarina.net/subs/documents/evolution/evolution_us.htm
http://www.subnetitalia.it/regiostoria42.htm http://www.youtube.com/watch?v=Mvu4XnHilXI&feature=related

Related titles published by Helion & Company

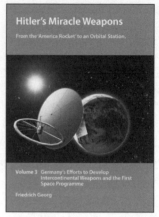

Under Himmler's Command. The Personal Recollections of Oberst Hans-Georg Eismann, Operations Officer, Army Group Vistula, Eastern Front 1945
Helion WWII German Military Studies Volume 2
Hans-Georg Eismann
144pp, photos, maps   Hardback
ISBN 978-1-906033-43-7

Hitler's Miracle Weapons Volume 3. From the 'America Rocket' to an Orbital Station. Germany's efforts to develop Intercontinental Weapons and the First Space Programme
Friedrich Georg
144pp, colour artwork, photos, diagrams, docs
Hardback
ISBN 978-1-906033-00-2

Forthcoming titles

Barbarossa Derailed. The Battles for Smolensk, July-August 1941
David M. Glantz   ISBN 978-1-906033-72-9

Entrapment. Soviet Operations to Capture Budapest, December 1944
Kamen Nevenkin   ISBN 978-1-906033-73-6

A Flawed Genius. Field Marshal Walter Model, a critical biography
Marcel Stein   ISBN 978-1-906033-30-9

HELION & COMPANY
26 Willow Road, Solihull, West Midlands B91 1UE, England
Telephone 0121 705 3393   Fax 0121 711 4075
Website: http://www.helion.co.uk